COUNSELLING AND IDENTITY

Also by Alex Howard and published by Palgrave Macmillan

Philosophy for Counselling and Psychotherapy
Challenges to Counselling and Psychotherapy

Counselling and Identity

Self-realisation in a Therapy Culture

Alex Howard

palgrave
macmillan

First published 2005 by
PALGRAVE MACMILLAN
Houndmills, Basingstoke, Hampshire RG21 6XS and
175 Fifth Avenue, New York, N.Y. 10010
Companies and representatives throughout the world

PALGRAVE MACMILLAN is the global academic imprint of the Palgrave Macmillan division of St. Martin's Press, LLC and of Palgrave Macmillan Ltd. Macmillan® is a registered trademark in the United States, United Kingdom and other countries. Palgrave is a registered trademark in the European Union and other countries.

ISBN 978-1-4039-3309-6   ISBN 978-0-230-62813-7 (eBook)
DOI 10.1007/978-0-230-62813-7

This book is printed on paper suitable for recycling and made from fully managed and sustained forest sources.

A catalogue record for this book is available from the British Library.

10 9 8 7 6 5 4 3 2 1
14 13 12 11 10 09 08 07 06 05

Contents

Acknowledgements

CHAPTER 1

Introduction: Identity and Why It Matters

> One of the distinct features of twenty-first century society is its relentless preoccupation with the question of identity. (Furedi 2004:148)

> I am I plus my surroundings, and if I do not preserve the latter I do not preserve myself. (Jose Ortegay Gasset 2000)

> The novelist Salman Rushdie asserts that the modern self is 'a shaky edifice we build out of scraps, dogmas, childhood injuries, newspaper articles, chance remarks, old films, small victories, people hated, people loved.[1] (Sennett 1998:133)

Who do you think you are? What are you to make of yourself? What do others make of you? Do you make too much of yourself? Are you complacent, or cruel, with yourself? Are you forgetful of yourself? Or self-obsessed? Critics of counselling complain that it encourages people to become altogether too preoccupied with themselves. A BBC guide to counselling was entitled *Let's Talk About ME*[2] and counselling, rightly or wrongly, tends to be seen as an essentially, and perhaps excessively, 'me-focused' activity. The counsellor can help me talk about (aspects of) me, clarify my agendas and options, pay attention to me and my concerns, help me to be more clear about who I am, where I am, where I came from, and where I am going. With a counsellor, above all, a client can reveal and explore some, or many, chapters in the Story of Myself. Mindful of ourselves, few seem to be willing or able to transcend their own life story, as mystics have perennially enjoined us to do:

> The sage has no mind of his own,
> He is aware of the needs of others. (Feng & English 1982:49)

Questions relating to personal identity are often, clearly, of central importance within counselling. People frequently come to counsellors to find, reclaim, remould, face up to, make something of, or control, (aspects of) 'themselves'. They want to see how they have been shaped, helped or damaged by their circumstances. They want to consider what they could do to put themselves in better shape and to determine what that better shape ought to be.

In this chapter I shall introduce a competitive range of contrary and contradictory voices, questions, themes, and ways of thinking about the subject of identity. I wish to show why the topic is so important, not just to counsellors, but to all of us. *The aim will not be to argue for a single 'answer' to the questions raised.* Rather, I wish to offer readers, counsellors and others, a richer vocabulary, and a wider variety of perspectives, so that they can explore the subject for themselves and make their own integrated picture. In other words, rather than providing a single account of identity, I seek to offer *a larger canvas, and a wider range of colours, with which people can paint for themselves the story of their lives.*

The book is critical, in places, of what I try to show is the dogmatic and/or simplistic slumber to be found in, rather too many, schools of counselling. But my aim, ultimately, is *to strengthen and support therapeutic talk and action.* Such strength and progress will come, I argue, when counselling is less dominated by quasi-professionals, and more *anchored in, aware of, and owned by, the cultures, communities and societies of which it is a part.*

Identity matters, whether you know it or not

> 'If I'm just a social worker, maybe you're just an ex-junkie. Is that all that's happening here?' (Ram Dass and Gorman 1985:123)

Issues around personal identity are not just relevant to those already predisposed to think or talk about themselves. Identity is often a centrally important problem for people, young and old, rich and poor, who may not feel good about, or think very often about, 'themselves' at all. By no means everyone is prone to introspection.

For example, many teenagers suffer problems in seeking to establish their identity, and in finding role models. Their struggle to do so is clearly important.

> Erikson has pointed out that the chief feature of adolescence is the renewed search for self-identity. The two year old has already gone through the preliminary stage. But later he has lost himself again, so to speak, in his family and gang loyalties. Now in adolescence the problem once more becomes more acute. The central teenage problem becomes 'Just who am I?' (Allport 1961:124)

Yet teenagers may rarely, if ever, go around consciously (or unconsciously) thinking that they are suffering from problems in establishing their identity. They may never introspect in any way about their self-image or their 'stream of consciousness'. Nonetheless, much of what they feel, think, do and don't do may be greatly determined by implicit, tacit, received and unthinkingly accepted or constructed views they have concerning:

- Who they are;
- Where they stand;
- Where they came from;
- Where they are going;
- What they are capable of doing; and
- What are their entitlements and obligations.

Most people, apart from those within the 'chattering classes', may never have reflected on any of these questions. They may never have thought about something so seemingly abstract as identity. But the counsellor, if she[3] is to help, may need to assist the client in clarifying these questions.

Identity matters, whether you discuss it or not

Why? Because counsellors will need to be aware of how constructs of identity crucially and unfailingly inform and affect what goes on between counsellors and clients. The counsellor needs to know how identity influences what she and clients do and don't do, see and don't see. To be aware, she will herself need to develop a broad, deep and sophisticated understanding of identity and its role in shaping or stunting the lives of clients.

We all, including small children, make assumptions and develop expectations about the identity of another very rapidly indeed. For example, children in a classroom will scent within a few minutes, or less, whether a new teacher will keep control effortlessly, or only after a struggle, or not at all. In this sense they share the rapid perception of a wolf pack concerning threat, opportunity and the strength of 'presence' of a newcomer. 'People understand: First things first. So how do you come in? Do you come *in*, or do you come *on*? No small matter' (Ram Dass and Gorman 1985:157).

Our first impressions of another are made very rapidly, and are primarily determined by non-verbal cues. Of course, these first impressions can often be driven by stereotypes that we have about other people that are simplistic, prejudiced and plain wrong. We cannot avoid forming first impressions, but the challenge is to ensure that the *first* impressions we form do not become our *last*. All too easily we assume that we 'know' what we want to know about another, and *then we just stop looking*!

This book will, therefore, seek to go beyond first impressions of identity, and will examine multiple answers and solutions to questions about self. It will encourage a sophisticated and cosmopolitan understanding of persons. It will discourage excessive self-preoccupation and any obsessive need to be consciously 'aware' of all that we do. It will challenge postmodern views that there is no identity to clarify; no truth separable from opinion; no author behind any text. It will explore the way constructions of self influence clients, counsellors and what goes on between the two. *More generally, this book seeks to consider how constructions of self influence all of us in every aspect of our daily lives.*

Identity structures what we do and don't do, see and don't see, attend to and ignore, prioritise and avoid. *Our view of ourselves will determine whether we treat ourselves kindly or forever see ourselves as 'no good' and requiring continuous punishment.* This is why I think the book will interest the lay reader as well as the counsellor and why I have tried to make it readable and relevant at every stage. Constructs of identity can be, if anything, more crucial for those suffering from low self-esteem. They may shy away from mirrors or any kind of self-preoccupation. They may well not think at all about concepts of 'self'. Sociologists and philosophers may like to explicitly conceptualise identity, but – let's face it – most people do not. Identity matters, whether we think much, little, obsessively, not at all of 'ourselves.'

Identity matters, even when you don't need to think about it

Our ideas about who we are, and the ideas that counsellors have about who we are, matter very much to out wellbeing and to the success, or otherwise of counselling. What others see in us, and what we see in ourselves, is crucially important, not least because 'WYSIWYG' can apply to people as to software – *what you see*, in yourself and other, *is what you are likely to get*. If you cannot, in the first instance, see yourself as doing, being, achieving . . . whatever, then you are less likely to achieve it. Of course, the reverse is not necessarily the case; grandiose fantasies about ourselves do not guarantee the reality unless we are also lucky, resourceful, competent, privileged, practised, informed, experienced, well trained and educated, highly motivated, etc.

Ideas and tacit understandings about identity, then, *particularly when we never think about them*, matter to all of us as we go about our daily lives. This is so, regardless of whether or not we are consciously preoccupied with or aware of any such ideas. Yet how much time is given over to the examination of self-concepts and identity in the training of counsellors?

Therapist views of identity

Most schools of counselling adopt, implicitly or explicitly, some model or other of identity. Freud spoke of 'Id, Ego and Superego', Rogers referred to an authentic 'organismic' self, Jung believed in a 'collective unconscious'. There are many other accounts of identity, and of what it is to be a person, as we shall see. But there are doubts about how far individual or collective identities remain fixed and unchanging: 'Psychoanalysis, a therapy that grew out of experience with severely repressed and morally rigid individuals who needed to come to terms with a rigorous inner "censor", today finds itself confronted more and more often with a "chaotic and impulse-ridden character"' (Lasch in du Gay et al. 2000:224)

Identities may change perhaps, and certainly there is a great variety in counsellor assumptions and theories of identity. However, I have seen very little systematic effort to compare, contrast or critique counsellor constructs of self. Some counsellors appear to accept without much question that there is an *authentic self* to be 'found' and that a counsellor is best placed to help a client find it. Also that the client is an *autonomous* being who can become more autonomous still by uncovering their defences, habits, contradictions, tensions, low self-esteem, negative attitudes etc. Finally, the belief is commonplace that the counsellor is able to engage in 'advanced empathy' with the client with very little investigation made of the highly problematic nature of empathy.

These beliefs, that we can become more autonomous, authentic and empathic, are a part of the underlying faith of most counsellors and schools of counselling. We believe we can be authentic, insightful and accurate in our understanding of ourselves, other people and the world around us. Counsellors, we assume, can assist us to know ourselves as we are, perceive our world accurately, and come to terms with the reality of our circumstances. Other people, likewise, we hope, can shake off their own defences, pretensions, prejudices and delusions. We can, therefore, meet other people free of spin, game-playing and image making. We can, with the assistance of a counsellor, really get to know one another, and find genuine intimacy with other human beings. And being genuine, we can find the distance between another and ourselves that is appropriate and right for each of us.

For example, Carl Rogers, the icon of person-centred counselling observed (1980:16) that: 'I feel a sense of satisfaction when I can dare to communicate the realness in me to another.' He later asserted (1980:173), for example, that: 'Her organism wants to be healthy and strong, but the introjected "I – the false self she has taken on to please others – wants to be, as she says at one point, thin and "intellectual".' One of his clients wrote (quoted 1980:209): 'Dear Dr. Rogers . . . I think that I began to lose me when I was in high school.'

Preserving identity from chaos – *and* naïvety

Authenticity, autonomy, intimacy and a foundational reality; here are the underlying core values of counselling. Within them, it is assumed, we find our identity. Without them we are lost to ourselves and to others. In many respects these values form part of the Enlightenment project of person-centred humanistic principles developed from the Renaissance onwards, which sought to recover and develop ancient Greek values lost, in the West, after the fall of Rome.

I will say, from the outset, that I do not intend to try to tear down these values. I do not seek to capsize counselling into that kind of postmodern relativism wherein nothing can be known, nothing can be done, nothing is intrinsically worth doing, and nobody is there to claim or do anything. But a great deal has happened since the Renaissance humanism implicit within counselling first began to break free from the authority of priests and scriptures. Beliefs about identity, authenticity, autonomy, intimacy, empathy and reality – have all come under the intense gaze of philosophers, sociologists, anthropologists, literary critics and cultural theorists.

Both psychology and counselling, place the individual as the main focus of their agenda. Yet the literature within counselling and psychology concerning identity and authenticity is surprisingly small. Sociologists examine wider social processes and it might be thought that they would spend less time than counsellors and psychologists in exploring concepts of identity. In fact, the reverse is true. I find that identity is a much more alive and intense subject of debate among sociologists than it is within psychology. Lewis (2002:370), for example, asserts, I think quite rightly, that:

> Postmodern cultural theory has been most acute in its analysis of the subject (self) and the fragmentation of modernist conceptions of a unified subjectivity. . . . The point here is that the self – an individual human being and his/her experience of life – has not been the same throughout history. The notion of 'who I am' is only conceivable in relation to other humans and the culture within which the individual functions. Members of oral, tribal cultures, for example, conceived of themselves as 'extempore', beings mysteriously connected to animals, objects and spirit beings.

For more than a century sociologists have recognised identity and authenticity as highly complex, important and problematic concepts. They have written a great deal about these topics and, I will try to show, substantial progress has thereby been made in our understanding of what it is to be a person and what it is to make genuine contact with another person. 'The issue of identity is central to cultural studies, in so far as cultural studies examines the contexts in which both individuals and groups construct, negotiate and defend their identity or self-understanding' (Edgar & Sedgwick (eds) 1999:183).

Likewise philosophers in the past century have revolutionised our understanding of these core ideas and values. Questions about identity are not mere 'leisure pursuits' or 'cultural entertainment' for those with the time and energy to pursue them. As Eagleton(1996:89), observes: 'Just to survive, the human animal cannot rely on instinct but must bring self-reflective resources into play.' Yet what notice do training programmes in counselling and psychotherapy take of these developments? Remarkably little recognition of sociological and philosophical thinking is to be found within most counselling prospectuses.

Sociologies of identity

To a considerable degree, I have to admit, this reluctance to engage with philosophies and sociologies of identity is understandable. Too much of the prose on offer on this topic is tortuous in the extreme. I have quoted extensively from materials that seem to be readable and relevant. But theorising about identity too often floats away into inaccessible, abstract prose that does not help counsellors, clients or laypersons who want practical, relevant and useful material with which to take stock of themselves and their circumstances.

This book seeks to maximise the *gain* in conceptualising identity while minimising the *pain*. I quote extensively from a very wide range of sources; sometimes to illustrate an argument; or in order to leave a question hovering in the background; or to set the reader thinking ahead; or shift an agenda, or stretch the issues. Always, I am seeking to show the diversity of thinking within a unified agenda and attempting to encourage the reader to make their own selections and establish their own priorities.

The book seeks to be practical, and the discussion will, I think, be of interest not just to counsellors but also to that much larger *general public interested in taking stock of themselves, for themselves.* This, I am certain, includes everyone at one or more stages in their lives.

Because of this ignorance of current discussion about identity, counsellors may still refer to 'getting in touch with myself' and 'making real contact with another' as though these were self-evidently simple, true and important ideas about which there needs to be little investigation. Moreover, counsellors tend simply to assume, rather than actually demonstrate, that counselling is a significant means by which people can develop insight, self-awareness, self-esteem and authentic relations with others.

Of course, a growing amount of research is done on effectiveness within counselling (of which more later). But much of this focuses on client self-reports. If clients are satisfied with counselling does that prove that counselling is effective? How far can I know myself? What does the statement mean? If I claim that I know myself better after counselling does that mean that I actually do know myself better? How far does my feeling of satisfaction about a service mean that the service is as authentic and effective as it claims? Who decides? Who defines? How? With what authority?

The person-centred counsellor, Brian Thorne, remarked (1991:4) that: 'At that time [during my primary school days] I simply experienced, with alarming frequency, the powerful sensation of knowing what it felt like to be in someone else's skin.' How well did he know this? How could he know this? How could, and did, he find evidence for what he 'knew'? How far is such 'knowing' actually possible? What we do know, is that not all those who claim to 'see the world as you see it' are able to convince anyone else that they are right. Also we know that a guru may convince disciples that they have finally 'found themselves' within the church or therapy of . . . yet few others may be convinced.

Worse yet, we know that even the majority opinion may not be reliable. Majorities, after all, may be saturated in sentimentality, prejudice, indolence, laziness, childishness, kitsch, ignorance and illusion of one kind or another. This does not mean that élites can necessarily be relied upon either to be reliably insightful, real, wise, sensitive or whatever. It is not easy to 'get real' with ourselves and find 'underlying truths'. The certificates placed on the walls of counsellor consulting rooms do not demonstrate that truth and authenticity can be relied upon after however many sessions of counselling.

> As we pay close attention, we notice that whenever we say, 'I am this,' or 'I am that,' there is to some degree a feeling of being an impostor. That whenever the 'I am' of just being is attached to this or that in the world, there is a feeling of falsity, of incompleteness, or somehow not quite telling the whole truth. (Levine 1986:17)

Nonetheless, I think we mostly, and rightly, persist in thinking that truth, knowledge and self-knowledge of some kind or another are real and important, however difficult they may be to achieve. We draw back from the chaos of concluding that there are only opinions and that no perspective is more valid, authentic and significant than any other.

I do think that progress can be made with these, and other, questions concerning knowledge of self and other. I believe that the Enlightenment agenda can continue to progress. In other words, I believe in the possibility of person-centred truth seeking and truth telling and that responsible mature choice and judgement by honest individuals is both possible and desirable. *I also believe that counselling, and the society to which it belongs, will never become more 'self aware' if it continues to ignore key ideas and developments made, not just within psychology but, more so, within sociology and philosophy.*

We live in a postmodern era. This, I will try to show, is a fundamental reality and not just an abstract debate that we can examine or ignore as we prefer. Postmodernism is a reality that is of profound importance if we really want to make progress in our understanding of what it is to 'be ourselves', to 'be real', to be responsible, to be free (insofar as that is possible and desirable), and to be virtuous. It is a reality that is of essential importance if we want to see how far empathy with another human being is possible. Empathy is of central importance for counsellors. Yet sociologists have looked far more carefully at empathy than psychologists. Counsellors really can no longer afford, therefore, to ignore sociology.

Who, or what, is this image and reality of 'self' that, probably without our realizing it, may be inspiring or hindering us in our daily lives? Who is this 'self' that we may be seeking to find, get away from, construct, let out, smarten, straighten, add to, subtract from, integrate, divide or multiply? . . . 'just as one's current sense of self is validated through the interpreted past, so too does one's self-image contain within it assumptions, goals, purposes and wishes that are directed toward one's future' (Spinelli 1994:174).

What is this 'self-concept' which, even when (particularly when) we know nothing of it, and never think about it, has such a powerful effect on what we think, feel, do and don't do? 'Self' is a highly paradoxical concept. *On the one hand, in all kinds of predictable ways, we know who we are very well indeed.* We can answer any number of questionnaires concerning our identity, as regards background, preferences, circumstance, fantasies, habits, consumer preferences, networks, contacts, affiliations, beliefs, hopes, fears, etc. *On the other hand, others may claim, sometimes with good reason, to see more clearly than we can the nature of our behaviour, intentions, character, personality and dilemmas.* 'The parts that I make up for you are creative parts that can do anything. I make up an unconscious that is concerned and caring and willing to work on your behalf, because I don't want parts of you that have limitations' (Bandler and Grinder 1981:162).

We may ourselves sometimes find something deeply mysterious about who we are. We may long to become more than we are. We may search vaguely for some connection to something 'more real' within ourselves. We may feel a deep emptiness within. We may feel overly full of ourselves, weighed down by our own weight, or tired of ourselves. We may, as T. S. Eliot put it (in 'Burnt Norton') feel 'hollow' and/or 'stuffed'. We may wish we could meet someone else or do something else that would bring out something fresh and new from ourselves. 'Stan, you are not a noun. You are a verb. A constant changing process ever unfolding into its next open moment' (Levine 1984:119).

Friends, family and colleagues may, in some respects, understand us more than we understand ourselves. Their understandings will differ, a little or a great deal, according to the different aspects of ourselves that we present to different people. Our relationships with different people 'brings out' different 'sides' of our personality. Also our roles differ. When I am in the role of 'father' I will, in many ways, behave differently, and see myself differently, from when in the role of husband, friend or colleague.

> There is nothing within this universe of change that I can call myself for very long, nothing I can say I am that is the whole truth. In fact, much of the time we feel like we are pretending to be someone else simply by pretending to be anything at all. (Levine 1986:17)

Jane may say to Joan, 'I don't know what Jean sees in John.' The John seen by Jean, Joan and Jane may be profoundly different. Is there a 'real' John beneath all these appearances? Is Jean's John a more accurate view of the reality of John than Joan's or Jane's John? Who decides? Is any one view as 'valid' as any other? There does not seem to be one absolute, objective, privileged view of 'the truth' about John. Neither does it seem acceptable that any description of John is as true and useful as any other.

> We are what we know how to do best. (Smail 1996:224)

We seem to be both a subject and an object, *and* the verb that links the two! We can think of ourselves and imagine looking at ourselves as an object. Yet who, then, is the subject, the observer? 'We think we are our thoughts. We call our thoughts "I". In letting go of thought, we go beyond ourselves, beyond who we imagine we are' (Levine 1986:21).

The John seen by Jean will, in part, be shaped by their dealings with each other and also by Jean's own personality, hopes, fears, experiences and expectations. Likewise with Jane and Joan. They may 'hit it off' and see each other in a highly positive way. They may, or may not, like the look and smell of each other. The chemical scent given off by their compatible or incompatible immune systems may attract or repel. They may reward or punish each other, and this will certainly affect how they see each other.

> The self in contemporary cultural discourse is not a single thing at all, but an open 'system' subject to change, choice, personal motivation, desire, freedom and an infinite raft of interactions and redirections. The unfixing of culture and the debordering of nations have opened the way for new formulations of the self and the 'identity' which constitutes the self. (Lewis 2002:370)

People may, or may not, much trust each other and this will strongly influence what, and how much, they reveal, and how honest they are with each other. They may wish to get *through to* each other, or get *the better of* each other, or *get away from* each other. We may well not wish to open ourselves to another. We may know from past experiences that they are not to be trusted and that we should remain on our guard. Even when there is trust, the way in which John is seen will also depend substantially on what Jean, Joan and Jane hope and expect to be able to give to and get from John.

Identity past and present

> We have always had theories about what it means to be a human being, and more particularly what it means to be an 'individual' human being. Theology and philosophy have speculated about the individual and the individual soul. Early modern theories suggested that each individual constitutes a natural and spiritual essence which is more or less fixed from the time of birth. (Lewis 2002:30)

Concern about the nature of 'self', its past, present and future, goes back a long way. In most poor, 'primitive', historic and prehistoric cultures a great deal of what limited amount of wealth was available was given over to looking after, reflecting upon, respecting, ritualising, burying and telling stories about selves whose bodies, at the very least, had died. Is there any 'self' remaining after the body has rotted away? If so, in what sense?

In most cultures people have not been willing to accept that John has gone when John has died. All manner of ideas have been embraced to show that, in some way or another, somewhere or another, John is still around. Ancestors remain present to us, certainly within our own memories, and this, understandably, matters to us a great deal. What are we to make of this widespread belief in the continuity of self? How are these various ideas best to be understood in a new millennium? Certainly they do not seem to be cultural luxuries. On the contrary, they appear to be central to the morale, wellbeing, and raison d'être of those who believe in them.

We may be able to face ourselves and our lives only because we feel reassured in the belief that our ancestors are still looking after us, or that our pharaoh, within his vast pyramid, keeps us properly hinged within the universe. Our ancestors, in stone tombs, may be littered all around us. In earlier times they may have seemed more present, more solid, more unchanging and more significant than all the ever-changing paraphernalia of our daily lives. In earlier times and for many still today, 'real' life only began in the 'afterlife', after we had died. In that eternal world we would all meet up again and really live. This imperfect material life on earth was just a preparation for the heavenly existence that was to come.

But perhaps we can come to terms with the idea that this life here on earth is not a 'rehearsal' for something more real? Perhaps we can accept that here and now is as 'real' as it will ever get; that this life is the actual performance and not a preparation. Perhaps we can accept that, for many of us, our life is already nearly over? And perhaps it is enough just to remember and be reassured in the thought that people, who are now gone, once cared for us and cared about us? We can be assisted by imagining what they *would* say to us now if we could ask for their advice.

We may see ourselves as shining and coping only because the light of God shines within and upon us. We may believe that we know ourselves within God and in no other way. Clearly there is no unanimity of view concerning the nature of self, and there is no reason to believe that our grandchildren will accept our current views about our identity.

There are, however, common features within most constructions of self; common assumptions, without which it is difficult to see how we could conceive of any kind of self:

> What exactly do people mean when they speak of the self? Its defining characteristics are fourfold. First of all, continuity. You've a sense of time, a sense of past, a sense of future. There seems to be a thread running through your personality, through your mind. Second, closely related is the idea of unity or coherence of self. In spite of the diversity of sensory experiences, memories, beliefs and thoughts, you experience yourself as one person, as a unity.
>
> So there's continuity, there's unity. And then there's the sense of embodiment or ownership – yourself as anchored to your body. And fourth is a sense of agency, what we call free will, your sense of being in charge of your own destiny. (Ramachandran 2003)

Within these basics, though, there is room for a great deal of debate. The last characteristic, our sense of 'agency', is particularly problematic. 'We are none of us as much in charge of ourselves as we think. The exercise of will may be an illusion' (Smail 1996:182). Social process, assumptions, values, negotiations and interactions will have a substantial influence on how we see ourselves, and on how others see us. No wonder then, that sociologists have so much to offer in the understanding of self. Just as individuals may develop little insight if they cut themselves off from the world around them so, likewise, psychology and counselling may make little progress in understanding individuals if they just focus on individuals. Individuals grow within the soil of the society of which they are a part.

> The personal is not opposed to the political – but constructed by the political. (Cohen & Taylor 1992:21)
>
> Displaced and dislocated within the wider global frame of post industrial capitalism, the individual self turns increasingly to consumption, leisure and travel in order to give substance to everyday life. (Elliott 2003:2)
>
> You can't lead a sane life in an insane society. Function is going to clash with dysfunction. (Hillman & Ventura 1993:205)
>
> I think we talk so much about inner growth and development because we are so boxed in to petty, private concerns in our jobs. (Hillman & Ventura 1993:13)

So, if a counsellor wants to know more about personal identity and personal growth they need to know something (rather a lot actually) about the soil that fosters or inhibits such growth, just as gardeners need to know about the conditions of growth for plants. These conditions of growth are not so much to be found inside the plant as in the soil and wider environment from which the plant will grow. Likewise, if we want to understand self we have to understand Society. Yet the counsellors' journal *Self and Society* has focused more on self and less on society than I think it should. Once again, we need sociology and a social psychology. We need to look at social processes. 'Modernism, of course, re-created the subject-self in terms of the subject–object split. Rene Descartes explained reality (and subjectivity) in terms of knowledge' (Lewis 2002:370).

How we are seen and received, and how we project ourselves will be a negotiated process of give and take. This will itself depend on our powers, roles, resources, accoutrements and skills as well as our character and personality. John, with jeans and an old jalopy, will see himself, and will see himself being seen, very differently from John in a Jaguar with other designer accessories.

The Jaguar itself will be seen differently, and will have different meanings according to the dreams, preferences, projects and stereotypes of different observers. To Joan, John-plus-Jaguar may equal a highly desirable partner. To Jane, the Jaguar may put John in the category of 'nasty exploitative capitalist'. The cold and heartless John that Jane then 'sees' will differ radically from the warm and witty John seen by Joan. John may pick up the hostility from Jane and may lose his tendency to warmth. Mutual stereotyping may become mutually reinforcing.

Will a counsellor be able to see beyond these prejudices? How far will a counsellor's needs, preferences, prejudices, knowledge, beliefs, affiliations, etc. affect not just her reactions to John but the very nature of the John that she sees and brings out? Will the counsellor seek to 'bring something out' of the client, or help the clients bring something out for themselves, or 'put something in' to the client?[4]

If people were totally knowable and known by each other then communication and interaction would be redundant. On the other hand, if people were a total mystery to each other then any kind of interaction would be difficult if not impossible. We proceed to engage with each other in a context of tacit and received understandings, expectations and recognisable roles and situations. We have social, personal, impersonal and professional projects to get on with and we deal with, and see, the people around us according to how we think and hope they can deal with us in our plans for the day.

In other words, *we never see another person in a social vacuum*, we never ourselves as observers exist in a social vacuum, and so we never observe as disinterested and disembodied observers. We see people in the context of their and our own, roles, plans, preferences, opportunities and constraints. What we see is partly determined by what the other person can, and cannot, do with and for us. What we become, and how we see ourselves, is partly determined by what we are, and are not, able to do for ourselves, and for others and with others.

> Identity is both a problem and a project. (Kidd 2002:93)

> The idea of multiple personalities and the sub-personalities attracted a great deal of attention by the end of the nineteenth century. (Hardy 1987:185)

A general who defeats Napoleon at Waterloo is likely to have a different self-image from a beggar who is ignored in the street. Their identity is to some degree an 'internal' matter known only to themselves. But in many respects their identity is a public reality, readily observable by others.

> A self is a repertoire of behaviour appropriate to a given set of contingencies. (Skinner 1979:194)

There are many respects in which our identity seems like an ever-moving and changing process, a mysterious context to the daily content of our lives and experiences, a tenuous idea, an enigma that always seems to signify more than our theories and descriptions of self. We 'bring out' different aspects of ourselves with different people and, depending on who they are and what they want, different people see 'in' us different qualities, opportunities and threats. Yet we also (generally) experience, or imagine, a continuity of self within ever changing circumstances. What is the basis, and validity, of this 'continuity'? Perhaps a certain degree of 'not knowing' about who I am is unavoidable and even desirable if we are not to become stale to ourselves?

> To what does this sense of 'I' refer? There is presence, a sense of just 'I am' which when you follow it back further and further will turn more into an 'am-ness' than 'I-ness'. (Levine 1984:118)

> The scientism and objectification of philosophical thought seem merely to have ossified the individual, reinscribing Christian articulations of the essential soul with an equally essentialist discourse of the self. (Lewis 2002:371).

Rapid changes in our circumstances can leave us with a profound identity crisis. Or, if our situation seems stuck or moribund, we can feel that the 'real' me is buried beneath tired or oppressive surfaces. We may feel that we are unable to grow into who we really ought to be. We may feel we are frustrated potential rather than a fulfilled actuality.

> celebrities perform all those roles that were once carried out by religion, ideology and history. It is now the spring from which we derive many of our multiple identities. (Sardar 2002:41)

Yet, (another paradox), the more self-obsessed we become the more sterile the process of 'personal development' may seem to be. We may become weighed down by our own weight, spoilt by our own comfort, jaded by our own good fortune, bored by the lack of surprise in our lives. And the more full of ourselves we become the emptier the experience of 'me' may be. *Perhaps we find ourselves by losing ourselves? But what does that mean in practice?* What is to be made of, for example, the Zen and Taoist observation that we should loosen ourselves from any idea we may have about who we are? 'both the existentialist and the Buddhist say that there is a deeper "basic anxiety" and in the view of Buddhism this is due to our deep-rooted attachment to the ego.' (de Silva 2000:110)

> Observing our own I, or self, we misconceive it to be inherently existent and through this misconception are drawn into afflictive emotions that motivate actions which tie us in tight bonds and cause us to be swept away by the four powerful river currents of suffering. (Gyatso, Fourteenth Dalai Lama 1984:141)

> It is rather a willingness to be open to forces greater than oneself and a readiness to co-operate with them. (Thorne 1991:16)

Single and multiple selves

This book will consider the range of conceptions and narratives of self offered within philosophy, social science and cultural history that can be put to real practical use, both by the layperson and by counsellors on behalf of their clients. The book explores the notions of self that are currently implicit within a variety of modes of counselling and provide practical ways in which these conceptions can, and should, be given more depth and range. The book will challenge a number of myths and fallacies that are currently powerful within counselling practice. It will show how a larger social, cultural, ethical and spiritual apprehension of self would improve the work of counsellors and the benefits to clients. I will examine self as integrated, divided, single, multiple, subject, object, process, prison, platform, performer, context, reality and illusion:

> The philosopher Kant argued that we never experience the knowing self in the same way that we experience the object-self. The knowing self is just there, a transcendental or pure ego. The knower apprehends but is not itself apprehended.
>
> The opposite solution, offered by William James and John Dewey among others, holds that there is no substantive knower apart from the process of knowing. The knower is nothing more than the organism itself. (Allport et al. 1961:129)

I will explore and critique Carl Rogers' concept of the 'organismic' self and show that conceptions of self make no sense if described purely within an individualistic or 'experiential' discourse.

> Ibsen's Peer Gynt strips himself of all identities and roles in the onion scene to find nothing – an empty space. (Blackman & Walkerdine 2001:118)

> The very number of present-day 'psychologies' amounts to a confession of perplexity. (Jung 1995:33)

Each chapter will refer, as appropriate, to constructions of identity from philosophers, sociologists and social psychologists that are of continuing relevance to contemporary concerns. Each chapter will include questions designed to link the theoretical issues raised with the practical dilemmas faced.

> Almost the whole time I am writing conversations with myself. Things I say to myself tête à tête. (Wittgenstein 1998:88e)

> The most intimate operation of your life becomes the potential grazing ground of the media (non-stop television on the Louds family in the USA, endless 'slice of life' and 'psy' shows on French TV). The entire universe also unfolds unnecessarily on your home screen. This is a microscopic pornography, pornography because it is forced, exaggerated, just like the close-ups of sexual acts in a porno film. (Baudrillard 1998:443)

In examining the history of ideas about self we shall see very clearly how each is a response/reaction to, or elaboration of, what went before. Ideas about self, just like selves themselves, need to be understood in context. The icon (and demon figure) of behaviourist psychology, B. F. Skinner, (1904–90) for example, stated (1979:195) that: 'The picture which emerges from a scientific analysis is not of a body with a person inside, but of a body which is a person in the sense that it displays a complex repertoire of behaviour.'

Skinner focused on behaviour, out of frustration with introspectionists like Wilhelm Wundt (1832–1920) who, he feared, made no testable or coherent statements at all. Skinner was tired of metaphysical claims about invisible selves that in some mysterious fashion 'occupied' bodies. We learned about each other, Skinner argued, by observing carefully what we *do*.

Even so called 'mind-readers' and 'mind-controllers'[5] do not read minds or control minds in any metaphysical, non-physical, sense. What they do is observe behavioural cues and verbal responses very intensely indeed, make inferences about intentions, and take actions, make judgements and predictions accordingly. Their control lies in the subtlety of their movements and speech, and the accuracy of their observations, not because of any non-physical 'emanations' coming out of a non-physical homunculus sitting somewhere behind the eyes.

So Skinner spoke of 'self' as a 'complex repertoire of behaviour'. The trouble is that objects that are not seen as selves also can elicit complex repertoires. Musical boxes have 'complex repertoires'. Computers much more so. Is a 'complexity of repertoire' alone enough to make something a 'person'? And what about the problem that, however much behaviourists might wish to pass them by, we do have private experiences, reactions, hopes, dreams, fantasies that others cannot access directly and which we see as a central feature of our identity?

Surely we do not reach an adequate understanding of identity if we see ourselves as no more than 'complex repertoires of behaviour'? People resent, I think rightly, being seen as mere 'portfolios of behavioural outcomes'. What about meaning, purpose, understanding? Yet the behavioural agenda is still alive and well and has, for example, had an enormous influence in recent years on the way in which education has been transmuted into training via, for example, the UK focus on 'National and Vocational Qualifications'.

> There is a conceptual thinness in its conception of the character of human being. It is a conception that sees human beings as mere performers rather than reflective actors. (Barnett 1994:77)

Early explorations of the problem of identity

The philosopher Rene Descartes (1596–1650) wanted to break away from superstition, uncertainty and empty speculation about self and others. Descartes asked, what foundation of certain knowledge existed from which we could build an understanding of the world? Descartes decided to strip away anything that lacked any kind of certainty. Then all that would be left would be bedrock of fundamental truth. Descartes thought that we could build up from this and, provided we took great care, we could establish a surer basis to our knowledge.

Descartes looked 'out' on all the objects of the world and found grounds for uncertainty. But then, he thought that even as he raised doubts about all the objects that he looked upon and thought about, surely one single thing remained beyond doubt? He could have doubts about all these objects around him, but he who doubted; the subject who observed and thought about all these objects; his existence was surely beyond doubt? Hence Descartes' famous assertion, 'Cogito ergo sum', 'I think, therefore I exist'. I am confused, uncertain, full of doubt, yet here I am, the quizzical doubter. That, surely, is beyond doubt?

> I thence concluded that I was a substance whose whole essence or nature consists only in thinking, and which, that it may exist, has need of no place, nor is dependent on any material thing; so that 'I,' that is to say, the mind by which I am what I am, is wholly distinct from the body, and is even more easily known than the latter, and is such, that although the latter were not, it would still continue to be all that it is. (Descartes [1637] 1965:27)

In this way Descartes' philosophy described an essential self that was non-physical; that was somehow 'connected to' but not physically locatable in, the body. The self could survive the death of the body. It could survey objects and bodies. It could not itself be directly observed. Its existence in others could be inferred. And, although non-physical, self was the most *essential*, central and 'real' fact of life. I could be aware of myself, even if not actually able to see myself, as an observer. I could observe my private experiences that others could not observe.

John Locke (1632–1704) likewise considered ([1690] 1998:ch. X) self to be an indubitable core of certainty: 'As for our own existence, we perceive it so plainly and so certainly, that it neither needs nor is capable of any proof.'

David Hume (1711–76) was much less certain: 'I never can catch "myself" at any time without a perception, and never can observe any thing but the perception' (Hume [1739] 1966: Book 1, Part 4, sec VI).

Descartes' 'self' was a subject, a thinker, an observer and a doubter. Locke shared Descartes' certainty that this self existed but Hume noted that subjects could not be observed as objects. Selves were neither physical objects nor objects of experience. *Hume observed bodies on the 'outside'; and heat, cold, etc. from the 'inside'; but never 'himself', inside or out.*

Immanuel Kant (1724–1804) profoundly understood Descartes' subject–object, mind–matter dualisms and Hume's scepticism about the whereabouts of these 'subjects' and 'minds'. What was to be done? Those who focused on minds and subjects were always in danger of empty speculation, untestable propositions, difficulties in achieving mutual understanding, undisciplined flights of fantasy. Those who confined themselves to objects and the physically observable, risked finding themselves in a disenchanting robotic world lacking in humanity, spirit, life, mutual recognition and the understanding that came from two subjects – selves, persons, homo *sapiens*,[6] really succeeding in making contact with each other. I did not reach you by referring to you merely as a 'complex repertoire of responses', nor by treating you as an object of manipulation.

Somehow, then, we hoped to make, and thought we could succeed in making, significant contact with other *persons*, other human *beings*. Yet, as Hume observed, could we even manage to observe 'ourselves'? Kant noted ([1781] 1991:ss12) that: 'The empirical consciousness which accompanies different representations is in itself fragmentary and disunited, and without relation to the identity of the subject.'

We experienced heat, cold and objects all around us, but what was this 'me' that the objects were around and the heat was 'within'? What held all this experience together into a coherent unity? What was the coherent 'self' around which this coherent experience cohered? 'Only because I can connect a variety of given representations in one consciousness, is it possible that I can represent to myself the identity of consciousness in these representations' (Ibid.).

I (who?) certainly did connect all these representations together. My experiences seemed to be threaded together into a 'string' or 'stream' of consciousness. And without this, how could I think at all:

> All general conceptions – as such – depend, for their existence, on the analytical unity of consciousness.
>
> the synthetical unity of apperception is the highest point with which we must connect every operation of the understanding, even the whole of logic, and after it our transcendental philosophy; indeed, this faculty is the understanding itself. (Ibid.)

Without such coherence of experience how could there be any understanding at all? Likewise, without a 'self' as 'that which understands' how could there be understanding? How could any object or activity be understood unless there was a subject that did the observing and the understanding? 'I am conscious myself of a necessary a priori synthesis of my representations, which is called the original synthetical unity of apperception' (Ibid).

Self, then, for Kant, was a necessary presupposition, and a necessary fact, given the degree of coherence that there was in the world. Moreover, for Kant, this coherence did not just stop with individual selves. There could be no real understanding or individual identity unless these were themselves embedded into something larger:

> there exists among the transcendental ideas a certain connection and unity, and that pure reason, by means of them, collects all its cognitions into one system. From the cognition of self to the cognition of the world, and through these to the Supreme Being, the progression is so natural, that it seems to resemble the logical march of reason from the premises to the conclusion. (Ibid.)

So, Kant agreed with Hume that when we thought, felt, did, or observed, we never came across 'myself' in the process of thinking. But the self was implied immediately in the recognition of there being any thought going on at all. This was because thoughts could not happen without a thinker to think them:

> I cognize myself, not through my being conscious of myself as thinking, but only when I am conscious of the intuition of myself as determined in relation to the function of thought. (Ibid.)
>
> All the modi of self-consciousness in thought are hence not conceptions of objects (conceptions of the understanding – categories); they are mere logical functions, which do not present to thought an object to be cognized, and cannot therefore present my Self as an object. Not the consciousness of the determining, but only that of the determinable self, that is, of my internal intuition (in so far as the manifold contained in it can be connected conformably with the general condition of the unity of apperception in thought), is the object. (Ibid.)

Perception and thought was a unified and unifying process and the perceiver and thinker was, in Kant's view, a unified and unifying entity:

> the I or Ego of apperception, and consequently in all thought, is singular or simple . . . [it] cannot be resolved into a plurality of subjects, and therefore indicates a logically simply subject – this is self-evident from the very conception of an Ego, and is consequently an analytical proposition.
>
> The proposition of the identity of my Self amidst all the manifold representations of which I am conscious, is likewise a proposition lying in the conceptions themselves, and is consequently analytical. (Ibid.)

A unified self, Kant believed, was built in to our very capacity to think, understand and negotiate at all. It was one of Kant's 'synthetic apriori' truths; a truth of logic and a truth about the world. It was logically unavoidable but it was also a fact about what existed in the world.

Likewise, Kant argued, it was a fact about the world and an unavoidable truth of logic that there were separate selves who distinguished 'me' from 'you' from 'it'. You were not me and you were not an object. My body was not me and it was an object.

> I distinguish my own existence, as that of a thinking being, from that of other things external to me – among which my body also is reckoned. This is also an analytical proposition, for other things are exactly those which I think as different or distinguished from myself.
>
> A thinking being, considered merely as such, cannot be cogitated otherwise than as subject. (Ibid.)

For Kant, selves, others and objects, and the fundamental difference between each, was embedded into our logic, our language and, not least, our world. Without them there simply could not be any logic, language, world at all. 'Self' and 'other' came with the set. Without them there was no possibility of there being any language, any object, any coherent world at all.

This was a very unifying picture and very reassuring if it was true and if you could believe it – and *understand* it! Kant, and those who followed him, thought he had settled the scepticism of Hume. Kant preserved self by showing that it was far more than a material object. But he anchored self into a material and coherent world, and thus ensured that self did not vanish into private fantasy, incoherent mysticism, or 'chaotic', romantic reverie.

Kant remains very difficult to read, yet his analysis is much more sophisticated than some of the naïve discussion about self that continues 200 years after his death.[7]

The problems about identity, we might hope, are solved and over. We can all go home and get on with out lives. We might not follow every word that Kant wrote about self. But we might rest reassured in the thought that, via Kantian Deep Thought, self has been preserved from chaos, non-existence, oblivion, fundamental uncertainty, emptiness, meaninglessness.

Perhaps, except that history suggests otherwise. Kantian thinking still has a place and has not, I think, been entirely unraveled. Yet others have rolled out all kinds of questions and doubts about identity subsequent to Kant. And these questions run and run and will not all be put down finally and constrained within the framework of Kantian thinking.

> Wouldn't it be absurd for an airline pilot to deny knowledge of the principles of flight, or for a physician to claim ignorance of the basics of human physiology and anatomy? Yet I, a neuro-psychologist, can give no satisfactory account of how the brain generates conscious awareness. Worse still, I find myself edging towards a doubt that it means anything at all to say that the brain generates consciousness. (Broks 2003:92)

> Some philosophers (dismissed by others as 'Mysterians') argue that the 'problem of consciousness' exceeds human mental capacity . . . (Ibid.:101)

So what are these questions and doubts? What are the problems? Is there a problem at all? Why don't I just get on with my life? Indeed, is it not the case that I do indeed just get on with my life? I rarely get up in the morning and say 'I've cleaned my teeth but I just can't go any further until I have established just who I am!'

The familiar *and* mysterious self

Here is part of the mystery of identity: As I have said, on the one hand I know myself in endless ways, and my identity is not generally, in daily life, a pressing problem for me. Except that sometimes it really is. And sometimes I might look back and regret the folly of time wasted in trying to 'be' and to 'assert' a 'me' that I no longer value, no longer believe in, no longer identify with, nor believe ever really existed. Clearly there is an issue about how to construe our identity since there is, without doubt, an enormous variety in the way in which selves *are* construed. For example:

> The doctrine of egolessness is the key to the understanding of the Buddhist psychological analysis presented in this work. (De Silva 2000:8)

> Forms of lamentation that are mandatory in Greece would be considered vulgar and shameful in England. (Nussbaum 1997:227)

> It was thought, moreover, [in Ancient Greece] that only in a male–male sexual relationship would one be likely to have a deep spiritual and emotional bond with one's lover: women were sequestered and relatively uneducated. (Ibid.:235)

> Hoggart's *The Uses of Literacy* is quite explicit in its nostalgia for the cohesion and dignity of the pre-World War II working class culture of England. (Lewis 2002:127)

If there is no problem about identity, how come there are so many different constructions of identity? How come we 'identify' ourselves with so many different causes, stories, characters, objects, principles, ideas, institutions and people? Though, on the other hand, why should we not? Perhaps a crucial feature of our identity is that it changes and that we can have a hand in changing it? We can 'make something of' ourselves. We can make 'more of', or something *else* of, ourselves. We can *find* ourselves, *lose* ourselves, *avoid* ourselves, *escape* ourselves, *know* ourselves, *not know* ourselves; and all these options can be both opportunities and constraints in different times, places and circumstances.

> The Leavisite legacy and the Frankfurt School critique share a certain pessimism, a fear that human society is disintegrating under the weight of mass-mediated messages and the dehumanising effects of impersonal, mass urbanisation. (Lewis 2002:122)

> Goffman, *The Presentation of the Self in Everyday Life*: Humans play many different roles. They follow certain scripts that are relevant in some situations but not in others. Individuals give 'front stage' and 'back stage' performances. Interaction – since it is social by nature – is a performance to an audience. (Kidd 2002:77)

> While psychoanalysis may not be overtly antipathetic to community life, social solidarity, and family ties, it certainly places no great value on them. (Fancher 1995:123)

Hegel (1770–1831) took unification still further than Kant as a means of preserving and defining 'self'. Our identity, according to Hegel, could not be found by isolated introspection or by fragmented observation of others or objects. We did not find ourselves alone, on our own, for we were not alone and we could not act alone.

Only Big System philosophy could get to the parts of self that other people and other ideas could not reach. Indeed 'self' was just a part in the Big System, and it had no meaning, direction, shape or coherence at all except within this system. This did not make self a static entity since a part of our very being, our reason for being, was that we strove towards a deeper apprehension of coherence, of oneness, of reunion, of realizing, feeling, knowing, not just thinking, our belonging to a bigger story, a bigger mystery.

We strove to come closer to 'the Absolute' of which we were a part. In a dialectical process of thesis, antithesis and synthesis, we developed a vision, but soon there would be doubts and opposition. This was not a step backward since a *synthesis* of proposition and opposition would eventually emerge that took us to a larger understanding of reality. The synthesis would then itself comprise a thesis against which more doubts, questions and uncertainties would surface. These themselves would ultimately be embraced within a still bigger picture, and a still more sophisticated account. This progress in our understanding of the world was mirrored in the progress in our understanding of ourselves. Indeed the two were not really separate, as Kant had sought to show.

> There is no inherent reason why internal dynamics, rather than one's place in society, must be the principal source of health or illness. (Fancher 1995:125)

> We have no logical basis, within behaviourism, for saying, 'The individual is in good working order, but the environment is awry.' (Ibid.:168)

Hume had been skeptical of Descartes, and Kant sought to synthesise Hume and Descartes. Hegel, too was a synthesiser. From whence would come the next antithesis? Or was Hegel right about all this? Could the opposition come up with an even bigger, broader, deeper 'Absolute' than Hegel's? It seemed unlikely, and indeed the argument went absolutely the other way, as we shall see. By raising doubts about his 'Absolute', were critics of Hegel showing that he was right and paving the way to the next enlargement of the picture? Was intellectual 'progress' inevitable? Were we getting a deeper grasp of ourselves and our world? Were we becoming more moral and responsible and aware beings? Or just going round in circles? 'Self-deception is a constant problem as we progress along a spiritual path. Ego is always trying to achieve spirituality. It is rather like wanting to witness your own funeral.' (Trungpa 1973:63)

Hegel argued that we found ourselves by integrating ourselves with, rather than differentiating ourselves from, the larger universe. But he did not see this as a conflict-free process leading to peace, salvation, a 'final' destination and resting place. It was not all heavenly choirs, choruses and harmony. On the contrary, conflict was built into the process. Thesis produced antithesis. Self produced Other. Dichotomies abounded. Yet the process did not have to lead to disintegration. On the contrary, a synthesis of the opposites could eventually be found, and a deeper harmony thereby embraced. Admittedly, synthesis was itself challenged by another 'other', another 'opposite', another 'different'. What seemed like a resolution became another thesis challenged once more by its antithesis. Progress, nonetheless, could continue as we finessed, refined, broadened and deepened our understanding. We could thereby move closer to an appreciation of the overall unity of existence praised by Spinoza, Leibnitz and so many theologians and mystics. For Hegel we engaged, via this dialectical process, with ever-deeper levels of reality in a fusion of thought, feeling and experience.

But were we really progressing in our knowledge of our God as an Hegelian Absolute? Or were we progressing by realising that 'God' was a superstition that we no longer needed?

The sociologist Emile Durkheim, (1858–1917), was ambivalent about how far a self could be founded and nurtured within secular modernism. On the one hand he believed that science, social science, educational reform, rational enquiry and empirical investigation could make a better world and more happy, aware and responsible individuals. In this sense he saw the torch of progress as being within the hands of secular modernists and less so as belonging to the church and its priesthood.

On the other hand, although he himself was agnostic, Durkheim could see the powerful social role of the church in holding individuals and communities together, giving them a sense of meaning, purpose and solidarity. Durkheim coined the term 'anomie', the sense of disconnection and alienation that seems to be so much a part of the modern experience. The division of labour, he thought, separated people off from each other even as they became more dependent on each other. They might not see the product or purpose of their work. They occupied just a fragment of the overall social space and might not see how it inter-linked with the wider world. Suicide appeared to increase when people felt less connected to their society.

> My mother pointed out some twenty years ago, in the height of my spiritual grandiosity, that I was good at loving humanity but not so good at loving individual human beings. (Zweig 2000)

> What is in fact a social phenomenon comes to be experienced by ordinary people as a personal problem. (Smail 1996:112)

> We are all haunted by the possibility of slipping from our perch. (Ibid.:229)

Suicide was not merely a personal and private decision. It could not be understood merely by looking at individual consciousness but was itself a product of social process and social disintegration. Technology and mechanisation could involve treating people like machines, like objects. How could ethics and social solidarity survive if we were all just seen as instruments of production? How could identity survive this destructive process? The disintegration of the sense of self was a product of social disintegration and it was the duty of sociologists not merely to understand the process but to propose remedies that would preserve and promote persons via improvements in the societies on which our identities depended.

Present day threats to identity

> Increasingly in the world as it is, people are just *reduced* to their private selves . . . (House & Totton 1997:167)

> I recall the word of Warren Bennis in the film of you and him, when he characterised your viewpoint as 'devilishly innocent'. How do you square this 'human and humane' world you predict with the fact that the suicide rate in this country has gone up 171% in the last 30 years? (Rollo May letter to Carl Rogers in Greening 1984: 16)

Sociologist Max Weber (1864–1920) explored the interconnections between our individual character and the society of which we were a part. What if we believed we were headed for Hell unless we made very substantial efforts to improve ourselves? What if we believed that we were miserable offenders who needed both to confess our sins and work day and night to make amends? What if we believed that we had no right to celebrate, spend, or distract ourselves in idle dissipation? Why, we would save, invest, work and work and work again. Society would accumulate capital; people would obey orders. Timetables would be made and followed. If other conditions were right, an entire capitalist revolution might be achieved. And so it was, or so Weber argued.

More recently, in *The Corrosion of Character*, Richard Sennett (1998) has taken a more negative view of capitalist revolution, seeing it as a way of frustrating human attempts to develop a mature and stable identity, as we shall see.

Such secular capitalist social 'progress' can both 'advance' and damage individuals and societies. The material and technical progress has been greatly evident and was indeed a revolution even though achieved at great price to those at the bottom of the social order. Others paid a price too. Weber observed the 'iron cage' of bureaucracy lowering itself, not just onto society but into the minds and identities of the bureaucrat. Georg Simmel (1858–1918) argued that a whole new 'metropolitan' type of individuality was emerging, which consisted in, and was created by, the intensification of nervous stimulation. Anthony Giddens suggests that now most of us can exercise 'cosmopolitan' freedom, and welcomes the prospect.

But how rational, and right, was it to treat people as 'instruments' for some larger, seemingly impersonal, purpose? What place was there for personal moral engagement, individual integrity, and personal responsibility in a world of big businesses, bureaucratic systems and impersonal procedures? What happened to our sense of magic, mystery and enchantment within a science whose central metaphor was the machine?

How was our humanity – our sense of uniqueness, of the sublime, of brotherliness, (and sisterhood), and of genuine personal relations – to be sustained in a world dominated by 'impersonalities', procedures, systems, techniques, and machines? What place was there, in all this so-called progress, for the human part of human beings? Weber and Durkheim raised the questions, and they remain as pressing now as they were a century ago.

The philosopher Martin Heidegger (1889–1976) was likewise deeply concerned about how identity could be maintained given the widespread alienation of individuals from society. There was always a danger, in any society, that we could become 'inauthentic'. We would attempt to 'be' someone who we were not: 'We take pleasure and enjoy ourselves as they take pleasure; we read, see, and judge about literature and art as they see and judge. The "they", which is nothing definite, and which all are, though not as the sum, prescribes the kind of Being of everydayness' (Heidegger [1927] 1995:164).

Instead of being with ourselves or with others we started to be *for* others. We created ourselves and presented ourselves and thought ourselves to be whatever it was we imagined others (themselves imagined) thought we were and ought to be. We became a mask, a presentation, a production, a plausible show, we lost our own true authentic selves in the crowd, in the imagined 'they'.

Such alienation was always a potential problem in any time and place, Heidegger thought. But it was a particularly pressing problem in a modern era that was so much focused on techniques, systems, bureaucracies, machines and mass organisation. In such a context, where we made such a fetish of machinery and technology, we could turn ourselves into a machine. We might come to see ourselves as no more than a skills-portfolio, a potential pattern of predetermined outcomes that 'they' wanted us to achieve. A patter of clichés predicted, prepared and preferred by Weber's bureaucracy. We might be asked 'what do *you* think, feel, understand, and want?' But the answers that we imagined were all our own might be simply a reflection of answers prepared in advance by spin doctors, public relations specialists, managers, marketing specialists, human resource consultants, social psychologists, motivational analysts or counsellors!

> A lot of therapies are simply another dose of hypnosis. Now we have the 'human potential top-dog' saying 'You should be open, you should be warm, you should love everyone.' (Stevens 1977:262)

> Consciousness has been reduced by certain popular dogmas to a psychobabbling subjectivity that legitimises the passing sensation, the available comfort, the half-truth. (Rosen 1977:222)

For Karl Marx (1818–83) individual identities were a product of culture, and this was itself shaped by the underlying economic structure; the 'material forces of production', including the *means* of production and the *relations* of production. For Marx 'it was the economy, stupid' even more so than it has been thought to be for recent liberal politicians.

Marx accepted Hegel's account of a dialectical process but argued that the forces at work were material rather than 'spiritual'. For Marx we were made, and broken, by the underlying material, socio-economic processes that comprised and contained us. Eventually we would emerge from false consciousness when the proletarians took over all the means of production. Millions followed and constructed their experiences, agendas and their very identities around the Marxist project.

Marx believed that personal worth was being boiled down into mere 'exchange value' and this, he thought, was highly damaging to individual identities. Our work had lost all individual character, and we had become mere appendages to machines. People might think otherwise, both rich (exploitative) and poor (exploited). But when they did so they were victims of 'false consciousness'. So, to get to the underlying reality that structured self one needed to examine the culture that shaped our ideas concerning who we were, what our life was about and to what we were entitled. We then needed to see how the culture was itself structured by the nature of the underlying economy.

> We are witnessing a fundamental shift in which higher education moves from being a form of cultural transmission to one in which it becomes a means of generating economic capital. (Barnett 1994:138)

Sociologist Theodore Adorno (1903–69) looked at this shaping process in more detail. The mass media, he argued, was the most important cultural formation that shaped individuals. These media controlled what we thought, how we thought, what we dreamed about, hoped for and expected of others and ourselves. They created 'pseudo individuals'. For Adorno, as with Schopenhauer, escape and liberation to authentic living was possible, not so much, as in Marx, via collective action of the proletariat, but through *art*. The artist was not merely someone who provided decoration, distraction and entertainment, but the best artists expressed our deepest, truest, most authentic longings, conflicts and concerns. Through inspirational art we could get a deeper understanding of who we really could become and ought to become.

For Louis Althusser (1918–90) it was not just the mass media that mattered. All social institutions were involved in the construction of individual and collective identities. Churches, schools, civil services, police, families as well as mass media told us who we were, where we were, and what was going to be on offer for us. *Structures* shaped individuals more than persons could, in isolation, change structures. So in order to understand the formation of identity it was less important to focus on the accidents of individual circumstances, decisions and 'stream of consciousness'. Far more important was the need to study the underlying social structures, collectives, communities and institutions. We needed to understand their interconnections, their dynamics, their priorities and the power relations operating between them. There was a 'science' of history expressed through class struggle and changes in the means of production.

We also needed to see, as Norbert Elias (1897–1990) argued, the ways in which social control became fundamentally lodged within the human psyche. Society and its structures wrote themselves deeply into each individual human being.

Jürgen Habermas and others in the Frankfurt School of sociology likewise tried, and try, to link individuals to societies by integrating Marx and Hegel with psychoanalysis and existentialism. Prominent thinkers from the 1920s and 1930s included Max Horkheimer, Theodore Adorno, Erich Fromm, Herbert Marcuse, and Walter Benjamin. Habermas, as we shall see, sought to preserve conceptions of humanity and individual dignity in the face of depersonalisation, mechanisation and (as he saw it) exploitation.

Identity matters

There are many other important contributors to the debates about identity, to be considered in the following pages. The aim of this book will be to provide at least a flavour of the nature, direction, conflicts and consensus that exists in past, present and possible future discussions about the nature of identity. As in my last book, (Howard 2000), I hope to show that these individual thinkers do not operate in a social and cultural vacuum, but react and respond to what went before, and create the circumstances around what is likely to be said next. So it is that they are best understood when the relations, reactions and alliances among them are appreciated. The identity, agenda and achievement of Habermas, Freud or anyone else can only be understood within the social and cultural context within which they were operating. This will become ever more evident as we proceed.

Above all, to repeat, I want to show why the issues explored in these chapters matter in practice for all of us as we shape our days, our dress, our accoutrements and our priorities. Many of the stories and characterizations that we think are 'us-and-ours alone' have been taken, off-the-peg, from thinkers, movers and shakers who may well be unknown to us. Our freedom, our range of options may be far less than some within the human potential movement for example, like to claim for us. However whatever freedom, insight and agency we may be able to manage is likely to be much enhanced when we have a larger awareness of the many and varied forces at work that shape us, assist us, frustrate us, define us and fill our dreams and days. 'Just because you feel good about yourself doesn't mean that you're doing good things; and doing good things doesn't mean that you're going to feel good later on' (Bandler & Grinder 1981:129).

Certainly counsellors, for whom questions about identity are so central, cannot afford to avoid any longer the lively debate among cultural theorists, anthropologists, sociologists and philosophers about the nature of identity. That so many counsellors and therapists have remained so relatively ignorant for so long of these developments is itself a symptom of the intellectual and social fragmentation that has itself been of major interest to many sociologists.

Questions for Counsellors

1. What theories and concepts about identity are implicit and explicit within your own training in counselling? What alternatives have you considered?
2. Do you agree with Brain Thorne that counsellors need to know what it feels like to be in the skin of the client? How do you go about checking that you have achieved this?
3. Do you, like Bandler and Grinder, 'make up' parts of the client's personality? Or do you 'observe' these parts? In either event, how do you justify this practice?
4. Are you seeking to help a client find their 'authentic' self, or merely a manageable account of (some aspect of) themselves? Are selves 'found' or 'founded'?
5. Do you share Locke's view that selves can be 'plainly observed'? Or Hume's that the self can never be 'observed' at all? Or are you uneasy with both these accounts?
6. Do you agree with Kant that 'self' is an integral part of our very capacity to think, talk, act and understand? Or with the Buddhist view that 'self' is essentially an illusion that gets in the way of clear understanding? Can both these views be, in some sense, true?
7. Is it possible, or desirable, to think about 'self' separate from social and spiritual context? In knowing your clients how do you find out about these contexts? How far can you rely on client descriptions of these contexts?
8. How far do clients bring what are essentially collective social and spiritual more than private personal problems to you? How do you know? What do you do about it? Think of specific examples.
9. The John seen by Jean, Joan and Jane may be profoundly different. Is the John seen by you, the counsellor, a deeper, more 'objective', more accurate perspective? Who is to decide and how?
10. How far do you agree with Salman Rushdie that the modern self is 'a shaky edifice'?

CHAPTER 2

In Search of Self – Counselling and Identity

This chapter will explore in more detail the central importance of identity in therapy and day to day living. It will challenge naïveté about identity and show how our constructions of 'selfhood' have highly practical consequences. It will, I hope, interest anyone wishing to take stock of themselves and their potential.

The following general questions matter, surely, to us all?

1. Who determines who is who?
2. In what manner are identities *established*?
3. In what ways *imposed*?
4. How do I create the story of my life?
5. How does that story create me?
6. Am I what I have been?
7. Am I what I am seeking to become?
8. What more is there to be made of me?
9. Can I, should I, get away from myself?
10. What do you know about me that I don't know?

Historical overview

> Pre-industrial societies have little notion of a person as a separate entity. (Storr 1988:78)

> Homeric man was not the introspective self-conscious being who populates Socrates' dialogues[1] a few hundred years later – indeed, *The Iliad* has no word for 'person' or 'oneself'. (Porter 2002:13)

Porter argues that 'self consciousness' of any sort is not fixed and has not always been a part of human experience. Moreover, for many centuries, 'coming home' or 'finding oneself' meant finding oneself *within God*. In a secular society it is so easy for us to forget how centrally important *Christian* philosophy and theology have been for most of the last 2,000 years of European history. Every conception of self and 'sanity' was rooted within a deeper apprehension of God: 'Reason was walking in harmony with God, derangement that state of mind when the soul, diabolically assailed, blasphemed against the Almighty' (Ibid.:24).

St Augustine, (354–430 AD), for example, observed that we could find no peace, no truth, no light, no awareness, or self-awareness, except within God. We could not trust ourselves; we had to trust in God. We could not know ourselves; except via knowing God. We could throw no light on anything ourselves; all light – of knowledge and insight – was the light of God, And the greatest weakness of mankind? 'The weakness of his soul was in relying upon itself instead of trusting in you' (Augustine 1998:122).

> Introspection [for Augustine] is impossible. There is no light within. I can only gain insight, or any other sight, via God, via prayer. By focusing on me instead of on God, I lose you and I lose us. Since 'we' are part of the ground from which 'I' am formed, I also lose myself. Instead I chase after illusions. (Howard 2000:81)

> The soul of man, although it bears witness of the light, is not the Light. (Augustine 1998:144)

> we are too weak to discover the truth by reason alone and for this reason need the authority of sacred books. (Ibid.:117)

We forget that, for so long, God, not 'self', was the starting place, the destination and the means to all knowledge. The reality of God was not an intellectual proposition; it was 'common-sense'. It was day-to-day experience without which a life could not be lived. What need of 'proof' was there when we knew God more than we knew ourselves and when we could only know ourselves via God? Without God, we could not survive for a day. We would be immediately assailed by the Devil in his many incarnations: 'Alchemists of the Middle Ages postulated that men were made up of *homunculi*, an assortment of tiny gods and demons. Indeed, the predominant views of the pre-Enlightenment West held that the individual self was subject to intrusion by devilish forces . . . (Brinich & Shelley 2002:3).

As soon as you start to need 'proof', then Christian teaching is no longer centre stage. With the rediscovery of ancient Greek, pre-Christian, humanist philosophy some kind of reconciliation was needed. St Thomas Aquinas (1225–74) tried to knit together the teachings of Jesus and Aristotle. His arguments required logic, analysis, textual knowledge, scriptural authority and not just the blinding revelation of God's Light. Self was still lit up by God, but books and book-men, it seemed, were needed to underpin God.

This was not the way of the world as seen by Rene Descartes. What could he know? How could he find certainty? How could he find himself? Instead of deriving 'me' from God, Descartes inferred that there must be a God given the blinding reality of 'Self':

> I observed that, whilst I thus wished to think that all was false, it was absolutely necessary that I, who thus thought, should be somewhat; and as I observed that this truth, I think, therefore I am, ('cogito ergo sum'), was so certain and of such evidence that no ground of doubt, however extravagant, could be alleged by the sceptics capable of shaking it, I concluded that I might, without scruple, accept it as the first principle of the philosophy of which I was in search. (Descartes [1637] 1965:27)

Descartes started with 'self' as the fundamental gateway to the world. Everything else might be uncertain. But here was I, looking out on the world. 'I,' the thinker, the observer.

Similarly John Locke:

> For man knows that he himself exists. I think it is beyond question, that man has a clear idea of his own being; he knows certainly he exists, and that he is something. (Locke [1690] 1998: Bk IV Ch X)

Locke's referral to 'man' includes women of course, if only as an afterthought. That was the common sense view three centuries ago, and much more recently. Locke believed that we each have privileged access to, and knowledge of, 'myself'. We, unlike outside observers, could 'look in on' ourselves. We could 'introspect'. We could survey our thoughts, feelings and intentions directly.

Others; strangers, friends, counsellors, had to *infer* our state of consciousness inside us by observing our behaviour 'on the outside'. But we, each of us, could know ourselves directly. We knew which mask we might currently be wearing for the benefit, or at the expense, of others around us. We knew the nature of our 'real face'. Others had to surmise this by staring intently into our eyes, or, more realistically, by attending carefully to our words and actions.

> We see and hear and speak through the face, creating the impression that consciousness, 'the stuff of the self', is concentrated there, even though there are no grounds for believing it is really any more 'there' than in the right elbow or the small of the back. This is because there is no 'self stuff' to be located. There is nothing in, or behind, the face except for organic matter . . . (Broks 2003:112)

David Hume was another who sought to 'find himself'. He confessed to failure:

> For my part, when I enter most intimately into what I call 'myself', I always stumble on some particular perception or other, of heat or cold, light or shade, love or hatred, pain or pleasure. (Hume [1739] 1966: Book 1, Part 4, sec VI)

This was in response both to Locke and to Descartes. Hume doubted that we could extract knowledge of self by attempting some inner journey to the centre of the self. What was this centre? Hume tried to find it and found only ideas and perceptions.

The extent of Hume's scepticism was new. But his *doubt* that we could journey alone, to the centre of 'myself' had been the common sense, for centuries, among Christians who believed that introspection was impossible without God. Without God our efforts at introspection were chaotic. How could we distinguish between fantasy and reality? More recently, twentieth-century behaviourists have been highly critical of the value of 'looking within'. Instead, they have argued, we should look out and attend to what people actually *do*.

Counsellors vary in their views about how far people can introspect and know themselves unaided. 'Person-centred' counsellors believe that people are well able to undertake this journey into themselves and merely need to be facilitated by the counsellor. Cognitive behaviourists, on the other hand, believe that client views about self, world and their possibilities need to be challenged systematically when, as is often the case, these views are unrealistic, incomplete, out of perspective, or just plain wrong. Likewise, psychodynamic (Neo-Freudian) therapists consider that client insight and agency is profoundly compromised by unconscious impulses, hopes, fears and beliefs. In these latter two schools, the counsellor must work hard to assist clients to see themselves and their circumstances more fully and accurately.

Locke believed it is beyond question, that man has a clear idea of his own being. But no major philosopher since Locke has accepted this naïve introspectionism. We do not look in and find a self. Rather we speak particular languages of self and experience self in different ways according to the ideas and vocabularies about self that we have picked up from others and, above all, *from the ways in which others treat us.* Some claim to experience their 'inner child'. Others, their id, or God, or 'bourgeois false consciousness', or 'existential bad faith', or whatever, because these are the conceptions that are shaping the very nature of their experience.

One of the aims of this book is to provide a larger range of vocabularies about self from which readers can choose to express, explore, create and come to terms with themselves. This may help people build on, cope with, or move beyond, the identity that they have been blessed with, burdened by, at any rate formed from, past experience.

Carl Rogers experienced his 'authentic self'. Saint Augustine experienced God. Both claimed that the experience was authentic, 'organismic', orgasmic, perhaps. They felt it 'in their guts'.

How is this Babel of constructions of selfhood to be assessed? Parmenides (b. c.515 BC) believed that the multiplicity of things and selves masked the underlying fact that there was only one single, eternal reality; all was essentially one. Change, multiplicity, individual isolation – all these were essentially illusions. Plato (427–347 BC) apprehended 'Forms' as being the most important part of life and the real world in which the true self was located. The (soulful) essence of self was that which participated in this Platonic world of forms lying beyond all appearances. The form of 'cat-hood', or 'cattiness', for example, was more real than the brief incidence of individual cats. Heraclitus (c.540–c.480 BC), and many Eastern mystics, experienced Flux as the raw reality. The self was no fixed object at all but simply part of the interconnected movement of an ever-changing universe.

Niccolô Machiavelli (1469–1527), Artur Schopenhauer (1788–1860) and Friedrich Nietzsche (1844–1900) apprehended, as a basic impulse, a raw hunger for *power*. The essence of self was to be found within this raw forcefulness; the 'I' was a kind of vast life energy in the universe erupting through this human body. It was indifferent to petty individual preoccupations and was always overcoming and destroying that which we currently thought we were.

For the mythical Greek god Apollo, to find oneself and one's calling meant finding a genuine, deep, healing engagement with the *aesthetic beauty of classical form*. At its best, truth, beauty and goodness were as one and we found ourselves and became as one, and at peace, when we connected to, and identified with, this deep reality of existence.

For the mythical Greek god Dionysus, on the other hand, we found ourselves via *hedonistic release*. Self was not to be found merely in conformity and good works. To find oneself meant engaging with our monstrous as well as our decent impulses. Life was unliveable, and life would drain from our lives, unless we allowed some release into lechery, violence, bacchanalian expressiveness, sensuality and liberating chaos. Saturday evenings in most UK cities reveal that this Dionysian philosophy of self-expression and self-discovery is still alive and well. A whole self acknowledged the daemon within us, that is, the good *and* the demonic. Hindu teaching likewise observes that we cannot be whole unless we see, and accept, that the serpent is a part of the whole story of self and existence.

Other gods and goddesses in Greece and elsewhere focus on *war*, *cultivation*, *reflective withdrawal*, *aesthetics*, *Nature*, and so on. Each expresses part of our potential identity. Each of us, to a greater or lesser degree, identifies ourselves with, or dissociates ourselves from, these various ways of making something of ourselves. The nature of self may change over a lifetime, as our story and characterisation moves on from child, rebel, warrior, lover, partner, householder, manager, parent, grandparent, aesthete, elderly hedonist, old wise person, bitter old hermit, and (second) childhood. In different respects I am who I was, and I am not who I was. I am the person who has always had this history. I am also the person who keeps rewriting this history.

Baruch Spinoza (1632–77) took the view that self could not be known except when it was known and felt as part of the overall unity of the cosmos. We found ourselves by losing ourselves within an ecstatic trust of, and release through, the larger mystery of existence.

For Gottfried Willhelm von Leibnitz (1646–1716) getting to the basics of life meant getting to that which was without extension or form but which comprised everything that had extension and form. These were 'monads'. They were the deep and delightful reality of existence upon which he invited us to meditate. They changed according to their own inner principles rather than because of external causation. They were harmonious within a larger world because of the pre-established harmony of this universe. Self-discovery and self-expression, for Leibnitz, therefore required that we recognise ourselves as souls, with other souls. We were voices within this universal harmony or chorus. For Leibnitz, as with Augustine, we could find, define and express ourselves only within a 'City of God'. You sang your part within the larger heavenly chorus – or you were lost.

Jean Jacques Rousseau (1712–78) thought that we could only find ourselves if we took ourselves away from the false values, superficialities, manipulations, deceptions and masks of supposedly sophisticated urban living. To find ourselves as we really were we needed to get out of town, get away from it all, get back to simple honest living, communicate with and once again become a part of, the authentic, wholesome life of the peasantry. Henry David Thoreau (1817–62) had a similar agenda, and scores of lesser writers have explored the genre. This retreat to rustic authenticity remains an important life-style option for self-expression and self-fulfilment via simple and/or transcendental experience. Details are to be found in countless magazines, TV documentaries and consumer purchase options. For those who cannot afford it on a full-time basis, self-discovery and self-expression by 'getting away from it all' and 'getting back to Nature' becomes an important story for many people on holiday.

> Much of our contemporary vocabulary of the person, along with associated ways of life, finds its origins in the romantic period. It is a vocabulary of passion, purpose, depth, and personal significance: a vocabulary that generates awe of heroes, of genius, and of inspired work. (Gergen 1991:27, in Brinich & Shelley, 2002:6)

History demonstrates that human beings can experience and feel certain about many things and yet authentically disagree with each other about what is certain, what is real, what is authentic. They may imagine that they have got in touch with their 'real' self, and yet hindsight, or more sceptical insight, might show that they were merely toying with fashionable conceptualisations. These were generally taken, 'off the peg'; from whatever authority figure they had actively chosen to follow. Or, even more often, people would passively adopt all and sundry within the climate of opinion that embraced them. People may retreat to the rustic rural in order to find their real selves and may be certain that they have found it right up to the moment that they change their mind and decide that they were chasing an illusion.

For Immanual Kant, (1724–1804), self was a 'synthetic a priori' category of experience, as we explored in the previous chapter. For Jeremy Bentham (1748–1832), personal development was organised around the larger project of maximising human happiness, for which legislation and good government was essential. John Stuart Mill (1806–73) likewise believed that good government was about maximising happiness. The liberal state was successful when it promoted individual development, diversity, liberty and freedom. People should be quite free to express and explore – provided that their actions did not damage others and the society on which all this personal development depended. Mill did not believe that this freedom would be destabilising; indeed he doubted that many people would take advantage of it: 'The general average of mankind are not only moderate in intellect, but also moderate in inclinations: they have no tastes or wishes strong enough to incline them to do anything unusual' (Mill 'On Liberty' 1989:126).

These many and various accounts of self and its story are not just 'head-trips'. When concepts are basic to the way we make sense of our world, they shape the very nature of our identity and our experience, just as our identity shapes what we see. People, all too often, and often very tragically, have been prepared to die to defend the identity they have constructed for themselves. They will kill others, after seeing them as 'less than human', because of their bad, wrong, threatening and alien identities.

Ronald Barnett considered that: 'Through his intellectual work, Stephen Hawking lives in a different world from most others; he does not just think in a different way.' Oliver Wendell-Holmes argued that fundamental thinking about identity actually enlarged our identity: 'More complex and intense intellectual efforts mean a fuller and richer life. They mean more life.'

Søren Kierkegaard (1813–55) 'observed'/proposed/felt that: 'The human being is spirit. But what is spirit? Spirit is the self. But what is the self?' (Kierkegaard 1989:43). How, for Kierkegaard, were we to get real and become truly authentic in ourselves and in our experience?

> So much is spoken about wasting one's life. But the only life wasted is the life of one who so lived it, deceived by life's pleasures or its sorrows, that he never became decisively, eternally, conscious of himself as spirit, as self, or, what is the same, he never became aware – and gained in the deepest sense the impression – that there is a God there and that 'he', himself, his self, exists before this God, which infinite gain is never come by except through despair. (Ibid.:57)

Like Mill, Kierkegaard believed that it was better to be a Socrates dissatisfied than a pig satisfied. Also, that we were truly human insofar as we moved away from the herd with its animal pleasures and towards the consciousness of a philosopher. Most people, in Kierkegaard's experience, did not achieve this level of being. Instead: 'They use their abilities, amass wealth, carry out worldly enterprises, make prudent calculations, etc, and perhaps are mentioned in history, but they are not themselves' (Ibid.:65).

Insight and authenticity were hard to find and silvery-hair counsellors had no reason to believe that they had a special vantage point:

> What affects the adult is not so much the illusion of hope as, no doubt among other things, the grotesque illusion of looking down from some supposedly higher vantage point, free from illusion, upon the illusions of the young.
>
> This 'we have been', which we so often hear from older people, is just as great an illusion as the younger person's illusions of the future; they lie or invent, both of them. (Ibid:89)

Looking for patterns in the debates about identity

This high-speed tour of some of the most influential philosophies of identity has, I hope, made it clear that *ideas about who we are, and what we might and should become, are continually contested and often change.* What may seem 'obvious' to us concerning our identity was not always so, is not obvious to others and will not necessarily be obvious to our children and grandchildren. Somehow, though, we will continue to seek patterns and principles in this story of the self. We will, I think, wish to avoid the chaotic premise that any opinion about identity is as valid as any other and any identity can be created on demand.

This book operates within the following basic assumptions:

1. Confidence about the nature of our identity waxes and wanes. Today's gut certainty about who we are may, later, seem like yesterday's prejudice and illusion.
2. The larger the range of narratives on offer to clients, the more the options available to them.
3. Imagination and creativity give us only a limited freedom from the very real constraints of social and material circumstances.
4. It is impossible to empathise with a client or anyone else, except insofar as you have some understanding of the world-view that they have adopted.
5. Actions speak louder than words. The way we treat each other reveals how we see each other and affects how we see ourselves. *Ethics and entitlements are central to identity:* we become human by treating each other as human beings, and by knowing the difference between value and price.

Here, then, is a study of ideas about identity, constructions of self, of continuing relevance today. Is there a pattern to be detected? Is there a coherent sequence and development of ideas over the centuries? Or is it all just a babble of competing voices? This book will have failed if it only shows diversity and fails to pick out some developments, patterns, principles and, even, some *progress*!

One development – we have generally moved away from 'God' as a prime condition for understanding self. Another emerging consensus – the self that we seek to explore and understand is not coherent and understandable unless we see its links to the society and the language within which it exists. My identity is, in part, formed by the identity of the institutions, communities, societies, nation of which I am a part.

Most important of all: Selves are embedded and embodied; I get to know you as one whole personality, by talking and interacting with you and listening to your story, your plans, your (changing) views of your past and future. I watch how you speak, act, react and interact. I note how you treat others and how they treat you. I see how you present yourself and what you consider to be important. *I don't look for, or need to find, some non-physical ghost that inhabits your body.*

Matthew Arnold ([1869] 1993) took the view that we best found and developed ourselves by studying the 'sweetness and light' to be found in our culture's best literary and philosophical works. Universal education, Arnold believed, was essential to stave off the ever-present threat of anarchy. Personal development lay in cultural development. A patterned self came from a patterned culture.[2] F. R. Leavis ([1948] 1993) likewise argued that the self was elevated and enhanced through high culture generally and English literature in particular. The ethics and aesthetics to be found within this 'Great Tradition' was not of mere recreational value. They gave us a deeper appreciation of what we *could* be; who we *should* strive to become; and our place in the larger order of existence.

More recently, Paul Ricoeur (1974) stressed the importance of in-depth interpretation of texts. Through language we could engage with other perspectives, other worlds, other options, other ways of expressing ourselves and thereby enlarge our understanding of ourselves, our world, its opportunities and constraints.

For Arnold, Leavis and Ricoeur, personal cultivation and integrity were inseparable from cultural, literary, artistic development and commitment. *It is only very recently that the notion of personal development has become linked with, and confined to, psychological, individualistic, and psychotherapeutic discourse.* Up to the middle part of the twentieth century character formation was an ethical, spiritual, cultural, social and political process. The recent fashion for individualism and individual psychology is, from a historical perspective, something of an aberration. It has, I think and hope, already passed its peak. Social, cultural and linguistic dimensions of character formation may displace psychology as the best way of understanding the self, persons and what it means to be a human being. *Counsellors, therefore, might be wise to link their activities more closely to this larger cultural practice and less to an individualistic, psychological agenda.*

But how can talk about societies, culture and language do justice to experience? What is private and precious for me, surely, is my mental, emotional, private life? This, no doubt, is related to the social, cultural and linguistic, but surely it is not identical to these? Carrithers (1985) explores Mauss's (1938) distinction between:

> The personne, that is, is a conception of the individual human being as a member of a (1) significant and 2) ordered collectivity. (Carrithers et al. 1985:235)

> The other term of art is moi, defined as a conception of (1) the physical and mental individuality of human beings within (2) a natural or spiritual cosmos, and (3) interacting with each other as moral agents. (Ibid.:236)

Yet how useful and 'real' is this proposed distinction between the 'moi' (physical and mental) and the 'personne' (collective) dimensions of identity?

> What was previously located within the inside has been folded outside into the realm of linguistic and social practices. The intra/psychic is located within language. (Blackman & Walkerdine 2001:114)

Is this right? Do I not have private thoughts and feelings and do these not lie at the very core of my identity? The philosopher, Ludwig Wittgenstein thought very carefully on this matter and observed (1998:24e) that: 'I really do think with my pen, for my head often knows nothing of what my hand is writing.'

Likewise, I develop my views on the subject of identity in the process of reading and typing. When the writing goes well it just goes. I don't run the sentences in my head before I type them across the page. Also, when the work is coming together I feel that in some way I have got 'myself' together.

> one is that with which one concerns oneself. (Heidegger 1995:368)

Conversely, when my projects are falling apart, it feels as though 'I' am in some way coming apart. Does this mean that some non-physical homunculus sitting somewhere behind the eyes is disintegrating? Surely not? A mental breakdown involves a collapse of meaning rather than the loss of a non-physical 'entity'.

> Whenever you feel yourself falling apart, it is your meaning structure falling apart. (Rowe 1996:150)

> The sum total of these pictures – our perceptions, ideas, opinions, conclusions, beliefs – give us our sense of identity. You are the structured collection of all the meanings you have ever created. (Rowe 1997)

Making sense of our world, finding sensible, meaningful, worthwhile people and things to do and to attach us to, all this does not simply occupy the self, it appears actually to comprise and construct the self. Recognition of this can be found within ordinary language. For example, we might say 'This job, that woman, this holiday (or whatever) was "the making of" John.' Or, conversely, 'that event, person was John's "undoing".'

Is there anything fixed about the self and, if not, how can we talk or think about self at all? Certainly there are many who have accentuated the fluidity of self:

> The self is not to be thought of as a fixed institution; it exists wherever and whenever there is in fact a boundary interaction. To paraphrase Aristotle, 'When the thumb is pinched, the self exists in the painful thumb.' (Perls et al. 1979: 427)

> we consider 'self' to be an impermanent, plastic construct that exists only as an outcome of relational forces. (Spinelli 1994:347)

> Who is *I'ing*? What do you mean by *I*? (Watts 1975a)

> we may call any inanimate object 'I' with which we are identifying our will and purpose. (Cooley, 1902)

Can identity ever be 'pinned down'?

There is a problem in that self does not appear to be a fixed object, and certainly not just a physical body. On the other hand mystical talk of selves as 'ghosts in the machine' (as Descartes described them) does not throw enough real light on the subject. Certainly we all experience ourselves as changing. We wonder what we might have in common with the younger self that we used to be. After major events we may feel quite estranged from the self we were. On the other hand, we also feel, and to a very substantial degree, a *continuity* with our past and, for that matter, with the future that we are busy trying to bring about. We might say (to ourselves?) 'I have changed a great deal in the last x years'. But we also believe that there is some continuity of 'I-ness' that these changing 'I's partake of. (The very word 'identity' presupposes that something now is in some way identical with something gone.) An elderly demented individual is no longer the person they used to be. But: 'It is precisely *because* it is quite clear that this is my grandfather that the thought of visits is such a nightmare' (Cockburn 2001:126).

We all tend to crave a degree of *stability* in this 'I' that I am. If I don't change at all I may become bored with myself. If I change too rapidly, I may become frightened and lose a sense of the 'I' that, I imagine, I am. In part we find this stability by *identifying* ourselves with significant and familiar objects, important projects, people and places around us. We 'take them in' and make them a part of us such that, if and when we lose them, we feel that we have, in some sense, lost a part of ourselves. 'So a boy flying a kite will say "I am higher than you," or one shooting at a mark will declare that he is just below the bullseye' (Cooley 1902, online at: http://www2.pfeiffer.edu/~lridener/courses/SLTHRS97.HTML).

The pilot or driver may initially feel that they are in their vehicle. Then it may seem as if they are wearing it. Finally it, and they, as veterans, become as one.

Just what we do, and do not, include as significant parts of 'me' is important in understanding how people see themselves. 'We may exclude parts of our body from our body image, or we may include non-existent part of our body in our body image' (Spinelli 1994:344). If we don't like parts of our body we may ***disassociate*** ourselves from that imperfect part. I might think, for example, 'I *have* a big nose, but that is not the *real* me. It just gets in the way. If only I could get rid of it and show myself better.' And many people, with the technology available via cosmetic surgery, are doing just that. Of course their perception of their inadequate bodies may be profoundly inaccurate. Many young women are convinced, against all the evidence to the contrary, that they are extremely fat. The fat person they imagine they see is not the real person they believe is inside them. If only, they may think, they could get a better body to show themselves off better.

Entire philosophies of self have involved disassociating, dis-identifying, disembodying self, in effect, from our bodies. We may say that we *have* a body, that we in some sense *occupy* this body, but that we are not a body at all. We are a non-physical 'soul', psyche, spirit, or whatever.

It is commonplace to imagine ourselves both as aggressors who must get hold of, and get a grip on, ourselves; and as victims who are worn down by, and beaten up by, the way we treat ourselves. We do to ourselves and are done to by ourselves. A great deal of unnecessary body tension arises from this split between the controlling and controlled self. I must raise my arms, so I tense my shoulders. But my arms can rise without this extra tension. *So much muscular tension appears to be a consequence of the civil war we conduct within ourselves*; tyrant versus victim and/or saboteur. Hedonist child plays truant in defiance of introjected authoritarian self. We binge in revolt against the authority inside us; then feel guilty, and buckle down to work, as the voice of that authority takes over once again.

By failing to locate the self and the problem it faces, we fail to mobilise muscles suitably. We grit our teeth in order to deal with a situation where there is nothing to bite. We tense our stomach against a punch that was never going to be physically delivered. We crouch down or droop against an abstract pressure that will not physically hit us. And so on.

Often, we *identity* ourselves with desired objects, people, projects, habits, beliefs, occupations, skills, networks, institutions or ideas that we own, embrace or are a part of. John's silver Jaguar becomes a part of John. John's core ideas and beliefs are a part of John. John's hobbies and interests may be a part of John. John's holiday experiences may contribute to John's sense of self. He may feel that he has 'made more of himself' via his various adventures. 'in the second half of the century leisure activity and/or consumer habits are being increasingly experienced by individuals as the basis of their social identity' (Chaney 1996:112).

Our principle projects and ideals may be seen as a part of who we are. Though how far might these have been sold to us without our realising it?

> the myth of Woodstock as a sovereign youth-culture state was part of a vast project of generational self-definition – a concept that would have been wholly foreign to those in attendance at Woodstock 94, for whom the search for self had always been shaped by marketing hype, whether or not they believed it or defined themselves against it. This is a side effect of brand expansion that is far more difficult to track and quantify than the branding of culture and city spaces. This loss of space happens inside the individual; it is a colonisation not of physical space but of mental space. (Klein 2001:66)

What is it that we choose and genuinely make for, and a part of, ourselves? What is there that is permanent, static, central and unchanging as a part of us?

> as the individual begins to identify with the recording and thinking and memory aspects of the organism, he begins to form a conception of himself as a static, permanent, persistent self; and that thought-self tended to feel separate not only from the impulsive world around it, but also from the spontaneous aspects of its own body. (Wilbur 1981:198)

We do indeed construct some kind of stability and persistence within our identity and our surroundings. For, otherwise, can we be said to have an identity at all? It is true though, that however much of a stable self we construct for ourselves, there is always that lurking, lingering, or at times positively overwhelming, fear that all that we have and hold will be ripped from us and we will cease even to be the self we think we are. 'In a deeper sense man is prone to some form of basic anxiety: anxiety is caused by an attachment to the belief in 'I' and 'me', which instead of giving us a feeling of security, creates worry and anxiety (*paritassana*)' (de Silva 2000:44).

We make a stable self-image in order to feel secure, yet we feel anxious about how stable it really is. What is the solution? Where is a balance to be found? Perhaps we should not cling too fiercely to ideas we have about ourselves? But should we go to the other extreme and abandon any efforts to construct a stable self? How could we live with such flux?

> A reasonably secure identity, as against a paranoically cohesive one, is a necessary condition of human well-being, and those postmodernists who fail to mention this fact are being morally irresponsible. Neither a subject which cannot name itself at all, nor one which can name itself only too well, is likely to be an effective agent of social transformation. (Eagleton 1996:126)

> It is one thing to decentre or deconstruct the autonomous, rational, masculinist self of Enlightenment culture; yet it is quite another to imagine that self as a category can be conveniently done away with altogether. (Elliott 2003:128)

We change according to circumstance. We show different aspects of ourselves to different people and in different situations. But is there no underlying continuity at all? Can we just wear any mask? Is there a 'real' face beneath the presentation? Or are we really two faced or fifty faced? 'We have become *actors* in the sense that the word had for the Romans – people capable of assuming the *externals* of *any personality* because they have none of their own' (Kamenka 1980:18–19, in Blake et al. 1998:83).

We are surely right to feel uneasy about such unprincipled willingness to take on just any persona that gets us a desired result?

So what are we to make of all the identity statements, options and 'life-style' choices nowadays available to us? Do these mean that we can make anything, or much more of, ourselves than the peasantry growing the potatoes? Do all these images and image options free us to make more of ourselves than our ancestors were ever able to do? Or do they take us further away from any kind of genuine contact with ourselves? 'In *Fatal Strategies* (1983), Baudrillard argues that images and simulations have become so intoxicating, so compelling, and so seductive that the self is crushed' (Elliott 2003:141).

We may feel pride in our achievements, yet pride may be oppressive, destructive and may itself belie our underlying feelings: 'When I am trying to impress someone with my self-importance, this is a signal that I don't accept myself, that I think I'm not very important as I am' (Stevens 1977:268).

Is there a 'real' me?

So what is real, within and around me? Or is this 'within' and 'around' itself unreal or/and a function of the language we happen to use? For counsellors and therapists talk is generally seen as the royal road, which can take us to a deeper understanding of ourselves and our circumstances. But do we *discover* ourselves via talk? Or is the 'self-talk' available to us itself the means by which self is *created* – and *constrained*? 'we do not use language to discover our subjectivity but are rather constituted as subjects by its impersonal operation' (Cohen & Taylor 1992:6).

Even if the language does not itself confine and constrain our understanding of who we are, do we in fact know ourselves very well? Does our therapist know us better than we know ourselves? How do we know? How does she know? 'Most people confuse self-knowledge with knowledge of their conscious ego-personalities. Anyone who has any ego-consciousness at all takes it for granted that he knows himself. But the ego knows only its own contents, not the unconscious and its contents' (Jung 1996:351).

Therapists often claim to know us better than we know ourselves, though the knowledge, the language, the methods, the concepts, the ideas about self and its nature, vary considerably between the (many) different schools of therapy. And it is not just therapy that is getting in on the act of creating identities. The entire marketing industry is getting involved. In our postmodern marketplace, global corporations do not just identify personalities and then find products and services to satisfy them. On the contrary, they find whole life-style packages and produce an entire suite of products and services that go with the image, the identity, the way of life. You find yourself by buying into our life-style. You become the person in the advertisement. You think as they do, you act as they do, you dream as they do. 'The ad tells teenage girls, for example, who they are and how they should act' (Lewis 2002:136).

Making something of yourself is a tough assignment. Cannot we just, instead, buy a self and a lifestyle to suit, off the shelf? Why, certainly we can. We can go upmarket, or just choose something noisy, short and flashy. If it's MTV, for example, we can have Euro-wide noise, light, sound, surrealism, style (but not much substance), instant gratification (of a sort), and it will all be over shortly – on an endless loop of wild celebration and hip happenings.

As Hebdige observes, (Kidd 2002) youth's focus on style is an important effort to create identity. But if street teenagers come up with something alive, original, genuine and significant, it will not be long before some corporation will move in, co-opt, and try to sell the style and statement back to them, or to someone else.

Klein (2001:133) notes that in the USA it is now a commonplace for poor black style to be used as a means of selling products (style) to rich whites. Street 'cool', credibility and authenticity are central components of teenage identity formation. They are frequently associated with designer products. Buy the product and you, too, can announce your cool. In postmodern society anything goes. You can, if you wish, become a 'wigger' (a 'white nigger') as the black/white comedian Ali G has done, with tongue in cheek, in the UK. He does not black his face but 'acts black' enough for a conservative politician in conversation to say to him 'you blacks'.

You can express your negativity as a 'slacker' (Kidd 2002:132). You, too, can tell the world 'I'm a loser baby, so why don't you kill me?' Or you can kill others, and progress as a criminal, in a variety of cyber cities, within computer software worlds that are becoming bigger business than Hollywood. Or you can watch as women and men all over the world bare themselves, with ever more forensic close ups, in photos and videos available online.[4]

Or perhaps, as a woman, you see more options opening to you than your mother had available to her? You see yourself as striving more successfully than the dull, daydreaming, drifting and depressive boys all around you. You can become a suited executive and find yourself a toy boy. You can emulate Madonna as a postmodern icon. You, like her, could endlessly reinvent yourself. You could become a 'bricoleur', adopting and adapting ever changing cultural forms, ethnic styles, religious images, deviant sexual practices. Will it be Zen this year? And Sufism later? Will you try designer lesbianism?

Who are you? A 1950s 'organisation man', now retired? A postwar baby boomer constructed around Woodstock and the 1960s carnival, now approaching early retirement, (as long as the pension scheme remains in place)? A 'Generation X' person (circa 1964–79)? That is, you are a child of the baby boomers? You grew up in the sixties? You are nihilistic? You see the future as bleak? You face a future of 'McJobs' with nothing worth committing to and identifying yourself with?

But surely there is more to life than style and words? What about deeds? Surely we can do something original that is genuinely ours and is not just a style statement sold to us by someone else? 'Language – I want to say – is a refinement, "in the beginning was the deed"' (Wittgenstein 1998:36e). Actions speak louder than words. But what significant actions are available to us in a world where machines are doing most of the physical work and where most of the remaining jobs themselves consist in words? There are the McJobs of course. The ever growing service sector keeps many busy but can people really 'be themselves' in these jobs? As train managers they read their script; as waitresses they learn their lines, as a supermarket checkout person they don't need to say anything; as a call centre operative they follow a tightly supervised and monitored script. They wait for talking machines, or graduates in India, to displace them.

As temporary part-time workers they are nobody, but they can try to be a 'somebody'. They can enlarge their curriculum vitae. They can add units and 'value' by completing a checklist of pre-determined outcomes. They can do this in a life-long learning programme that never ends: course modules, in-service training, continuing professional development, parenting training, 'third age' recreation. They can say 'I am accredited, and continuously updated and re-accredited, therefore I exist.'

As consumers they are, of course, Kings and Queens (for as long as the cash or credit holds out). So, when they get home, they can explore and express themselves by choosing from scores of interactive TV stations, interactive computer adventure games, holiday, leisure and life-style packages. Or they can drink themselves into a Dionysian frenzy. Or they can be voyeurs, watching others talk, sleep, flirt, having sex, winning a fortune, defining themselves to their audience in their 15 minutes of fame.

How much room is there, in any of this, for an individual perspective, a personal choice, a human achievement? At work, certainly, all that many people can do, and are required to do, is to achieve the employers' defined outcomes or the vendors' predetermined package options. They are not required, and are not allowed, to put their own personal mark on their work since quality control requires that every product and service unit is identical within the parameters selected by the manager for the consumer.

How far, in any case, do individuals even *want* to take a genuinely individual perspective or make a distinct, particular and personal mark? There are already enough 'unique' choices and permutations of colour, style and cool. Why bother to search for an identity statement of my own when there are so many stylishly prepared and colour coordinated statements for me to choose from? 'Under all the packages each of us carries, a different self can be discovered. *You are* not any of the things you have set aside. You are no content at all!' (Gendlin 1982:79).

This is less than reassuring. I can 'be' from any number of possibilities. I can choose from 64 channels. I can go anywhere in the world, except that everywhere is beginning to look more like everywhere else. I can go to 'unspoilt' environments and 'find' myself, except that the unspoilt is expensive and carefully planned, groomed and coordinated. Almost no space or option is left that has not been intensively and extensively designed and coordinated by professional consultants 'with me in mind'. So much for my free choice. 'It may not be so much that we are *doing* things as that they are happening *through* us. Maybe we're not so much *willing* our actions as *witnessing* them' (Smail 1996:183).

If that is so, what about personal agency and moral responsibility? Yet it does sometimes feel as if it is so and that we do *witness* our life rather than *determine* it. Certainly marketing and motivation researchers, and other hypnotists, appear confident that they can substantially control, predict and shape that which we will 'freely choose'.

> If I look meaningfully at somebody in a session and say 'Now, look, there's a part of you that finds this a little scary and I can understand that,' that's a huge lie. 'Part of *what*?' I don't know what that means.
>
> These descriptions are just useful ways of organising experience. (Bandler & Grinder 1982:46)

A hypnotist takes hold of a person's imagination, circumstance and identity and creates very surprising results and an alarming degree of control. They dance between strategic vagueness, where the client fills in the detail, and a specificity that anchors the client's attention. How much hypnosis goes on that we are not even aware of? Look at the trance states of viewers and consumers, (and clients?) How much of what we think are our ideas about ourselves and others are ours at all? Mill celebrated the possibility of individual diversity in a liberal democracy. He did not, however, believe that many would opt for the genuine article. I suspect he would be confirmed in his worst fears if he came back to see the current state of 'personal development' in these liberal democracies. 'I'm convinced that multiple personalities are manufactured by parents and well-meaning therapists; they are not spontaneously derived' (Bandler & Grinder 1981:189).

Yet surely there is an underlying integrity, authenticity and reality to be found somewhere in all this froth of appearance, sub-personality, image-making and focus on style at the expense of substance? Is there not a real self struggling to get out?

> According to Gestalt theory the natural state of growth for a person is towards integration, which is a state in which all the parts of a person function interrelatedly. There are no parts of the person alienated when integration is achieved. Such divisions, however, are common. Sometimes a person will no longer wish to identify with a part of himself and try to disown it. (Passons 1975:136)

Our very notions of maturity and wisdom imply that character building, virtue, discipline and genuineness are possible and desirable, albeit difficult. Are we chasing illusions? Is a wise and mature person merely an old, or dead, middle-class white male with patriarchal, Euro-centric, oppressive and exploitative tendencies? Obviously not if maturity and wisdom are genuine and worthwhile goals.

Rainwater (1981) refers to an 'Old Wise Person' exercise, where we imagine, engage with and learn from an old wise person. This, she claims, is a device to bring out the best in the person concerned. The person's own wisdom is projected into the imagined other. Or is it? Who decides? Perhaps what is projected is just prejudice? A sub-personality? My inner child (when I might be better off with my 'inner adult'). Or my stuffy old super-ego, when I might be better off with my inner child? Or my id? (whatever that may be).

Rainwater and others, offer the chance for us to have conversations with parts of ourselves. We can talk to our genitals, our ugly nose, our legs, anything. And they, in our imagination at least, can talk back to us as though they were individual persons – sub-personalities – in their own right. In so doing we can, perhaps, unravel some kind of insight, or unconscious preoccupation concerning these parts. Or else we can create psychodramas with no reality to them at all? We may merely be indulging our imagination, or prejudice, to no real purpose?

This capacity of imagination in human beings is enormously powerful and significant. The way we see ourselves fundamentally influences what we do, and don't do, and the situations we seek to create for ourselves. There is a dynamic relationship between identity, circumstance, choice, attitudes and behaviour. Much of what we choose and don't choose arises as a consequence of our imagined identity. *We do what we do because these are the things that are done by the sort of person we see ourselves to be.*

For example, I remember two public[5] school boys aged around eight or nine on a train from York to London. They occupied space on the train, and took in the world around them, with a confidence, demeanour and maturity that would be much harder to achieve for most children from less-privileged backgrounds. They were not loud, or aggressive, but it was clear that they already knew that, whatever the details, they would be occupying one or other of the most choice, powerful, stimulating and lucrative corners of adult life. They had, no doubt, been treated as sons of the powerful since birth. They could see what they were 'entitled' to. Others could see that they could see, and would no doubt go on responding with suitable deference.

'*I can see myself*', or '*I can't see myself* doing x' is crucial if x is to be done. This is important for counsellors. In order to help clients see themselves as doing x, the counsellor must herself be able to see the client doing this. She must then be able to communicate this to the client. If we are to help each other, we need to be able to see the other doing something that they, currently, are unable to see themselves doing. I may, thereby, help you because I see more in you than you see in yourself.

We will be unwilling (and possibly unable) to do something if we think that 'this is just not *me*'. Conversely, we will be unwilling to *stop* (trying to) do something if we think that 'this *is* me'. Imagination takes us beyond what is currently really there. But it also needs to be informed by real constraints if it is to be useful to us. An architect imagines a building from pieces of stone, metal and cement. But the architect's imagination, if it is to produce a building that really will stand, must be constrained and informed by the real limitations of stone, metal and cement. Creativity does not defy reality; it works with it. So, for example, self-help books that advise us that we only need to imagine we are super and we will become so, are encouraging a magical denial of reality rather than an imaginative engagement with it. Successful architects imagine the building, and imagine *themselves* creating it. But their imagination is highly disciplined and concerned with real, achievable, options.

The ways we see ourselves is far more an act of *imagination* than it is an act of simple *perception*;[6] but this imagination, likewise, must engage with, rather than ignore, real opportunities and constraints.

Finding ourselves and losing ourselves

Human beings, unlike other animals, deal in abstractions and possibilities as well as specific here and now opportunities and threats. This imaginative capacity allowed us to triumph over the sabre-tooth tiger. It can also, if we allow it, turn us into chronically anxious neurotics frozen with fear and tension concerning all the dangers we may face. Our problems can be imagined as vast objects looming over us, or as tiny challenges dwarfed by our vast stature or (more often) as something in between. We can, in imagination, and according to the metaphors we choose, look *down* on our problem, or *up* to it. We can look at it as though it was dangerously close to us or at a comfortable distance away. Accordingly, our anxiety levels will rise or fall, and we will be confident, panic stricken, or complacent.

Descartes argued that we always put ourselves into our imaginative frame; seeing involved a seer, hearing a hearer, thinking a thinker etc. – 'me'. Yet is this really the case? When we attend closely to anything, there may be no awareness, appearance or representation of 'me' either perceived or imagined. The object of my attention, the project in hand, can take up *all* my attention. I may have no awareness of myself at all. We may be lost in thought, lost in what we see, hear and do. I may be so wrapped up listening to a piece of music that there is only the music.

> There are many different ways in which the person or I appears to our minds. In one way, the I appears to be permanent, unitary, and under its own power; in this

> mode of appearance the I seems to be a separate entity from mind and body with the person as the use or enjoyer and mind and body as what is used or enjoyed. No Buddhist school of tenets accepts that such a person exists. (Gyatso, The Fourteenth Dalai Lama, 1984:162)

> This same 'disappearance' of the self may occur when we are deeply *immersed in an activity* such as long-distance running, driving a car, or gardening. (Spinelli 1994:345)

This experience of losing ourselves by immersion in some activity that we value and enjoy is, hopefully, one that we are all familiar with. Within such an experience, have we lost ourselves or, as the Buddhists suggest, have we merely lost sight of an *idea* of self that was never real and true in the first place?

How strange to be 'me'! I am familiar and mysterious. Continuous and discontinuous. Always present and never here. I am the subject who attends and the object of my attention. I am the process of attending and the context of attention. I am at one and divided. I am aware, and ignorant. I am wise and a fool. Detached and committed. I am at home and true to myself – and/or no more than a series of fables and fictions?

> Our minds are perpetually restless, our attention is always distracted, so wherever we are, whatever we are doing, we are never completely *there*. In short, we are not truly conscious of anything, including our own self. (Sardar 2002:151)

> Pseudo individuality is rife: from the standardised jazz improvisation to the exceptional film star whose hair curls over her eye to demonstrate her originality. (Adorno & Horkheimer 1999:154)

> This notion of the autonomous subject, sure of its own identity and continuing throughout the individual human being's life, was dominant not just in philosophy, but also in political thought (not least as a grounding assumption of liberalism and psychology) (Edgar & Sedgwick 1999:184)

Of course, we have mirrors – and flat water and shiny surfaces. We can, with these, see ourselves as, we imagine, others see us. We can remember what we saw. We can then, in imagination, place ourselves outside our own body and look in on our body and on what we are saying and doing. This imaginative capacity itself provides us with opportunities and threats:

> At present we are dissociated, dualistic personalities with a dualistic language, a dualistic mentality, a dualistic existence. The deep split in our personality, the conflict between deliberate and spontaneous behaviour, is the outstanding characteristic of our time. (Stevens 1977:46)

We can, as Perls observes, engage in 'retroflection'; splitting ourselves between doer-of-things-to-myself and masochistic object-being-done-to-by-myself. We can spend, in imagination, more time looking in on ourselves than we spend looking out on the world. We can become overly self-conscious. We can paralyse ourselves with all this meta-observation. We can lose necessary spontaneity. We can do unto ourselves and be done to, done and undone, by ourselves. On the other hand, when our imagination is being used constructively we can imagine how we are being seen, or will be seen, by others and modify our actions accordingly.

In some respects, the 'I', then, is like a cursor of attention. 'I', can be like the variable 'x' in algebra, it takes on different values, shapes, identities in different circumstances. The sentence "I am . . ." can be completed in millions of different ways, it changes all the time, and the 'I' thereby changed accordingly. 'The self is not the figure it creates but the creating of the figure: that is, self is the dynamic relation of ground and figure' (Perls et al. 1979:470). 'In ideal circumstances the self does not have much personality. It is the sage of Tao that is 'like water', assuming the form of the receptacle' (Ibid.:485).

In important and fundamental respects we construe both our world and ourselves. But what about continuity? Within this ever-changing 'I-ness' we assume that there is a thread that holds the whole process together.

> For Scheler, the person is never to be thought of as a Thing or a substance; the person is rather the unity of living-through which is immediately experienced in and with our Experiences. (Heidegger 1995:73)

The keyword here is 'unity'; we look back on our memories, on our stream of consciousness; we know that much remains unconscious, that much we did not attend to in the first place; that much we have forgotten. We now know that, in remembering something, we *reconstruct* it more than we *retrieve* it. But, through all this we see a continuity of 'I'. I am the *same* person who remembered, forgot, did or did not attend. I may change and change again; and sometimes so radically that I hardly know myself as I was. Yet in all this change we continue in the belief that it is this same 'I' that has been involved in all this changing. Even when we hardly seem to know who we are, we tend to persist in the view that we are the *same* 'me' who no longer knows myself.

> A person is in any case given as a performer of intentional acts which are bound together by the unity of a meaning. (Heidegger 1995:73)

We certainly seek for such unity of meaning, but do we *find* it or do we *impose* it on a chaotic substratum that is not so united and stable as we might wish it, and ourselves, to be?

> The self is literally *constructed* out of our experience with the object world. This 'self' which we take to be 'me' and which feels so present and so real to us is actually an internalised image, a composite representation, constructed by a selective and imaginative 'remembering' of past encounters with significant objects in our world (Bruner 1964). In fact, the self is viewed in both psychologies [object relations theory and

> Buddhism] as a representation *which is actually being constructed anew from moment to moment.* (Wilbur et al. 1986:22)

How strange that our own identities, which we presume to be so basic to us, are contested so profoundly with some denying the real existence of a self. After all, we may ask, in an uncertain world surely I can be sure that there is a 'me' here and now who is not sure? I rely on there being an 'I' who was here yesterday, is here today, and may hopefully be here tomorrow. If I cannot even rely on my own presence then what can I rely on?

Postmodern identities

We must look, if only briefly, at what so many sociologists, and some (French) psychoanalysts, are doing to us; to the 'I' who is supposedly so much at the heart of therapy, democracy, consumerism, our deepest hopes and dreams. Perhaps I should indeed give up on me and go off into cyber-space and be whichever fictional personality, name, place and history I present to some (real or imagined) other? 'This is more real than my real life,' says a character who turns out to be a man playing a woman who is pretending to be a man. In this game the self is constructed and the rules of social interaction are built, not received. (Turkle 1997:10)

Rolande Barthes (1915–80) explored the ways in which myths are of such central importance in contemporary culture. Much, he argued, of what we see as foundational realities about our world and ourselves are fantasies; mythical stories that it suits us to believe in because they simplify and make safe an otherwise intolerably unstable, chaotic, and ever-changing flux.

Jacques Derrida (1930–) argued that our perennial efforts to *pin down* meanings and identities are doomed to failure. We might as well try to pin down and freeze the waves in the sea. Derrida argued that we are always looking for a starting point, reference point, centre, self, which we can use as a 'keynote' from which to start, end and frame our patterns of meaning-making, our symphonies of understanding (my metaphor). We imagine that these keynotes, centres, foundations are basic truths about the universe. But they are more nearly truths about our need to make patterns. In order to understand we simplify and simplify. We create binary opposites – for example, self/other, good/evil, light/dark, masculine/feminine, right/left, being/nothingness, reason/madness, word/silence, culture/nature, mind/body and imagine that these binaries have been *found* rather than *created*. We generally value, privilege and give priority to one of the pairs over the other and then imagine that the tensions between them are real rather than *created*.

Derrida proposed that we 'deconstruct' these binary opposites, by which he means that we take them apart in such a way as to show that they are not opposites at all, but rather that they are each a part of, and dependent upon, the other. Each is defined in terms of its relationship with the other. There is, therefore, no 'essence' to find – in anything or anyone. Things and selves are defined and understood not in terms of what they essentially, finally, foundationally and 'really' are. Instead, things and selves are defined in terms of how they *differ* from other things we have bound them together with in a binary. I am 'me' which means I am not *you* or *it*. When we find meaning in anything and understand anything, we do not break it down into an essence; we compare it with something else. It *is* . . . (whatever) because it is *different* from . . . (whatever).

Derrida talks of différance, which, in French, encapsulates both *difference* and *deferring*. We make meaning by making comparisons, examining differences. We also *defer* meaning. Meanings are deferred first in that they are never final. Second, in that one half of a binary defers to the other, as the more central, significant, and superior side of the binary. Meanings are additionally deferred in that other differences, other comparisons, can always be considered. Different comparisons, different binaries will show up different kinds of meaning, other ways of understanding. Nothing, therefore, finally or singly means anything, but meanings are enriched by multiplicity of meaning. This process is not chaotic. On the contrary, it constructs a far richer world. All our current philosophies themselves defer to whatever comparisons, contexts and binaries we choose to explore next. Meaning, like life, is always on the move. The process is not merely intellectual, but passionate and aesthetic:

> Taste is first and foremost the distaste of the tastes of others. (Pierre Bourdieu 1987)

Such construction and deconstruction of différance implied that there was no finally true, fixed and essential self to find. I only feel more or less 'real' right now in relation to a specific other 'not-so-real' with which I am making a comparison. Hence it is possible to say, as advertisers do, 'Coke, the *real* thing' if it is defined as more real than, say, a cheaper cola, with none of the traditional advertising dream connotations of 'real coke'. We can also say that Coke is not at all real if we offer different, more traditional criteria. Coke, we may say, is less real than 'traditional' ginger beer brewed by farm girls in rustic, romantic, rural farmhouses.

But nothing is finally traditional or modern or artificial; it all depends on the comparison, differentiation and criteria that you have in mind. Today's traditional was yesterday's modern and the avant-garde of the day before. On the other hand, it does not follow that *anything* at *any time* is as real, true, or genuine as anything else is. You have to offer criteria, a context, a purpose, an argument and others can criticise all of this. Lives and selves, in a postmodern context do not have to become *chaotic*; but they are certainly more *complex* than we might have preferred and they certainly depend much more than we thought on contexts, comparisons, perspectives and intentions.

Michel Foucault (1926–84) argued that the process of our making sense of ourselves and our world could not be separated out from the exercise of power and control over our world. We are never, in other words, disembodied and dispassionate observers with no axe to grind. We are always grinding our axes because this is what it is to be human. We always have purposes, intentions, interests to protect and promote, and all our understandings of our circumstances, ourselves and others are shaped, very strongly, by these needs to survive and prosper. And, moreover, this 'we' is not something that comes *to* language, but, more so, our identity comes *from* the language that we are using, or which others are using at our expense. My story tells me more than I tell my story.

Who we are is not so much *found* and *described* by language as *shaped by* language, which is why there are as many selves as there are languages to describe self. Identity is shaped by the 'gaze' of various discourses and, thanks to the burgeoning therapy industry, there are more discourses of self than, for example, I will have space to refer to in this book. Moreover, as we read any text we are ourselves as reader placed, positioned, situated and constructed by the text. The text will itself contain implicit assumptions about who we are, where we are and what we want.

Jacques Lacan (1901–81), like Jacques Derrida, argued that there is no essential or foundational self to be found; that meaning is always deferred and never finally found. Identities are unstable and open; they change as circumstance changes; their meanings depend on contexts and intentions. Selves, subjects are never finally found and stable, they never arrive at some final destination. There is never a final home to go to. There is always a sense of 'lack' as we move on to satisfy our next needs and desires. There is no way that desire will ever be finally satisfied and this is because of the nature of desire rather than the nature of the world.

Jean François Lyotard (1924–98) developed this deconstructionist agenda by arguing that, since meaning is always deferred and there are no final 'foundations', then there can be no final meta-narrative about the world or about ourselves. Foundations exist only within the context of the temporary and conditional and context-sensitive binary – 'foundation/superstructure'.

For Jean Baudrillard (1929–), technology had made any notion of an underlying reality unsustainable. Advertisers attached realities to products, and people imagined that, by buying the product, they could buy into the reality and the identity. Postmodern identities, therefore, were bought, off the shelf, within a particular, coordinated, lifestyle package. Television, the Internet, computers, and all the other media were coming together to create 'hyperrealities'. These constructed worlds, and selves, were more real and vibrant than reality. Reality, as one information-technologist observed, was 80 million pixels. Copies were so perfect, so indistinguishable from originals, that the notion of a copy had lost its meaning.

Imitations of imitations abound; reflections of reflections are everywhere. Self looks at self looking at self being looked at by selves looking at selves being looked at. It is a recipe for giddiness. Is there a foundational self and real world to be found? Should we celebrate in response to all these cyber opportunities? Or despair? Is self an illusion as Baudrillard suggests? Is the deconstruction of identity a postmodern road to anarchy? Or a traditional Buddhist insight concerning the illusory self?

> 'Part of me, a very important part of me, only exists inside PernMUD,' says one player. (Turkle 1997:12)

> 'RL [Real Life] is just one more window,' he repeats, 'and it's not usually my best one.' (Ibid.:13)

For many, the most real part of their lives is their essentially imaginary relationships with celebrities: 'We may well know more about Merv, Oprah, Johhny, and Phil than we do our neighbours. Celebrities are not our community elders, they are our community.' (Gergen 1991:56)

Stuart Hall suggests that self is something that we *produce*. For Goffman, self is a presentation. For Zweig, self has died. Does anyone still believe in Descartes' view of self as a non-physical mind inhabiting a material body? Or, do most people still believe in Descartes' account even though they may not even have heard of Descartes? The idea of the ghost in the machine at least gave integrity to the concept of self. The postmodern self, on the other hand, appears fragmented, unreal, disintegrated.

Diversity and integrity of identity

John Paul Sartre (1905–80) stressed the integrity of identity by viewing self as *a little God which inhabits me and which possesses my freedom as a metaphysical virtue*. Sartre distinguished between 'Being-*for*-itself' – that restless spirit that moves on from whatever we had made of ourselves, and 'Being-for-others' – the me that is an observed object for others making something of themselves. Is the self that we are seeking to *become* more crucial than any self that we can currently *define*? Kierkegaard argued that self is a balancing act between infinite potential and finite actuality and that integrity was found by finding a suitable balance.

Martin Heidegger argued that integrity was achieved via the integrity of our environment and our projects. Spaces and objects did not just *surround* us; they *characterised* us. Home, work-ware, leisure-ware, car, all made up part of who we are and helped to hold us together. Buddhists, on the other hand, argue that all these accoutrements are distractions, a set of imaginary props that create an imaginary self. *Perhaps there are no final and foundational answers to many questions about the nature of identity, but answers conditional upon the circumstances, comparisons, contexts and intentions within which the questions are being specifically asked?*

Social class, gender and race, obviously, are enormously significant in establishing the integrity of our identity and in forming the great diversity to be found in human identities. What can I make of myself as black, female, working class, poor? What, more importantly perhaps, do all these circumstances make of me?

The 'nature' versus 'nurture' argument goes on as regards gender identity in particular. For example, do females focus on emotions and relations because of society or biology? Do males have 'inevitable' male characteristics or are they formed by social expectations and as a result of being treated 'like boys'? We know that humans are far more malleable by environment than other animals, but also that nature and nurture are so intertwined that they cannot, even in principle, be disentangled.

Freud provided his own extraordinary account of the identity formation, which stressed the inevitability of internal conflict and the difficulty, therefore, of achieving any kind of integrity.

> Not one to shrink from grand claims, Freud argued that Oedipal desire is universal. . . . the Oedipus complex is viewed by Freudians as essential to the constitution of selfhood. (Elliott 2003:58, 59)

Freud suggested that we are all formed by our struggles for control of the female body, our fears of castration (if male) and our envy of the penis (if female). Males saw themselves as rivals to their father and sought to possess their mother. As for females: 'The discovery that she is castrated is a turning-point in a girl's growth.' (Freud 1991:424)

This bizarre account of identity formation, among all the many others explored in these pages, had an enormous influence on twentieth-century western elites. There has been more than enough written about Freud elsewhere and my own views can be found in previous work.[7]

The pace of change in society is accelerating. As a consequence, our own sense of self can change at a dizzying rate. How far can we cope? How can we maintain our own integrity? Anthony Giddens sees great opportunity within this rapid change. But perhaps most people, fearful of global cosmopolitanism, will become casualties, and/or will promote a fundamentalist backlash? Douglas Kellner argues that, either way, identity is becoming accelerated, unstable, disintegrated, fragile, superficial and illusory.

Self as subject and object

Rogers, and many others, propose that self is not an object. In crucial respects this is true. It is also surely true that selves often see themselves and are regarded as objects. They may greatly resent their treatment or invest their entire identity around being the (beautiful, brilliant, skilful, sensitive, or whatever) celebrity object of attention that they are seen to be. Physical beauty attracts partners, employers, customers and clients, opens doors, and keeps you out of gaol.[8] Vast and growing expenditures are devoted, for good or ill, to improving appearances, on clothing, cosmetics,[9] even by surgery[10] if necessary. Some of us, undoubtedly, define ourselves as me-as-seen-and-approved-of-by-others. 'I am seen and gazed upon, therefore I exist.'

Introverts, on the other hand, may prefer me-as-others-do-not-know-me-and-as-I-keep-hidden-from-the-world. But many, in contemporary society, seem to equate a 'real' and successful identity as being a *celebrity* identity. They crave their 15 minutes of fame and spend a large part of their own lives dreaming of the triumphs, tragedies and absurdities of the rich and famous.

> To think that there is an ego where there is only a changing psychophysical complex is to create the conditions that generate sorrow, grief and dejection. (de Silva 2000:57)

This is the Buddhist position: Self-as-illusion. It is a perspective that has something to offer us. But the question remains; what makes this particular 'changing-psycho-physical-complex' different from that other changing-psycho-physical-complex? And when people ask 'who are you?' this is often a fair question, *whose precise meaning depends on the context in which it is asked.* It will usually be unreasonable to reply that 'I am only a changing-psycho-physical-complex'!

The Zen teacher asks the disciple, no longer a beginner, *who are you?* The disciple replies *I have no idea.* The teacher responds: *You are of course free to cling to that idea of no idea.* Self as a changing psycho-physical complex is an idea worth apprehending. It is not an idea worth clinging to.

> For thought, being initially static, seemed to offer something that neither nature nor flesh would: *permanence.* The word 'tree', for example, stays the same while all actual trees change, mature, and die. Thought promises eternity by delivering its substitute: permanence. No wonder [Otto] Rank could say that all ideologies were immortality projects. (Wilbur 1981:199)

We cling to ideas, including ideas about self. I seek to offer a very large array of ideas about self. I do not seek to push one of these ideas at the expense of all the others. I seek interconnections and interrelations between these ideas so that they 'pull together' in enhancing our understanding of identity. But I certainly do not wish to suggest that any or no idea is as good as any other. Instead I wish to *explore how and when different ideas about self have currency and how to use the currency that works best in the context.* A deeper understanding of self does not mean that we lodge ourselves within some imagined 'essence' of self. Rather we *move around and around these various ideas and see the dynamics of their operation.* For if one thing is certain it is that self involves *both* change and continuity, it is both a subject and object.

> The notion of a unified subject – that is, the unity of the 'me' or 'I' of the world – is generally assumed in pre-Freudian descriptions of the self. Western culture has produced a substantial vocabulary which describes this condition of fixity: origin, essence, consciousness, structure, centre, being, substance, truth.
>
> Psychoanalytic theory, especially the adaptations of Freud by Jacques Lacan and Julia Kristeva, opens the way for theorising the subject as 'unfixed'. Psychoanalysis also theorises a more precarious and indeterminate relationship between subjects and the language which connects them. That is, the subject no longer exists as an absolute condition, a deeply rooted and basically unchangeable entity; the subject is dynamic,

> mutable, open and formed through various relationships and experiences, all constituted in language. Derrida, therefore, is highly dubious about the possibility that a subject 'originates' in some essential form. Rather the subject exists as a contingency of language. (Lewis 2002:165)

The postmodern accounts of self described by Lewis and others tend to be ignored by many counsellors and therapists. This, I am sure, is a serious mistake. The criticisms postmodernists make of the supposedly unified, essential, self are very important, and mystics have made them for centuries. Postmodernism does not, I think, require that we entirely reject modernist and earlier theories of identity. We need to understand what purposes were served by earlier accounts, and how to recast our understanding of essence and unity of identity in the light of more recent insight. We can adopt a Hegelian view of thesis and antithesis each being absorbed into a larger synthesis. We need to ask what is a postmodern identity that is not a *chaotic* identity. 'Identities become detached – disembedded – from specific times, places, histories, and traditions, and appear "free-floating". We are confronted by a range of different identities, each appealing to us, or rather to different parts of ourselves, from which it becomes possible to choose' (Hall et al. 1992, cited in Lewis 2002:138).

Hall is, I think, right. There is far more opportunity to change our identity than was ever the case when the opportunities were fewer, and the pace of change in society was much slower than it is today. But if we are to avoid chaos and/or a fundamentalist backlash, both very real possibilities, then we need to see the role of unity and continuity and, even of 'essence'. We do not pick an identity in the way that we pick up objects from a supermarket shelf. There is a 'we' (who?) that is doing the picking. This 'I' is not merely 'a changing psycho-physical complex' and there are, or should be, principles, *including moral principles* by which choices are made. There is the matter of our *duties* and *obligations*, which themselves will, and should, restrict and shape our choices.

We may have no right to detach and disembed ourselves from family and social commitments in order to chase after morally trivial ways of creating a new identity. This is a crucial ethical point for counsellors, who have duties, not just to their clients, but to the client's wider network of contacts and to the society to which we all belong and to which we all have obligations. We may have no right to dissociate ourselves from our current past and present actions and their *essential* consequences, by imagining that 'I'm moving on, now, man'. 'perhaps one of the saddest indictments of psychotherapy and its century of valiant efforts to plumb the depths of the human mind, is its moral triviality' (Dryden & Feltham 1992:261).

We need, also, to remember that there is no consensus about the nature of postmodernism, (almost by definition) and that its anarchic and nihilistic tendencies are strongly, and I think rightly, contested. For example, Jürgen Habermas rejects postmodernism altogether and focuses on the importance of how we seek consensus via language and how we require democratic public spaces if we are to thrive as individuals.

For centuries there have been accounts of the need to know oneself as one really is.

> In the *Gospel of Thomas*: 'the Kingdom of God is inside of you and it is outside of you. When you come to know yourselves, then you will be known, and you will realise that you are the sons of the living Father. But if you will not know yourselves, then you dwell in poverty, and it is you who *are* that poverty. (Pagels 1982:136)

Christian accounts of self describe 'self-within-the-Kingdom-of-God'. Secular humanist accounts retain the need to find an *essential* self, an *authentic* self, and an *integrated*, *mature*, *wise*, and '*best*' self. No doubt we need to refine these concepts in the light of postmodern criticism. But, I am convinced that we are making a grave moral and epistemological error if we reject these concepts in their entirety. How, if we do so, will we locate and reject amoral and cynical manipulation, deception and opportunism?

> 'The divorce between soul and body,' says Brown, 'takes the life out of the body, reducing the organism to a mechanism.' (Wilbur 1981:215)

> The working man has no time to be anything but a machine. (Thoreau, in Reinfeld 1964:105)

There is great concern that science treats people as mere machines, objects of manipulation and creates a disenchanting world lacking in meaning and purpose. The 'soul' has been taken away from the story of humanity. In traditional accounts of self, the soul was seen to be central, essential. Even today, when we say that there is no 'soul' in someone's actions we imply that the life, the heart, the zest, the fire, the commitment, the understanding, has gone out of the whole process; we are behaving as robots, following a script, absent and uncaring. With such alienation, we have lost ourselves as active, reflective, responsible subjects and turned ourselves into robotic objects of manipulation.

How, then, to make sense of humanness; a crucial component in the nature and story of identity? This involves recognition of the importance of *continuity* in identity, and of the fact that there are ethical, empirical, logical – essential – *priorities* in the formation and expression of identity, as we shall see. We do not have to go back to some Neo-Platonic, Cartesian or Hegelian construction of soul and spirit in order to provide a soulful account of self. We just need to look at persons as intrinsically cooperative, language using, meaning-seeking and meaning-making beings:

> What I want to suggest is that this giving and discussing of reasons is a fundamental aspect of human life. It is basic to the way we conceive of ourselves and others.

> We think of ourselves and others very much in terms of the sorts of reasons we and they have for our actions. Our assessments of character are very much based on the types of reasons people have for what they do, and their constancy or inconstancy in applying them. This giving and taking and defending of reasons is more fundamental to us as human beings than science. It is a critical part of every human life, part of what makes us human. (O'Hear 2001:20)

> In the Thatcherist society we each become a Faust, whose endless and innumerable desires can all be satisfied provided only that he gives up his identity, his soul. (Boyle 2000:28)

Self, autonomy and agency

Yet, whether 'soulful' or secular, how much *agency*, and *autonomy* do individual selves actually have?

> Foucault considered the whole idea of autonomous selfhood to have been an invention of the modern era and a consequence of the death of God in an industrial age. (van Deurzen 1997a:92)

> It is not clear whether the farmer has a house or whether the house has the farmer. (Thoreau, in Reinfeld 1964:106)

How far, in order to be *responsible*, do we actually need to be *conscious* of what we are doing? Within Christian teaching our autonomy was greatly limited, though God had given us the freedom to choose to sin and to avoid sin. Within secular humanism great play is made of the ability of people to choose for themselves, to create themselves, to mould themselves into what they would most wish to become.[11] Within most forms of contemporary therapy it is assumed that people do have a great deal of autonomy and freedom to choose. Without this freedom therapists could offer little more than consolation or, if more proactive, an active 'training' and conditioning of clients.

Within postmodern debates about self there is controversy about how much agency we have. Some argue that we can make of ourselves what we will. Others that we, and our choices, are made by corporations or other contexts and that we have only an illusion of autonomy.

> Butler says that the self is produced in the act of performing sexuality, doing gender, and enacting desires. There is for Butler 'no doer behind the deed'; people only come to see themselves as possessing inner lives and psychological identities through a set of repeated gender performances. (Elliott 2003:117)

> it is through the display of the dress, and the gender performance that this necessarily entails, that the woman is necessarily constituted as a 'bride'. (Ibid.:118)

Some belief in agency is essential if the notion of moral responsibility is to have any meaning at all, and lawyers are well aware of this. Certainly we are very busy in our actions and interactions with others. Unlike other animals we have the capacity:

- to imagine how we appear to other people;
- to imagine how the other person *judges* this appearance; and
- to feel *proud* or *ashamed* or *resentful* or whatever as a result of this imagined judgement.

We are continuously judging, being judged, imagining and judging the imagined and real judgements of others. These judgements are negotiated, refined and revised in the light of arguments and actions of others. When they involve what we consider to be essential issues we consider this to be an ethical matter and the ethics matters to our identity. We like to see ourselves as 'good' people in ethical, and in many other, respects and this quality of goodness (however we may define it) is a key component of our very identity and well-being. Moreover, an active agency seems to be essential if the concept of understanding itself is to have any meaning: 'Understanding . . . is active, is an engagement, is a form of agency, and is a form of self expression' (Barnett 1994:110).

Note that Barnett also sees understanding as a crucial part of our identity. We identify ourselves with that which we understand. Where would 'I' be if there was nothing in my world that I understood? We tend also to 'identify' ourselves with our virtues, as we shall see.

Identification is central to identity, it seems, yet *dis*identification is also of crucial importance. We have the capacity to disidentify from ethical, intellectual, emotional or any of the other components of our identity. We can enjoy the daemonic freedom of 'throwing off the traces' and running free of dreary social, ethical constraint.

Here is another central feature of human experience; our capacity both to *attach* and to *detach* ourselves from any and every imagined component of identity. Buddhists tend to be attached to the concept of detachment; but presumably both capacities have a place. The trick, once again, is to know when attachment or detachment is most appropriate, to what degree, in what circumstances. *Our autonomy and agency depend on this ability both to attach and detach.* Some undoubtedly suffer because they are overly identified with some limited component of their lives. They suffer by clinging too hard to that which must pass away. Others, though, suffer because they do not identify, commit to, defend, promote, or stand by, anything, anyone or any aspect of their own personality. If, for example, we did not grieve as a result of the loss of people to whom we were attached then what would become of our humanity?

Some, though, seek detachment from everything and everyone. They see themselves as infinite potential and prefer this to finite actuality. Therefore they avoid any choice which would limit their options. The trouble is that all choices limit options by immediately excluding many alternatives. The person who never identifies and never becomes attached becomes a spectator to his or her own life. But if you are a spectator there is very little for you to observe since there is very little that you will be doing that is worth observing. You will certainly be absent from all that you observe. You will become invisible. No one will be reacting or responding to you. Perhaps you will prefer it that way? Perhaps you would rather be a passive object rather than an active subject? Perhaps you would rather be invisible? Kierkegaard (1989) explores these dilemmas very graphically in his accounts of the existential dilemmas of human experience, choice, action and inaction.

Jeanette Rainwater (1981) drawing from Roberto Assagioli (1980, 1985) shows the value of disidentification exercises; whereby we detach ourselves from people, places, ideas, actions, aspects of our identity with which we have become constrained, blinded or bogged down. This is all very well. But equally, and perhaps more, problematic in a postmodern context is the need to *identify* with people, places, issues, ideas, principles, moral obligations. For, if we do not, we find that our lives have become stale, flat and unprofitable, morally trivial, dependent on distraction, superficiality, and cheap excitement. Ultimately such uncommitted lives appear to be, because they *are*, empty, pointless and meaningless.

Questions for Counsellors

1. Do you think that your clients, generally, have a clear and constructive idea about who they are? Do you, in some ways, see more in your clients than they see in themselves? Be specific with examples.
2. Do you see it as a part of your job to help your clients see more in themselves they can currently see? Be specific with examples, concerning what you see and how you help the client to see it likewise.
3. Do you share Rousseau's view that we might find our authentic selves better if we sought a simpler, more honest, more authentic way of life? If so, in what might this consist?
4. Do you share Kierkegaard's view that many people use their abilities, amass wealth, carry out worldly enterprises, make prudent calculations, etc, and perhaps are mentioned in history, but they are not themselves? Do you find yourself forced to assist clients in remaining plausible rather than in getting real? Be specific with examples.
5. How far do you believe in the validity of 'gut feelings' – in yourself, and in the client? How do you assess their validity? Be specific with examples.
6. Do you agree that clients would benefit if you had a larger range of narratives about self to offer them?
7. How far do you agree that personal development has ethical, spiritual, cultural, social and political dimensions? How do you do justice to these larger priorities when responding to concerns as perceived by individual clients? Be specific with examples.
8. Do you agree with Rowe that whenever you feel yourself falling apart, it is your meaning structure falling apart? How, and with what kinds of skills and knowledge, do you assist clients to 'rebuild their meaning structures'? Be specific with examples.
9. Do you find that your clients hold on too tight, or too carelessly, to their ideas about who they are? Be specific with examples.
10. Which of your clients make too much, or too little, of themselves? Which are too attached to, or too detached from, ideas about themselves? Be specific with examples.
11. Have any of your clients constructed a mainly DIY identity? Which have taken a view of themselves 'off the shelf' – and from where? Be specific with examples – and evidence.

12. Do you agree with Bandler and Grinder that multiple personalities are manufactured by parents and well-meaning therapists; they are not spontaneously derived?
13. Do you agree with Rainwater that we can locate an 'old wise person' within? Are you, like the Dalai Lama, sceptical that there is a permanent unitary 'I' that is under its own power? What evidence could you offer?
14. Do you agree with Smail that maybe we're not so much *willing* our actions as *witnessing* them?
15. Are you a subject who observes? An object of observation? The stage on which subjects observe objects? Or 'all of the above'? Do you agree with Perls that 'the self is not the figure it creates but the creating of the figure: that is, self is the dynamic relation of ground and figure'?
16. *Who are you?* Who might ask this question?

    What answers would you give to whom?
    How many answers could you give?
    Which answers would you keep to yourself?
    Could you ever give a 'complete' list of answers?
    How far have your answers, (and you), changed over time?
    In ten years do you think you will still be 'you'? In what ways?
    In ten years do you think you will have changed? In what ways?
    Who might know you better than you do? In what ways?

17. *Who are you?* What would be your answers if the question were asked by:

    A policeman?
    Your new employer?
    An amorous friend?
    Imagine all the many others who would ask this question. Imagine the context of the question and your answer.

18. In what ways do you see yourself as the *same* person that you always were? In what ways do you see yourself as becoming *different* from the person you used to be?
19. Think of times when you have felt very sure of yourself. When you knew who you were and where you were going. What was the basis of this confidence?
20. Think of times when you have felt very unsure of yourself. When you had lost confidence in your sense of yourself. What was the basis of this unease?
21. The 'postmodern self' – disintegrated, degenerate, de-centred, sophisticated, cosmopolitan? What do you think?
22. Do clients tell their stories? Do their stories tell, and tell on, them? Or all of the above? Give specific examples of the consequences and implications.
23. I have been assisted by counsellors who have said 'Tell me your story' and by others who have said '*don't* tell me your story'. Can you think of instances where each of these is most appropriate?
24. When, and in what ways, is self a haven or (as Schopenhauer suggested) a prison? Be specific with examples from your experience.
25. Do you agree with Spinelli that self is more a *product*, than a *source* of experience? Think of examples in each case drawn from your own experience.
26. How often does your client's agenda for personal development conflict with their and your wider moral obligations? How do you know? What do you do about it? Be specific with examples from your experience.
27. Which of your clients are too attached to, identified with, whatever? Which are too dis-identified from whatever? How do you judge? Be specific with examples.
28. Which of your clients have a confined identity, restricted by the finite actualities of their circumstances? Which have yet to develop an identity by failing to make a genuine decision and commitment? (Because they are still clinging on to infinite potential). Be specific with examples.

CHAPTER 3

Telling What's Wrong – Narratives and Metaphors of Sickness and Health

> We have, each of us, a life story, an inner narrative – whose continuity, whose sense, *is* our lives. It might be said that each of us constructs and lives, a 'narrative', and that this narrative *is* us, our identities. (Sacks 1985:105)

> the vocabulary of human deficit has undergone enormous expansion within the present century. (Gergen 1991:13)

We seek to find ourselves, express ourselves, actualise ourselves, develop ourselves, connect ourselves, advance ourselves. We wish to move 'forward' rather than backward! We want to be well and live with commitment and energy. We want to be healthy and happy. We want to be good at, good for, and good. We want to be good people living the good life. We don't want to be sick, depressed or 'dysfunctional'. So much for the generalities. The details vary more than a little.

Counsellors and therapists promise to try to facilitate, help or train us to live more 'satisfying' and 'resourceful' lives. They do not claim to cure us of physical ailments, but may be able to assist with mental distress. However, the distinction between mental and physical is not itself straightforward. 'The distinction between mind and body is an artificial dichotomy, a discrimination which is unquestionably based far more on the peculiarity of intellectual understanding than on the nature of things' (Jung 1995:85).

Counsellors and therapists promise to help sufferers from chronic anxiety and dissatisfaction and those who simply want a third party to help them take stock of some aspect of their life.

> There are about as many modes of care as persons wanting help or practitioners wanting to offer some particular vision of what life is about. (Fancher 1995:93)

> Ever more people who, in times past, would have been considered normal – if troublesome or unhappy or unlucky or even evil – are considered candidates for the ministrations of psychotherapeutic professions. (Ibid.:95)

Health and 'satisfaction'

So how satisfied with ourselves can we expect, and do we want, to be? How satisfied do we have the right to be, or deserve to be? How far is it sensible and rational for us to be 'satisfied'? What do we want to be satisfied about? And how far does our 'inner' resourcefulness depend on external resources, allies and (favourable) circumstances? 'You gain confidence from having, or having had, people being confident in you. Courage comes from encouragement' (Smail 1996:190).

When people think and talk in general terms about sickness and health they also tend to have specific goals and views about what comprises this healthiness. This chapter seeks to look at some of these specifics insofar as they relate to our identity. As we shall see, there are many vocabularies, metaphors and narratives available when telling the story of individual sickness and well-being. The details are highly revealing concerning our views about technologies of health, our ethical priorities and our conceptions of just whom we think we are, whom we could be, and whom we ought to become.

Certainly people in the West increasingly appear to be looking for a remedy even if they cannot clearly identify the problem. They will tend to favour the cure they have selected, of course, and will almost inevitably be disposed to believing in its efficacy. They will generally record their satisfaction with the treatment. This faith can persist quite stubbornly even, in the most extreme case, after the healer has confessed that the entire enterprise was a fraud:

> Crystal homeopathy – strongly defended by its supporters in response to an outside 'critic' who in fact deliberately created this bogus therapy in order to test the extent of people's gullibility! Details on www.ukpagan.com www.the-crystal-changer.net. The crystal homeopath now states: 'Nothing in this site makes any sense. It was all made up in a few hours to test susceptibility and gullibility.' (*New Scientist* 2003:92)

The writer R. D. Rosen experienced the same phenomenon when he invented a caricature of a cure that he called 'Sansuki' (Rosen 1977). Despite many absurd details and claims, he received many inquiries after press publicity. *For a growing number of people, the sickness seems to consist in always to be looking for, and taking, a new cure.*

Quantities versus qualities of health

Perhaps, then, we need to sober up and find more scientific, numerical and disciplined ways of measuring our satisfaction?

> The EuroQol team have generated values between 0 and 1 for 243 quality of life categories. (Tolly & Rowland 1995:129)

> Attempts have been made to produce a 'gold standard' quality of life scale for use in producing QALYs,[1] such as EuroQol, but progress has been slow. (Ibid.:131)

Progress, Tolly and Rowland (1995) admit, is indeed slow in putting hard numbers around many of the imponderables of a healthy existence and its 'quality'. But there are growing numbers of measures of health and wellbeing[2] and economists, too, are now becoming interested in them. Quality assurance is a big agenda within every organisation in the twenty-first century, but many consumers and employees remain unconvinced that the assurances, protocols and measuring devices match, describe or deliver, the reality. Shakespeare's Hamlet may ask: 'To be, or not to be. That is the question.' But we are not yet able to deliver an answer in terms of a quality of life score. We cannot yet say: 'Hamlet, why not be, that is the answer. You are scoring 0.93 on 243 quality of life categories, and you probably have another 23.4 quality adjusted life years in which you can live resourcefully and with satisfaction.

Perhaps we will get there eventually and, to be fair, attempts to pressure people to place numerical scores against the intangibles of various health care options can certainly concentrate the mind. But attempts to attach numbers to everything can also turn complex, paradoxical human dilemmas into banalities; can crush the subtlety out of the issues; and can abolish any real understanding of quality in the never ending fetish for *quantity*.

Hamlet asks why he should go on with his life and he is, surely, looking for a narrative, a story worth telling and living and a character in the story worth being. He is looking for reasons, moral principles, projects and qualities in themselves intrinsically worth living for. None of this is made clear by collapsing the entire account into a single score. We may lose the plot. We may not really 'get it' any more. If we score everything we may lose what we score. We certainly won't know what the score really means until we look at and understand what it is that is actually being scored. Perhaps we can give a score to all of Shakespeare's plays. Hamlet gets 0.73, or 73 per cent. So now will you read it?

> Critical theory highlights the danger of the hegemony of instrumental rationality, which in our society tends to displace communicative rationality, creating a force for objectifying, commodifying and depersonalising. (Sutherland 1997:11)

Many critics, as we shall see, complain about the loss of humanity and the forces of depersonalisation acting in contemporary society. They deplore the focus on numbers, skills-portfolios and behaviours at the expense of the (supposedly) inner life, the individual identity, meanings, understandings and purposes that make human beings *human* beings. They deplore the treatment of people as though they were machines without autonomy. Certainly some behaviourists, and more recently many postmodernists, question how much autonomy we really have.

> What is being abolished is autonomous man – the inner man, the homunculus, the possessive demon, the man defended by the literatures of freedom and dignity. His abolition has long been overdue. (Skinner 1979:196)

> He is indeed controlled by his environment, but we must remember that it is an environment largely of his own making. The evolution of culture is a gigantic exercise in self-control. (Ibid.:210)

Critics of Skinner argue that, when he talks of self-control he actually means *social* control. But is social control all that is available in a world where the very existence of a self is regarded with such postmodern scepticism?

> In the end the transcendental subject of cognition is apparently abandoned as the last reminiscence of subjectivity and replaced by the much smoother work of automatic control mechanisms. Subjectivity has given way to the logic of the allegedly indifferent rules of the game, in order to dictate all the more unrestrainedly . . . Reason itself has become the mere instrument of the all-inclusive economic apparatus. (Adorno & Horkheimer 1999:30)

> In the culture industry the individual is an illusion not merely because of the standardisation of the means of production. He is tolerated only so long as his complete identification with the generality is unquestioned. (Ibid.:154)

Health and humanity

Sociologists have for over a century explored the place of the human part of human beings in a society that has become so increasingly locked within the metaphor of the machine. Are our machines assisting us, or are we ourselves slaves to the machines and/or being turned into machines? And, if so, is this not itself a serious sickness in society and a fundamental threat to individual human health and wellbeing? 'Neglect of what is genuinely human is the major reason why so many people in American business right now feel more victimised than helped by the latest management techniques and company-wide processes for improvement' (Morris 1997:109).

Economists may answer by offering numerical measures of the overall 'wellbeing' in society. We can look at our 'gross domestic product' and congratulate ourselves that it is increasing. We may alternatively consider that it is indeed 'gross', given the gross and growing inequality of wealth that exists within and between nations. Is all, most, or only a little, of our economic product of real value to us as human beings? Stigliz (2002) complains, along with many other critics, that economists' measures of output and wealth do not take into account the *costs* of producing the benefits. What about the environmental, social and health costs? Nor do economists consider whether the products and the benefits are in fact of very much real benefit to the humanity, integrity and well being of human beings. What is the real value of our domestic product *net* of the costs and *net* of those products that do not produce any real (worthwhile) wealth; that do not produce any genuine well-being?[3] *Our gross domestic product is indeed gross, for all these reasons. Our net domestic product nets in much less than we may imagine, when costs and valuable ends are factored in.*

Of course, the traditional answer from classical economics is that 'the market' is the means by which human productivity and human wellbeing are maximised. How so? Because the market is presumed to consist of rational, autonomous individuals who are best placed to decide which goods and services they want and need, and which combination of purchases will maximise their 'utility'. These rational autonomous individuals are also best placed to decide how to sell their labour power. In this way, it is argued, a market society may fall far short of perfection but it will produce the best of all possible worlds. We are advised that it will certainly be better than anything that will come from meddling professionals, experts and government officials. So if people insist on 'crystal homeopathy' then, in a market economy of rational autonomous individuals, crystal homeopathy is what they should have even if its own creator insists that the product is entirely bogus.

Self evidently 'the market' is very far away indeed from maximising the health and wellbeing of humanity. It lavishes health care on the dogs of the rich while failing to provide food, water, shelter, employment or security for the poor. This expenditure on dog-food in no significant way 'trickles down' to the poor. Market economies provide a surplus and surfeit of health care and emotional attention on the privileged and do very little about severe stress and psychosis suffered by those who cannot pay. In the UK though, at least, there is some socialisation of health care. Services are provided free at the point of demand and according to need rather than on ability to pay. The market, it is assumed, does not deliver best value in health and wellbeing. Certainly, the experience of health and sickness in the USA suggests that markets, on their own, can be relied upon *not* to look after the health and wellbeing of poor people.

Individual health and social progress

We can measure health care expenditures, but how far does growing health care investment, even in a socialised health system, correlate with growing health and wellbeing? Are we spending more on health, not because we are healthier but because we are sicker?

A balanced account is needed.[4] We are certainly living longer, in Western nations at least, and this must be a sign of improving physical health regardless of its causes. Inevitably death catches us in the end; if infectious diseases don't kill us then atrophy of one kind or another quite probably will. If we live longer, the costs of keeping us alive in our last year, with ever more sophisticated and expensive technology, tend to increase dramatically.

'The major shifts in the population's health have been a function of social, not medical, advance' (Pilgrim 1983:122). There is a general consensus that social change, more than medical progress, has been the most important source of improvements in health statistics. The body, if not actually more healthy, is presumably being protected more effectively and for longer, from lethal sickness. What, though, of the overall health of the 'psyche', 'mind', 'soul', 'self'?

> our culture is obsessed with emotions, from soap operas through chat rooms to an apparently endless series of self-help books dealing with anxiety, stress, assertiveness and relationships. (Craib 1994:86)

> Our emotions are constantly engaged in sentimental and formulaic narratives. (Lewis 2002:89)

Emotions appear to have people more than people have emotions. This focus on feelings, at the expense of perspective and self-discipline, is surely not a sign of health, genuine sensitivity or maturity.

> Our relatedness is overcome by a kind of paralysing self-consciousness because it can no longer point beyond itself to any kind of purpose. (Smail 1987:97)

> Expressive individuation has become one of the cornerstones of modern culture. (Taylor 1996:176)

Critics on the one hand deplore the threat to the individual identity of human beings lost within the machine. They also focus on what they see as a growing self-obsession. Can both tendencies be operating? Arguably they can. *Questions about identity are less pressing when individuals live in stable and supportive environments that offer fulfilling opportunities.* We get on with what we value and we do not need, so often, to ask, 'Who am I?' and 'What is it all about?' The *self-obsession may arise when self concepts are under threat*, when the distractions do not provide the desired wellbeing and fulfilment, when changes are so rapid that the self we thought we were is no longer sustainable.

> Children and the young who are well cared for don't worry about the meaning of life during the exciting rush of their daily projects and adventures. For them the meaning of life is simply living it. (Raabe 2001:145)

> The degradation of sexuality and the aridity in human relations lacking genuine concern, affection and tenderness is a crucial source of the identity crisis. One's sense of identity is enhanced by productive and creative human relations, whether these relate to love, work or amusement. (de Silva 2000:119)

Perhaps we are dissatisfied because we too often attempt the impossible? We attempt to achieve autonomy and wellbeing in a social context that very greatly frustrates our efforts? 'The difficulties of living the fiction of the autonomous self is presented as signs of personal inadequacy and failure' (Blackman & Walkerdine 2001:104). Or do we suffer because we behave so badly? Because we have lost sight of the importance of ethical principles in social and individual wellbeing? 'Unless we can now tame and transmute the potential for evil in the human soul, we shall be lost' (Peck 1988:263).

Perhaps the very nature of progress within society creates problems of meaning, purpose and identity for the individual? How can we 'boldly go where no one has been before' when everywhere is well trodden, tamed and controlled? How can we enjoy the excitement of the hunt when hunting is no longer a viable means of making a living? How can we feel good about bringing home the necessities of life when machines have already provided the necessities – cheaply and in great abundance? How can we feel at one with the rhythm of the seasons when we are almost entirely cut off from nature? How can we find meaning and purpose when most of what we work for is far less than necessary?

'What man actually needs is not a tension-less state but rather the striving and struggling for some goal worthy of him' (Frankl 1987:107). For most of history the worthy goal was obvious for each and all of us. It was merely to *survive*! If we had food, shelter, a few allies, a degree of security; then we could feel justly proud of our day's work. As Rousseau observed, after a busy and physically energetic day the most basic food tasted wonderful, and just sitting down felt like a blessed relief. But perhaps it is harder now to find worthy goals? First, because we are mostly not battling for physical survival, and second because we are mostly small and insignificant cogs in a large and impersonal process. Perhaps we are oppressed by banality and moral triviality in our lives? And/or are we weighed down by the impersonal ugliness of much of the built environment?

Organisations appear to provide less and less space for individual autonomy, individual initiative, and individual ways of tackling the work. Everything that increasing numbers of workers are paid to do is carefully prescribed in advance by protocols, procedures, quality assurance checklists and strict hierarchies. Everything is planned in advance. You are paid to achieve a standard that is not in any way *your* standard. You fit in to the organisation. The organisation does not do much, or anything, to fit itself around you. It is, perhaps, a recipe for emptiness, dissatisfaction and boredom. A very large part of very many people's lives now consists in filling in forms which, by their very nature, leave no room whatever for an individual contribution, a personal touch.

> In actual fact, boredom is now causing, and certainly bringing to psychiatrists, more problems to solve than distress. (Frankl 1987:108)

> 'The Sunday neurosis,' that kind of depression which afflicts people who become aware of the lack of content in their lives when the rush of the busy week is over and the void within themselves becomes manifest. Not a few cases of suicide can be traced back to this existential vacuum. (Ibid.:109)

Are we under more stress than ever or was life always 'stressful'? Do we have a new illness simply because we have invented a new word?

> The invention of stress as a non-specific form of disability induced by modern living and working conditions can be dated to the middle of the twentieth century. This is not to say that it is not a real condition, but that it is constructed in how we talk about the experience of modernity and is therefore to some extent a self-fulfilling prophecy. (Chaney 2002:24)

Perhaps the very fact of social progress concerning larger matters of life and death leaves us with more time and inclination to fret over smaller concerns? Perhaps social change simply relieves us of traditional life and death problems but provides us with new pressures?

'George M. Beard (1839–83) popularised the concept of "neurasthenia", nervous breakdown produced by the frantic pressures of advanced civilisation, which drained the individual's reserves of "nerve force"' (Porter 2002:151). 'Neurasthenia' is no longer on the list of ailments we can claim to experience. But many have continued to write about the pressure of 'advanced' civilisation. Is it a greater pressure now? Are we in fact advancing? Or are we complaining too much as a result of a loss of 'moral fibre', courage, integrity and tenacity? Is the sheer comfort of modern life weakening and debilitating us? Does it make us stale and inert? Are we suffering from a chronic lack of physical exercise with all the mental and 'spiritual' ailments that accompany it? Do physically and morally weak individuals now survive who previously would have perished? Is the strength of society thereby adding to, and preserving, the inherent weaknesses of individuals?

> The emergence of pessimistic philosophies is by no means a sign of great and terrible misery. No, these question marks about the value of all life are put up in ages in which the refinement and alleviation of existence make even the inevitable mosquito bites of the soul and the body seem much too bloody and malignant and one is so poor in real experiences of pain that one would like to consider painful general ideas as suffering of the first order. (Nietzsche, *The Gay Science*, Book One, Knowledge of Misery)

> Classic hysteria, so common in Freud's day, may also have disappeared, but it has perhaps metamorphosed into new and primarily female conditions, notably anorexia nervosa, somatization disorder, and bulimia. (Porter 2002:88)

Some ailments change, some continue. But melancholy can be something of a fashion statement and there is evidence that it was so both in the nineteenth and eighteenth centuries. Hume refers to 'agreeable melancholy' and Porter (2002:87) observes:

> Fashionable melancholy had a bright future ahead of it in various incarnations. On both sides of the Atlantic, eminent Victorians sank or wallowed in hypochondria

> (mainly male) and hysteria (essentially for the ladies). By the fin de siècle, it was trendy to be 'neurasthenic', much as, in superior Manhattan circles, one might till very recently lose face unless engaged in 'analysis interminable' with a chic shrink. Private 'nerve' clinics, hydros, and spas sprang up for rich breakdown cases in Europe and America alike, paralleling the TB sanatoria in the Alps.

In his great novel, *The Magic Mountain* (1924, 1999), Nobel Prize winner Thomas Mann, provides an unforgettable and hugely subtle account of sickness as a way of life and death within the closed world of a TB sanatorium. Trivia, tragedy, obsession, withdrawal, denial, authenticity, a full gamut of (prosperous) humanity is portrayed.

Porter (2002:85) traces an eighteenth-century source back at the trivial end of the health specturm: 'In his *Treatise of the Hypochondriack and Hysterick Diseases* (1730), the Dutch-born practitioner and satirist Bernard Mandeville examined the kind of modish melancholy with which the elite like to flirt.'

Certain kinds of mental distress or dissatisfaction appear almost to be a statement of cultural sophistication and individual sensitivity. They are, perhaps, a product of comfort rather than of real stress. But it is unfair, I think, to sneer about this. The ennui and anxiety may be real enough and the process needs to be understood. Certainly the number of non-physical ailments being recorded (or invented) by professionals has been growing very substantially in the past few decades. Porter (2002:214) notes the enormous growth of that bible for clinical psychologists and psychiatrists, *The Diagnostic and Statistical Manual:* 'The first edition was some one hundred pages; DSM-II ran to 134 pages, DSM-III to almost 500; the latest revision, DSM-IV-TR (2000) is a staggering 943 pages! More people seem to be diagnosed as suffering from more psychiatric disorders than ever; is this progress?' Perhaps it is? Once a culture has tackled the basic problems of food, shelter, security and raw physical health perhaps it can, and should, move on to more subtle, and (lower priority?) issues concerning morale, wellbeing, identity? Advances in technology result in the declining need to employ everyone as farmers and fighters. Therefore the questions 'who am I?' and 'who shall I become?' begin to involve real choices. There is little point in providing career, lifestyle, and life-choice counsellors in a traditional pastoral community where the vast majority of the population will be either a farmer or a farmer's wife.

But with technological advance, more and more people are freed up to focus their attention on less essential, more cultural, more luxurious, more civilised and comfortable services, occupations and products. As people become ever better supplied with the necessities of life then still further growth in the economy requires the production of goods and services that people certainly do *not need* for bare survival, but which they may have good reason to enjoy and appreciate. To be human, after all, is surely to do far more than merely survive? But in focusing on more cultural and aesthetic products and services should we seek to lift, renew and inspire the human spirit, however we might define this, or merely provide entertainment and distraction? 'The obsession with identifying oneself with fast-changing and transient objects, the restless search for diversity and the consequent boredom is nowhere given such graphic expression as in Soren Kiekegaard's *Either/Or*' (de Silva 2000:119).

In the UK, I regularly received an 'Innovations' catalogue that made all kinds of jokes about the frivolity, triviality and absurdity of most of the products on offer. This 'lite' approach to wealth creation sometimes appears to be the shape of things to come. When you already have all that you need and more, then what else is there to be bought? And how do you feel about yourself when you play a (vanishingly small) part in producing products and services that you know that no one really needs?

Can we at least produce something that, if not necessary, is at least valuable? How do you feel about yourself if you have to spend all your time and energy trying to persuade people to buy a product or service they would never otherwise dream of looking for? How are we to make sense of the fact that more is spent on public relations and advertising than on education? How are we to feel about the prospect of education itself being a means, less of self-expression, but more of producing 'flexible' and 'motivated' staff? 'With the disappearance of the public place, advertising invades everything (the street, the monument, the market, the stage, language)' (McNeill & Feldman 1998:443). In order to feel good about the look of ourselves, we like to believe that we are doing something worthwhile and that we are not just fodder for the advertising industry.

Are we all proletarians now?

> Abraham Lincoln[5] wrote: 'I see in the near future a crisis approaching that unnerves me and causes me to tremble for the safety of my country . . . corporations have been enthroned and an era of corruption in high places will follow.' (Monbiot 2001:6)

The sociologist Georg Simmel (1858–1918), noted that the division of labour within industrial economies might increase productivity, but it produced a very one-dimensional individual, skilled in a very limited range of accomplishments. What happens to a personality who spends so much time with so little variety in their working life? The nature of our health and our identity is surely closely related to the nature of our work?

In our advanced society I wonder if many of us may be, as individuals, less skilled than prehistoric man who had to be multiskilled in order to survive at all! We are so utterly dependent on others to cope at all in the world. This interconnectedness may be reassuring, it may be efficient and highly productive, but it may also be very frightening. Is this security and specialisation making infants of us all? Soon, with in-car global positioning and navigation, we won't even need to know where we are. We will be able to let a machine tell us. But if we don't use our ability to locate ourselves, will the ability decay? If we don't use it, won't we lose it? What would our ancestors think of that?

We may imagine that we are more independent, individual and autonomous, yet in fact we are more dependent on others and helpless on our own than at any time in history.

> Owing to the extensive use of machinery and to division of labour, the work of the proletarians has lost all individual character, and, consequently, all charm for the workmen. He becomes an appendage of the machine, and it is only the most simple, most monotonous, and most easily acquired knack, that is required of him. (Marx [1848] 1998)

With the development of computerisation, this proletarianisation of work has been vastly extended from manual labour, where it began, into professional employment. There is ever less chance to use your own words, write your own prose, make your own decisions. More and more we are supervised, monitored and we fill in forms and follow procedures more than taking individual initiatives of our own. This includes elite workers as well as those low-down in the hierarchy. Routines substitute for individual creativity, initiative, responsibility and autonomy which organisations nowadays tend not to trust.

In both work and play there is less opportunity to make one's own mark, and more of a requirement to follow along the tracks already clearly marked. Of course, when responsibility is taken away from people, we ought not to be surprised if they become depressed and demotivated. When anything goes wrong we can be sure that no one will want to take responsibility; it will be 'the system' that is at fault. And a system that is full of demotivated individuals will often fail! Look around you.

More than ever, perhaps, we are, as Louis Althusser argued, positioned and defined as individuals by social institutions such as education, police, family, mass media and, less so now, the church. This cannot but have a profound impact on how we see ourselves, how we are seen, how we struggle to be seen, and how we seek to claim some sort of individuality for ourselves. There are ever fewer open roads left on which we can travel. We are monitored, checked, identified, positioned, by CCTV and by our every credit card transaction.

Language is a powerful way of positioning people. Consider, for example, the word 'we', which I have used frequently in the above narrative. 'We' positions you the reader as being one of 'us'. You are not 'other' in this discourse. But perhaps you don't wish to be positioned in this way? Images, likewise, position people. Unless you consciously check the process, you will allow yourself to be positioned in the position of the camera lens. The 'other' is over there, above, below, near or far from you. But perhaps you are, 'in fact' one of the others? Perhaps you don't 'really' belong, or wish to belong, where you have been placed? How many of your political positions are the results of the positions within which you were placed by cameras, over many years, within the tableaux of political disputes?

Faced with all this positioning, defining and monitoring,[6] it is no wonder, perhaps, that we are self-obsessed and make (pathetic?) attempts, by kitchen colour scheme, car colour and accessory combination or whatever, to announce our individuality to the world. The cars advertised to us position us and are presented as protecting us from a grey urban world; or merging us invisible within it; or propelling us onto an open road we shall rarely find. The commonest reality of motoring, where we are marooned in yet another day of congestion, is rarely presented.

No wonder, also, that we break out into violence[7] or intoxication at times, or obsess about money and pleasure. In all these ways we can release tension or give ourselves some sense of control or distract ourselves:

> Sometimes the frustrated will to meaning is vicariously compensated for by a will to power, including the most primitive form of the will to power, the will to money. In other cases, the place of the frustrated will to meaning is taken by the will to pleasure. That is why existential frustration often eventuates in sexual compensation. (Frankl 1987:109)

No wonder, too, that we may be tempted to give up in the search for an individual identity and just do as others do, as others expect us to do, as circumstance most obviously allows us to do: 'To develop ones own personality is indeed an unpopular undertaking, a deviation that is highly uncongenial to the herd' (Jung, in Storr 1986:198). Sociologists often seem to be profoundly pessimistic about the possibilities of individual expression in a postmodern and post-industrial world.

Talcott Parsons, (1902–79) introduced the concept of 'social inclusion' as a key determinant of personal and social health and well-being, a term which is now central within so much contemporary UK government policy. Parsons, like many other sociologists, expressed concerns about the fate of socially excluded individuals and groups; welcomed the growing role of professionals in explicitly tackling social problems, and arguably under-estimated the damaging consequences of professional self-interest.

It was Parsons, too, who spoke of the dangers of 'the sick role'. Sickness, Parsons correctly appreciated, was not merely a physiological or psychological phenomenon. It also had important sociological dimensions; one literally took a new social role when one was sick. A mental breakdown, for example, involved, above all, announcing to the world, and having the world accept, that one could not go on with one's existing roles; that one needed to be cared for, to take time off, to slow down, to rest and recuperate, to become dependent.

Subsequently, medical theorists talk of the notion of 'secondary gain', that there are certain benefits in adopting a sick role, and it can become a habit that is difficult to break as one becomes more skilled in being sick than in being functional and well.

Jean Baudrillard paints a much blacker picture in his assertion that the individual subject is now silent, asleep, atomised, cut off from others and the world, lacking in sensitivity, unable to speak in any individual way. Individuals have no basis for, or interest in, political action. They are not merely cut off from the world, they are cut off from any coherent sense of who they are or what they might become.

Hebdige notes that we share a sense of community by sharing mass cultural products, such as soap operas, and through these try to find a feeling of connection, some roots, and a past. Yet I would suggest that now even watching TV together and experiencing the same TV programmes is becoming a thing of the past. We may not eat so much together. We may not live so much together, or for so long. Everywhere there is fragmentation and all our efforts at nostalgia, or 'heritage', or romantic escape, or exciting release or quiet tradition, come in packaged units carefully constructed by marketing and motivation specialists. They offer us[8] constructed visions of the past or future, which allow for little individual interpretation or response on our part and which may have little to do with any real past.

But, if our circumstances are, as alleged, so bad, would we, given the chance, take a time machine back into the past? To which place and time would we take ourselves? Would we rule out all those places without modern medicine and painkillers? Could we cope as individuals in any other environment, given that our identity is so shaped by the place and time to which we belong? Pessimistic accounts of our lack of individual health and our sickening world need careful attention. But I will attempt, before the end of this book, to move to a more hopeful note.

Myths of a healthy 'golden age'

Henry Thoreau asserted in *Walden* (1854, 1992:3) that:

> The mass of man lead lives of quiet desperation. What is called resignation is confirmed desperation. From the desperate city you go into the desperate country, and have to console yourself with the bravery of minks and muskrats. A stereotyped but unconscious despair is concealed even under what are called the games and amusements of mankind. (Ch 1:Economy)

Is this so? Was it always thus? What would Thoreau make of the last 150 years of urbanisation? Would it be reassuring to us if we decided that people are *not* in fact getting their lives together and becoming successful celebrities, as seen on TV? Adorno and Horkheimer (1999) argue that, in contemporary society 'love is downgraded to romance', but is there really less love than there ever was? The changes made in the past century appear to dwarf all previous eras of change; yet some patterns remain familiar. Here, for example, is an observation made about religion in America compared with more secular Europe:

> Here and there in the midst of American society you meet with men full of a fanatical and almost wild spiritualism, which hardly exists in Europe. From time to time

> strange sects arise which endeavour to strike out extraordinary paths to eternal happiness. Religious insanity is very common in the United States. (de Tocqueville 1830:Chapter XIII)

We[9] express concern about the effects of religion. We express concern about the effects of the decline of religion. The common thread is that we express concern. Perhaps we always did, perhaps we always thought that the future is in doubt, that the good old days are past, and that the youth of today are (another) cause for concern:

> Inability to face the inner vacuity of the so-called ego results in flight from anxiety. Compulsive gregariousness, frantic club-joining, filling one's leisure hours with feverish activity – all these are facets of covert anxiety, all help people to avoid being alone. The love of solitude and the way of silence advocated by the Buddha is anathema to large numbers of people who live in the 'lonely crow'! (de Silva 2000:49)

Michael Moore (2001:86, 103) bewails contemporary illiteracy, along with many other concerns: 'There are forty-four million Americans who cannot read and write above a fourth-grade level – in other words, who are functional illiterate . . . Only 11 per cent of the American public bothers to *read* a daily newspaper, beyond the funny pages or the used car ads . . . 163 New York City schools opened the 2000–2001 school year *without a principal*!'

Are we to be reassured, or further depressed, by the fact that, for example, Emerson (in Reinfeld 1964:69) was expressing similar concerns more than a century ago? 'Because our education is defective, because we are superficial and ill-read, we are forced to make the most of that position, of ignorance. Hence America is a vast know-nothing party, and we disparage books and cry up intuition.'

Goffman talks, more positively, of the contemporary phenomenon of 'civil inattention'. In urban settings we are circumspect with each other. We approach each other with enough attention to show that the other is there, and not so much as to invade their space. We each go about our own business with a kind of polite, brief and glancing concern. We are co-present but separate. We mix and mingle together but avoid enmeshment. We look, but not too much. We are aware but not engrossed. We are courteous but we do not converse. Is this a cause for concern? Surely not? Without these skills and attitudes, this metropolitan courtesy and civility, how could we exist in cities at all? And, for all our complaints, is there not much to celebrate in becoming cosmopolitan, urban and urbane individuals? Do we all really want, or need, to withdraw to a country cottage and grow roses?

We can lose our sense of ourselves by too much immersion in 'the other'; but we can also lose ourselves by being too much cut off from others. Mystics propose withdrawal in order to find one's true 'trans-egoic' self, escape from fantasy and come truly alive. Sociologists tend to recommend engagement. Durkheim, for example, argued that we found the best in ourselves from involvement in our social world, and that we suffered 'anomie' when we were disconnected or when social norms and frameworks were weak or absent.

Elias (1939) talks of a highly controlled decontrolling of emotional controls in modern society. We let loose, let our hair down, explore and express ourselves, but only within a confined and determined social context. We may imagine that 'anything goes' but this is anything but true. Is this a cause for concern? Marcuse (2002) suggests that it is, but perhaps it is a sign of civility and sophistication that we allow freedom of expression yet within a safe and disciplined context? Chaney (1996:114) suggests that: 'The discourses of individuality that are so fundamental to Western thought have not, however, existed for all time.'

Others make a similar point. Art from the Renaissance onwards shows this emergence of artists as individuals rather than as just anonymous creatures of the Church and its teachings. The entire programme of secular humanism from the Enlightenment onwards celebrates and promotes individual identity, autonomy, integrity and virtue. Democratic political organisation claims to serve and promote personal development.[10] Progress, it is argued, has been made on all these fronts. Is this really a cause for concern and gloom? Is all our gregariousness feverish and false? Does it all cut us off from our true identity? Or do we not also find ourselves through our affiliations? Should we not take a larger perspective on the progress made concerning individual and social health and wellbeing when considering the problems and setbacks?

To a very large degree, Christian notions of health and well-being are being replaced by more secular narratives. Is this not a cause for celebration? Do we really want to go on seeing ourselves as miserable offenders who have no health in us, and who can be spared only if we go on and on confessing our faults? Porter expresses concern that not only Christian narratives are in decline but so, too, are broader humanist accounts of health and wellbeing. He fears that we are becoming too dependent on purely psychological discourse in making sense of ourselves and our personal development: 'The idioms of the psychological and the psychiatric replace Christianity and humanism as the ways of making sense of self – to oneself, one's peers, and the authorities' (Porter 2002:218).

Porter is not optimistic about the powers either of psychiatry or psychotherapy to help us move towards healthy living, at least not without a much broader and deeper curriculum. He notes (Ibid.) that: 'public confidence in the psychiatric profession is low. Is Folly jingling its bells once again?' Blackman and Walkerdine (2001) likewise note that psychology is one of the grand metanarratives of modernity. Is it so grand? What have we gained with it? what have we lost as a result of its hegemony? What evidence is there of its efficacy?

Porter argues that, at least by creating a 'sick other' we can reassure ourselves that we are healthy. But is our reassurance of real value to us? 'Setting the sick apart sustains the fantasy that we are whole' (Porter 2002:63).

Finding our own narratives of health

Porter observes the damaging consequences of our loss of the control of health narratives to health professionals. We have a right, and a need, to find our own language for health and wellbeing, and to use the rich range of vocabularies available in everyday speech. This is lost when health professionals monopolise the story of our health and wellbeing; especially when they move from physical ailments to more general philosophical observations about what a good and healthy life ought to consist in. He notes (2002:158) that the problem goes back a long way: 'Visiting an Irish lunatic asylum around 1850, the inspectors were buttonholed by an inmate alleging theft: "they took my language from me".' 'It seems a pity that psychology should have destroyed all our knowledge of human nature' (G. K. Chesterton in van Deurzen 1997a:94).

Now professionals of every kind are snatching away our language, and thereby our individuality, substituting their own and selling it back to us, while retaining control. Foucault explores the consequences of this linguistic imperialism in great detail, with a variety of case study instances. He seeks to free us from the 'discourse' ('sociologese' for 'language') of professionals, and argues that we cannot be ourselves if we cannot talk for ourselves. Robert Frost (in Reinfeld 1964:172) shows a similar awareness of the problem:

> They say the truth will set you free,
> My truth will bind you slave to me.

The problem is implicit within all language, in that words both direct and blinker our perceptions in certain directions. Psychotherapists need to be aware of the risk of limiting individual liberation and personal development since they each have their own specialist visions of, and vocabulary for, the nature of personal development. 'if we're not careful, the principle contribution of psychotherapy becomes to inflate the importance of private experience and help imprison people within it' (House & Totton 1997:167).

Clients are soon learning to speak and think in the approved style.[11] They thereby may become disempowered (whose language is that?) and dependent on the vocabulary, metaphors and accompanying script/narrative, of their therapist. The authenticity that they eventually find is the authenticity as defined by the therapist. They finally reach their destination at whatever 'stage' the therapist has described as being necessary. If the therapist is to go on helping, and to be themselves helped by the client's continuing financial support, then there will always be room for more personal development, more wellbeing, in future sessions.

> By establishing the idea that happiness, emotional balance and mental adjustment are the norm, psychology and psychotherapy serve only to add an edge of despair

> to the distress most people encounter at least sometimes in their lives. The contrasting view of life as tragic, reflected in particular in the great artistic and literary works throughout the ages, is probably not only more accurate than the cosy smugness of so much therapy and counselling, but is actually a solace to those who value the discovery that they are not alone in the boat. (Smail 1996:204)

Conceptions of health have moved way beyond a survivalist view of health as absence from debilitating pain, disease and deformity. The World Health Organisation offered a famous definition of health as a 'state of complete physical, mental, and social well-being, and not merely the absence of disease or infirmity' (WHO 1948). Does anyone ever feel this good? Perhaps they do after a particularly fulfilling sexual encounter or after a major success, or on hearing exceptionally good news. Most of the time, though, we are less than vibrant, ecstatic, blissful or full of zest and determination. Perhaps that is just as well, both for us and for others who would otherwise have to put up with us.

Nowadays we use the word 'health' to describe far more than the functioning of bodies. In everyday language we talk of healthy attitudes, conscience and character. We refer to healthy, or unhealthy, communities, cities, societies and environments. People are thought to have a healthy, or unhealthy, sense of their own self-esteem. We have healthy, or unhealthy, expectations, goals and habits, both physical and mental. We can be healthy, or otherwise, in our hopes, intentions, and our self-image, in our judgements, life-style, in the wise or foolish management of our emotions. The morale of individuals and organisations is seen as healthy or unhealthy. Immoral behaviour is sometimes considered to be unhealthy. Our perceptions, priorities, purposes and relationships can be assessed as healthy or unhealthy. Virtue is associated with health. There are leaders who create, or destroy, healthy organisations and individuals. Some of our opportunities are healthy; the lack of opportunity is generally seen as unhealthy. It is healthy to belong to supportive networks. Some stories, films, books are seen as good for us, and as sources of inspiration and improvement. Others are considered to be corrupting and damaging to our emotional, moral and spiritual health.

Conversely, we talk about 'sick' brains, buildings, communities, hearts, minds, networks, organisations and societies. Dysfunction, morbidity, impairment, and dependency are all seen as forms of sickness. Yet the word 'clinical', carries both positive and negative connotations. 'Clinical' suggests efficiency, cleanliness, objectivity, and concern for evidence and results. It also connotes sterility, impersonality, coldness and inhumanity. It is thought to be unhealthy if we always try to treat everyone in a clinical way with clinical detachment. There is concern about amoral behaviour. We can save people's lives with a clinical approach to problems. We can also exterminate people with clinical efficiency, skill and competence, thoroughness and detachment. Twentieth-century history has shown that health and educational professionals living under dictatorships have frequently been aligned with, rather than in opposition to, oppressive and inhumane regimes. Such cooperation has, of course, helped to advance the careers of the professionals concerned.

There are endless arguments concerning the healthy or unhealthy state of the popular media, of avant-garde art, of the portrayal of sex and violence etc. Perhaps it is true that one of the best ways of achieving a healthy life is to emulate the virtuous. We no longer pay much attention to saintliness, but mentors, role models and inspiring leaders are an essential part of the health of individuals, organisations and societies. They provide a vision of possibility. They offer a view of what defines a well-lived life. They provide hope when hope is in danger of draining away. They see more in their followers than ordinary people may be able to see in themselves. Let us remember that the key words 'whole', 'hale', 'healed', 'healthy', 'holy'[12] share the same roots and have long been associated with each other.

Integrity and health are interconnected but integrity is not the same as 'perfection'. To be a whole person is to come to terms with one's endless incompleteness, imperfection, and capacity for destructiveness and despair. 'Mental health and well-being are so rare as to be remarkable. For most people, even a single day of unalloyed well-being is a rare event' (Charlton 2000:2).

Health is seen as far more than a purely bodily, physiological matter. A growing number of professionals now attend to various aspects of the health of their clients. Teachers look out for healthy personal development as well as learning outcomes. Social and community workers attend to unhealthy family relationships and communities. Psychologists define 'disorders' of behaviour that have no known physiological abnormality: 'An important fact of clinical [psychological] practice is that in no case whatsoever is diagnosis made on biological grounds' (Fancher 1995:278). The list of psychological disorders lengthens all the time. We have 'attention deficit/hyperactivity disorder', 'disruptive disorders', 'behavioural disorders', 'emotional disorders', 'separation anxiety disorders', 'depressive disorders', 'psychiatric disorders' and 'developmental disorders'. As Foucault observes, in some cases people may be diagnosed with (accused of) one or other of these 'disorders' not because there is any 'disease' but simply because others wish to control them and do not wish to tolerate their behaviour.

A broader view of health

Health issues cannot all be reduced to a physical defectiveness, deficiency, failure or abnormality. Doctors themselves are rediscovering that when considering the health of a patient it is not enough just to see them as machines with bits that have gone wrong, and medical training is changing accordingly. Hence the current medical efforts to broaden conceptions of health and to include a humanities curriculum within medical training. People want to be treated as whole persons, they want a dialogue, and they want to understand.

They often want the story of their health to be told within more than just one vocabulary, by more than just one specialist.

> Peacocke (1985) puts it nicely: the essence of reductionism is a 'nothing-buttery' approach, the belief that an understanding of complex phenomena – such as human action and interaction – can be reached by seeing the phenomenon in question as nothing but discrete entities understandable in relatively simple conceptual schemas. (Barnett 1994:14)

Psychology is reduced to biology, sociology is reduced to psychology, and all our understandings are reduced as a result. We do not like to be treated just as objects. We do not like to be manipulated. And whether we like it or not it is wrong and it reduces us as individuals, as we shall see. Unfortunately, the treatment of people as objects of manipulation, without individual human respect, is a frequent experience:

> In the terminology of Jürgen Habermas, instrumental reason colonises the life-world, which would otherwise be the domain of open, interpersonal reason. Instead of engaging with each other and with the world in mutual interaction, we end up always having an eye to the main chance and by getting out of our transactions with each other and with the world what we can get away with. (Barnett 1994:78)

> Industry is interested in people merely as customers and employees, and has in fact reduced mankind as a whole and each its elements to this all-embracing formula. (Adorno & Horkheimer 1999:147)

We reduce ourselves and others, we engage in unhealthy practice, we fail to fully treat the health of individuals if we try to make people well purely through physical manipulation. In health education and therapy we can too easily succumb to operationalist thinking, where people are treated merely as 'cases'.

> Terms such as insight, understanding, reflection, wisdom and critique are neglected in favour of skill, competence, outcome, information, technique and flexibility. (Barnett 1994:16)

> Understanding is replaced by competence; insight is replaced by effectiveness; and rigour of interactive argument is replaced by communication skills. (Ibid.:37)

This reductionistic, mechanistic, materialistic, manipulative and impersonal approach to health is itself unhealthy and damages our sense of ourselves as individuals. Yet mechanistic talk about health care is everywhere. Managerial and instrumental talk about health predominates. We have inputs and outputs, best value, and 'mechanisms' for 'delivering' health care 'packages'. The doctor–patient, therapist–client, I–Thou relationship somehow disappears from the script.

Patients, clients, people like to tell their story of their health and *dis*-ease, as they see it. Sometimes they may need to establish their story. Sometimes they may need to move on from it. But how far do researchers and health care workers provide human beings with the opportunity to tell their story of their health, and in their own words? Are health care workers merely 'delivering' health care? What is the significance of the metaphor of delivery? Where is the personal touch, the personal relationship? What happens to the roles of wisdom and insight? 'Without insight, interpretation and understanding, information is blind' (Barnett 1994:42).

In all our feverish descriptions of inputs, outputs, performance targets and deliveries of packages, the concept, and implications, of a 'conversation' get entirely lost. Yet it is in dialogue and conversation that we express, find and share our individuality. The exchange is open ended, personal, engaged, flexible, exploratory, tentative, mutually respectful, attentive and intrinsically worthwhile. These features fail to show up in too many accounts of health. Yet they are themselves intrinsically healthy and human, and without them we lose track of who we are, both as recipients and providers of health care.

Habermas refers to the ideal speech situation of communicative reason where each can question anyone else to see how far what they say is true and sincere, and how far they have a right to say it. This aim is a re-statement of democratic humanist values made in the face of, and in response to, post-modern cynicism about truth, entitlement and sincerity.

> Nothing destroys the development of an effective relationship more rapidly than the diagnostic, pathological ideas we communicate to patients. (Sabo & Havens 2000:19)

> Clients should be conceived of as subjects of their own affairs, not as objects on which skills are wrought. (Barnett 1994:81)

Too often we look upon people as 'performers' rather than as reflective individuals who think and choose for themselves. Yet we lose our sense of ourselves as individuals if we are expected merely to complete the tick-boxes previously prepared. It is inherently depersonalising to see people as mere packages of skills. Skills-talk takes the individuality and humanity out of human life. Of course skills are important, but skills are meaningless except within a context of intentions, principles, purposes, priorities, values, experiences, understandings, identities – all that kind of soft talk that technologists back away from and humanists embrace. A skilled doctor can become a good poisoner, as Plato observed. 'Ideally, and this is characteristic of adult education, the relation of educator to learner is one of subject-to-subject, a peer relationship, rather than one of subject-to-object' (Sutherland 1997:13).

Of course competencies are important; but health and education discourse is crammed with competencies. *Persons* can only thrive within humanist discourse; so persons get left out. Ask the teachers, doctors and others weighed down by forms, checklists, competencies, skills, outcomes, but with less and less time and opportunity to engage with individuals or to be individuals themselves. Ask yourself, what am I to make of this disenchanting competency and skill talk, devoid of vision of individuality and purpose? Is it healthy? 'Competency stands for a prior determination of outcomes and of standards; it is a form of imposition. For understanding, read openness; for competence, read closure' (Barnett 1994:111).

The growth of counselling is itself greatly due to the decline of ordinary human dialogue, time, care and attention in so many aspects of our personal and working lives. Doctors, managers, colleagues, spouses, nobody, it seems, has time to pay attention, except within the context of a pre-planned and premeditated agenda. The priestly role has lost authority and credibility. So counsellors are drafted in to play the role of human beings with time for an open dialogue. But this is an absurdity. *Humanity is itself, in any case, lost if it is defined as a professional speciality.*

Counsellors insinuate themselves, and are pushed to demonstrate, professional expertise. The claim is generally bogus, as we shall see, and the human touch is, in any event, lost. The whole *point* about the enlightenment humanist agenda[13] is that we are *all* to be seen as human beings, worthy of, capable, and with a duty to provide, respect and attention. It is madness to think that being an accessible human being capable of dialogue with others is a professional skill. *It is irresponsible to throw this ordinary, though vital, human responsibility onto the shoulders of a new group of technical specialists.*

Evidence of health and sickness

The efforts to measure the overall state of mental health and general human wellbeing in Western society yield some alarming statistics. Here, for example, are some highlights from Roth and Fonagy (1996):

- During a 6-month period 6 per cent of the (US) population have a DSM-III-R diagnosis of an affective disorder (p 58);
- Anxiety: one year prevalence of 8.8 per cent (p 115);
- Eating disorders: subthreshold diagnoses 5 to 15 per cent prevalence (p 171);
- Personality disorders: 10 to 13 per cent (p 200);
- Alcohol dependency and abuse: Lifetime prevalence of 13 per cent (p 217);
- Sexual dysfunction: 4 to 9 per cent male erectile disorder, 4 to 10 per cent inhibited male orgasm (p 236);
- Psychiatric impairment among children and adolescents estimated at 10 to 33 per cent (p 263);
- It is likely that at any one time, 20 per cent of children in the UK and the US suffer from psychiatric disorder (p 270);
- Old people: At any one time: Severe depression 4.3 per cent mild/moderate depression 13.5 per cent (p 322); and

- Between 1967 and 1980, the proportion of the US population using mental health services increased from 1 per cent 10 per cent (p 37).

This kind of casualty rate suggests that there is a war going on! Clearly many people are not living the good life as seen on TV or as imagined anywhere else. They are not healthy as health is defined by the World Health Organization. And notice the last figure, a ten-fold increase in the take-up of mental health care in the US in just 13 years! Compare these with figures from Dineen (1999:7):

> In the early 1960s, 14 per cent of the US population (25 million) had received some psychological service. By 1976, that number had risen to 26 per cent; by 1990, to 33 per cent. And by 1995, according to the American Psychological Association, 46 per cent (128 million) had seen a mental health professional.

What is happening? Is our mental health really deteriorating as fast as these figures suggest? Are we simply less tolerant of imperfect health? Is health care improving and therefore picking up cases/people that/who were previously ignored? Are health professionals inventing ailments and creating dependency in order to further their own careers? Are changes in expectations of normal health affecting health statistics? It seems likely that all these factors are at work in some combination or another.

Is health to be equated with norms and normalcy? Are 'normal' people healthy? Or are they simply, and suitably, as mad as the world they live in? Baudrillard, Hebdige and Fromm all question concepts of 'normality'. Homosexuality was, until not so long ago, seen as a pathological condition. Both 'normal' and 'expert' men considered women to be inferior to men in many respects. Owning slaves was considered a normal and healthy kind of activity for many centuries. It is still 'normal' to pay people in many parts of the world what might (abnormally?) be considered to be an exploitative pittance. Even if normal people are less than happy with this they normally think that there is nothing much that can be done about it. These normal people would probably have accepted slavery too if born in an earlier time.

Perhaps real health requires, not that we are edged and positioned into some conception of 'normalcy', but instead that we be inspired to become more than we might normally expect of ourselves. Perhaps 'inspiration' should be used as a keyword more often within health narratives. We want to become healthier? Then what if inspiring buildings, cities, healers, landscapes, mentors, music, novels, speeches, teachers, views, ideas, actions, people, vistas, visions, and arts and crafts uplifted us? Even the *thought* of these might be (mildly) inspiring!

Health, we[14] have observed, is associated with integration, integrity, and wholeness. Yet this is an era of fragmentation and specialisation. Knowledge is fragmented, in talking therapies as elsewhere, with competing claims. Everyone claims and promises more than they can deliver in order to survive in a competitive market place. *Such fragmentation and competitiveness in health-care and elsewhere may in itself be evidence of an underlying societal sickness.* 'as the academic community splits apart into so many "tribes and territories" (Becher 1989), the university intensifies the fragmentation of cognitive capital present in society at large' (Barnett 1994:16).

The problem of fragmentation may, though, be older than we think. Here is Thoreau (in Reinfeld 1964:101) from more than a century ago: 'A college deals with branches of knowledge – all the branches and none of the roots.'

Psychiatry in particular has been assailed since the 1960s for its fragmented and materialist construction of mental illness. Goffman, Illich, Szasz, Laing, and others from what has been called the 'anti-psychiatry' movement have made trenchant criticisms of positivist-modernist narratives of health and well-being. Irigaray claimed that (for example) schizophrenics are not biologically ill but are overwhelmed and controlled by language being used against their health and interests. Likewise women generally suffered because of what she saw as the masculine bias of language. Laing, similarly, considered that people went mad when they were driven into 'double binds' by others; put into impossible situations, defined by others in a way that gave them nowhere to go, nothing to do, except snap.

Laing's alternative therapeutic community did not, however, stand the test of time. We should not be seen merely as pieces of biological machinery to be treated and 'cured' like sides of bacon. But it seems very foolish indeed to deny that we are embodied. Biological narratives have their (centrally important) place within all the other languages of health and sickness.

Brains can indeed become 'dysfunctional' in a variety of ways. Sadly our knowledge of brain function is tiny in relation to our vast ignorance. But when brains malfunction, something may need to be done about the brain, first and foremost, rather than the narrative, the self-concept or whatever. Drugs or surgery may well be the first priority in some cases. Dialogue, life skills training, psycho-education, marital education, sex education, counselling skills training, management strategies for anxiety, depression, obsession, or panic attacks; all these may merely be adjuncts to the primary task of fixing a malfunctioning brain.

However, *even when there is a dysfunctional brain to treat, there is also an individual person with whom to communicate.* And if communication is to be successful it may require us to show ourselves as functioning both within and beyond our role. We show the appropriateness of our role, and also its limitations. We thereby provide a human touch. This does not require that we become enmeshed with the other person. *To be human is not to be overly, invasively, intimate. It is to find the most appropriate distance and level of engagement with another person.* In so doing we retain our individuality and show our respect for another individual human being.

> Learning to communicate is something to which we bring the whole of ourselves: our sincerity, commitment, personal values and other qualities (even virtues) are all

> at stake. To learn to communicate as a matter of practising skills or techniques, by contrast, is to learn to play on people's susceptibilities, to manipulate them and achieve certain effects (in this sense the skilled communicator is indeed effective). (Blake et al. 1998:57)

We do not like other people practising 'communication skills' upon us. Such abuse is itself evidence of a sickness in society. We feel used and abused, and we *are* being used and abused even when we are not quick enough to spot the skills that are being employed on us. We want dialogue, sincere contact, and dialogue is absolutely essential in the development of whole, hale healthy communities.

Sincerity and humanity, though, does not consist in pretending to be closer emotionally to a person that we really are. Sincerity does not require that we promise more than we can actually deliver. But a person with a dysfunctional brain or other body part still wishes to be approached as a person and by another person. That person will be within a role, but will show that they are more than just a role. They will do so without having to tell their entire life story, or listen to your own, as though there could ever be the time, the need, inclination or reason to do so.

Persons need to *make sense* of their having a dysfunctional brain. They need to include this event in the story of their life. They need to relate to this fact and come to terms with it. They need to clarify their reactions to it. They may have to try to sort out where they have responsibility and where their behaviour is symptomatic of their illness. They have to both integrate themselves with their illness and differentiate themselves from it. This is easy with a broken leg. It is much more difficult with a damaged cortex since this part of the brain plays a far more important part than the leg in the expression and development of individual identity. I can incorporate the damaged leg into the story of my life. But, with a damaged cortex, my capacity to tell my story at all may be impaired, or destroyed.

'A child deprived of stories is deprived, as well, of certain ways of viewing other people' (Nussbaum 1997:89). Not just children, but all of us are continuously seeking, refining and upgrading our narrative account of who we are, who others are, where we have come from and what we are about. Our identity is closely related to our story, though we can become both too attached to, or too detached from, our account. We are story tellers and we go on trying to account for what is happening to us even after the most serious and disruptive trauma. Somehow, we go on trying to make sense of our world even when, as a result of brain injury, many of the pieces in the jigsaw of our lives have gone missing: 'Confabulation is the inadvertent construction of an erroneous self-story, signifying the neurological breakdown of the storyteller' (Broks 2003:52).

The dynamics of our circumstances are at least as important for counsellors to understand as our own 'internal' dynamics. For example a person may feel very strong emotions indeed that will be incomprehensible unless it is also known that they are both *responding to* a cortical injury and *expressing the symptoms of* this injury. Disentangling these two can be difficult for patient, counsellor and surgeon.

Surgery can be healing. So too can dialogue, plays, novels, paintings, poems and pieces of music. The promise of quick fixes can be far from healing, though the hopeful fantasy may sustain for a while. The recognition of tragedy and limitation will be far more helpful. The imposition of a particular story or vocabulary of health may be far from healing. An integrated, committed and flexible exploration of narratives of sickness and health may empower the client to take other perspectives and try other responses.

> the confrontation of tragedy is a highly cathartic experience. (de Silva 2000:110)

> Tragedies acquaint the young citizen with the bad things that may happen in a human life, long before life itself does so. (Nussbaum 1997:93)

Healthy and unhealthy narratives of health

Above all, respect for, and use of the client's vocabularies and narratives can be healing. The healer should start from there and suggest alternatives with sensitivity and regard for what a client is ready, willing and able to engage with. Sometimes an entire language that, to us, seems appropriate may strike another as alien and unhelpful. For example consider the following remark from Andrew Marshall, president of the Men's Counselling Association quoted in Sands (2000:42): 'Counselling is a female language. It's what women do naturally over the kitchen table without even being aware of it. Men don't have the language.'

Particular vocabularies might be alien to men, to women or to both from particular classes and social backgrounds. Tonnies, more than a century ago, distinguished between traditional society, where people tend to know each other face to face ('Gemeinschaft'); and our modern 'normality' where contact with each other is based on contracts ('Gessellschaft'). Hence in a modern world we interact with each other less in a regular face to face way but more as consumers or as sellers of our labour power. The shopping mall has replaced the village green. The skills portfolio and curriculum vitae have replaced the local network of assumptions, expectations and opportunities. These changes have profound effects on our sense of who we are and our understanding of what a healthy life ought to consist in. There is still a great deal of (healthy? unhealthy?) nostalgia for a (healthier?) past where everyone knew everyone else, where our world was not too large to cope with, and where we knew where we were, where we belonged and where we were likely to stay.

Willis argued that conceptions of sickness, health and the good life varied between social classes. Traditional working class values, for example, involved a view of masculinity that gave priority to physical strength, skills and prowess learned via experience rather than from education. Working class values gave particular priority to humour, 'having a laugh' in order to get through each day and cope with the boredom of repetitive work.

Miller likewise wrote of working class masculinity, preference for immediate gratification and excitement, and fatalism about what the future might bring. These self-concepts and views of the good life do not fit easily within most counselling narratives and (middle class) counsellor perspectives. Neither do they survive very easily in an economy where unskilled manual work is fast disappearing – in Western economies at least. Suicide rates among young working class males are increasing. Working class teenage boys are often demotivated, sullen or positively rebellious at school (assuming that they agree to go to school at all). Is this because of some psychological change in the 'psychodynamics' of these boys? Or because of their (rational? predictable?) response to, and grief about, social change and their diminished opportunities in a New Work order?

If this kind of social malaise (sickness?) is to be treated, how is this to be done? Does it require, above all, management? Or empathy? Or both in equal measure? Do we look for *causes*? Or for underlying *meanings*? Do we look at what social changes mean to us, or what they look like from the perspective of the people suffering from the effects/consequences/meanings of these changes?

> Weber argued that all sociological explanations should strive to be 'adequate' on two levels: at the level of 'meaning' – called verstehen; and at the level of 'causality' – called erklaren.
>
> Weber's major contribution to sociology was the idea of trying to achieve verstehen in social research. This idea can be described as 'seeing the world through the eyes of those involved.' Many action sociologists since Weber have taken up the idea of verstehen. (Kidd 2002:55)

Likewise, empathy is seen as important from the perspective of many schools of therapy. It is important, though, to see that empathy can, and should, be practised both on individuals and on entire communities. Counsellors, to be effective, need to see how they are seen from the perspective of communities for whom middle class liberal talk is not a part of their equipment, self-image or view of what a well-lived life is. Counsellors, to be effective, need to see what they can *learn from* as well as what they can *offer* such communities.

Traditional working class life is already a story past and gone. Individuals, communities, societies all change. The pace of change continues to accelerate. Social class may still be highly significant but working class people now seek to be consumers with their own kinds of status symbol products as much as, or more than, anyone else. Consumerism chimes with working class values in its instant gratification of needs. Consumerism, and consumer products, nowadays place and identify working class people as much as others.

Consumer decisions become a central part of our imagined identity and life-style. Consumer products are sold within a context of 'good' and 'healthy' life-style 'packages'. But does consumerism offer us a healthy narrative of health and the good life? Increasingly we are invited to buy, not just individual items, but entire matching sets of goods and services that, taken together, announce to the world whom we are, what we value, where we are trying to get to, and what we have achieved. UK working class people arguably identify with, and actively admire, North American consumer values more so than middle class Europeans anxious to preserve their own cultural values, identifies and status in response to North American hegemony.

Different forms of therapy, whether therapists realise it or not, focus on different consumer segments of the therapy marketplace. They will be attractive or not depending on the existing self-image of the potential client. But how (truly) healthy are these health narratives? 'Psychoanalysis was ideally suited to the treatment of highly functional, highly educated urbanites' (Fancher 1995:74). The narratives on offer may be untrue and unhelpful even if they are highly attractive to the target client group: 'Freud's fanciful pseudo-explanations (just because they are so brilliant) performed a disservice' (Wittgenstein 1998:62e).

Clients may buy into a narrative of sickness and health that is itself unhealthy, inadequate and untrue. They may fail entirely to see what is missing in their narrative of choice. For example,

> Joy, hope, disheartenment, pride, regret, and a host of other apparently important emotions almost never appear in psychoanalytic writings and are never given an explanatory role. Pleasure and pain, anger and lust, anxiety and guilt – this is about the size of the psychoanalytic emotion vocabulary. Similarly, motivation terms are equally limited: Sexual longings, aggression, attachment, and defence against their negative dimensions are fundamental motivations. Honour, grace, compassion, decency, and a host of other apparently important motives rarely appear, and, again, never as primary explanations. (Fancher 1995:118)

We can be empowered and/or impoverished by our health narrative of choice and our satisfaction with our therapy may have little to do with its real efficacy. The narrative may make more or less of us, but when we become confined within the narratives of any particular therapy we are generally quite unaware of the nature of our imprisonment. Here, for example, is a sample of the wide range of deficiencies in the health narratives, as described by critics who are invariably drawn from *outside* the therapy under question:

> I have experienced this feeling of falseness with a friend who has recently done a counselling course. It is tragic. We are in the middle of a feisty, vigorous and sensitive talk about our feelings and relationships, and suddenly the counselling tape switches itself on. (Sands 2000:41)

> As a newcomer in the dining room, I looked round for a comfortable looking table of faces to join. Without thinking, I found myself in the one group that did not consist of counsellors. These were journalists on a quite different in-service course.

> This group was relaxed and easy. The counsellors were busy with a subtle competition to see which of them was the most caring, sensitive and authentic. They were thereby blinded to their competitiveness, defensiveness and status anxiety. They wanted so much to be 'good' people that it was unsettling to be with them. The journalists were much less bothered about being good and genuine souls. Consequently, they were good to be with and, within sensible limits, more genuine. (Howard 1996:74)

> Whose truths do we investigate during therapy? The client's, or that of the therapist, or of the particular school of thought which the therapist follows? (Sands 2000:51)

> Perhaps this optimism about the world (and the belief that fear is the greatest problem) accounts for the prevalence of assertiveness training in behaviourism – and the absence of, say, patience and humility training, or resignation to one's lot training, or loyalty training, or training in fidelity to one's station and its duties. (Fancher 1995:162)

> The basic norm of cognitive therapy is this: Except for how the patient thinks, everything is okay. Reality is not pathogenic. Just think straight and life can be good enough. (Ibid.:231)

> Many of us were taught that reliving unpleasant experiences makes them less harmful, and that absolutely, categorically, is not so. (Bandler & Grinder 1981:197)

> I think the reality that humanistic psychologists have built is incredibly indulgent and not useful. That kind of indulgence is dangerous. (Bandler & Grinder 1981:221)

> Have you heard about 'unfinished business'? It's finished; you just didn't like the way it came out. (Bandler 1985:8)

> A lot of people go to therapists asking to feel more confident, when they're incompetent. That lack of confidence may be accurate feedback about their abilities. (Ibid.:138)

Nussbaum (1997) argues for liberal humanist values in education and therapy and sees better role models in earlier practice than in much of what goes on today: 'The central task of education, argue the Stoics following Socrates, is to confront the passivity of the pupil, challenging the mind to take charge of its own thought' (Nussbaum 1997:28). But it is difficult to get a mind to take charge of its own thought. It is much easier to take charge of a mind by filling it with one's own thoughts (or the thoughts as written down in the training manual). In a great deal of skills training, this is precisely the purpose of the enterprise. Lip service may be paid to responsibility and autonomy, but only if people autonomously and responsibly make the right decisions and take the right actions; that is, the actions and outcomes desired by the trainers.

Some therapists position themselves as trainers, some as educators, some as facilitators. *Currently therapists have so many profoundly* different *views about what constitutes health and wellbeing that it is hard to see how the same word 'therapy' can be used to describe so many diverse activities.*

'The most destructive split within Western man is the one that is created during childhood between the controller and the controllee, or, in gestalt therapy jargon, between the top-dog and the under-dog' (Stevens 1977:135). Is this right? Sometimes perhaps? Or is 'me getting control of myself' the most *constructive* achievement of Western man? Is counselling an essentially psychological activity? Should psychologists therefore preside over, control and manage therapists and counsellors? 'Existential counselling is a philosophical investigation rather than a medical or psychological one' (van Deurzen 1991:28).

Should we, as the behaviourists claim, focus on symptom relief or removal? Or should we rather accept and learn from our symptoms? 'I always think of symptoms as being people's friends, not their problems, because I think of symptoms as being communication channels. Symptoms, like people, don't always realise the difference between what they intend to communicate and what they do communicate' (Bandler & Grinder 1981:143).

How far back should we go in our study of narratives of sickness and health? 'Hellenistic philosophy several millennia ago set out as a disciplined search for the well lived human life, or eudaimonia' (Mace 1999:216). The entire liberal humanist educational system, not so long ago and for centuries, put the study of the classics at the centre of a child's education. Students invariably studied Homer's *Illiad* and *Odyssey*, and Virgil's *Aeneid*. The aim was to inspire readers by showing them what heroism and virtue consisted of and the importance both of public and private life. Few would argue now for a return to such a curriculum, but as regards a well-lived virtuous and healthy life what do we in the UK currently offer? Traces of faded Anglicanism? Ethics needing God in order to be justified? A shallow civics curriculum tacked on to the edge of the mainstream skills-programme of individualism, consumerism, technology and hedonism? In the past century, what progress have we made in our understanding of the composition of a healthy, wealthy, wise and well-lived life?

There is, and always has been a (healthy and unhealthy) 'battle of the narratives' as regards what constitutes a healthy and well-lived life. Not surprisingly, therefore, this battle is itself replicated to some extent between competing schools of therapy. 'the Playpower of the sixties has given way in the field of psychotherapy to the power plays of the nineties' (House and Totton 1997:172). Clients, likewise, bring reports of their battles with others, and they generally want the therapist to take their side, their perspective, in any such conflict and represent their own concerns without looking at wider interests. The therapist may, or may not, choose to confront the client on this and other issues.

Therapists may also compete against the health narratives of other specialists, for example within sociology. Should we look first and foremost at individual health or the larger health, or sickness, of the wider context? Elias, for example, has shown that we are wired up, within the musculature of our faces, to smile and to frown. This suggests that we are, first and foremost, a *social* species. Our smiling and frowning might best be understood by looking at the dynamics of social interactions, social processes, social norms, social roles, social hierarchies, social and cultural symbols and products, values, priorities and purposes.

We may have little chance of understanding frowning, smiling, hopes and fears merely by looking at individual dynamics. The society, within which we work out who we are, precedes us and outlives us. We emerge *from* it; we do not begin as intact and whole autonomous individuals who then go off *to*, and negotiate a contract *with*, a society of our choice. We are embedded in our world, which creates and constrains us far more than we create and constrain it. Never mind individual history, the whole of *homo-sapiens* itself emerged as a social species from social species. *In the beginning was Society, and therefore the possibility, with suitably large brains, of constructing a Word.*

Given the power of society, how far does a healthy response require that we change the situation that causes us problems? How often would we be wiser to change our *attitudes* to the situation we face? The answer, obviously, varies, but so too do schools of therapy vary in the extent to which they believe that individuals and/or societies can and should be challenged, changed and confronted.

Sociologists Blumer and Mead argue that selves are always in the process of change, but that the change is essentially a response to *social* change. In order, therefore, to understand the dynamics of change we need to look at changes in language, in patterns, opportunities and constraints in communication, in roles and social opportunities for, and restrictions on, interaction. If this perspective is accepted then, in order to understand a client and their healthy or unhealthy way of life, therapists need to identify and examine what is going on in the client's social world more so than in listening to the client's view of themselves. *Perhaps therapists need to become more like social anthropologists than individual witnesses to confession?* In this respect, family therapists, social and community case workers come closest to the social systemic approach that, sociologists argue, is essential in understanding the ever-changing self and its projects.

The sociologist Emile Durkheim observed that in the modern world the individual was becoming sacred. This has positive and negative features. Therapists concentrate on the positive: individual freedom, opportunity, diversity, autonomy, responsibility and maturity. But the negative aspects of liberal individualism also need attention if a whole and complete account is to be given that will be in the long-term health both of individuals and societies. As Fancher (1995) argues, honour, grace, compassion, and decency are also essential components of a healthy society. But all of these require that, at times, we privilege others rather than ourselves, place ourselves less at the centre of events, and take a more humble, and realistic, view of our own part in the larger scheme of things.

In sum, therefore, a healthy view of health requires that we attend to, and integrate, individual health with the health of communities, institutions, families, networks, classes and societies.

Healthy points of view

However healthy or unhealthy, we remain skin-encapsulated and embodied. We are likewise embedded within the context of our life, its past, present, and the resources available to create a future. Only in memory and imagination can we move beyond here and now, and survey our options from a larger perspective. But with these powers of memory and imagination we show ourselves to be truly exceptional apes.

There are so many (viable, healthy or unhealthy) ways in which we can construe ourselves, so many perspectives from which we can survey our circumstances. So many *more* than we generally realise. The question of which *kind* of perspective works best in which circumstances deserves more attention that it often gets.

'If you look closely at the face of the player, you will see that his cheek muscles are tightening and his lips are pursed in effort and attempted concentration. But face muscles aren't required to hit the backhand, nor do they help concentration' (Gallway 1986:19). Gallway argues that if you wish, for example, to become a good tennis player, it is a bad idea to watch yourself learning to play tennis. You need to avoid being a spectator watching your performance. Instead you need, above all, to watch the ball and, in the process of watching it, you do not need to have any kind of conversation about the matter. Words will not catch the ball; words do not move the arm, only a fast physical movement via effective hand-eye co-ordination.

> We have arrived at a key point: it is the constant 'thinking' activity of Self 1, the ego-mind, which causes interference with the nature *doing* processes of Self 2. Harmony between the two selves exists when the mind itself is quiet. Only when the mind is still is one's peak performance reached. (Ibid.:22)

> Trusting your body in tennis means *letting* your body hit the ball. The key words is *let*. (Ibid.:41)

> the key to better tennis – or better anything – lies in improving the relationship between the conscious teller, Self 1, and the unconscious, automatic doer, Self 2. (Ibid.:18)

We are still very often Cartesians[15] without realising it. We imagine that we must go on thinking consciously in order to exist and that, in the process, we should always be observers of ourselves in action. Yet this process of 'spectatoring' and providing running commentaries all the time can seriously inhibit effective performance. We can be spectators and commentators and sometimes these perspectives have a role. But we can also be, and we often need first of all to be, actors, doers and performers. And often this doing does not require comment, conscious rehearsal, or any kind of 'me-keeping-an-eye-on-myself'.

> If you can stop the internal talking and maintain internal silence, you will arrive at a simpler appreciation of the facts and your reaction to them. (Perls et al. 1979:143)

> At this point I want to say something of how I experience wholeness on the infrequent occasions that I do. I am sensorially aware of the present; I see, hear, smell, touch and feel without the intrustion of thoughts. (Stevens 1977:136)

Perls, Stevens and Gallway celebrate self in the mode of unselfconscious awareness and action. We can see, hear and touch without saying to ourselves 'I am seeing, hearing, touching.' The danger, though, is that this mode can then become over-accentuated at the expense of other ways of being. 'My self-understanding necessarily has temporal depths and incorporates narrative' (Taylor 1996:50). Sometimes we need to do more than just attend to the immediate present moment, the immediate swing for the ball. We need to step back in imagination and explore the story of how and why we came to be here swinging the ball and where we intend to go next. Sometimes we can just let ourselves go to the next target. Other times we need to engage in conscious deliberation. This might involve going back, via memory and imagination, to some previous point in the story.

> Associated means going back and reliving the experience, seeing it from your own eyes. Dissociated means looking at the memory image from any point of view other than from your own eyes. (Bandler 1985:40)

> Dissociation is particularly useful for intensely unpleasant memories. (Ibid.:43)

The cave dweller can go back to yesterday's encounter with a sabre tooth tiger. Where shall they place themselves? At the moment just prior to when they were nearly bitten, and looking out from just where they were standing at the time? From this perspective they will re-stimulate a fight–flight alarm response that may be important to store. Or they may paralyse themselves once again in terror. 'Survivors have to learn the trick of observing themselves as if the events of their lives were happening to someone else' (Lasch 1985:96). Perhaps if they looked at the whole situation as though they were looking down from the safety of a nearby cliff? This might make them too blasé about the risks of fighting tigers. Or it might help them to stay calm enough to see that, had the tribe all worked together with their spears, the tiger could have been killed.

Alternatively, the tiger incident can be surveyed from the imagined point of view of the cave dweller's gods, far up in the clouds perhaps. This may provide a large and calming perspective on this individual incident. Or it may provide the humans with added confidence, in the belief that their gods are on their side. Or it might make them careless, or fatalistic, in the expectation that the gods will provide.

How and where we see ourselves in imagination can influence how successfully we will place ourselves in our next real encounter. The imagination needs to be disciplined by the real constraints of the situation. We might imagine killing the tiger with a mere angry growl of our own. This thought might make us feel good and improve our confidence. But it won't help us kill the tiger, won't improve our tiger killing skills, and may make us reckless in the face of real danger.

The point of view we take on ourselves depends not just on how, and from where, we *see* ourselves in our imagination. It also, crucially, is determined by the way we *talk* about ourselves, as we are now, as we have been, and as we seek to become. For example, do we describe ourselves as active *agents* or as passive *victims* or *hostages* of our circumstances? We are *both* active and passive and, if we are to be wise, we will have the courage to change what we can (and should) change, the grace to accept what we cannot and the wisdom to know the difference.[16]

Our physiology has evolved in response to both negotiable and impossible circumstances. A manageable threat will trigger an alarm response; adrenaline will bring the body very rapidly into action; within seconds we will be ready to fight or flee. An overwhelming circumstance or trauma will trigger endorphins. We will anaesthetise ourselves, go still, contemplative, passive, fatalistic, waiting, in calm, peace and with little pain, to see if help is at hand.

Different schools of therapy provide extravagant, realistic, or pessimistic views of the extent that we have autonomy, agency, and control over our lives and circumstances. Existential humanistic schools place great stress on the importance of realising that we are in charge of our lives and ourselves. We need to change old habits of helplessness and passivity. We need to get on our bikes. We need to think and talk about ourselves in an *active* rather than a *passive* way. For example, here is a large agenda of language change described in detail by Passons (1975):

- Personalise pronouns: change 'It' to 'I', 'You' to 'I', 'We' to 'I';
- change verbs: change can't' to 'won't', 'need' to 'want', 'have to' to 'choose to', 'know' to 'imagine';
- change passive voice to active voice;
- change 'but' to 'and';
- ask 'how' instead of 'why'; and
- omit qualifiers – 'may', 'possibly'.

This is the language of people who see themselves as acting on, rather than being acted upon by, their circumstances. It is the sort of active language that people need to learn if they are too passive and fatalistic in their lives. But is everyone so passive? Are there not also people who take on too much responsibility for their predicament? Who expect too much of themselves? Who do not appreciate the crushing forces of the situation they face? Perhaps it would be better for such people to turn around the above active language agenda in precisely the opposite direction? ***Fatalism may be a wise strategy of survival for those who do indeed have almost no control over their fate.***

> There are no magical solutions to the damage life inflicts upon us . . . [Therapist] influence is minimal, limited for the most part to the simple solidarity they can offer to people in distress . . . Overcrowding, poor housing, bleak, dangerous neighbourhoods can quickly crush the spirits and extinguish the optimism of those who have to suffer them. (Smail 1996:37, 145, 202)

Depending on the circumstances, doctors, counsellors and others will encourage clients to take more, ***or*** less, ***responsibility for the situations they face.***

We can take any number of points of view upon, from 'within', or beyond ourselves. But health of any kind is not just a matter of our point of view, or just of our thoughts or emotions. Health and a healthy identity are found, perhaps above all, in what we *do*. We are not Cartesian ghosts in a machine. We are embodied, physical and social beings. We express ourselves in words and actions. When we act wisely, and with integrity, our points of view, our thoughts, our constructs, feelings and actions all work together within some kind of overall unity. This is what makes us one person living one life and not an army of warring individuals battling within one body and trying to lead many different lives.

Behaviourists and cognitive behaviourists have a great advantage over other schools of therapy in stressing the need to focus on actions, on what people actually do with themselves, with others, with their lives. Talking about oneself, taking a perspective on oneself, constructing and reconstructing oneself; all this can, if we are not careful, become a substitute for, rather than an aid to, actually doing anything with oneself and one's life. 'Making something of oneself' requires, above all, some *action*.

> If they are to feel differently, something will have to be done. (Smail 1996:210)

> Questions about the meaning of life can never be answered by sweeping statements. 'Life' does not mean something vague, but something very real and concrete, just as life's tasks are also very real and concrete. Our answer must consist, not in talk and meditation, but in right action and in right conduct. (Frankl 1987:77)

> That's what reframing is all about: finding out what else needs to *happen* so that the client won't need the symptom anymore. (Bandler & Grinder 1982:137)

So, the narratives and metaphors of sickness and health that we carry around with us are important. But narratives describe actions, within a meaningful story. And, if we want to be a part of the story of our lives, we cannot just be a storyteller or invisible observer. We have to be an actor, a participant, doer, central character perhaps, in our story. Otherwise we may become just another postmodern couch potato, a voyeur on the pretend lives of others, active and interactive only in cyber-space; and elsewhere merely a cipher, form-filler, a follower of procedures.

Therapy may help a person take stock of who they are, where they want to go, and what they want to do next in order to make something of themselves. But therapists all have views of their own about what constitutes sickness and health. However non-directive they may claim to be, these views will be highly influential. Therapist perspectives on what constitutes a good, healthy and well-lived life, like those of everyone else, *differ*, and often profoundly so. That is why it is so important to have some knowledge of the range of options available.

For example, Carl Rogers (1902–87) is the originator and icon of person-centred, non-directive therapy. But *the person-centred movement is centred on a particular view of who persons are*, what they can become, and what are the stages in their personal development. You can be sure that this philosophy informs all that person-centred therapists do. You need to be able to assess for yourself how far this philosophy is actually true, useful, healthy, morally acceptable and socially responsible. You will not be able to make such an assessment of the health agenda of person-centred therapy if you are steeped only in person-centred therapy. The same is true, of course, of any other school of therapy. *Hence my repeated efforts, in this and previous publications, to encourage therapists, clients, and people generally, to look more broadly at ways of thinking about identity and wellbeing.*

Rogers (1961, 1979) enjoins us, in a series of sub-headings, 'To be the self which one truly is':

> Away from facades p 167, Away from 'oughts' p 168, Away from meeting expectations p 169
> Away from pleasing others p 170, Towards self direction p 170, Towards being process p 171
> Toward being complexity p 172, Toward openness to experience p 173, Acceptance of others p 174
> Trust of self p 175, Social implication p 178

Rogers' account provides a particular philosophy of life, health and identity that is very much a product of the humanistic, individualistic and hedonistic zeitgeist of the 1960s. It has some merit, and more than a few substantial defects. *How to find one's own way among all these competing philosophies of health and the well-lived life?* This takes us on to the next chapter and the question of how far my reality relates to yours and how far we can and should achieve some consensus about what is real.

Questions for Counsellors

1. Which of your clients are advancing into sophisticated and cosmopolitan agendas of health? Which are retreating into immature self-obsession that is in many ways less healthy than the health of our ancestors? Be specific with examples.
2. Which of your clients are exceptionally pressured, and/or exceptionally privileged, by their circumstances? And with what consequences on their mental, moral and spiritual health? Be specific with examples.
3. Are you aware of the 943 pages of psychiatric disorders listed in DSM-IV-TR? How often do you need to refer clients to professionals 'trained' to deal with these disorders? Which, if any, of these disorders are 'unreal' and/or could be better treated by (which kind of) counsellors?
4. Do some of your clients bring to you problems that, from most people's perspectives, are luxuries that most people do not have the time or money to pursue? What examples come to mind?
5. How far do you seek to assess the influence of social context on the health of your clients? Do you rely entirely on the accounts given by your clients? If not, what other sources of information do you utilise?
6. What evidence do you have of the health making, and health damaging, effects of city life/rural life on your clients? Be specific with examples.
7. What evidence do you have of democracy/lack of democracy, justice/injustice at work and in society, having a healthy/harmful influence on your clients? Be specific, with examples.
8. In what ways does your vocabulary of health assist your clients? In what ways does it constrain them and detach them from their own narratives? Be specific, with examples.
9. Do some of your clients have an unhealthy wish to be more healthy, joyful, happy than is realistic? How do you judge and respond? Be specific with examples.
10. How far do you agree with Marshall that 'Counselling is a female language'? If it is, what can be done about this?
11. How far do clients from working class backgrounds feel comfortable with your health narratives? How do you put them at their ease?
12. In what ways do honour, grace, compassion and decency show up in the agendas you negotiate with clients? What is the role of patience and humility training, or resignation to one's lot training, or loyalty training, or training in fidelity to one's station and its duties? Is Fancher correct to argue that these are missing within so much therapeutic discourse?
13. How far do agree with Bandler and Grinder that 'the reality that humanistic psychologists have built is incredibly indulgent and not useful.'?
14. How far do you agree with Fancher that 'The basic norm of cognitive therapy is this: Except for how the patient thinks, everything is okay.'?
15. Do you agree with Bandler and Grinder that 'A lot of people go to therapists asking to feel more confident, when they're incompetent. That lack of confidence may be accurate feedback about their abilities.'? Have you experienced cases like this and, if so, what did you do about it?
16. Do you utilise association and dissociation when clients recall previous experiences? Can you think of clients who associate too often for their own good? Who dissociate too often? Be specific with examples.
17. Can you think of clients who are take too much/too little responsibility for their actions? Be specific with examples.
18. Is a person-centred therapy centred primarily on persons or on person-centred therapy? Justify your answers.

CHAPTER 4

Truth Telling – Identity and Reality

> Psychotherapy is . . . at bottom a truth-seeking venture. (Yalom in Feltham 1995: 115)

> Telling clients that we can help them is assuredly helpful even if it is not strictly true. (Kottler in Dineen 1999:177)

> One waits in vain for psychologists to state the limits of their knowledge. (Chomsky in Dineen 1999:248)

This chapter will consider how reality, as perceived by the counsellor, is negotiated with reality as seen by the client. It will also look at how constructs of reality interconnect with conceptions of self. Can, and should, counsellors be entirely non-directive concerning client realities? Counsellors can no doubt be dogmatic and invasive with their own views and interpretations. Counsellors can also, presumably, be too reticent about challenging what may be unhelpful, damaging or positively immoral assumptions, expectations, beliefs and behaviour in clients? *How, then, to find a balance between these two extremes of invasion and inertia? When does challenge become disrespectful? When does support become collusion, or enmeshment?* Who judges what is real and authentic about a client and their circumstances and with what authority and evidence?

> Neoclassical economics as now taught – I do not exaggerate – comes perilously close to being a design for concealing the reality of political and social life from successive generations of students. (Galbraith in Melman 2001)

Classical economists, Galbraith argues, conceal political and social reality. Counsellors and psychologists, as we shall see, likewise argue that the realities of *rival* schools of counselling are inadequate and 'unreal'. So who has a handle on reality?

> France now has twice as many professional astrologers and fortune-tellers as priests. And it is the same in the USA. (Zeldin 1998:339)

> We don't typically sink our intellectual and emotional roots deep enough into reality. So in times of surface drought we have no source of nurture, strength and refreshment. (Morris 1997:179)

Secular and spiritual realities

For two thousand years conventional reality, common-sense reality, was the reality of the priests. It was the Christian Church, in Europe at least, that was considered to be the repository of our deepest wisdom, insight and understanding. If you wanted to reconnect to underlying realities, and see beneath and beyond day-to-day triumphs and disasters, then you consulted the priest, who could help you to survey your situation from a larger perspective and support you in coming to terms with your deeper motives, aspirations and fears. If you could not get real and be authentically yourself within the church then where else could reality be found? The most real reality would, of course, come later, after you had died, in the eternal life to come. There you would find reunion and endless bliss, unless, of course, your sins on earth had led you to utter damnation.

This, then, was, until quite recently, the most commonly held view, in Europe, about what was real and authentic. Now, as Zeldin observes, fortune-tellers, astrologers and other New Age (old superstition?) practitioners outnumber the priesthood. Therapists of some schools may seek to heal you by reconnecting you to your 'past lives'. Is this progress? Or are all such practitioners equally far removed from a real understanding of human beings and their circumstances?

'one's perception of material objects is shot through with one's psychological nature . . . the perceptions of the ordinary man are contrasted with those of the arahant, who "sees the world as it is" (de Silva 2000:24). Padmasiri de Silva offers a Buddhist psychologist's view of reality. According to Buddhist teaching, some individuals see the world as it is, and most do not. 'The Buddha traces this predilection of the "anxious man" to his inability to grasp the basic truth of egolessness, which is the key to understanding any form of anxiety. The belief in "I" and "mine", though it gives a superficial feeling of security, is the cause of anxiety, fear and worry' (Ibid.:49).

Most of us, the Buddhists argue, are fixated on a false idea of who we are. We defend this imagined self, we seek to keep the bits we like fixed and unchanging. And in the process we thoroughly distort our understanding of what is actually going on all around us. We don't know who we are and we don't know what is happening.

> Exposure to a never-ending variety of stimuli increases the sense of diffuseness which invades the self. Absence of an inner purpose directing one's life makes it possible for parasitic desires and artificial life-styles to eat into the soul. By a consistent refusal to look at ourselves closely, we create blocks and barricades which prevent the growth of self-knowledge. (Ibid.:114)

We are bombarded by stimuli and distraction. We lose sight of who we really are and what is important. We lose ourselves in the anonymity of living in the mass. So perhaps the Buddhist teacher is the person to find if we want to know ourselves better, be more authentic and maintain a better understanding of life? Certainly Buddhism is a stronger influence on many Western intellectuals than Christianity. 'that wholeness, according to Buddhism, is what is real and all that is real. A radically separate and isolated and bounded entity does not exist anywhere' (Wilbur 1981:151).

Likewise, Hinduism teaches that most people are cut off from underlying realities and fail to achieve a whole, integrated grasp of the one interconnected universe. Within Hinduism, many gods are available to assist the masses cope with their partial, shallow and incomplete understanding of reality. But for the élite, the Brahmans, reality lies beyond the world of appearance with its finite selves and warring gods; all of which are essentially illusory. Reality was a transcendental unity that embraced all appearances and conflicting partialities. Through moral action we began to understand this interconnected unity, beyond all dualism, and ultimately we found ourselves to be identical with Brahman. The essential 'me', within so many spiritual and mystical traditions becomes identified by, identical with, the essential unity of the universe. Even within Christian teaching, we hear from a variety of sources that the Kingdom of God is *within* you.

In every discipline, accusations are made that reality is lost or is actively being concealed. Will reality eventually catch up with us? Or can we evade it indefinitely? Evasions of reality, we are advised, occur within every discipline, and within individuals, institutions, communities and whole societies. 'the Private Finance Initiative . . . could be viewed as what accountants call "an off-balance sheet fiddle": a debt hidden from public view but which the government will eventually have to pick up' (*Financial Times* December 11 1997).

Psychologists, presumably know more than laypersons about human nature. But which kind of psychologist do we need? If a Buddhist psychologist is not available what kind of Western psychologist would be best? 'The psychologist knows no more about "human nature" than the next man, and if he is wise he will not let his claims outrun his discretion' (Eysenck 1953:224–5). Surely self-awareness and self-understanding are important parts of psychological training? Surely psychologists, in their efforts to understand others, have to have a better than average insight into themselves?

> Trainees will develop skills and theoretical understanding but at no time will they be expected to understand themselves in any coherent way. (Pilgrim & Treacher 1991:97)

> The irony of our profession is that though the 'currency' of our work is with emotions, our background is an academic one which places the onus on objectivity (the

> applied scientist) as opposed to listening, giving space and listening (the practitioner). (Walsh 1990:7, cited in Pilgrim & Treacher 1991:137)

Or perhaps psychologists can extract the truth from clients by hypnotising them and thus 'getting behind' their 'defences'? 'Memory under hypnosis is *not* more accurate than in a waking state' (Dawes 1996:167).

So perhaps it is wiser to make use of psychoanalysts who, within their training, do have to undergo a very substantial self-analysis?

> His [Freud's] place is not, as he claimed, with Copernicus and Darwin, but with Hans Christian Anderson and the Brothers Grimm, tellers of fairy tales. (Eysenck 1986:130)

> In my experience, a psychoanalytic approach can weaken our sense of connection with the world and our faith in the validity of all our judgements and perceptions. (Sands 2000:34)

> If you are led by psychoanalysis to say that really you thought so and so or that really your motive was so and so, this is not a matter of discovery, but of persuasion. (O'Neil 1995:143)

In any case, within the most avant-garde French postmodern psychoanalysis, the very search for a 'self' as a destination in therapy has been abandoned. 'The ego or self, says Lacan, is a fiction; selfhood is frozen as an image of something that does not exist' (Elliott 2003:54). So maybe psychiatry would be a preferable source of support in the process of making sense of ourselves? 'When I first worked in psychiatric hospitals in the early seventies, I was astounded by the profession's ignorance of patients' desire for existential meaning' (van Deurzen 1997a: 184).

Cosmopolitanism or chaos?

Clearly there are many different voices, perspectives, opinions, within every discipline concerning what is real and important. How to draw all this together and produce an integrated picture? Is there not just too much material now to bring together? Is there a deeper truth of any kind that underlies any of these conflicting voices?

> What is deeply pernicious in today's academy . . . is the tendency to dismiss the whole idea of pursuing truth and objectivity as if those aims could no longer guide us. (Nussbaum 1997:40)

Are notions of 'deeper' truth themselves a remnant of a modern age now past and gone? Should we focus more on, and come to terms with, our relative *ignorance* about our world and ourselves? After all, Socrates, arguably the originator of the Western humanist tradition of ideas, asserted that he knew more than most only insofar as he knew that he knew almost nothing. 'Our primary goal should be to produce students who have a Socratic knowledge of their own ignorance – both of other world cultures and, to a great extent, of our own' (Ibid.:147).

Certainly our advances in knowledge do very often seem to highlight what we do *not* know. Intellectual progress seems to de-centre human beings ever more. Our growing knowledge dissects, ever more clearly, our fallibility, prejudice, power ploys and partiality. We are endlessly and constantly susceptible to rationalisation as we seek to justify our search to secure, promote and defend our own interests. 'Even an infant's crying is described differently – as anger when the observer thinks the baby is male, as fear when the observer believes it is a female' (Ibid.:187). The child is angry? The child is afraid? Which? Both? Does mother know? Does the therapist or psychologist know? The truth, it seems, is very hard to find. Yet what could be more basic than the sound of a crying child? Is there *a* truth at all, or just a series of perspectives? Can we say only that 'The child is angry *in my opinion*'? Surely to abandon the distinction between truth and opinion is a recipe for chaos?

'The postmodernist attack on truth threatens the very possibility of ethical and political criticism' (Ibid.:296). When the only 'truth' on offer was that to be found in the local church it was a relatively simple matter to seek counsel and guidance. There was the church, and not much else. But now there are so many different ways to make sense of our lives. We are overwhelmed by the choices on offer via the various media. The entire world, and all that it ever thought and did, appears to be available to us at the press of a button. How can we make sense of all this? How can we find our way through it? If the client is lost, what can the counsellor offer that will help?

> For Frederic Jameson (1990, 1991) our sense of presence in the culture and in meaning-making has been seriously compromised by the proliferating omnipresence of the media and information systems. (Lewis 2002:7)

> It is undoubtedly true that for many people film relationships provide the most emotionally wrenching experiences of the average week. The ultimate question is not whether media relationships approximate the normal in their significance, but whether normal relationships can match the powers of artifice. (Gergen 1991:57)

Can we 'return to nature' and thereby 'reconnect with ourselves' and find peace, calm, serenity and insight? Barthes argues that: 'a distinction between nature and culture is no longer valid, since even natural objects (water, stars, trees) are rendered meaningful by human sign systems' (Lewis 2002:7). The nature we find is generally constructed by human agency and, in any event, it is a presentation of nature mediated by heritage industry, tourism and other marketing specialists eager to link the narrative scene with the consumer's own dreams and expectations about what comprises 'getting back to reality'. We have come a long way with Rousseau's romantic view of the essential nobility of peasant life.

> From property values in certain sorts of villages, to ways of dressing at country shows, to picture postcards to mass media dramas of rural life, authenticity is continually being sought and presented in a huge variety of social and cultural symbols that mean that discriminations between image and reality can never be absolute. (Chaney 2002:157)

> The noble savage motif, for example, has become a central part of Third World tourism. Tourist promotions frequently sell their product through images of 'natural' and 'primitive' lifestyles. The discourse of tourism abounds with essentialist and Romantic idealism. Artefacts, rituals, dance performances and agricultural lifestyles are imagined as 'authentic' or paradisaical. (Lewis 2002:120)

> The naturalness of rustic environments was, of course, as artificial as any cityscape with the development of representational traditions as in the influence of Gertrude Jekyll on English country gardens. (Chaney 2002:157)

> our ability to make sense of the world we live in is now absolutely dependent on our relationship with the media. (Lewis 2002:12)

Yet are we wise to rely on realities as presented by journalists or by feature writers with links to marketing and lifestyle promotions? Who will offer a dispassionate account? Did such an account ever exist? It is false to imagine that 'tradition' in previous centuries was any more authentic than the many pastiches that are served up to us now. For example, Whigs had been inventing, and concealing, their histories from the Glorious Revolution of 1688 through to 1900. Heraldry, with all its fantasies and flummeries, was always just a show to impress the masses and rationalise one's own opportunism, sharp practice and good fortune.

Even when we seek to train as a counsellor, and thereby locate authentic identities, we can be sure that each institution will be keen to market their *own* training course and their own brand of counselling. Their funding will depend on it. No one, it seems, is paid to be dispassionate about anything. Worse yet, many postmodernists do not even believe that there is anything to be dispassionate, or passionate, about. 'Man is an animal suspended in webs of significance he himself has spun' (Weber, in Lewis 2002:68)

Can we at least escape into a simple authentic intimacy within the haven of hearth and home and, best of all, in bed? Here, away from all the pretence and manoeuvring of working life, we can be ourselves and be at one and as one with another?

> Although we may laugh at the story of the lover who turns contentedly to his partner after consummation and says, 'You tell me your fantasies and I'll tell you mine,' or

> nod knowingly when we hear Freud's comment about sexual intercourse always involving at least four people – the two lovers and the two imagined lovers – nevertheless we are cautious about admitting that fantasy had quite such salience in our own life. (Cohen & Taylor 1992:106)

Fantasy can come between two people whether they are in face-to-face contact or not. The Internet can facilitate the creation of fictional selves, but people can also be at least as sincere when they write as when they meet each other.

> Surely face-to-face encounter is not a requirement of what most people would consider 'real and important' relationships. Some of the world's most intense affairs of the heart (Héloïse and Abelard, Elizabeth Barrett and Robert Browning) were carried on largely by written word. Nor does reciprocal exchange seem essential for significant bonding; consider people's relationships with religious figures such as Jesus, Buddha, and Mohammed. (Gergen 1991:56)

Deconstructing, or destroying, 'truth'?

> This above all – to thine own self be true,
> And it must follow, as the night the day,
> Thou canst not then be false to any man.
> (Shakespeare, *Hamlet*, I.iii.75)

Instead of trying to construct a truth, should we merely 'deconstruct' the efforts of others to make sense of their world? Jacques Derrida suggests that we look at language and rhetoric. Rather than searching after (what we may imagine to be) the real, we should instead look at the binary opposites of 'real' and 'unreal'. Who is using them? When, where and with what purpose?

Instead of considering what is reasonable and right we should look at the binaries 'reason' and 'unreason', 'right' and 'wrong'. What are the distinctions being made? Which half of the binary is privileged? Which is seen as superior? Instead of looking at civilisation we should look at the binary 'civilisation' and 'barbarism'. Rather than looking at what is 'authentic', we need to consider how it relates to, and what is defined within its opposite, 'in-authenticity'. And so on. 'The interest in the authenticity of a concept enters into the judgement about this concept. Whatever is authentic in this concept also becomes so only under the perspective of something that is different from it. It's never pure in the concept itself' (Adorno 1973:123).[1]

Reason, many postmodernists claim, only exists as a dyad with 'unreason'; right because of 'wrong'. And so on. Neither half of a binary can exist without the other. They are each coupled with, and defined in relation to, the other. The relation is what is fundamental just as 'fundamental' is only so when braced with what is defined as 'superficial'. Nothing, it is claimed, is everlastingly true since there is only truth within language. We never look at the world without language, we never escape the language, which empowers and imprisons us. We can never look in on language except with language. We never look at ourselves except with the language we happen to use to describe 'self'. 'But what is it to 'look inward' and to identify what one 'really means'? Can one identify an 'inner state' not already prefigured in the public language? (Gergen 1991:105).

'Truth' itself only exists in contrast with what is construed as 'false'. According to this argument, we can never get to any kind of 'foundational' truth, either about ourselves or anything else. All we can do is clarify what we are right now holding to be 'foundational'. We never get to a true and real place outside of language. We only ever unravel the language we are using. The unravelling is itself another usage of language. And the 'unraveller', 'I', is itself a construct of language. 'Time and again Foucault debunked the idea of a true self; he was scathing of what he called the 'Californian cult of the self' (Elliott 2003:91).

According to postmodernists, we never get to a real, fundamental, extra-linguistic meaning of anything. We only locate the meanings that currently exist in the language (a cultural product) and in the actions, expectations and practices of families, friends, groups, networks, institutions and societies, which place and define us all.

> Derrida doesn't claim that we can think outside or beyond a particular concept, for to do so would entrap us in the (false) gesture of origination. (Lewis 2002:165)

> language, according to Derrida, is not of itself constructed out of truths, essences or ultimate reference points – there is no origin that lies behind language. Rather, language is a restless and ever moving mass of imprecise details, constantly seeking, but never quite achieving, some approximation of meaning. (Lewis 2002:164)

> Give the people a new word and they think of a new fact. (Willa Cather, in Fancher 1995:26)

This postmodern view about reality has been developed from, among others, the philosopher Ludwig Wittgenstein. (For a fuller account relevant to counsellors, see Howard 2000). Wittgenstein had originally (1922) searched for reliable foundations to our understanding of reality and truth. He wrote of logical 'atoms', deep-structured realities, and saw propositions as 'pictures' of reality. Linguistic/logical propositions were models of reality. Representation and reality shared the same logical form. Logic was a mirror image of the world and provided a model of the structural scaffolding of reality.

But Wittgenstein (1953, 2002) wrote an entirely different philosophy. Now there was no foundational reality, no scaffolding, no deep structure, no pictures or representations of the 'real' world. Philosophy should no longer search for 'essential realities' underlying societies, words and deeds. It should merely describe the actual use of language and its links to action. Language was used in many ways. Actions were many and various. Linguistic analysis was decoupled from logical analysis. Truth and reality were not found, via analysis, in foundational logical atoms outside of language and society. Neither was it found via individual introspection. Truth was found within societies, within languages, within communities of intention, negotiation, agreement and conflict. The word 'truth' was used in many ways, to make many contrasts. We had to get to specifics and these varied, along with the languages used to describe them.

But now that there are so many new and different words, and so many kinds of language with which to think and talk about identity, what is to be done? What 'facts' are to be identified and prioritised?

> Frederic Jameson . . . believes that the proliferation of televisual images is producing a cultural condition he calls 'historical amnesia'. Jean Baudrillard . . . believes that the same qualities are producing a hyper-reality in which there can be no referent, no truth and no direct or materially oriented human experience. (Lewis 2002:218)

> Douglas Kellner . . . characterises postmodern identities as: accelerated, extended, unstable, disintegrated, fragile, superficial, illusory. (Kidd 2002:93)

> The marketing of consumer culture makes authentic goods – such as the artefacts of Tibetan craftspeople – available to global audiences, and yet in so doing turns their craft into another tourist industry. So that overall the plenitude of culture means that we are constantly aware of the play of meaning and the possibilities of enhanced meaning while simultaneously suspecting that the simulations of cultural industries render our environment fundamentally meaningless. (Chaney 2002:176)

Are there many truths or should we assert that there is no such thing as truth? Do we merely have opinions? If so on what basis do we assess them and what is the point of academe at all? Who with authority can announce that there is no authority? How can postmodernism be of any use at all if it is so relativist and sceptical as to claim that nothing of significance can be said? And if such a claim is made why should we consider it to be significant?

Postmodernism, then, at its most sceptical, destroys its own case even in making it. But postmodernist observers do make a number of important points about what, and how, we come to know anything. Clearly language is significant, clearly power and interest are significant. Clearly, as we progress in our understanding of 'truth'. 'reality' and 'authenticity', we have to abandon naïve views about what defines these. Objectivity can never be as complete, foundational or as final as we might prefer. We seek it only within our limitations as interested, prejudiced and partial human beings. Therefore we never 'finally' find it. 'As soon as I have expressed something in a word, an alienation takes place, and the fullest experience has already been substituted for by the word' (Fromm et al. 1997:109). Yet there is no justification in abandoning the search for knowledge, and sinking into the absurdity of asserting that no assertion is any better, or truer, than any other.

It is interesting, and I think constitutes progress, to look at Derrida's language binaries, and to see how we carve up our world and our views of ourselves, according to these fundamental (and arguably neo-Kantian) distinctions. It is useful to be able to become aware of our imprisonment within our language even though, in the very process of seeking to loosen our chains, we remain enchained in words.

Every word, every concept, every binary, by its very nature, opens certain doors of insight for us and closes all the others. Kant was well aware of the dangers and limitations. But he did not collapse into chaos and despair. Neither should we. He believed that, despite human limitations, human progress in action and understanding was possible and desirable. So should we, and not just as an act of blind faith, but with a well argued case. Counsellors, in particular, who rely so much on the subtleties of language as negotiated between themselves and clients, need to pay much more conscious attention to the relationships between language, truth and authenticity. 'It would be catastrophic to become a nation of technically competent people who have lost the ability to think critically, to examine themselves, and to respect the humanity and diversity of others' (Nussbaum 1997:300). Nonetheless, it is undeniable that the search for what is real (and what is meant by 'real' in a particular context) is made all the more difficult given the glut of information and the extent to which so much of what we understand is mediated by someone else.

> [For Baudrillard] all idea of what is 'real' has come to an end. TV images may even appear 'more real' than one's own life. He finds this collapse of meaning exciting, alarming, and even humorous. (Kidd 2002:110)

> Seduction lies at the core of Baudrillard's account of the hyperreal: fantasyscapes such as MTV, Disneyland and McDonalds become more vivid, more intense and more real than that which we typically think of as 'reality' . . . For example, the very idea of Coca-Cola – the 'Real thing' – holds more power and seductiveness than does the actual drink. (Elliott 2003:141)

> Many people who engage in netsex say that they are constantly surprised by how emotionally and physically powerful it can be. They insist that it demonstrates the truth of the adage that ninety percent of sex takes place in the mind. (Turkle 1997:21)

Yet we have *not* abandoned all ideas of what is real. We do (generally) still distinguish between TV realities, computer-generated realities, and reality. And so we should. We do express real, and reasonable, concern if someone cannot distinguish between what is on their computer screen and what is to be seen out of their window!

> If the French poststructuralists, like Derrida, are correct in their analysis of narrative, the hermeneutic turn will end in the recognition that there is no unified or centred

> subject behind any text. Attention to narrative ends not in analysis of the self but in its absence. If, on the other hand, critical theorists like Habermas are correct, narrative dissolves into social discourse. (Fancher 1995:132)

Compare this with an earlier observation by Thoreau, who certainly did believe that there was a centred subject behind his text, and who thought that this self was best known via the text. Thoreau claimed to find himself on Walden Pond, but advised that others would do best by finding him in his books: 'You may rely on it that you have the best of me in my books, and that I am not worth seeing personally, the stuttering, blundering clodhopper that I am' (Thoreau, in Reinfeld 1964:103).

The idea that there is no subject is an invitation to psychosis. But nowadays we have far more sophisticated views of persons, authors, subjects of texts than the common-sense naïvety about personhood that passes for knowledge in so many schools of counselling. 'Everyday life has become a field or a site of struggle in which meanings are contested or reclaimed from ungraspable others. It is important in this context to look at what might be called struggles of identity' (Chaney 2002:175). We can, and should, avoid both naïvety and nihilism. There are better and truer accounts of identity than those offered by naïve empiricists, naïve introspectionists, and sophisticated yet sophistical postmodern nihilists. Habermas provides one such option, as we shall see.

Yet the path is more difficult than common sense might prefer. Naïve confidence in our own self-awareness will not suffice. For example, clients are often asked to provide self-reports about their satisfaction with counselling. On the basis of these reports, counsellors and counselling organisations claim that counselling 'works'. Fancher notes that self-reports are not particularly accurate. Indeed counsellors from many counselling schools claim that clients need counselling precisely because they are so deluded and so incapable of providing an accurate account of themselves. It is only human, of course, to take a more positive view of the insight of clients when they start to give you positive feedback and praise the efficacy of counselling! But are such positive accounts accurate? And, indeed, are we being necessarily accurate when we are positive?

How much truth can we stand?

> In the past fifteen years, a substantial body of data has accumulated showing that depressives are actually much more accurate than non-depressed persons in their appraisal of themselves and their circumstances. Most people's characteristic ways of understanding themselves are, in fact, inaccurate and overly positive. (Fancher 1995:213)

> Human kind cannot bear very much reality. (Eliot 1994: 'Burnt Norton')

What is the basis, then, of cognitive therapist challenges to the depressive attitudes of clients? 'The cognitive therapist assumes, without doing any empirical investigation, that she has a more accurate grasp on the patient's life than the patient does – even though the patient always has more data about his life than the therapist has. (Fancher 1995:214). Surely, though, there are cycles of negativity that therapists need to challenge? 'There is nothing irrational about concluding from a long history of failures that this is one's lot in life' (Ibid.:215).

It may well be rational to be negative, but perhaps it is not always realistic to be 'rational'? Perhaps we have to take an unrealistically positive attitude simply to survive at all? Perhaps we have to go on hoping even when (*particularly* when) there is no real and rational basis for hope? 'It may well be that the capacity for denial and self-deception provides powerful adaptive advantages (Slavin and Kriegman 1992; Dennet 1995)' (van Deurzen 1997a:185).

Is truth really our first concern? Is it not a far deeper truth that we want to get through each day in one piece, to tell a manageable story, preferably with a few triumphs, and remain plausible to ourselves and to others? And when I say 'we' I mean organisations and institutions as well as individuals. These, too, want to retain credibility, to find solutions, to complete the contract, to develop the programme, to capture, secure and protect the business. And if truth of any kind, from any source, gets in the way of these fundamental objectives, then truth needs to be buried, burned or bypassed. I certainly discovered the power of this process when I attempted to get an entire organisation to face up to deeply unpalatable truths about its activities. Never mind truth, there are mortgages to be paid. That, for many, is the deepest truth you can get.

'I characterise the culture of cognitive therapy as middlebrow' (Fancher 1995:230). And so we construct our idea of ourselves not 'simply' from the evidence available, but from a careful *selection* of our past:

> our interpretations of the past serve to validate our current understandings of ourselves. We 'manipulate' the past, shape and reshape it, so that it 'fits' who we believe ourselves to be (or who we believe we must/must not, can/cannot be) . . . sedimented beliefs are the foundational 'building blocks' of our constructed self. (Spinelli 1994:173, 348)

Our search for truth about the world around us is profoundly interconnected with what we consider to be the truth about ourselves. What we look for and take an interest in is driven by who we think we are. And what we see and remember reinforces our ideas about who we are. Each is cause and effect of the other. *Identity is closely interconnected with epistemology*, and we go on seeking to maintain our identity even when, perhaps through brain injury or dementia, we find it ever more difficult to make sense of ourselves and our world:

> Consciousness is so compulsive a story-teller as to be a master confabulator – it will always invent a story in terms of cause-and-effect relations, even when it has no idea what is going on, and the available data are inadequate or contradictory. (Charlton 2000:200)

> Abysses of amnesia continually opened beneath him, but he would bridge them, nimbly, by fluent confabulations and fictions of all kinds. (Sacks 1985:104)

How conscious do we need to be?

> *In general, we're least aware of what our minds do best.* It's mainly when our other systems start to fail that we engage the special agencies involved in what we call 'consciousness'. (Minsky 1987:29)

We construct an identity. We make sense of ourselves and the world around us. The two processes are interlinked. But how conscious do we need to be of any of this? Mostly we are *not* conscious of what we are thinking, feeling and doing. Mostly we do not *need* to be conscious of our activity. But it does not follow that, when we are doing something without conscious thought, we must have been doing it as a result of 'unconscious thought'. Much more likely, we are doing something without any kind of thought or mental activity at all! When we become skilled and competent we don't have conscious thoughts about what we are doing, and we don't have 'unconscious thoughts' about it either. There may not be any mental activity concerning what we are doing. We may simply be *doing* what needs to be done and thinking, if we do, about something else altogether.

'"Body and Mind": This split is still popularly current, although among the best physicians the psychosomatic unity is taken for granted' (Perls et al. 1979:288). This is a crucial point for counsellors to appreciate. Many imagine that, if there is not a conscious mental life associated with an action, there must have been an 'unconscious mental process' that could, and maybe should, be 'dug up' if the action is to be properly understood. Generally, though, there is no unconscious mental activity to be retrieved or dredged into surface awareness. Instead, in the process of counselling, or anywhere else for that matter, we can reflect upon previous actions and generate any number of thoughts, feelings, opinions and understandings of them. However, these are not, generally, unconscious thoughts that we were having at the time. Rather they are conscious thoughts that we are thinking now.

> There is no reason to assume that there is such a thing as full consciousness of anything, nor that there is such a thing as an unconscious reservoir of phenomena. (van Deurzen 1997a:152)

> Why tax the conscious mind? It's the limited and undependable part of the person. (Bandler & Grinder 1981:179)

> It's really strange to realise that we are all hypnotised, that we are all in the process of waking up, seeing and hearing perhaps ten percent of what goes on. (Stevens 1977:269)

In all our actions, and certainly in skilled and complex activity, there will be many levels of control and monitoring of activity in the *brain*. But most brain activity is not associated with conscious (or unconscious) *mental* life at all. I don't consciously (or unconsciously) think 'now breath in, now breath out, now hit the ball, now stop at the traffic lights, now walk around this obstacle' etc. *There are no, conscious or unconscious, mental thoughts or representations associated with most of the brain's control functions.* Indeed, sometimes the mental activity seems to be more a bye product, or effect, of the activity than any source of decision or control. 'No one knows yet just what consciousness does and does not do; but we are sure that it does not provide a mirror into how we think' (Fancher 1995:240).

Let's suppose that we are asked to move our finger with conscious intention. We might assume that the brain events associated with conscious intention would come *before* any other brain events associated with moving the finger. After all, if conscious intention is the *cause* of finger movement it must come prior to the movement. But as Ramachandran's 2003 Reith lectures made clear, this does not seem to be the reality of the situation:

> the brain events are kicking in a second prior to your actual finger movement, even though your conscious intention of moving the finger coincides almost exactly with the wiggle of the finger . . . natural selection has ensured that the subjective sensation of willing is delayed deliberately to coincide not with the onset of the brain commands but with the actual execution of the command by your finger, so that you feel you're moving it. (Ramachandran 2003)

Ramachandran argues that the brain events come *before* the consciousness, but, as he acknowledges, there are still questions to ask about what we mean by consciousness. The trouble is that much of counselling and psychotherapy is still saddled with a dualist view of the world. Actually dualists imagine that there are *two* worlds. One is made of physical stuff, the other of mental stuff. Counsellors who subscribe to this kind of philosophy will imagine that much of their time needs to be spent exploring the client's 'mental world'. This mental world is itself often broken down into two kinds of stuff – conscious mental activity (thoughts and feelings), and unconscious thoughts and feelings. The counsellor then seeks to help the client bring the unconscious mental stuff into consciousness. To understand my actions, according to this philosophy, I must find the thoughts that I had at the time that 'drove' and made sense of the actions. Perhaps the driving thoughts were unconscious? If so I must make them conscious.

This entire dualist account (it goes back to Descartes, and links much earlier to Plato and many others) is, I think, closer to myth than to fact and is not taken seriously by most neurologists. The binary 'mental–physical' deserves investigating and sometimes makes distinctions worth making. But it creates nothing but confusion and misunderstanding when conscious and unconscious mental 'worlds' are imagined to run in parallel to physical actions and to the process of speaking and writing.

Of course we can imagine, anticipate and remember. In so doing, we experience visual, auditory, tactile, olfactory and taste constructions and reconstructions of events. But none of this requires that there be a mental 'world' accompanying, controlling or running in parallel with the physical. Nor that there be thoughts accompanying, preceding or following all our actions. To repeat, our brain controls most of our actions without our needing to think anything at all. Even highly cerebral activity does not necessarily require thought! When the work is going well it is the action that predominates. A scholar puts down words on pages and this is how we judge their work. Who knows, or cares, what they think other than via what they *say* and *write*? We have to think more about what we are doing when we don't know for sure what to do. When we really know what we are doing we seem to need to think less! 'With complete assimilation the knower and his knowledge are one. There is no "application of knowledge" to a situation, like ointment to a wound or cold cream to the face, but only the person-in-action. The person and his knowledge are in healthy confluence' (Perls et al. 1979:154).

So, this text, for example, stands or falls all by itself, when it is read and assessed by you. It did not need a 'mental life' on my part to get it on the page. You do not need to access the inside of my head in order to assess the text. No sentence had to be preceded by a sentence, thought or other representation that I 'ran inside my head'. I find out what I think, like you, when I read the text. I may then, of course, revise it some more! I find out what I think when I write. I don't locate a thought 'in my head', assess the thought, and then write it down.

Evidently there is a time and place to be conscious of what we are doing. But being conscious often involves paying active attention to what we are *doing* and what is to be *perceived* all around us, more than attending to a thought. Of course, from time to time, we consciously try to make sense of what we are doing. Whatever we do takes place within hierarchies of projects and concerns.

When I am getting on well with my projects I can simply *act* without having to *reflect*. Likewise when I am cooperating well with others I do not have to try to consciously assess what they are thinking, feeling and doing. When cooperation is going well, we respond to each other appropriately, helpfully, and perhaps without words. But doubts and uncertainties may soon set in. We find we need to say 'please pass me the hammer' rather than just hold out our hand. We find we have to start trying to imagine and trying to anticipate how all this hammering is seen from the perspective of our carpenter apprentice. This does not require that we enter a parallel mental carpenter's apprentice world. But it does mean that we must listen, speak, show, attend, and *try to imagine also how we are being seen* from the other side of the workshop. Making sense of how others make sense is necessary because we are essentially *social* creatures: 'we need also to construct models of other people's minds because we're intensely social creatures, us primates. We need to do this so we can predict their behaviour' (Ramachandran 2003).

We need to predict the behaviour of others. We need also to predict what behaviour they would like to see, and promote, in us. It is this prediction of actions and interactions that is so important in social life. What will this person do next? How does this person interpret and make sense of what I am doing? Do they understand what I am doing? What do they want me to do next? Arising from these questions we start to formulate ideas about the *intentions* of others. Much of this mutual understanding (and misunderstanding) is non-verbal, and can even take place between humans and animals.

For example, my cat is standing by its bowl. It looks at me. It looks at the bowl. That is all it does. I am sure it *wants* to be fed. I do not have to know what is happening in the brain or mind of the cat to know this. I merely have to make sense of its behaviour. But what if I ignore the cat? It follows me. It meows. It walks back to its bowl. It looks up at me. It looks again at its bowl. What more evidence do I need? I feed the cat and now it lies down to sleep. We understand each other.

> maybe the solution to the problem of the self won't be a straightforward empirical one. I don't want to sound like a New Age guru, but there are curious parallels between this idea and the Hindu philosophical view that there is no essential difference between self and others or that the self is an illusion. (Ramachandran 2003)

Why won't truth stand still?

One of our greatest difficulties arises from our wish to pin down meanings and understandings and make them more permanent than they can in fact become. In this sense the Buddhists are right. Meaning making appears to be a *dynamic* rather than a static process. We are continually learning and developing and that which we seek to understand and make sense of is continually changing. 'Meaning is inevitably altered constantly. Nothing means the same from one second to the next. Things never attain a solid or reliable single meaning. This is not dissimilar to Heidegger's remark that we are always no longer and not yet' (van Deurzen 1997a:86).

In constructing meanings we are more like surfers on a beach than secure occupants of a stone fortress. Meanings, like butterflies, are best understood in flight rather than pinned down on a table.

> He who bends to himself a Joy
> Doth the wingèd life destroy;
> But he who kisses the Joy as it flies

> Lives in Eternity's sunrise.
> (William Blake *Gnomic Verses*)

In the process of making sense of our world we are continually faced with the highly professional efforts of others who want to make meaning for us and who want us to understand what, as, when, and how, they want us to understand. Our apprentice carpenter starts to sing the famous song 'If I Had A Hammer', and dreams of hammering out justice and freedom all over the world. We may start to ask, 'Is this guy skilled in carpentry? Perhaps he would better off as a poet?'

> If the practitioner clicks into therapy-speak, the exchange starts to feel discordant. It is difficult then to continue with what one wants to talk about. Telling a practitioner that one finds his language inaccessible, or pretentious and insincere, may not feel like a viable option. One may then feel obliged to choose between engaging in a conversation which seems phoney, asking the therapist to rephrase what he has said, or saying nothing at all. (Sands 2000:41)

> Most of the hypnotic realities that people have built for themselves and live in most of the time – what they call the waking state – are not profoundly useful. (Bandler & Grinder 1981:221)

In any event, meaning making is not purely a linguistic activity. Actions speak louder than words; and actions may belie our words. Gestures, movements, muscle tensions, the set of our head, mouth and jaw; our voice, eyes, nose, arms, hands, torso, legs and feet, our autonomic responses; all these can give a clue to what we are about, and what we really mean, more so than what we may say we are about.

> When one fears contact with actuality – with flesh-and-blood people and with one's own sensations and feelings – words are interposed as a screen both between the verbaliser and his environment and between the verbaliser and his own organism. The person attempts to live on words – and then wonders vaguely why something is amiss! (Perls et al. 1979:139)

> Speaking at length about something does not offer the slightest guarantee that thereby understanding is advanced. On the contrary, talking extensively about something, covers it up and brings what is understood to a sham clarity – the unintelligibility of the trivial. (Heidegger 1995:208)

In understanding the making, and communicating, of meaning, then, the non-verbal is arguably more important than the verbal. Why say 'Pass me the hammer' if merely reaching out with one's hand will produce an instant and appropriate response? Moreover, this non-verbal meaning making is an essentially social rather than a psychological process. Garfinkel, for example, argued that people make sense of the world together, and they are very methodical about it even though they are rarely conscious of the process. The emotions of psychological discourse are not the most fundamental reality of a social situation. What is still more fundamental is the way people make sense of a situation. This is so because the way we feel about anything or anyone is the result of the way we *construe* the situation or person and their motives. Arguably, therefore, *understandings* should be the currency of therapy more so than *feelings*.

> A topic that receives systematic attention in some regimes of communication training is 'talking about feelings' – the assumption being that the feelings themselves are 'there', the established property of an already-existing self, and what is lacking is only the level of communication skill needed to do them justice. (Cameron 2000:6)

Garfinkel argues that, in our everyday lives, we all utilise an enormous amount, and variety, of 'background' knowledge – about people, situations, projects, institutions and so on. This tacit knowledge does not so much exist as an unconscious thought or idea in an individual mental world. Rather it is ready 'to hand' in our shared understandings of the world. Therapists so often seek out unconscious, personal knowledge in their attempts to understand a client. Sociologists, on the other hand, when following on from Garfinkel, look out for tacit, shared, public knowledge and understandings. Therapists arguably need to adopt what C. Wright Mills described as a 'sociological imagination'.

Garfinkel experimented to see how people would respond when students pretended, like Martians, no longer to be familiar with what others expected of them. He found that students very rapidly produced reactions of enormous irritation, anger, and moral outrage when they did not use the background knowledge essential to make sense of each other's actions and words. If I ask for the hammer and my apprentice carpenter, preferring the role of philosophical sceptic, says 'what do you mean by hammer?' I am likely to get rather baffled, and impatient. I may well ask 'what do *you* mean by asking?'

So much of what we understand depends on our understanding of the *context* in which things are said and done. Without the context, the words and actions are meaningless. Life is too short to explain and make explicit every assumption, context, circumstance and implicit rule of evidence and reasoning. *Unless a great deal of context is taken 'as read' then it is impossible to read any situation, speech or action.*

Hence perhaps, the considerable irritation with philosophers when they seek to make assumptions explicit without explaining *why* they are doing this! Hence the *justified* irritation, when philosophers nit-pick at questions, assumptions and issues without any serious underlying purpose. Major philosophers, by definition, avoid this, but mediocre philosophers will sometimes repeat questions and arguments previously aired while losing sight of any significant rationale. 'Living comes before thinking. Practice precedes theory' (van Deurzen 1997a:170).

We have to 'fill in' the bits of a person's message and action that requires our understanding of the context. A person waiting at a bus stop is asked 'Have you been waiting long?' If they were to answer by asking 'Waiting for what? A job? A partner? A pension?' the questioner would be baffled and irritated. It is *just obvious*, given the context, that the question relates to buses. We do not have to, and do not wish, to precede our question with the self-evident statement: 'I see you are waiting at a bus stop and I imagine that this is because you are waiting for a bus.' Less yet do we say 'And when the bus stops at the bus stop, which I think it might, I imagine that you will get on it.' Much of what people say to each other makes little sense unless we understand the context, conventions, institutions, circumstances, and history of events, actions, intentions, projects and plans leading up to what they say and do.

Notice that it is the *tacit social context*, not the *unconscious personal content*, that matters most. We don't have unconscious thoughts about all, or any, of this tacit knowledge. On the contrary *we generally have the necessary knowledge to understand one another without consciously or unconsciously thinking about it at all.* I don't consciously or unconsciously think 'this is a bus stop and there is a bus company in this society'. I see the bus stop and I question the person waiting at the bus stop. I expect and assume that she will know that I know that I am asking if she has waited long for a bus and not a buzzard. I also know, when I think about it, that if I simply write down the question: A: (to B) 'Have you been waiting long?' then in the absence of any context it is impossible to know what the questioner wants to know.

Garfinkel talks of the importance of trust in the collective making of meaning. We trust that others will seek to try to make sense of what we are doing by paying attention to, and taking due account of, the circumstances in which we are operating. We can only understand each other to the extent that we live in a shared universe of understandings about what words, actions and institutions mean. These shared understandings need constantly to be worked upon to be maintained, and we trust and require that everyone will do the necessary work so that we can go on making sense of each other. This work rarely requires conscious or unconscious thought. More often it requires careful *attention* to what is happening here and now and to what *was* happening that led up to, and relates to, these here and now words and actions. That understanding may require that we have to hand a broad and long-term picture of the context, including the intentions and expectations of actors. The larger the cultural, and the longer the temporal, context of understanding, the deeper the understanding is likely to be.

Notice again that the depth of understanding is more a depth of sociological and cultural insight than of 'depth psychology'. Actually it is pretty well impossible to go deep into any individual psychology without bringing in a large social and cultural agenda. You will not understand carpentry by looking inside the head of the apprentice, or the carpenter. This probably explains why sociologists, anthropologists and cultural theorists have had so much more to say about identity than counsellors and psychologists.

Notice also that empathy with another has little to do with any sort of 'tuning in' to their 'stream of consciousness'. It has much more to do with a committed understanding of what and why they think, feel and act as they do given their circumstances and their understandings of their circumstances. We communicate via our shared interaction and our communion of intention, by what we say and do, more than by exchanging supposedly 'inner' experiences.

Another important point to understand about understanding is this: We do not so much assemble 'facts' and then create an understanding. More often we begin with a large tacit, and shared, understanding and then select and create facts, about wood, hammers, saws, customers, perhaps, that we see as relevant to further developing this understanding. Facts are thus, to a very large degree, socially produced. Our background knowledge creates and brings certain facts into the foreground of concern, and the entire process generally takes place with no conscious or unconscious thought at all. The facts just 'pop up' into consciousness, not so much from our 'unconscious', but more so from our shared social world. This vast activity of background and tacit knowledge stays, of course, in the background and remains tacit. We almost never think about how much we need it, and how much we utilise it, in order to make sense of anything and anyone. Neither do we think about it unconsciously. We simply don't think about it at all since we rarely have any need to do so. 'Without consciously thinking about it, we play by the rules' (Nussbaum 1997:238).

Psychologists and counsellors seeking to understand this collective process of mutual negotiation and understanding will make little progress if they confine their efforts to studies of individuals in clinical settings. The process of negotiating tacit understanding only takes place in recognised and social settings. *If understanding is not studied within societies and institutions it is not understood at all.* Hence the tendency of psychologists to carry out experiments that everybody else considers to be trivial or obvious, of use only to visiting Martians. Hence, also, the tendency to be irritated with psychologists who pretend to *be* visiting Martians, and who refuse to engage with a social world of tacit understandings. Hence the common failure of psychology to produce experimental results that are considered to be of much practical use or relevance in everyday life.[2]

Hence, not least, the irritation with psychologists, or other social scientists, who claim that they can observe as a kind of neutral 'fly on the wall'. No human being looks at the human world as though a Martian from outer space. Each of us belongs to institutions and communities of concern, and we see, and are seen, accordingly. Nobody has a right to observe people as objects of observation. What makes us human is that we are subjects. None of us are disembodied or disinterested.

However psychology is not the only discipline that takes a narrow and naïve view of how best to find truth and discover reality. Other specialists, too, tend to assume that their own 'take', metaphors, constructs and perspective on the world should be given special privileges at the expense of others. Economists collapse too many questions into the confines of economics, sociology is reduced to psychology. Psychology is reduced to physiology. Physiology to chemistry. Chemistry to physics. Physics to maths. And then we will have a 'theory of everything'? This is what happens when specialists of any kind fail to understand the context of, and particular role for, their own specialist studies.

> Having trapped itself into narrow definitions of knowledge, [higher education] is unable to provide the wider definitions of knowing and intellectual development which it supremely should have been in a position to supply and which now are required by society. In short, a higher education for a rational society requires that higher education expand its own sense of rationality. (Barnett 1994:24)

A great deal of the truth that we seek is not that which is stated explicitly within any particular specialist discipline at all. It is that which is *implicit*, to be inferred, deduced, discussed and debated within the true and fictional *stories* we hear of, read and tell each other, and narrative, by its nature, transcends disciplinary fragmentation and specialisation. We make sense of each other and of other broader events via *narrative* truth perhaps more than any other kind of truth. *This happened and then this and this. So, what do you make of that? What is the moral of the story? Why am I telling you this? Why are you interested in this? Here is the news . . .*

Narrative helps us understand, helps us identify ourselves, and others and our place in our world. It helps us bond with, and distance ourselves from, others. In so doing we identify and express ourselves.

The myth of the 'detached' seeker after truth

Positivist psychology still trades under the fantasy that there can be an impartial, detached, neutral outside spectator, making notes and developing 'scientific' knowledge free of personal interest, power relations or prejudice. No such human being exists, or could ever exist, yet psychologists have wasted years in the illusion that they can and should aspire to such an inhuman, and inhumane, status.

> There is no authentic person to be liberated, no self to be uncovered, but instead other narratives who write subjects differently. (Blackman and Walkerdine 2001:97)

> it is next to impossible to see what it could mean to read a drama of Sophocles, or a novel of Dickens or George Eliot, in the detached way. (Nussbaum 1997:104)

Much of twentieth-century psychology modelled itself on nineteenth-century physics and failed to notice that physics, and the philosophy of science, changed profoundly after Einstein's theories from 1905. Hence it clung on to mechanistic and materialistic paradigms and notions of objectivity and rigour. These were already outmoded in physics in 1905 and they were never helpful in a disciplined study of persons (who are neither machines nor ghosts in machines). Psychologists, in their efforts to be realists and materialists, failed to understand that they were victims of a naïve metaphysics of realism and materialism. As a result, their brave charge against the bastions of psychological ignorance was something like a Somme offensive: costly, inappropriate, barren, unproductive, essentially a monumental failure. No wonder many have given up psychology altogether and taken up physiology.

> Psychology's realist assumption – that there are stable, enduring psychological capacities waiting to be discovered via scientific method. These capacities are ahistorical, untainted by culture, and lie beyond language and signifying activities. (Blackman and Walkerdine 2001:102)

> Much of counseling psychology is pseudoscientific reification, and amounts to no more than suspect social intervention. (Marinoff 2002:355)

Coupled, and interconnected, with the myth of the detached seeker, is the myth of the detached 'fact' that sits around in the world waiting to be found. The more facts we can find and 'gather', like so many blades of grass, the more factual fodder we will have and the more informed we would be. But the gathering of facts, of information, leads to the question 'so what?' Machines can store millions of facts but they know and understand nothing. Knowledge requires that you make some use of the information at your disposal. Where are you trying to go today with all your knowledge? If you are going nowhere with your information is this information 'knowledge' in any significant sense at all? If you are just regurgitating facts with no personal mark, evaluation, perspective, understanding, reaction or intention in relation to any of them, then is this knowledge at all?

> That information cannot amount to wisdom is clear enough. But Midgley points out that information cannot amount to knowledge either. Without insight, interpretation and understanding, information is blind. (Barnett 1994:42)

> Emotional (subjective) and real (objective)': this split is again a general scientific article of faith. It is the result of the avoidance of contact and involvement and the deliberate isolation of the sensoric and motoric functions from each other. We shall try to show that the real is intrinsically an involvement or 'engagement'. (Perls et al. 1979:288)

Truth telling, the search for authenticity, understanding the 'reality' of self and circumstance is, as we have seen, a much more complex and fluid process than naïve intuitionists or empiricists may imagine. 'It is naïve to assume that one can create a neutral environment, as neutrality itself is a particular choice of signal' (van Deurzen 1997a:190).

To illustrate the relevance of all this to counselling, I want to show what happens when counsellors fail to engage with the scale of the epistemological problem they are faced with. I think that they do so fail, more often than they succeed, and I want to demonstrate this by taking an example, not of poor practice, but of what has often been seen as *best* practice in counselling.

Gerard Egan's bestselling *The Skilled Helper* (3rd edn 1986) is one of the most successful, influential, practical and systematic training manuals in counselling that has ever been produced. Egan seeks to be eclectic, though in a disciplined fashion, and he focuses both on empathy and on results. He is popular because he provides a clear, step by step method, rather than too many awkward and intractable questions, dilemmas, uncertainties and ambiguities for people to wrestle with.

His work continues to be highly influential within a very large number of counselling training programmes. He is not, then, a straw man and easy target. Yet although I am impressed with Egan, certainly in relation to most other counsellor training programmes I have studied, I remain concerned about much of his work. I think it is terribly naïve in relation to the problem counsellors and clients face in establishing truth, authenticity and client identity. Of course, naïvety sells well. If your chosen expert is not much bothered by deep-seated philosophical and sociological questions then why should you bother your head about such questions? Why don't you just enrol for the programme and then hang out your shingle?

Much of Egan's book is taken up with case study illustrations of the points he seeks to make. The problem with all case studies, of course, is that they are presented from the point of view of the author. How can we know that the case is seen in the same way by the client or other observer or participant? As one might expect, practitioners present far more cases of success than of failure. Do others see them as successes? Would the reader see them as a success? Is the reader ever given enough information to make an independent assessment of the case? Here are some illustrations of the problem:

> Frank goes to his minister. The minister sees quite clearly that Frank is scared and confused. (Egan 1986:98)

Would we see the same in Frank? There is no way of knowing either from the text quoted above or from the original. Here is another (I have inserted the question marks in brackets):

> Client: I'm here because I have to be. You're here either because you're dumb and like to do stupid things or because you couldn't get a better job. You people are no better than the people on the street. You're just more 'respectable'. That's a laugh.
> Helper: So (?) nobody could really be interested in you. (?)
> Client: I'm not even interested in me!
> Helper: And (?) if you're not, no one else could be, including me. (?)
> [She emphasises her contempt for the kind of people that try to "help" her.] (Ibid.:124)

> As he talks, it becomes fairly evident that part of the problem is that he is so quiet and unassuming that it is easy for his supervisors to ignore him.
>
> Client: I am not as flashy as some others, but I'm just as substantial.
>
> Once he becomes aware of the self-limiting dimensions of his social style, he might be in a position to do something to better manage the problem situation. (Egan 1986:212–13)

Is it 'evident' that he is 'quiet' or that he is 'not flashy'? Is his social style 'self-limiting'? Should he become as 'flashy' as most Europeans seem to consider most Americans to be? Partly it will depend on where he is living, and what he wants to do. *But, once again, a naïve counsellor trainer collapses complex judgements and social contexts into simple and unproblematic 'perceptions'.*

> The client begins to react defensively then catches herself and lets the truth of what is being said sink in. (Ibid.:215)

Does the client react defensively or, for example, does she respond with intelligence to puerile homilies? Is it really acceptable, in a counsellor-training manual, or anywhere else, to imagine that truth 'sinks in' in some unproblematic way? If truth merely has to sink in to us, how come that we all, including everyone in the endlessly varied and competing schools of counselling, have so many different 'takes' on what constitutes the truth? Truth matters, it is worth pursuing. But it is not a final 'destination' that we reach, and it does not 'sink in' like sunshine, natural oil or anything else. The establishing of truth is a highly complex process and we only say otherwise when we no longer want a discussion of the matter. I do hope that this point has truly 'sunk in', before I move on!

Truth is generally a contested area, especially within counselling. It is absurdly naïve ever to suggest otherwise when considering case studies. It is particularly ironic when, in the process of discussing some of these cases, Egan is considering what he imagines to be 'advanced empathy'!

> Some clients cannot face the world as it is (?), and therefore distort it in various ways. For instance, Arnie is afraid of his supervisor and therefore sees her as aloof, whereas in reality (?) she is a caring person. (Ibid.:221)

It is assumed of course that counsellors, and readers of counselling texts, can face the world 'as it is'. It is assumed that Arnie's supervisor is a caring person 'in reality'. Who has the last word on this? The counsellor? Why so? Who provides any evidence? None is presented in the text. I have again inserted comments below in brackets:

> Nancy perceives her stubbornness (?) as commitment. (The old adage: '*I am firm, thou art stubborn, he is pig-headed*' – at least acknowledges the problem.) (Ibid.:221)

> Eric, a young gay male who has been beaten up a couple of times by people he's met in gay bars, sees himself as a sexual victim. He blames his problems on an older brother who seduced him during his early years in high school. (Perhaps he is right?) (Ibid.:221)
>
> Eric: I want people to leave me alone.
> Cousellor: I don't believe it because I don't think you believe it . . . Be straight with yourself. (Why should the counsellor not believe it? Maybe the counsellor is the bully here and he too is not leaving Eric alone?)
> The counsellor bluntly but caringly (?) *invites* Eric to let go of the past (psychobabble) and let himself think more clearly about the present. (Ibid.:222)

The word '*invites*', positions, coaches and may coerce the recipient, without them ever thinking about this consciously or unconsciously. Why won't you accept an 'invitation'? Moreover, everyone is now imagining that they can, should and will 'let go of the past' as though this abstraction was like a shopping bag they could just put down! Never mind letting go of the past, will the past let go of you? Is any of this talk useful given that time, and its 'contents', is more like a dimension of our identity than a line along which we travel? You might with as much sense talk about letting go of 'up' or 'sideways'.

Egan concludes his book by saying that: 'Both of these – knowing both yourself and others in caring, reflective, unvarnished ways – will help you develop the wisdom that enables you to move beyond the technology of helping, the helping alliance, and even the "real relationship" to the kind of authenticity celebrated by Rogers in *A Way of Being*' (Ibid.:362). So, for all of Egan's focus on technique, he still, ultimately succumbs to Rogerian naïvety and romanticism concerning the nature of authenticity, agency and knowledge.

The search for enlightenment

Egan, like so many other counselling writers, ends on a heroic, hypnotic hokum of hurrah words. They create good feelings but they are 'lite' on content. They often offer empty tautologies in that the alternatives are inconceivable. For example, will anyone opt for uncaring, unreflective but highly varnished ways of being? Of course not. These are (the flip side of the binary) 'boo' words. They create bad feelings even though they too may be devoid of content. When we approve of our 'varnishing', we call it 'cultivation', 'maturity' or 'polish'. This phenomenon of hypnotic linguistics is important because it must be remembered that one of the most effective ways of making clients feel good, and thereby 'show' that counselling 'works', is to shower clients with 'hurrah' words that do not tax them too much. (For other success strategies see Howard 1996.)

'The client's "capacity for self-determination" is held in the highest regard in the British Association for Counselling Code of Ethics and Practice. Yet the nature and individual extent of this capacity is nowhere examined' (Feltham 1995:122). The nature and extent of our capacity for agency, autonomy and personal responsibility is very rarely examined anywhere within counselling texts. It is assumed. It is insisted upon. It may thereby become yet another source of stress on people who are already overtaxed by circumstance and who, in fact, have very few resources indeed with which to cope. 'We need to free ourselves from the illusion of utter individual autonomy' (Morris 1997:180).

The reality often is that counselling 'works' best for the young, active, verbal, intelligent and successful who wish to find new ways to celebrate and utilize their already more than adequate resource base and network of options. Life is indeed basically good for the privileged of the earth for whom life is basically good. It can be basically appalling for those whose circumstances are much worse, and which are not likely to become much better in the foreseeable future.

Is this a reality that we can take? If it gets in the way of a (relatively) profitable career as a counsellor perhaps it is a reality we would prefer to avoid? Political activism might be a more worthwhile and significant option, but it might not pay so well and, within a consensus of global corporatism ('there is no alternative') it may be a dispiriting career choice. Such is our real optimism about the future. Tend your own garden, your own career, your own (imagined) personal interior, because public space is in decline, is squalid, is unprofitable and is dangerous. And in the longer run? Let's not think about it. Let us instead proceed to some enticing 'psychic interior' or another as set out by counselling gurus. Rogers (1970, 1973:127) provides the classic account, though others offer variations:

> The Process of the Encounter Group
> Fifth Stage. Many feelings are freely expressed in the moment of their occurrence and are thus experienced in the immediate present. These feelings are owned or accepted. Feelings previously denied now tend to bubble through into awareness, though there is fear of this occurrence.
> There is a desire to be the self-related feelings, 'the real me', and a questioning of the validity of many personal constructs.

Here is Rogers describing the 'fifth' stage of personal development. (Don't you too want to get to 'stage 5'?) Feelings are 'here and now'. But what about those feelings which are inappropriate, invasive or indulgent? Feelings are accepted. But what if they are unacceptable? There is a desire to 'be' the self-related feelings. But what if it is inadvisable to identify oneself with particular feelings?

Feelings 'bubble through'. But is this metaphor appropriate? Are we a kind of soup through which feelings bubble to the surface? Is it not more true to say that feelings are themselves a *consequence* of our understanding and interpretation of our situation? Feelings are not foundational, fundamental nor any more real or permanent than any other component of our actions, circumstances and experiences. Feelings do not exist in an autonomous unconscious mental world. Feelings should not, and cannot always be 'let go of' or 'released' like so much excess steam from a boiler.

Feelings may be an infantile, inappropriate and incorrect response to misperceptions and misconstructions of people and events. When expressed and indulged, feelings may feed off themselves and strengthen rather than being 'let go'. This entire Rogerian fifth stage metaphor is not an approach to 'deeper reality'. It is a very particular form of discourse and philosophy of life that arguably has done far more harm than good. Likewise the process of 'getting in touch with' the 'inner child' when, as I have argued elsewhere, we might do better with the metaphor of an 'inner adult' or 'inner warrior'.

> If we can easily sympathise with a character, the invitation to do so has relatively little moral value; the experience can all too easily deteriorate into a self-congratulatory wallowing in our own compassionate tendencies. (Nussbaum 1997:98)

Note also, that Rogers provides a very directive discourse for all his rhetoric of being 'non-directive'. There are stages you go through on the programme and, if you reject the narrative, in whole or in part, the system and its practitioners do not know what to do with you.

> R. Kegan (*In Over Our Heads: The Mental Demands of Modern Life*. Harvard UP, 1994) and others have challenged the very idea of non-directiveness as an impossibility. A major problem with the person-centred approach, then, at least in its purist form, is that it is arguably not *person*-centred at all, but centred on so-called 'person-centred' dogma. (Feltham 1995:88)

Closed systems like this tend to be incapable of engaging with any other narrative that is not itself a part of the system. And so it is with most other therapy narratives. This is where philosophers score. They are trained (educated) to dance within and outside particular conceptual boxes, to analyse, explore, compare and contrast particular narratives on offer. This is real freedom, real authenticity and real agency – insofar as we really have any of these available to us.

> The Sixth Stage
>
> Another characteristic of this stage of process is the physiological loosening which accompanies it. Moistness in the eyes, tears, sighs, muscular relaxation, are frequently evident. Often there are other physiological concomitants. (Ibid.:147)
>
> The Seventh Stage

> the situation is experienced and interpreted in its newness, not as the past. (Ibid.:152)

Is it actually possible, or desirable, to perceive and experience anything without being informed by one's past? The physiological, psychological and cultural evidence suggests not. But what is certain is that clients learn the script on offer from the institution they have signed up with, and before long they are 'going through' the 'stages' as outlined in the manual. For example:

> Art: No, I'm so darn used to living with the shell, it doesn't even bother me. I don't even know the real me. (Rogers 1973:32)
>
> Art: (Crying): I take the shell, and the real me, and put it in my pocket where it's safe. I guess that's really the way I do it – I go into my shell and turn off the real world. And here – that's what I want to do here in this group, y'know – come out of my shell and actually throw it away. (Ibid.:32)

Well here is the 'real' Art (crying)? Or is this the Artwork of the author and the group that is normalised around the author's text? Does Art 'really' put his 'shell' in his pocket? Or behind the fridge, or does he get it photographed and framed? Let's get real about this!

> I am increasingly at peace with myself and my world, and more sure every day that this is no fluke. It's real: I am in a very dynamic process of becoming. I'm not on top of the world yet (maybe, as Joe suggests, I'm somewhere around five in the process scale), but now I know I will be. The cavern is filling with experiencing, and feeling – and I'm in there – ME – A PERSON. (Rogers 1980:209)

The CAPITAL LETTERS announce the enlightenment. Is the peace to be described according to the Rogerian script? Or is it more to do with the way social groups form, storm, norm, perform and reward players who convince themselves and others that they have achieved group goals?

Should we be positively moved by this announcement that 'I'm in there – ME – A PERSON.'? Or should we wretch? Or weep? Or despair? Or shrug with indifference? Is this a statement of (finally achieved) insight into individuality, authenticity and reality? Or is it drivel, psychobabble, simplistic nonsense? Might it just be a wet goo of hurrah words, producing good feelings but devoid of real content? After all the claims of personal enlightenment derived from Rogers, and so many other carnival and alternative gurus from the 1960s and on, do we now live in a better, wiser, more real, more responsible and authentic world?

Rogers (1980) tells us about the qualities of the person of tomorrow. They will be open. They will desire authenticity. They will reject the hypocrisy, deceit, and double talk of our culture. Hurrah! Of course, I am not aware of anyone who proposes that they wish to become closed, inauthentic, hypocritical, deceitful double-talkers. Why? Because these are hurrah and boo words. The moral disapproval is built into their very meaning. When we approve of hypocrisy we call it 'flexibility'. Deceit becomes 'tact', inauthenticity becomes a 'brave face', closed and intolerant becomes 'determined', and so on. *Our ethical position is often implicit within the very meanings of the words we have chosen to use. What we see as 'real' is both cause and effect of what we see as 'right'.*

It is true that we can fly from our feelings. So some might need to 'get in touch with' them. But it is equally true that we can take flight *into* our feelings. And when we do we might be wise to detach, dissociate, take another perspective, think, feel or do something else more authentic and more constructive. So the truth? Truth gets around. It's on the move all the time and shimmers with different qualities from different angles. What is truly helpful in one moment to one person might be no longer true and no longer helpful – moments later!

> we feel as though we should be constantly restructuring our selves, examining and justifying our relationships in a search of intimacy and commitment. What I want to argue is that these are illusory tasks and goals set by late modernity, carrying on the myth of self-control and of the powerful self that can control itself. (Craib 1994:117)

The peace, love, joy and autonomy agenda of the 1960s and 1970s human potential movement may, in recent years, have shrunk back into a more survivalist mentality. Has counselling changed accordingly? 'From the perspective of today's therapeutic ethos, therapy is much more an instrument of survival than a means through which enlightenment can be gained. Individuals are not so much cured as placed in a state of recovery' (Furedi 2004:204).

Rogers, and most others within the counselling movement, fail to see the limitations of autonomy and the complications of authenticity. Rogers also rather naïvely tends to equate being authentic with being intimate. I might authentically (and correctly) decide that it is unwise, unsafe or inappropriate to be very intimate with you. I might best stay armed and armoured against you. Yet there is no cause to be cynical about authenticity and autonomy. The words exist and there are surely important and significant meanings concerning how they can and should be used.

Here, for example, is Barnett's view of understanding, and its connection with autonomy, authenticity and identity:

> Understanding . . . is active, is an engagement, is a form of agency, and is a form of self expression. It is an expression of individuality; and it strikes against the conventionalism of competence, insofar as competency is a fulfilment of standards determined in advance. (Barnett 1994:110)
>
> Since understanding is personal and has to be owned by the individual, we cannot predict in advance any particular understanding a student may frame for herself. It

> will be distinctive, come what may. No other understanding on earth will be identical. (Ibid.:110)
>
> Understanding does not kow-tow; it does not defer; it does not accept willy-nilly others' agendas. True understanding is tough and resilient. What counts is the better argument. True understanding is also not afraid to adopt an attitude of humility. (Ibid.:111)
>
> It is not that the understandings lie behind the action. It is the much stronger claim that the actor's understandings are constitutive of the action. (Ibid.:76)

So, for Barnett, if you are to understand this text, Rogers' text, or any other, you will not merely repeat back someone else's script and dutifully follow through all the 'stages' of development. You will not blindly accept all the outcomes and procedures anticipated for you. You will pay careful attention to other scripts. But if you are to show you understand them you will write, identify with, commit to, and live through your *own* script.

The very process of understanding is an achievement of authenticity, at least in that small area of life that has been understood. Without out own understanding, we inevitably lose our autonomy because we become passive instruments and echoes of other people's agendas, narratives, forms, questionnaires, protocols, timetables and understandings.

As regards authenticity among counsellors, here is a little gem: 'Counsellors seemed to be more effective than their clients in hiding things that they did not want/feel comfortable to discuss, by adopting facilitative non-verbal behaviours, such as relaxed, open posture, head nodding, etc.' (*Counselling and Psychotherapy Research*, vol. 2, no.1). Is this because counsellors have not reached the 'fifth stage'? Because they are hypocrites? Because they are not so naïve as to actually believe in the script they sell to others? Because they simply fail to be as self-aware as they imagine they are? 'When you know the truth about anything, the real inner truth – it is very hard to write the surface fluff which sells it' (Helen Woodward, influential copywriter in the 1920s, quoted in Klein 2001:345).

Assuming that we wish to do so, how are we to avoid simulation, appearance, manipulation of others, and ourselves, and manoeuvres with the plausible? Adorno, Horkheimer and others of the Frankfurt School of critical theory (above all Jürgen Habermas) argue for the need for dialogue. This is the process whereby we seek to understand ourselves and others according to the principles set out by, for example, Barnett above.

When we engage in dialogue, we do not observe each other as disembodied flies on the wall. We do not treat each other as objects of manipulation. We do not treat others or ourselves as bodies to be managed from which we dissociate ourselves. In our attempts to understand, we seek to cooperate and achieve some consensus, both to make sense of ourselves and of others. We appreciate that to operate as individuals, to express ourselves as individuals, we must acknowledge that we are social beings. The social is the context from which we emerge and which sustains us. It is not a separate entity, which we discover and with which we make a contractual relation. We cannot make a contract with society because we are already contracted, constructed, constrained, composed, provided for and promoted by this societal context.

Realising this, we may realise that ethical behaviour is central to our identity, as we shall see later in more detail. Ethical discourse is not a negotiable 'package', which can be added to, or subtracted from, society at will. To the extent that there is ethical behaviour there is a society. To the extent that there is not there is only chaos. This does not mean that ethical decisions are always easy to make.

Adorno and Horkheimer were pessimists as regards the possibility of dialogue providing a means by which an alienating, bureaucratic, mechanistic society could be humanised: 'Modernity, far from redeeming the promises and hopes of the Enlightenment, had resulted in a stultification of mankind and an administered society, characterised by simulation and candy-floss entertainment' (Adorno & Horkheimer 1999:back cover). Habermas, though, as we shall see, was more positive.

Questions for Counsellors

1. Compare and contrast Christian, Buddhist, person-centred, behaviourist and psychoanalytic concepts of self. What are the strengths and weaknesses of each?
2. Do you agree with Derrida that we cannot think about the self outside a particular concept of the self? If so, in what way might this be a problem?
3. Can we 'return to nature' as a way of 'connecting more with ourselves'? What might this mean and what insights and illusions might this quest engender?
4. How far do you agree with Kellner that postmodern identities are accelerated, extended, unstable, disintegrated, fragile, superficial and illusory?
5. Do postmodernists destroy their case in the very process of making it? If so, how? If not, why not?
6. Is Fromm correct that as soon as we have expressed something in a word, an alienation takes place, and the fullest experience has already been substituted for by the word?
7. Do you think we should abandon realities that may lie beyond language and instead focus on the fundamental binary distinctions made within language?
8. How far do agree with Baudrillard that all idea of what is 'real' has come to an end? If this is the case, *should* it be the case?
9. How do you distinguish between a psychotic individual who has lost touch with reality and a French poststructuralist philosopher who denies that there is any foundational reality to be contacted?
10. Compare Derrida's view, that there is no unified subject behind a text, with Thoreau that the best of himself may be found in his text? Are Thoreau's and Derrida's observation consistent or inconsistent with each other?
11. What, if any, are the connections between client *satisfaction* and counselling *efficacy*?
12. Do you agree with T. S. Eliot that human kind cannot bear very much reality? If so, how do you, and should you, protect your clients? Be specific with specific illustrations.
13. Fancher argues that there is nothing irrational about concluding from a long history of failures that this is one's lot in life? If so, how do you assist your clients? Be specific with specific illustrations.

14. Assess Slavin's assertion that the capacity for denial and self-deception provides powerful adaptive advantages. If so, how do you assist your clients in this respect? Be specific with specific illustrations.
15. Do you agree with Fancher's characterisation of cognitive therapy as 'middlebrow'? What do you think he means by this?
16. Is the conscious mind, as Bandler and Grinder argue, a limited and undependable part of a person? If so how does this affect your practice? Be specific with specific illustrations.
17. Is Stevens correct to say that we are all hypnotised, seeing and hearing perhaps 10 per cent of what goes on? If so, is this a problem or a useful adaptation? Can and should we try to do anything about it?
18. If the relevant brain events *precede* consciousness, as Ramachandran and other neurologists have shown, where does this leave the notion of conscious will power?
19. How can we talk intelligently about mental events and processes if there is no mental 'world' at all?
20. When we say that a person has 'made up her mind', what, in fact are we saying? That she has run a particular stream of conscious thoughts through her head? Or, if not, what? Describe and distinguish the different uses and meanings of 'mind' in the following:

My *mind* is made up	I've a good *mind* to . . .	I *mind* very much indeed
I have made up my *mind*	That *reminds* me	This brings to *mind*
I'm *mind*ed to consider	*Mind* out	*Mind* your ps and qs
I'm in two *minds* about	I've lost my *mind*	What's on your *mind*?
I can read your *mind*	A *mind*less fool	Use your *mind*
It's on my *mind*	I have it in *mind*	*Mind*ful of this
Bear that in *mind*	Never *mind*	Do you *mind*?
That is *mind*-bending	Love with all your *mind*	I bend my *mind* to this
Can you call to *mind*?	Absent *minded*	He operated cleverly on my *mind*
It just sprang to *mind*	My *mind* ranged wide	In my *mind*'s eye
Bad influence on his *mind*	*Mind* over matter	An unsettled *mind*
Turn your *mind* to this	Focus your *mind*	My *mind* was shaken
Make up your *mind*	My *mind* is settled	Set your *mind* on this
Speak your *mind*	Disease of the *mind*	We are all of one *mind* on this
Slipped out of my *mind*	A troubled *mind*	Call to *mind*
You're out of your *mind*!	Blotted out of *mind*	My *mind* is set on this
I've changed my *mind*	Blissful state of *mind*	A perfectly balanced *mind*
It has crossed my *mind*	I've a good *mind* to . . .	My *mind* is busy on this
His *mind* is closed	Narrow *mind*ed	Broad *mind*ed
Relieved my *mind*	A noble *mind*	Empty the *mind*
Given a piece of your *mind*	Hold in *mind*	My *mind* is in a state
Apply your *mind*	Pure in *mind*	Impression on my *mind*
Right frame of *mind*	Sharp/dull *mind*	My *mind* was drawn by . . .
Time out of *mind*	Force of *mind*	He's touched your perfect body with his *mind*.

Do any of these accounts of mind require belief in a non-physical ghostly substance?

21. If we cannot pin down truths and meanings does this mean that we are doomed to chaos and the triumph of opinion over truth? If not, why not?
22. How can you avoid 'clicking into therapy-speak', as Sands describes it?
23. Do you agree with Bandler and Grinder that most of the hypnotic realities that people have built for themselves and live in most of the time – what they call the waking state – are not profoundly useful? If so, what is to be done? Are Bandler and Grinder's realities, or your own, any more useful to the client? How do you decide?
24. Do client *actions* count for far more than their *words*? If so, how do you monitor their actions?

25. Do you agree with Garfinkel that empathy has more to do with shared social interactions and tacit assumptions than with unconscious personal contents? If so, how far can you enter the 'life worlds' (Habermas) of your clients if you never actually see them operating in their daily world?
26. How far do you see (for example) Egan's and Rogers' case study illustrations as highly contestable? What are the implications?
27. Does it surprise you that counsellors seemed to be more effective that their clients in hiding things that they did not want/feel comfortable to discuss, by adopting facilitative non-verbal behaviours, such as relaxed, open posture, head nodding? Should clients learn to match counsellors in these skills?
28. Do you agree with Adorno and Horkheimer that modernity, far from redeeming the promises and hopes of the Enlightenment, has resulted in a stultification of mankind and an administered society, characterised by simulation and candy-floss entertainment? How often do counsellors provide a challenge to, rather than a component of, the entertainment?

CHAPTER 5

Honoured and Esteemed? Identity and Happiness

> The profession of psychology has propounded a simplistic philosophy of life. This philosophy maintains that the purpose of life is to maximise one's mental health, which is dependent wholly on self-esteem. (Dawes 1996:33)

We hear a great deal nowadays about 'self-esteem'. In the process of 'finding ourselves', or 'getting more in touch with ourselves', it is argued that people want to learn how to feel good about themselves. We want to feel at home and at peace with ourselves. Identity and self-esteem, then, are closely related since it is thought that a lack of self-esteem is an obstacle on the road to finding our identity. We find ourselves when we feel good about ourselves and when we believe that we are good for something and that the something is good.

Freud and his followers took the view that we were, to a great degree, ignorant about aspects of our identity. This, he argued, was because, in many ways, we could not face up to ourselves. We therefore operated with all kinds of defence mechanisms. We utilised these in order to avoid looking at unpalatable truths around and inside us. The role of the therapist, therefore, was to assist the client in coming to terms with themselves as they 'really' were. For Freud, this might mean no more than an advance from hysterical misery to common unhappiness. If this was not a happy state it was, at least, a less unhappy one and Freudian therapy was, therefore, seen to be a positive move.

Subsequent to Freud, therapists have tended to promise rather more; from acceptance, to resourcefulness, to satisfaction, to 'self-actualisation'. At the top end of the spectrum of promises we are offered the prospect of oneness, nurturing relationships, spontaneity, joy and bliss.

How deserved is your self-esteem?

> A wonderful person who does not happen to think particularly well of herself or himself (for whatever reason, such as a religiously based modesty or an absence of pride) is a failure. A conceited ass, in contrast, has good mental health. (Dawes 1996:34)

It might well be easier to face up to ourselves if we could feel good about the self we were facing up to. But how good about ourselves is it reasonable and realistic for us to feel? 'Numerous observers have claimed that American children are systematically flattered, fed on a diet of empty phrases and therefore become demotivated' (Furedi 2004:157). Counsellors tend to offer an agenda wherein we will *raise* our self-esteem. We will feel better about ourselves. But what if we have good reason to feel bad about ourselves? Should the self-esteem of a Mafia criminal be raised, or lowered? Are we to argue that people do not really feel good about themselves when they commit bad actions? Would the Mafia criminal feel better if he behaved better? If so, where is the evidence? Many of those who commit crimes appear to think very highly of themselves and do *not* suffer from low self-esteem.

> Other researchers have shown that deviance may actually increase the self-esteem of low-income boys. In a study of tenth grade adolescent boys, Morris Rosenberg and his colleagues found that the more juvenile delinquency the boys reported engaging in at one point in time, the more their self esteem had *increased* two years later. (Swann 1996:143)

Does pride always lead to a fall? Must hubris lead to nemesis? Or do many bad, cruel, selfish and complacent individuals go to their graves with their complacency, self-satisfaction and happiness intact? Are we ourselves part of this feel-good no-good community? What does it mean to talk about facing up to ourselves? Which part of me is looking at which other part? Or am I creating all the parts? Or am I (who?) buying in to the parts created by someone else?

Counsellors tend to concentrate on the importance of building self-esteem and of supporting clients. But self-esteem may be unrealistically high, may promote over confidence, may lead to serious errors of judgement, and may result in anti-social and immoral behaviour. Counsellors surely have a role in *challenging* clients as well as supporting them.

> In *The Wealth of Nations* Smith wrote of the 'overweaning conceit which the greater part of men have of their abilities . . . the chance of gain is by every man more or less overvalued, and the chance of loss is by most men undervalued.' Frank and Cook report in this regard a recent study of a million American high school seniors in which 70 per cent thought they had above average leadership ability and 2 per cent thought they were below average. (Sennett 1998:90)

So much of the vocabulary to describe personal development, happiness and self-esteem is couched in overly individualistic terms. Yet what of all the social and ethical aspects of personal development? If we are to develop and find fulfilment we do so in a social context since we are inherently social creatures. What, then, of the role of concepts like honour, duty, dignity, discipline, citizenship, civility, compassion, empathy, decency, family and kinship ties and commitments, grace, restraint, justice, moral worthiness, loyalty and solidarity in developing happy, mature persons with appropriate levels of self-esteem? These traditional virtues do not appear to show up very much on counselling agendas. *In an overly individualistic, self-regarding and atomised society, counselling has become a symptom of societal disruption more than a solution to it.* Consequently concepts of 'self-esteem' have been misunderstood and overrated both in contemporary society and within counselling.

Within the consumerist philosophy that now permeates so much of counselling, feeling good about ourselves tends to involve making 'more' of ourselves, being more of a someone. But sometimes less is more. Traditionally, a mature and wise person, a well-developed person, has also needed to know about the role of resignation, of patience, of humility, fidelity, moral worth, refinement, and character formation in developing self-esteem. The term 'personal development' is relatively new. But serious attention concerning the nature of character building, maturity, wisdom, love and commitment goes back thousands of years. For example: 'Is there anything more precious to you than yourself? You will agree that there is nothing. Then if you possess yourself, you will have something you will never want to give up and something which Fortune cannot take from you' (Boethius (480–524) 1962:29).

It is not at all obvious that our current psycho-technologies concerning human development are a great improvement on earlier insights. Certainly it is depressing that so much counselling focuses on personal 'skills', deployed in an imagined social vacuum, rather than on social, cultural, political and historical contexts and values.

As Bertrand Russell observed, in a social world, self-realisation cannot be the supreme principle of ethics. Therapists, in replacing the priestly role, might need to adopt also the traditional priestly understanding of the importance of *shame*. If we are to heal ourselves of wrongdoing, forgive ourselves and be forgiven by others then we may need to feel suitably bad about ourselves before we can feel, and have any right to feel, good about ourselves.

Both challenge to, and support of, the client are necessary to build genuine self-esteem. We cannot feel good about ourselves if counsellors 'prize' and celebrate parts of ourselves that are not praiseworthy and do not deserve to be celebrated. However, a certain amount of self-deception may sometimes be necessary to survive at all. The truth may sometimes set us free, but sometimes it might be just too painful to bear. 'Usually, making a group work means suppressing at least some of the interests of its members, and that may be easier if individuals can hoodwink themselves' (*New Scientist* 'Isn't self-deception marvellous? Where would we be without it?' 22 December 2001). Perhaps to be happy and to feel good about ourselves we need to have some capacity to hoodwink ourselves? 'Self-deception is also useful in self-promotion, according to Trivers. If you can convince yourself that you're better than your opponents, you have a better chance of carrying off the bluff' (Ibid.).

Presumably it is much easier to retain reality contact about one's self and one's circumstances when both really are rather good. Otherwise the temptation to retreat into cyber realities, or celebrity watching, or drug induced alternatives is all the greater. Self-esteem can rise when real social opportunities are increased. A crucial component of self-esteem is *social inclusion* and this is not something that it is in the hands of excluded individuals to change by their own efforts alone or with the help merely of counsellors.

We may suffer from low self-esteem both because of what we think we are, and from what we think we are *not*. Either way, we may need social resources, social support and real social *opportunity* if matters are to be significantly changed. We may gain courage by being encouraged, we may become resourceful by gaining resources, and we may gain self-esteem by receiving social esteem. But the esteem is of most value when it is real and when it is deserved. It can only be deserved as a result of our deserving actions. Counselling focuses on the need for people to *feel good* about themselves, but how and why should they feel good unless they *do* some kind of good in, with and for, the social world around them? Actions count, and come first. Emotions follow. A virtuous circle can then be engendered.

But old habits are hard to break. People can most easily love, support and empathise who have themselves experienced love, social support and empathy from an early age. On the other hand, what if they have learned only that they have no reason to trust others, that they are not loved and that no support is available from others? With such a traumatic past, how much time and attention will they need before they can ever learn to love themselves, love others and trust the world around them? Sometimes the damage done seems to be so great that it is beyond repair.

Freud spoke of a tripartite self – id, ego and superego. And if you, likewise, accept these constructs and Freud's' narrative then you too will talk about struggles with your id, etc. According to Freud, these parts of the self took different views about what constitutes happiness and the good life. For the id, the most animal part of the self, goodness was pleasure. Happiness was the enjoyment of pleasures. If the id wrote books on ethics and lifestyles, it would extol hedonism, instinct, instant gratification, power, lust, primal urges, perhaps a certain amount of torture. Certainly there is evidence that the id gets its way at times. Certainly there is plenty of evidence of marketplaces in goods and services happily selling, and selling out, to the id, when the id carries the money. The customer is king, it seems, and if the customer also suffers from regal folly, childishness, selfishness and animal needs for gratification then markets simply adjust their product lines accordingly.

For the superego, happiness was to be found in virtue. Happiness and the good life consisted in doing good and being good. Ethics and lifestyle books written by the superego would consist in accounts of sacrifice, self-discipline, courage, restraint, sensitivity to others, duty, honour, humility perhaps. Arguably, the demands of the superego are precisely the expectations of the Christian church and those of most ethical teachers within most other spiritual and secular traditions.

These superego teachings predate Christianity. For example Aristotle argued that the good life consisted in being virtuous and that we could not feel genuinely happy if we did not honour obligations, see our place in the broader scheme of existence, recognise our duties to others etc. Also, and interestingly, that we could not feel happy if we had unrealistically large expectations about our rights to, and possibilities of, happiness. Come to terms with misery, as the Stoics argued. It is a part of existence and you will be most happy if you accept this. If you do not then you will be forever demanding more of the world than it can provide. You will therefore add, needlessly, to your misery by feeling perpetually disappointed, disillusioned, despairing. 'For Szasz[1] most if not all psychotherapy is a denial of the tragic nature of life, refusing to accept the possibility that life is full of adverse circumstances which can only be met with courage and realism' (Feltham 1995:132).

For Freud, there was a third character in this ethical play, the 'ego'. This was the part, Freud argued, that we generally experienced as 'the self'. ('Ego' does, after all, mean, 'I am' in Latin). Ego had to come to terms with the demands of the superego, of the id and, also, of the world and other people around us. Ego was a kind of compromise liberal government. It took the view that the superego was too much of a perfectionist and that its standards of virtue were unachievable in the 'real' world. It also recognised that the urges of the id, if unrestrained, or, conversely, if entirely ignored and allowed no release, would lead to chaos. So the ego sought compromise. It was a pragmatist. It was a reflection, as you might expect, of the liberal ethical principles that Freud himself believed in. Only by attending to, and acting on, the realistic recommendations of the ego could we live a life that, if not happy, was as near to happiness as we could find. This would require that we behaved in a virtuous fashion – within reason – up to a point. But happiness also required acceptance that we were animals in many ways, with animal instincts, that could not always be ignored or controlled.

Within a Dionysian revelry, the 'I am' of the ego might disappear and be replaced by the 'I am' of the id. Mr Hyde replaced Robert Louis Stevenson's Dr Jekyll (1886). We would identify with the animal within us. We became the animal. And, from the superego's point of view, darkness reigned upon the earth.

So who were we 'really'? The ego, the id, the superego? Or none or all of these or much more besides? The Church argued that we were miserable offenders, animals who should confess our faults and hope, with divine grace, to become more super, more angelic. The church, within Freud's terminology, saw us as ids who needed to try to become superegos but who would, more often than not, fail in the attempt and be suitably damned into eternal misery in the life hereafter.

Happiness and goodness

Freud argued for ethical realism led by the ego rather than the ethical perfectionism insisted upon by the superego. But who decides what is ethically realistic? Which part of the self is the 'real' most authentic self? To whom should 'we' listen? Who is the 'we' that is talking? Within our own internal conflict, who is making whom happy or unhappy, and with what justification? It seems evident that identity, happiness and ethics are all inextricably intertwined. If we are to face ourselves perhaps it helps if we feel good (enough) about ourselves? If we are to *feel* good perhaps it helps to *live* a good life? This presumably requires knowing what is good, for us, and for others? If so, then ethics should be given *far* more attention within counselling than is currently the case. But we still have to ask, who is facing whom? The 'I' appears capable of receding in an infinite regress as I keep an eye on I keeping an eye on I – until my imagination or interest is exhausted!

In any event, our notions of what is good are central in determining both wellbeing and identity. Ethics, therefore, should not merely determine *how* counsellors should conduct themselves. Ethics, our notions of the good, evidently construct the rationale, nature and direction of counselling, whether we realise it or not. Therefore, ethical concerns range far beyond professional codes of practice. Ethical assumptions structure the foundations, the methods, the direction and the success criteria in counselling. Counselling is quintessentially an exploration of aspects of who you are, what would make you happy, and what it would be right for you to do; and all three questions interconnect.

Ethical assumptions within various schools of counselling do, of course, vary. The differences need more meta-ethical attention than they generally get. For example, a lot of counselling appears to have moved on from an ethic of humanist liberation to one of impersonal consumer servicing and management. None of this underlying ethical change shows up in professional codes of practice, and moral philosophy is given little attention in the training of counsellors.

A great deal of misery can arise if, to use Freudian terminology, the superego endlessly, cruelly and unreasonably punishes us for not being good enough. If the superego's supervision is cruel rather than kind, we can become a kind of underdog (to use Gestalt terminology) under the lash of the 'top dog' superego. But where does this superego come from? What if its ethical injunctions are too good to be achievable or not even good at all? Who assesses the assessments and judgements made by the superego?

Freud argued that we take within us the teachings of key people in our lives – parents and others. This is fine if what they teach is loving, caring, forgiving, accepting, generous, tolerant, virtuous, and realistic. But what if these key persons do not love themselves and do not love us? The New Testament teaches that love is a key concept. Perhaps that is right? But love sits awkwardly within counselling codes of practice and efforts to be professional. Also, the New Testament Christian teaching that we should love our neighbour as we love ourselves is of little value if we do not love ourselves at all.

The Old Testament teachings were full of punishment, self-loathing, intolerance, and cruelty. In our wish to be respectful of Christianity, we nowadays tend to draw ourselves away from just seeing how absurd, offensive and destructive of human beings so much of Christian teaching really is. The notions of The Good Life as put forward by many Christian fundamentalists are extremely alarming and anything but good. de Tocqueville's early nineteenth-century concerns about religious insanity in the USA[2] are as relevant now as they were two hundred years ago. Fundamentalism within Islam may be a source of unease. But we need to pay more attention to, and be seriously alarmed about, fundamentalism within Christianity. The USA, as a hyper-power, is continuously vulnerable to fundamentalism, fascism and imperialism which will not, and does not, create a good life for the many that deserve better. The dogmatism, aggression and intolerance that characterises fundamentalist teaching shows up in institutions, in laws, in foreign policies, and, (when using Freud's terminology) within the punishing superegos of individuals.

For example Laura Schlessinger is a US radio personality who dispenses advice to people who call in to her radio show. The following is an open letter to Dr Laura penned by a US resident, which has been widely posted on the Internet. It is tongue in cheek, of course, but the underlying concerns are serious.

Dear Dr. Laura:

Thank you for doing so much to educate people regarding God's Law. I have learned a great deal from your show, and I try to share that knowledge with as many people as I can. When someone tries to defend the homosexual lifestyle, for example, I simply remind them that Leviticus 18:22 clearly states it to be an abomination. End of debate.

I do need some advice from you, however, regarding some of the specific laws and how to follow them:

a) When I burn a bull on the altar as a sacrifice, I know it creates a pleasing odor for the Lord (Lev. 1:9). The problem is my neighbors. They claim the odor is not pleasing to them. Should I smite them?

b) I would like to sell my daughter into slavery, as sanctioned in Exodus 21:7. In this day and age, what do you think would be a fair price for her?

c) I know that I am allowed no contact with a woman while she is in her period of menstrual uncleanliness (Lev. 15:19–24). The problem is, how do I tell? I have tried asking, but most women take offense.

d) Lev. 25:44 states that I may indeed possess slaves, both male and female, provided they are purchased from neighboring nations. A friend of mine claims that this applies to Mexicans but not Canadians. Can you clarify? Why can't I own Canadians?

e) I have a neighbor who insists on working on the Sabbath. Exodus 35:2 clearly states he should be put to death. Am I morally obligated to kill him myself?

f) A friend of mine feels that even though eating shellfish is an abomination (Lev. 11:10), it is a lesser abomination than homosexuality. I don't agree. Can you settle this?

g) Lev. 21:20 states that I may not approach the altar of God if I have a defect in my sight. I have to admit that I wear reading glasses. Does my vision have to be 20/20, or is there some wiggle room here?

h) Most of my male friends get their hair trimmed, including the hair around their temples, even though this is expressly forbidden by Lev. 19:27. How should they die?

i) I know from Lev. 11:6–8 that touching the skin of a dead pig makes me unclean, but may I still playfootball if I wear gloves?

j) My uncle has a farm. He violates Lev. 19:19 by planting two different crops in the same field, as does his wife by wearing garments made of two different kinds of thread (cotton/polyester blend). He also tends to curse and blaspheme a lot. Is it really necessary that we go to all the trouble of getting the whole town together to stone them? (Lev. 24:10–16) Couldn't we just burn them to death at a private family affair like we do with people who sleep with their in-laws? (Lev. 20:14)

I know you have studied these things extensively, so I am confident you can help. Thank you again for reminding us that God's word is eternal and unchanging.

Your devoted disciple and adoring fan.

People do not necessarily practise what they preach, as all the scandals about child abuse within churches has made clear. But, in any case, quite often what they preach is, or ought to be regarded as, morally offensive. In a secular society we still give a great deal of weight to the ethical teachings of Christian leaders. This is partly due to a legacy of deference to an old tradition and partly because nobody else appears to carry much ethical authority. Who, in a secular consumerist society teaches what is right, what is good, what is a good life, what 'wealth' really consists in, and what will therefore help us come home to, and be at peace with, ourselves?

Yet when ethical teaching is drawn from the Old Testament it is often absurd, offensive, deeply dangerous. At the time of writing, there is a great moral panic about Islamic fundamentalism. We are all, supposedly, engaged in a 'war on terror'. Fundamentalism is indeed a problem but Christian fundamentalism is, arguably, still more of a threat than the Islamic version. Why? Because the Christians have access to the use of terror via much more lethal weaponry – aircraft carriers, missiles, nuclear, biological, economic – everything.

Anglicanism in the UK, at the time of writing, is not much of a vehicle for Old Testament fire and brimstone. Also, it is less and less the Tory party at prayer. Instead it tends to teach a more liberal social democratic ethic than that embraced by the current Labour government. It argues for public space, public investment, and public responsibilities as a means towards the good and happy life. It challenges shallow secular consumerism on the grounds that this panders to the illusions, superficialities and urges for instant gratification of the not-sufficiently-inner-child within us all. I am sympathetic.

But when we look for the source of this priestly authority where do we find it? Should we look in the Old or New Testament? Actually, we should look at critical theory from the Frankfurt school. The current Archbishop of Canterbury, Rowan Williams, appears to be drawing from Habermas, Adorno and Horkheimer far more than from Jesus. I approve of his choice of counsel. But I think Anglicans ought to be more honest about the secular authorities they are using when engaging in supposedly Christian teaching. And we ought to ask why Christian teachers are given so much moral authority when the morals from which they are drawing are not taken primarily from Christian sources at all!

Insofar as there has been progress about ethics in the past several centuries it has come from secular humanist, Enlightenment sources rather than from the Church. Indeed, despite important and honourable exceptions, the Church has tended to side with conservatives, reactionaries, authoritarian and dictatorial kings.

Happiness, consumerism and the good life

But, whatever the failings of the Church, the alternative of secular consumerism gives just as much cause for concern. It appears willing to honour, gratify, sell and sell out to, the id. It acquiesces in the belief that happiness and the good life can be found via Dionysian consumption. From a historical perspective, there is something relatively new in this idea that we ought to be, or could be, or deserve, or have a right to be, 'happy'. The ancients believed in the occasional celebratory feast but did not imagine that we could be happy all the time. *Arguably we are being made seriously miserable in the belief that we could or should be feeling good and happy more or less continuously.* 'escape the ravages of the pursuit of happiness' (Smail 1987:123).

So within societies and individuals there is a culture war concerning what constitutes the good and happy life. *The punishing fundamentalist authoritarian, with a perpetual frown on his face, does battle with the undisciplined, unprincipled, amoral and hedonistic consumer. Each polarises in response to the other and moves deeper into their own kind of indulgence.* Surely we can do better than this in our search for what will make us feel good and happy with ourselves? Where, then, does counselling fit into this debate?

Back in 1993 the British Association for Counselling proposed, in its code of ethics that: 'The overall aim of counselling is to provide an opportunity for the client to work towards living in a more satisfying and resourceful way.'

Almost by definition, of course, we prefer to *increase* our satisfaction and resourcefulness. Who could possibly argue in favour of becoming *less* satisfied and less resourceful? But how satisfied and resourceful can we realistically be? And, above all, what should we *do*, what should we *believe in*, what should we *aim for*, if we are to become more satisfied and resourceful? Should we join a fundamentalist church? Should we cheer ourselves up by buying something new (retail therapy)?

What would a counsellor suggest? What insight, ethical principles and skills empower them to suggest or assist at all? Would they suggest nothing? Would that not itself sometimes be immoral? How much happier should we realistically try to be? Would we not be happier if we focused less on happiness and more on the projects, actions and values that would help us to be happy – though only as a byproduct?

'Precisely the most cold-eyed appraisal of the facts has caused his depression. (In my own experience, this kind of situation is rampant in clinical situations)' (Fancher 1995:216). The depressed person comes to see the counsellor. He or she feels despair, misery, hopelessness, defeat, unhappiness, pessimism and pain. The counsellor responds. How? As we saw in chapter 3, the depressed person may have a more accurate perception of 'reality' than the more optimistic individual.

'The male fly has 24 per cent of its time available for its promenades and a full 20 per cent for grooming itself. That adds up to 44 per cent of leisure. After many centuries of struggle, Westerners have not done much better' (Zeldin 1998:352). This is a somewhat tongue in cheek view of humankind's progress towards fulfilment and happiness. But it is one way of raising the question of how far we have reason to be more or less happy with social progress. On the one hand we can ask 'what is the good life'? On the other, we also need to consider, 'are we moving closer towards, or further away from, this better life?' The answer is almost bound to be a mixed one. But the details do matter as clients turn up at counsellor practices and consider how far their search for a more satisfying and resourceful way of living is in their hands or beyond their powers to achieve.

> Richard Sennett of the London School of Economics argues that flexibility and short-termism in the workplace – the American graduate, for instance, can expect to move jobs up to a dozen times, unlike his dad, who held a post for life – are bound to have an impact on personal relationships. His fears are borne out in a survey conducted last year by the magazine *Management Today*. Half of those questioned said they were too exhausted to do anything but work and sleep; 76 per cent wanted more time with their families, while 43 per cent reported that they had adopted a strategy of ruthless self-interest, a loyalty to their own careers rather than to their employers. (Yvonne Roberts, *New Statesman*, 18 March 2002)

Counsellors must therefore develop at least an overview of the social as well as the personal dynamics that influence the wellbeing and unease of their clients.

Happiness and wealth creation – the pessimist's perspective

Do we have a greater wealth of resources to live a satisfying life or are resources being removed from us? In order to answer the question we need to clarify what comprises 'wealth'. From an economist's perspective we (in the West, some of us) are indeed becoming more materially wealth. But what are the costs that we are paying in order to receive these benefits? In what way are we becoming impoverished in the very progress of pursuing (our conceptions of) wealth?

'In the early part of the Industrial Revolution, a Scottish industrialist wrote of "the utmost distaste on the part of the men to any regular hours or regular habits", and incomprehension that "they could not go in and out as they pleased, and have what holidays they pleased' (Zeldin 1998:351). Zeldin observes that these poorer people had been rich enough to choose their hours, choose their holidays, as and when they pleased. So were they richer or poorer than the person who works 16 hours a day under an atmosphere of continuous pressure?

> The present division of a lifetime seems fixed forever only because it has been forgotten how recent retirement and the weekend are. The English inventors of the weekend (the word dates from the end of the nineteenth century and was imported into French in 1906) have forgotten also that the number of their holidays fell sharply in the sixteenth and seventeenth centuries, that their Bank Holiday Mondays are token survivals of the reign of Saint Monday. (Zeldin 1998:355)

Zeldin tells us that we have fewer holidays than many of our ancestors and that we work harder even than the humble fly. This is not exactly a cheering thought, but there are presumably compensations? We will come to these. Counsellors, when looking at client satisfaction and resourcefulness, focus on the individual narrative, but more attention needs to be paid to the social context which, more than anything we can do, nurtures and/or denatures and restricts us more or less profoundly.

Happy families may support happy infants growing into happy adults. But families themselves need nurturing and support. Is the social context in which families seek to survive becoming more or less supportive? There appears, for example, to be less secure employment to economic providers than there used to be. What is this doing to the security, resourcefulness and wellbeing of individuals?

> the chances of a major disruption in your life – marriage breaking down, losing your job – are nowadays far higher. Our lives are much less predictable than those of our parents or grandparents, and we can't fall back on the kinds of social structures that may have supported them; extended families, geographical communities and faith communities are all less conspicuous now. We carry more of the burdens of life alone and all that saves us from breakdown is our own personal resilience.

> According to the Mental Health Foundation's 'Who's Life Is It Anyway?' report, work's corrosive effect on our lives is widespread. Their survey uncovered 'a picture of loss on a large scale': relationship breakdown, loss of friendship, poor relationships with children, not being able to spend time with a terminally ill friend or relative – even cases where long hours at work precluded people from having a child or meeting a partner in the first place.
>
> Such is the extent of this problem that one has to ask: why on earth are we all putting up with it? (*Guardian*, 'whose life is it anyway?' 30 April 2003)

Governments and companies compete with each other to argue that individuals must stand more on their own two feet and must expect less support from employers or from the State. 'Transnational corporations, which control more than 33 per cent of the world's productive assets, account for only five per cent of the world's direct employment' (Klein 2001:261). They subcontract to employers whose terms and conditions of employment are inferior to those of the transnational corporation. This improves 'flexibility', increases profits, and drives down the costs (of large corporations). But what costs does it place on those families and individuals who are trying to look after their own resourcefulness and well-being? These costs, passed on by corporations to individuals and families, may be very substantial indeed but accountants are not paid to measure them.

'60 per cent of (U.S.) income gains over the period from 1980 to 1990 went to the top 1 per cent of the population. The UK shows similar trends in less extreme form' (Giddens 1998:105). What does this do to people's overall morale, resourcefulness and wellbeing? What happens to morale when one begins to believe that the society in which one lives is becoming less just and fair and is providing fewer real opportunities for many of its citizens?

> Few of us can easily surrender our belief that society must somehow make sense. The thought that the State has lost its mind and is punishing so many innocent people is intolerable. And so the evidence has to be internally denied. (Arthur Miller in Pilger 2003:97)

> Erich Fromm (*The Sane Society*, 1963, Routledge) posited the view that what we have come to regard as normality may in fact be a kind of pathology, and argued that greed and ambition, which we easily exalt as capitalist virtues, are forms of insanity. (Feltham 1995:145)

Counsellors focus on individual wellbeing, but this is surely inseparable from the wellbeing of society as a whole, and the direction in which it is travelling. The health, wealth and wellbeing of an entire society have enormous impact on the wellbeing of individuals. This influence is far greater than the influence any one individual can have on society. If there is to be further moral and material progress in human existence then we can be sure that what we consider to be 'normal' at present will be seen as a moral outrage and absurdity by our great grandchildren. Just as we look back in horror at slavery, child chimney sweeps and other injustices, so they will have difficulty in understanding how we tolerated such poverty and suffering, so easily in our power to alleviate.

The cats and dogs in the West are far better fed, sheltered, medicated and cared for than many human beings elsewhere. Our material wealth leads us to trivialise our own lives with material distraction while ignoring serious material poverty elsewhere. Yet we remain seriously poor in many, non-material, respects and therefore seriously unhappy and unfulfilled.

'We have to think not only about how we will earn enough to live, but also about why we live, and what makes life worth the living' (Nussbaum 1997:172). Philosophers, sociologists and other cultural theorists ask what is a good and well-lived life and, crucially, what social contexts allow individuals to thrive. The clients who seek out counsellors wrestle with this question as it manifests in their lives in one way or another. Yet counsellors just attend to individual dynamics, individual narratives, as though any individual stories can effectively be told without reference to the larger stories within which we are all characters.

'Sense, imagination, pleasure, beauty are what the soul longs for, knowing innately that these things would be its cure' (Hillman & Ventura 1993:131). Here is a hint of the kinds of wealth that do not show up on an accountant's balance sheet or within individual salary cheques. Money is a means to wealth, in many forms. But in order to transform money into wealth we need to know what wealth consists in. Yet, amazingly, *in a 'wealth creating society' where politicians and managers continue to exhort us to create wealth and 'add value', people almost never ask what wealth actually consists in*! How could we add wealth and value in our lives so that we felt more satisfied and resourceful and, sometimes perhaps, positively inspired?

As it stands, it is assumed within secular consumerism that consumers are the best judges of how to turn money into wealth. Consumers know what is good for them and what will make for a good life. Spend, spend, spend and then things can only get better. Fundamentalists, within Islam and Christianity know that this secular consumerist philosophy of life undermines health, wealth and happiness but their alternatives are, I believe, still less appealing.

Clearly the politicians and managers are right in that wealth creation, and the adding of 'value', are very important topics indeed. Unfortunately their conceptions and philosophies of wealth are deeply impoverished and inadequate. This matters profoundly because it is impoverishing, damaging and disempowering to all the individuals who waste their lives chasing fools' gold, surrounding themselves with distraction, and undertaking work that does not add to the wealth and wellbeing either of themselves or of others.

> Rather than explore resistance too much, it works better to genuinely marvel with people how they manage to make it at all. (Sabo & Havens 2000:85)

> What's left is little more than a vaguely sarcastic way to eat Pizza Pops. (Klein 2001:83)

> Whatever reconnects you to the natural world is the surest way to regain perspective on your life as just a part of a greater whole. (Marinoff 1999:232)

If this latter is true then many of us are becoming increasingly impoverished. We can no longer, most of us, look up and see a night sky. We cannot easily find peace and quiet. Whether we are 'indoors' or 'out of doors' we remain in a manmade environment. Indeed, increasingly, even when we are out in the open this open is still closed off. We remain in a mall, or in a car, train or plane. The very concept of outdoors is less certain for many urban dwellers and the rural is itself being turned into a great factory cum theme park.

So the life style that poor peasantry took for granted, time off, stone, leather, rural vistas, peace and quiet, is in many ways becoming reserved for the privileged few. Others make do with virtual views and recordings of peaceful lakes, hillsides, streams and coastal scenes or high-density packaged holidays. No wonder we seek to 'get away from it all' and watch TV programmes of people who attempt to escape the rat race. However, there may be no escape since the effort to 'escape' is itself turned into a large, and highly managed, business. Tourism is to become and to remain the largest business in the world:

> This relentless commercialisation and professionalisation has created an army of 'escape attempt managers' who supervise and regulate these routes to psychic discovery. (Cohen & Taylor 1992:21)

> There must be something wrong with Reality, if so many people want to escape from it. If we cannot change the reality, what can we do? (Turkle 1997:242)

According to the consumerist philosophy, each individual consumer is sovereign, is autonomous, has agency, and is responsible. Consumers, we are to believe, make rational choices in the marketplace and can best determine how to turn money into wealth. Yet salesmen and women, motivation researchers, public relations specialists and others in the sales force see things differently. They focus on the insecurities, doubts, uncertainties and ignorance of consumers. They seek to *create* demand rather than merely *respond* to consumer demand.

Dialogue involves mutual respect, care for the perspectives, concerns and arguments of the participants. Selling involves knowing more about the motives of the consumer than the consumers know themselves. Selling involves persuading consumers to buy in a way that keeps the consumer almost entirely ignorant of the manner in which they came to their 'decision'. Selling, if this is the best way to make a sale, may involve appealing to the lowest common denominator, the vulnerabilities, weaknesses and insecurities of the customer.

Selling does not generally involve respecting the consumer or encouraging them to make mature and genuinely wealth-creating decisions. It involves finding a way past their defences so that they will buy your product or service regardless of whether or not they 'really' want or need it. If they do really want it, all well and good. But success in business involves making sales to those who may well be wiser is they bought something else, or saved the money, or spent less time earning money.

It is simply not the case that consumers reliably know what will make them healthy, wealthy, wise, good and what will take them to a good and better life. Moreover, the ethic of secular consumerism tends to encourage consumers to remain childlike and indulgent. 'Our "aspirational age", as they say in marketing studies, is about seventeen. This applies equally to the forty seven year old baby boomers scared of losing their cool and the seven year olds kick boxing to the Backstreet Boys' (Klein 2001:70).

Moreover, the ethic of secular consumerism, although it panders to short-term gratification, relies on longer-term dissatisfaction, anxiety and unease. We are always being told by the advertising industry that we need more than we currently have, and that others who have what we do not are living a better life than we are. We are never told that perhaps we already have most of what we (materially) need and would be wiser to occupy ourselves more profitably. *We are never told that most forms of wealth exist outside the world of consumption.* We are never told that we might be happier and more fulfilled, more satisfied and more resourceful if we resisted the hypnotic process that draws us ever deeper into consumerism, debt and workaholic efforts to go on making the payments.

'We seem to live in an impatient and unthinking age where either impulse or apathy often rules' (Feltham 1995:124). Patience and individual reflection are not virtues in a consumer society. They are obstacles to the sales imperative. As a salesman, I want you to buy now. I don't want you to wait, or question the purchase. Borrow if you cannot pay up front. The entire Western economy is currently dependent on people borrowing more than they can sensibly afford and being impatient and unthinking.

The entire economy is based on the ethic that people want, if they can afford it, to be 'cool' and sophisticated. It is not based on the aim of making people *wise*, or *mature* or *good*. Yet ethicists, from Aristotle on, have argued that true wealth does indeed require that we cultivate virtue, wisdom, self-discipline, insight, perspective etc.

For Aristotle, our aim in life should be to achieve 'ataraxia', which was an inseparable combination of excellence and virtue. We certainly hear plenty about 'excellence' among business consultants and business motivational speakers nowadays. But no longer is this concept welded inseparably to virtue, Aristotle spoke of the good and well-lived life as 'eudaimonia'. This combined virtue and excellence but it was expressed in *action*. It was observable in the actions and interactions of a civil and civilised society. It was not merely a state of mind but a name for the well-judged activities themselves. The question was not so much what could we best think and feel, but what could we best *do*?

Compare this with today's fragmentation where action is secondary to style, to pose, to presentation, to plausible sounding descriptions. Yet, beneath the cool? 'The quest for cool is by nature riddled with self-doubt ("Is this cool?" one can hear the legion of teen shoppers nervously quizzing each other. "Do you think this is lame?") Except now the harrowing doubts of adolescence are the billion dollar questions of our age' (Klein 2001:69). The youngsters buy their 'cool' products and seek to look cool. The advertisement makes it clear that, with this cool product, their lives will really start to come together. The advertisement does not make it clear that the very next advertisement will be explaining to them that there is in fact something else in their life that they still lack. If they really want to be cool they will have to go out to the mall once again and buy. Where does the process end? When are we ever encouraged to think, 'enough; I can, sometimes at least, do something better with my time than working, borrowing and spending'?

'Happiness is about doing something you love with people you respect'. (Morris 1999:322). But this philosophy gets dangerously close to saying that 'the best things in life are free'. Do something you love with people you respect by all means. But how can you respect anyone who is not cool? And how can you do what you love without a comprehensive kit of matching accessories and additional status features? Every leisure pursuit has now been fully managed, constructed, coordinated and supervised by the advertising industry. Even fresh air and exercise requires a considerable investment in matching equipment, status declaration, market segmentation along with every other kind of leisure pursuit.

Moreover the sales pitch is now rarely for single objects and services in isolation. Increasingly we are invited to buy into entire sets of matching goods and services that, taken together, make up an integrated statement about who we are, where we belong, what we believe in, what we aspire to, what we value and what we like to do.

> Since Lauren began marketing his concept of the 'total environment' in 1984, he has presented us with several such 'perfect worlds': 'New England', 'Jamaica', 'Thoroughbred', 'Log Cabin', 'Safari' and 'Marina', to name his earliest projects. Each is meticulous in its detail, complete unto itself. (Silverman 1990:247)

> the products that will flourish in the future will be the ones presented not as 'commodities' but as concepts: the brand as experience, as lifestyle. (Klein 2001:21)

> The fashion magazines of the 80s are yet another example of how this process of defining and redefining style has become extended to the whole of social life. Readers of *Vogue*, for example, will find regular, monthly columns on Beauty Style, 'Food Style', 'Health Style', 'Travel Style' even 'Driving Style' among others. (Silverman 1990:255)

We do not merely buy single products and services; we buy into entire environments of life style product and service. We buy an entire identity. Moreover, the shop is no longer an item in a larger public environment; it now increasingly constitutes the entire environment. The public space has disappeared. The town centre has, often quite literally, been privatised, sold to the mall. The mall now *is* the town centre, and as like as not the public services that once comprised the public space have themselves been transformed into privatised consumer services. Everyone becomes atomised as a consumer. As a result, concepts of public service, public interest, public ethics, public priorities simply disappear.

For example, a public meeting, with public dialogue will only take place if the managers of the mall grant permission. If the meeting is consistent with the marketing aims of the mall; if it shows that there is a vibrant, bright and interesting 'community' of users in the mall; if it does not waste floor space that could be better used in a marketing opportunity, then all well and good. But if there is a hint of 'controversy', of strong feeling, of serious public concern, of blasphemous criticism of consumerism within the secular cathedral of the mall, then of course the public meeting will not be permitted. There is no public space. There is no public. There is no society. There are only production, marketing and purchase opportunities.

This invasion of public spaces includes the invasion of schools: 'They are fighting for their brands to become not the add-on but the subject of education, not an elective but the core curriculum' (Klein 2001:89). In cash-strapped schools companies provide high-quality learning materials that simulate the benefits of manufacturing, managing, accounting for and selling the company product or service. Schools have always been a preparation for work but they did once allow people to explore non-work perspectives on work, and they did once have other agendas too. Work was seen as a part of a larger social agenda of being a citizen, a householder, a parent, a community participant. All these roles were integral in the personal development and identity formation of school pupils. Now school is a place where children learn about and for the world of work and for little else. Training matters in the workplace. Education, on the other hand, might be somewhat inconvenient in a world where opinions are to be managed and appearances are to be professionally constructed and controlled.

The invasion goes further. Schools themselves can actually become a marketing opportunity; a chance for pupils to sell the product and identify with the brand. '"*Pepsi – Official Soft Drink of Cayuga Secondary School*". The school has a clause in its Pepsi contract committing the school to "make its best effort to maximise all sales opportunities for Pepsi-Cola products"' (Klein 2001:91). Fixation of an entire school around caramel fizz. Is this the best way of learning how to create wealth and assist in producing a genuinely wealthy society?

Happiness and wealth creation – the optimist's perspective

Schopenhauer described optimism as a bitter mockery of the unspeakable suffering of humanity. The pessimists concerning contemporary life, social change and its influence on human identity and happiness make some telling points, which deserve careful attention. But so, too, do the optimists. There is plenty of room for hope and enthusiasm, and current ennui and despair needs to be placed into a larger perspective: 'In the 1820s and 1830s "young people found a use for inactive strength in the affectation of despair," as Alfred de Musset put it: "Scoffing at glory, religion, love, at everybody, is a great consolation for those who do not know what to do".' (Zeldin 1998:372).

There is nothing new about expressions of concern about human greed, folly and ignorance. Yet profound dissatisfaction may be part of the human condition, part of what makes us human rather than an obstacle to our being able to live a human existence. If we were too satisfied and balanced we might still, as I have previously observed, be balancing somewhere in a tree. To change anything at all, to improve anything at all, we need to have strong wishes to make changes despite all the difficulties. As a result of all that humanity has previously wished to change we have changed a great deal. And then, of course, we sometimes wish that we didn't have to deal with the consequences of the changes. There are always many unintended and unanticipated consequences of change that, often, could never have been foreseen. And whenever we wish to change anything there is a price to be paid. We ask ourselves 'will I succeed? What if I fail?' So we experience anxiety even if we later achieve success. 'Powerful and strong wishes are as capable of creating anxiety as actual disappointments' (de Silva 2000:91).

Choices, growing opportunities, themselves raise further anxiety. When we have no choice we avoid both the burdens and the benefits of choice. 'Only a privileged few can ever pose the question, "What will I work at? What do I want to do? What is worth doing?"' (Sloan 1987:159). It is the more materially prosperous who have the time and energy to ask what they are doing and who consider the options, the point, and the purpose of their lives. 'Feeling that life is meaningless is in a sense a luxury. If you were scrambling to hold body and soul together, you'd never pause to question the meaningfulness of your actions' (Marinoff 1999:232). Likewise, if we coast along the surface of our lives, and restrict ourselves to habitual patterns of living, we may feel relatively peaceful and relaxed. But as soon as we start to ask deeper questions about what we are doing and who we are, then the unease may, once again, establish itself.

'The experience of "inner emptiness", boredom, loneliness and nausea is part and parcel of contemporary art and literature' (de Silva 2000:120). These are symptoms of cultural elites who have the time and energy to look beneath the surface of everyday existence. In so doing, they may create an anxiety about who they are and what they are about that they did not previously experience. Human progress, it appears, involves a preference for being a Socrates dissatisfied rather than a pig satisfied. However many changes we ever successfully make, we go on wishing for more. And so any reduction in dissatisfaction tends to be temporary at best. This may be due to human temperament more than human circumstance. And circumstances, in many ways at least, have surely improved for many and perhaps for a majority.

People live longer, they have a more secure supply of food, water, shelter. Whether they are more secure within their society is less certain. Social change creates new instabilities and therefore new sources of stress. The pessimists argue that, for example, families are in decline therefore overall human well-being and identity are gravely threatened.

The optimists, like sociologist Anthony Giddens for example, argue that these changes provide new opportunities for people to create new, more cosmopolitan, identities and sources for security for themselves. People stayed in marriages because they did not have the opportunity to get out. This does not mean that they were happy. They may not have been actively dissatisfied simply because it never occurred to them that they had any real choice in the matter. Given that there was no escape, there was no possibility of feeling anxious about change or dissatisfied with the status quo. When there is no alternative we do not have to expend emotional energy worrying about the alternatives and considering whether any of them are worth struggling for.

> Against the conservative critique of irredeemable breakdown, Giddens sees the self opening out to constructive renewal. (Elliott 2003:39)

> In *The Transformation of Intimacy* (1992) Anthony Giddens anticipates some significant changes to human sexual relationships, arguing that the deconstruction of formal and institutional notions of marriage will enhance relational potential. (Lewis 2002:314)

Computers, the pessimists argue, take us away from real life and prevent us from contributing actively to improving our real life here on a real earth. The optimists take a different view: '"On this MUD (Multi user domain) I'm relaxing, shooting the breeze. On this MUD I'm in a flame war. On this last one I'm into heavy sexual things. I'm travelling between the MUDs and a physics homework assignment due at 10 tomorrow morning"' (Turkle 1997:13). For optimists, this is an expansion of identity, which provides greatly expanded opportunities for challenge and well being. For pessimists this is a sad and withdrawn individual who thinks that fantasies in front of a computer are a substitute for a real and committed life with flesh and blood individuals living in real communities. 'your identity on the computer is the sum of your distributed presence' (Ibid.: 13).

Certainly we can now have a presence, of a kind, in discussion forums with people from all over the world. If you are interested in a rare species of bird you will soon be able to converse with everyone else in the world who shares your interest. Will this broaden your identity or constrict you into becoming an even more introverted and obsessive specialist than you were before?

Computers can help us focus more effectively if we already are inclined to focus effectively. Computers can also help us waste time on a grander scale than ever before if that is the kind of person we are. We can become more informed, we can take a broader view, or be more obsessed, or more introverted, or more dogmatic (sharing our dogmatic views and paranoia with like-minded dogmatists). Computers, along with all our other technologies, are first and foremost tools. It is we who decide to use them for good or for ill. They can expand our sense of who we are, or leave us even more fragmented and confused than ever. Optimists look for ways of building on the opportunities and coping with the constraints.

Pessimists are concerned that we are indulged by consumerism, seek instant gratification and run away from responsibilities. Instead of real intimacy we share fictions and fantasies on computer screens with unknown others. Optimists see new communities generating, new forms of solidarity and commitment and a new willingness to cope with the ever-increasing rate of change. Pessimists retort that this kind of cosmopolitanism may be OK for a tiny few who are already very well resourced, but that most people are inevitably limited in the extent to which they can cope with change. Hence, they argue, the rise of a fundamentalist backlash wherein people try to seek refuge in traditional simplicities rather than engaging with the changing circumstances that threaten to overwhelm them.

Theodore Zeldin argues that we need to ask how to sustain love and longevity in relationships, and that this is the most pressing agenda for the twenty-first century. Arguably he is right that this is central to (true) wealth creation, social stability and individual identity, wellbeing and security.

A rise or fall in gross domestic happiness?

Gross domestic product, in the West at least, and as measured by economists, was on an upward trend, with just a few hesitations, throughout the twentieth century. Without question there is more money to spend and more material goods and services to spend it on. We are living longer, with longer periods of retirement to enjoy our wealth – though that may change. We should mostly be feeling that we are 'more of a somebody' – with all our status acquisitions – than our grandparents, and their limited accumulation of goods. So does all that make us wealthier than we were? And does it make us happier? We have a greater wealth of goods and services, but what other forms of wealth do we have more or less of? And what is the effect, overall, on the self-esteem, health, wellbeing, satisfaction and happiness of each of us?

Economists and other social scientists are slowly beginning to take more interest in these broader questions about, and measures of, wealth and happiness. Richard Layard, in his March 2003 lectures at the London School of Economics, refers to the commonly observed phenomenon of 'rising norms'. To put it crudely, as we have long known, the more we get, the more we want, the greater our expectations. So when we achieve something we were long wanting we are, briefly, happier. But then we take what we have for granted, and, in any case, it does not delight us as much as we might have hoped. We soon locate new targets for acquisition.

Happiness appears to have more to do with the *gap* between what we have got, on the one hand, and what we want, think we can get, and think we deserve, on the other. This gap is briefly closed by our most recent success, and quickly re-opened by our most recently formed appetite for more. Rising material wealth, therefore, leads to rising expectations. What was yesterday's luxury becomes today's necessity. We become hostages of our comfort, security, ease and prosperity. We expect good times to go on for us. We may also suffer a latent unease concerning how long we can continue to stay up on our perch and successfully cling on to all our wealth. 'those most blessed are often the most sensitive; unless everything works out perfectly, they are impatient at disappointment and shattered by quite trivial things' (Boethius 1962:29).

These issues are relevant to our sense of identity in that what we have and hold, the property, the people, the perks, the power, the experiences and opportunities – all this becomes taken in, 'introjected', and construed as a part of who we think we are. I am a 'somebody' because of the long list of status symbols, successes, experiences, networks, people, and 'stuff' of all kinds that I have assembled around me. As we grow more materially wealthy we add 'experiences', places we have visited, people we have met, holidays we have enjoyed, to our list of items to be consumed.

I consider myself to be doing well if I have got more than I had before. I also measure how well I am doing, by comparing with those others whom I define as competitors all around me. In the great horse race of human existence, we do not compare ourselves with those who are way ahead of us or those far behind. The queen of England may have more stuff than us. The peasant in Africa may have less. But what really matters to us are those who we can see on our radar as it were, who are in competitive range of us, a little ahead or a little behind. If we draw closer to, and overtake, someone a little in front of us we celebrate. If someone creeps up on, and overtakes, us we may feel anxious and depressed.

We measure our 'wealth' relative to our expectations and in contrast with the defined competition. In a rich country, a given amount of wealth – say £5,000 – might leave us looking relatively poor. In a poor country, that same amount of wealth could define us as relatively rich. Layard observes that people would rather be richer in a poorer country than poorer in a richer country, though there are no doubt other factors at work as well. A certain amount of wealth can make us happy, but we can be happier still if we can observe not only that 'I am rich' but that, as comedian Harry Enfield observed, 'I am considerably richer than you!'

Of course, there are different kinds of wealth even within the limitations of the philosophy of consumerism. What may be 'cool', or impressive or elegant to John may be 'gross', irrelevant, ugly, or ostentatious to Joan. We learn to rationalise about the grapes that are beyond our reach – they are sour in any case and not a part of the personal statement we want to make at all. We console ourselves that we are perhaps more sensitive, or intelligent, or attractive, or experienced than the competition. We avoid racing in races where we will lose. We seek to find some area where we can be a winner. If necessary we can choose to win by being more miserable, more unlucky, more amoral, more defiant, more indifferent, more violent, more courageous, more stubborn than our competitors. If we can't be a successful winner we can try to be a successful loser. Whole communities may declare themselves to be more or less at war with a surrounding society that offers them little but the prospect of waiting at the back of every queue. In the end we may say, 'I am less concerned about winning than you (so I win)'.

Michael Bond[3] observes this problem of rising expectations about happiness:

> People think they should be living on the edge of joyfulness all the time. You get people who are actually happy, but they think happiness is so important that they strive to be even happier. Yet we're not built to be joyful. We're built to be positive, but not to be stuck in a kind of euphoria. We should be in that mid-range so that when something good happens, we can go up.

He confirms the limited link between happiness and income: 'Every study that's ever been done on this has always found that happiness increases with income, but in the West the effect is always a small one. Elsewhere, among slum dwellers in India, for example, the effect is much more substantial.' But losing one's major role in society, for example, as an employed person with a contribution to make to the wider community, can exact a high price. The loss of role and of opportunity for commitment and for social contact is more damaging even than the loss of income: 'Unemployed people show a big negative drop. They come back, but not to where they were before. Widows and widowers come back, but it takes them quite a few years' (Ibid.).

Of course, I have not defined 'happy' since it clearly has a broad range of meanings dependent both on culture, context and expectations. If we are wise we will not be happy about a life of simple 'pleasure'. We will want to make more of ourselves. We will want to feel a range of emotions, including the strong 'negative' ones. We will want tough and easy experiences, challenges as well as consolations, storms as well as tranquillity, doubts as well as certainties. We will be happy only if we also know sadness. We will be happy if we are satisfied with the scale of the challenges and projects that we have set for ourselves.

We will be satisfied if we have sometimes been dissatisfied and uncertain, yet have come through the process. We will be satisfied if we have learnt to come to terms with defeat, disappointment. We will be happy if we come through the storms of existence, battered but, more or less, unbowed.

We will be less than happy if, after a long and tranquil life, we come to the conclusion that we never really put our boat out to sea at all, but stayed in the harbour of our immediate, and overly safe, surroundings. We will be happy if we decide that we did try more or less well to live a fully human life, taking on a reasonably full gamut of human emotion, triumph and tragedy.

We will be happy if we know that we discovered the truth that it is better to have loved and lost than never to have loved at all. We will be happy when we realise that we became more of a someone by living through, learning from, and more or less surviving, the tragedies, frustrations and limitations of our existence. 'The word "happy" doesn't have an exact equivalent in some languages. In English, happiness has a number of different meanings. It depends on the context. It might mean "satisfied", it might mean "joyful", it might mean a longer-term happiness' (Ibid.).

Personal happiness and social progress

> Our minds were 'made up' before the invention of agriculture, and there has been insufficient time for natural selection to change them. (Charlton 2000:3)

> We now live in a mass society full of strangers who have no reason to trust as they are neither family nor friends. Although resources are vastly more abundant, they are linked to status and there are massive inequalities in their distribution.
>
> This means that there is a much higher proportion of intractably low-status people in modern societies than in the societies in which humans evolved. (Ibid.:10)

Rising personal and cultural expectations are interconnected. In addition to believing that we can and should be happy there is the related belief that society as a whole can and should get 'better' year on year. The culture as a whole should become more democratic (as in Abraham Lincoln's government *of* the people, *by* the people, *for* the people), more just, wealthier, more powerful, and more knowledgeable. From the seventeenth- and eighteenth-century Enlightenment onward, but not before this time, we have taken the view that, be the use of human reason, we can gain more insight and control of our world and make a better society for all. This belief has been greatly strengthened by the technological advances of the nineteenth and twentieth centuries so that it has been increasingly taken for granted that 'experts' will steadily increase their expertise and, in so doing, make life more comfortable and more interesting for us all.

This belief in social improvement closely relates to our implicit expectations about personal improvement. As the social tide of progress rises, we all expect to be lifted from where we were previously placed. And so it has proved to be, certainly from a technological perspective. We have endless new ways of distracting, amusing, communicating, entertaining, exploring, discovering, studying and expressing ourselves. It is less than obvious that the progress made in technology has been matched by progress in ethics, politics and overall human wealth and wellbeing. Lincoln would not, I think, believe that the US government is by the people or for the people. A large fortune is needed if you are to become a politician in the US, and the fortunes of wealthy lobby groups predominate in government affairs. This, essentially, is government by the rich for the rich and European governments offer no better.

As regards ethical progress generally, there is much debate as to whether or not we have become 'better' people. It is a mixed picture. On the one hand, we are less exploitative of women, perhaps, and more tolerant of homosexuality, which 'we' no longer see as a form of sin or medical pathology. Perhaps we are less overtly racist, but that is debatable. Changes in social etiquette are a poor measure of virtue. But it is not at all obvious that there is more civility in public spaces, more respect for public places, more respect generally for individuals.

Are we more, or less, kind to others than we once were? It is true that we don't push young boys up chimneys or down mines. We have abolished slavery, and we demonstrate occasional concerns for the poor and oppressed. There are more global organisations than ever concerned to reduce human suffering and injustice. TV pictures can bring the suffering of individuals very close to us. But TV pictures can also distance us from what may really be happening to people. We can become deadened by violent images. The images are generally from the perspective of the wealthy. We think little of dropping bombs from 15,000 feet. We do not know, and do not seem much to care, how many people Western nations have killed in the last 50 years via war, sanctions and by unjust economic relations.

Oliver James (1998) argues that British society (and indeed, most of the Western world) is unhappier now than it was 50 years ago and that much of this unhappiness is due to the *lack* of genuine social progress. He suggests that many of the most important social changes in recent years are difficult to cope with. They go against a human nature that, over many years, evolved and adapted itself to a very different world to the one that we now inhabit.

> New patterns of parental behaviour, such as the increased divorce rate or pressure to succeed at school, have almost certainly increased the proportion of people emerging from childhood with high and medium risk of low serotonin[4] compared with 1950. (James 1998:9)

Families have been destabilised, modern life, as so many sociologists have argued, is alienating. We feel cut off from it, impotent in relation to it, insecure because of the rapid rate at which it keeps on changing. As social animals our happiness is linked to social status and social standing, but little stands for long in a rapidly changing world and social status itself is less secure than it once was. All this, James argues, leads to depression.

According to James, people born between 1945 and 1955 were between three and ten times more likely to suffer major depression than those born between 1905 and 1914. Suicide rates among young men have trebled in Britain since 1970. Violence against individual persons has increased fivefold since 1950. Drug and alcohol use has increased in most countries.

Of course, statistics are very difficult to compare between decades and between nations. Happiness, as we have seen, is a complex concept. In any case, what matters most is not that we achieve some 'final' comparative description of different historical periods. That may be impossible. It does, though, matter that we attempt to identify the severity of the threats to human well being that we currently face. Are we, for example, really suffering from greater levels of stress that are damaging, and even disintegrating, our sense of who we are? Or have we discovered a new word – stress – for the perennial human condition?

Do we define ourselves as mentally distressed and sick because we really are suffering more than we once did? Or do we have more reason, and opportunity, to declare and define ourselves as unwell, with the sickness benefits and respite that goes with it? Or do we declare and define ourselves as distressed because we now have higher expectations about wellbeing? Or because we are sickly neurotics who simply would not have survived in earlier, tougher, times? Or do others categorise us as distressed because those others, in a burgeoning health industry, have an interest in bringing into existence new categories of client?

Perhaps there is some truth in all these possibilities and although we can never have any finally certain answers we could indeed benefit from a better understanding of the nature of human wellbeing than currently exists.

Social scientists, from many backgrounds, are taking an increasing interest in the relation between human wellbeing and the social influences that add to, or detract from, this secure and positive sense of self. There is no consensus. Some commentators, like James, bewail the destruction of a unified self, which he sees as arising from impossible social pressures and changes. Others, Deleuze and Guattari, for example, see the movement away from the idea of a unified self as a form a liberation. Like R. D. Laing they have a somewhat romantic view of the radical potential within schizophrenia. The schizophrenic sees beyond oppressive, limiting mind-sets. Or so we are asked to believe. I do not believe.

Some critics see the increased focus on self as a sign of growing social progress and prosperity. This self-preoccupation and increased introspection and self-care, are luxuries that we previously could not afford but which we should now, rightly, celebrate. Others (for example, Lasch (1980)) argue that this growing preoccupation with 'me' is a symptom of social decay. We retreat, rather than advance, into self because nowhere else seems safe anymore. Nowhere else seems like home when even the family home is detonated into fragments by divorce. 'Masses of people are concerned with their single life-histories and particular emotions as never before; this concern has proved to be a trap rather than a liberation.' (Sennett 1986:5). Critical theorists of the Frankfurt school are likewise sceptical about the benefits of social progress, as we saw in the previous chapter.

Greed has been seen, since ancient times, as a major human vice against which we should be endlessly on our guard. But *greed does not even exist as a concept within consumerism.* Much of the economy is now organised around the need for consumers to be greedy. We cannot afford for people to exercise material restraint. Greed and shallow material distraction has now been re-branded as 'retail therapy', and it is a social duty that we get out there and do our bit for the consumer economy. We may know that our purchases are morally trivial, humanly degrading and plain silly; and many postmodern, self-referring and surreal advertisements play with the underlying absurdity of our consumer concerns.

Surreal advertisements make jokes about the endless need to make a sale, but go on and on, nonetheless, in their highly professional efforts to make the sale. We may well accept that, in making these purchases, we may only be *playing* with different ways of expressing our identity. Our statement this month about who we are will not survive for long. We will change and change again, explore other aspects of ourselves and, in the process, we will need to find new sets of designer goods and accessories and fashion options. We will reinvent ourselves over and over again, perhaps not as often as Madonna, but as often as we can afford. In the process, we will be doing our bit to maintain prosperity in the consumer economy and thereby increase the gross national wealth of society.

Who are *you* trying to be today? Whoever it may be, you can be sure there are cohorts of companies out there who are only too keen to provide you with the necessary accoutrements of objects and activities. 'Because you're worth it!'

> Weinstein (1991) borrows the term 'bricolage' from structural anthropologist Levi Strauss to discuss how subcultures borrow, refine and use styles and symbols from cultural groups other than their own. Bricolers are social actors who create meaningful cultural myths, stories and so on in order to think about and understand the world around them. (Kidd 2002:124)

This is the song of the postmodernists, and it has been taken up enthusiastically by postmodern business because it provides enormous new opportunities to increase sales and create new markets. After all, if you believe that there is a stable self then, once you have established this identity, you will feel little inclined to break it all up and start all over again. Your car, house, furniture, clothing etc. are all statements of the kind of person you are. If you don't change very much then why should they?

If you become this kind of stick-in-the-mud-self then your motivation to revisit the mall will decline as the amount of stuff in your home accumulates. This is bad for the economy. It is much better to throw away all those old, and now unfashionable or archaic personal style statements. You are a new you on a new day. So get out there and find out what is new for you to make this new you. And so the cash registers can still ring their positive messages to global corporations that you are alive and well, because ever changing. *You are still swiping your ever-changing identity through the credit control system of the global village.*

It this to be welcomed? Is it not good news that we can – more and more of us – become global, cosmopolitan consumers and thereby continue to invent and reinvent ourselves? Or is Kidd (2002:96) nearer to the truth when he suggests that: 'Postmodernism provides a thinly veiled justification for the false needs created by the capitalist economy.' Ferrucci (1982) asserts that there are many 'sub-selves' that deserve to see the light of day and we can be sure that a large and diverse consumer opportunity will be provided for each of them. Perhaps you can take self-1 to the mall on Monday, then follow through the week with self-2, 3, 4, 5 and 6? And, no, there is no day of rest, so self-7 can visit on Sunday where the purchasing activity will be as feverish as ever. Ferrucci, though, seeks and sees (1982:58) an underlying integration to all this division within the self: 'We increase our integration by allowing our subpersonalities to become synergistic rather than antagonistic with each other.'

But, as Baudrillard observes, there can be no final integration and 'arrival' for our postmodern consumer if the economy is to prosper. Consumers exist because they consume, and they must go on consuming ever anew. It is the buying that matters, not the decision that one is happy with what one has and needs no more. Hence consumers are deluged with images and signs without end. Consuming is never, and never must be, consummated. It must never be complete. We must always feel a gap, a lack, and an empty space. We must always yearn for more.

May (1973) argues that, in the process of personal development, we do need to *differentiate* ourselves, to make a statement about who we are, to draw ourselves as separate from the social and cultural context from which we come. But we also, he suggests, need to *integrate*, to see ourselves as at one with, as a part of, something much bigger than ourselves. This appears to be a deep spiritual need, indeed it might be seen as a defining characteristic of spirituality, this sense that we have of our identity as being both at once separate from but, more fundamentally, *at one with*, the larger mystery, pattern, process of existence. The word 'religion' itself is rooted in the Latin 're ligare', to reconnect, and this sense of connectedness is arguably the most important feature of the religious sense, without which our sense of ourselves seems to be without a real root. We will look at this more systematically in chapter 7.

'All through life a person is engaged in this continuum of differentiation of himself from the whole, followed by steps toward new integration'. (May 1973:120). This sense of the transpersonal, as being an essential context to establishing the personal, is arguably far more valuable to us than fundamentalist dogmas, medieval beliefs that are palpably absurd in the light of modern knowledge, and immature fantasies about father substitutes. It is not an area that the philosophy of consumerism can do much with. Integration may reduce sales and may not be welcomed. What is better is to encourage a positive 'Tower of Babel' of New Age, Heritage Traditional, and Modern Scientific remedies for problems real and unreal. And why don't you just try them all? Buy your crystals, your meditations, your conventional and complementary (though expensive) drugs. Buy them all. Try Sufi dancing this week and bionic radionic energetic whatever next week. In this way a growing care service sector will continue to grow. You can binge eat in celebration this week and visit a health farm later.

And if you want to complain about this consumerism and its damaging consequences on identity and wellbeing why then, in a democratic society, you can arrange a public protest and hold a public meeting. But no, the mall is not a public space and they don't like controversy and especially not anti-capitalist rallies. Well you have free speech so you can write to the media. But media features are tied in with sales promotion campaigns. The advertising finances the papers, not awkward comments that we've heard before. A national or global conglomerate owns your 'local' paper. You have a right to speak, but you are unlikely to be heard: 'Concentration of media ownership has successfully devalued the right to free speech by severing it from the right to be heard' (Klein 2001:280). You remain free, however: 'Freedom without opportunity is a devil's gift' (Chomsky, in Klein 2001:185). The constraints remain invisible. The images and language made available to you drive out any accurate sense of the state you are in.

But, even as the state is itself being rolled back, there are corporations that care. 'In its press material and ads, there is an almost messianic quality to Nike's portrayal of its role in the inner cities: troubled kids will have higher self-esteem, fewer unwanted pregnancies and more ambition – all because at Nike "We see them as athletes"' (Klein 2001:371). Buy the shoes, buy the chocolates, and you, your community and your school will prosper. As a child, I remember the promises:

- Anytime, anyplace, anywhere, there's a wonderful world you can share, with the right one, with the bright one, with Martini.
- Sugar, jelly, real fruit flavours, that's what Bassett's jelly babies are made of.
- You'll wonder where the yellow went when you brush your teeth with Pepsodent
- The ESSO sign means happy motoring.

These little ditties go back nearly 50 years. They are lodged deep in my brain. They, along with scores of others, have sought to crawl in and become a part of who I am and who I want to be. And in those days there was only *one* commercial television station in the UK. How much of younger brains has been filled with the corporate promise? We are dressed in the uniform of the corporation and we are beckoned to find our true selves with the products of the corporation: '*Because you're worth it*!'

I also remember lines of verse and extracts of plays we were forced to learn as children. I was convinced at the time that this was 'square',[5] not modern, not a part of my agenda of personal development. How wrong I was. How much I have treasured these, more thoughtful and helpful lines. How much I wish I had learned more of them. How much I wish I were less infested with idiotic jingles and images. Yet how much worse has this problem become in the past 50 years? Corporations intrude so much now into public and personal spaces and identities that they are ubiquitous and therefore have become invisible. When the first company uses a school as a marketing opportunity we sense that something is wrong. When every school is marketing products and is itself being managed or inspected by a company that also monitors rail safety, the whole problem appears to disappear.

Corporate advertisers may become more contemptuous of individual human beings as their power grows. Their own self-esteem rises as they pay themselves ever more than the average and their comments about consumers become positively offensive. Consumers, we are to believe, become ever more resistant to advertising the more they have to live with it. Klein (2001:9) reports the view of one marketing executive: '[They] are like roaches – you spray them and spray them and they get immune after a while.'

But a test question always needs to be asked: If the current social and political circumstances are as bad as some argue, are they actually worse than all the other places and times past? Where and when do we wish we would rather be living? Giddens highlights the crucial role of day-to-day civility in preserving social cohesion and in promoting individual wellbeing and development. We notice when people are being uncivil to each other but perhaps we take ordinary civility too much for granted? Perhaps it is more ubiquitous than we may think, and perhaps we are better at it than our ancestors?

As Elias (1939) observed, we have progressed a long way from medieval texts on social etiquette and good manners. These suggested, for example, that before we sat down, we should check to see that our seat had not been fouled. If there was a tablecloth we were advised that we avoid using it to blow our nose. There was less in the way of advice about the need to wash one's hands before eating from the common dish, and no comment was passed about spitting on the floor, or breaking wind at table. Women in the West reveal far more of their bodies than was allowable in medieval times or later. Does this indicate a moral decline? Or does it suggest that modern man has internalised such a high degree of civilisation and restraint that such 'provocative' clothing can be worn in relative safety?

Elias does not take social progress and civilisation for granted. Our civilisation, bureaucratisation and organisation have made 'civilised' mass murder another production process requiring little sweat by, or disturbance of, its perpetrators. The 'final solution' strategy in Germany during World War II is an obvious example. But what of progress since that war? In the organisation of targets, their monitoring, assessment, the 'collateral' damage, it would appear clear that *the killing of thousands of people now takes place in exactly the same depersonalised way as the production of biscuits. The language used is bland, anodyne, instrumental, and analytic in terms of cost and benefit options and probability outcomes.*

War is just a managed process like any other managed process. People watch it in a detached way on television. They may be at home. Or deep inside an aircraft carrier. Or piloting two or three aircraft remotely from a TV set ten thousand miles away on the ground. The computers indicate the likely death count. There will soon be no difference between wars simulated by computers and 'real' wars mediated by computers. Perhaps tomorrow's pilots will be able to work from home? There is no technical reason why they should not.

They may not need to be told whether the war they are fighting is a real one or a simulation. The 'only' difference, of course, is that in real wars thousands of people get killed – usually at a great distance from their killers. This large-scale death has little more emotional impact on the killers and their allies than the pretend deaths of simulated war games.

We no longer swing axes directly into the faces of our enemies. This was bloody stuff but nothing like so bloody as today's push-button options. Killing was pedestrian and personal; and it gave us pause to reflect as the flesh of another dropped into our own face. Tomorrow's ground-based pilots will have had years of practice killing people in the combat flight simulator games that they will have grown up with as children. Trainers are already stating how impressed they are with the hand-eye coordination and IT skills of student pilots. Given the quality of simulations, the pilots of tomorrow may never know whether the war they are fighting is real or virtual. Is this a path to virtue? *Clearly, technical progress may have nothing to do with moral and social progress.*

It is not surprising then that there is growing concern that science and technology are not inevitably beneficial to humanity. There have been too many examples in recent decades of technological change benefiting only the rich, or no one at all. Larger numbers of 'general publics' are taking the view that each new invention needs careful attention. It may or may not be beneficial. But its costs need to be carefully assessed. We have to ask Who gains? Who loses? What are the long-term implications? What might be the unforeseeable consequences? What are the risks, to whom, and are they worth taking? Are scientists always dispassionate researchers, or are they too often in the pockets of the companies who employ them?

> One study, published in 2001, found that only 16% of scientific journals had a policy on conflicts of interest, and only 0.5% of the papers they published disclosed such conflicts. The same researcher found that 34% of the lead authors of the scientific papers he studied were compromised by their sources of funding. In other words, the great majority of the scientists with conflicts of interest are failing to disclose them. It gets worse. In 2002, the *Guardian* revealed that British and US scientists are putting their names to papers they have not written. The papers are 'ghosted' or cowritten by employees of the drugs companies, then signed, for a handsome fee, by respectable researchers. In some cases, the researchers have not even seen the raw data on which the papers' conclusions are based. (Monbiot 2004)

The days when people tended to say 'gee-whizz, here is another brilliant invention from our boffins', have well and truly passed. Rather than uncritically accepting new technological tools we have to ask how they will be used, by whom, and for whose benefit. Also, we must ask: what are the costs and risks, who will be required to bear them, can costs be shared and how?

Further social progress will almost certainly require further technological development. The idea that we could, or should, try to survive without the technological achievements made so far is absurd. But a great deal of social progress requires no 'technology' per se, and unless we use technology wisely, with a concern for justice and humanity, it may lead us to a dystopia that positively diminishes individual human happiness and wellbeing.

We talk of the urban jungle, but, nonetheless, in so many urban societies people learn to glide respectfully past each other, people create highly complex webs of mutual dependence and mutual support. In an age that is supposedly about individual development, we actually depend on each other more than at any time in human history. We go off and buy all we need for ourselves perhaps, but others have produced all that we buy. Our own individual capacity to produce the daily essentials for survival, never mind for prosperity, has never been more limited. Increasingly we are not even capable of repairing objects that malfunction. For that matter, the process of repairing goods is being replaced by – replacement of the goods.

Likewise we talk about the isolation of families, the decrease in the size of families. But *families, just as much as individuals, are further away from being autonomous social and economic units than they have ever been in history.* We have suffered a period of politicians blithely declaring that there is no such thing as society, that public is bad and private is good, yet we require a larger public to survive at all. Not so, say those on the political right. We require markets, not public services or public spaces they argue. Yet markets only exist at all within a public space, where there is public trust, public laws, public civility, and a modicum of just government. *Markets cannot define the boundaries of our social space since markets only can exist* within *a (tolerably stable) social space.*

The more stable the society, its laws, ethics, civilities and expectations become the more invisible it may appear to be. When societies care so comprehensively for individuals, then individuals themselves may imagine that they can, and do, care for themselves alone and do not need to care for society. But, were society to falter, they would soon discover that any notion of individual autonomy is an illusion. We can be 'autonomous' only within a stable and supportive social space. And this social setting needs continuous care and maintenance. It can decay. It can disintegrate. We may then find, perhaps too late, that what we so much relied upon has been lost. *If we are concerned about personal development and personal happiness, we had better pay far more attention to social stability and social progress. The personal and the social are inseparable.*

So, if counsellors want to raise self-esteem and enhance personal development and happiness, let them pay active attention to social contexts by defending democratic values and nurturing critical intelligence.

Questions for Counsellors

1. How many of your clients suffer from excessively low self-esteem? And excessively *high* self-esteem? How do you deal with each? Be specific with specific examples.
2. How far do you, as Fancher suggests, recommend resignation, patience, humility, fidelity, moral worth, refinement, and character formation in developing self-esteem?
3. How far do you recommend that clients identify with the 'superego'/Aristotelian route to happiness via virtue?

4. How far do you recommend that clients identify with the id/Dionysian route to happiness via hedonistic pleasure seeking?
5. Which of your clients, in their efforts to be 'good', are needlessly hard on themselves? Which are overly kind to themselves concerning their bad behaviour? How do you judge and what do you do about it? Be specific with specific examples.
6. Which of your clients belong to a faith community? Does this faith, in your view, assist your clients to be good and to feel good? Or does it make them feel bad without improving their behaviour? Be specific with specific examples.
7. Do you agree with Smail that we need to escape the ravages of the pursuit of happiness?
8. Do you agree that you should always seek to increase client satisfaction? If so, how do you combat client smugness, selfishness and complacency?
9. On balance, do you think that society is opening up new opportunities for individual fulfilment or, because of overly rapid change, undermining the basis of individual happiness and security? Who is gaining and losing?
10. Do you as a counsellor, see it as part of your role to inform clients of the social and political dimensions of individual happiness and misery? What, specifically, can and should you say in what specific circumstances? What examples come to mind?
11. What kinds of wealth do your clients possess and lack? What can you do to show them the way to wiser forms of wealth creation? What specific examples come to mind?
12. How far do you agree with Klein that what's left is little more than a vaguely sarcastic way to eat Pizza Pops? What do you think she means by this?
13. Do you agree with Cohen and Taylor that there are now armies of 'escape attempt managers'? Are counsellors a part of this army? Are some clients attempting to escape into, or via, counselling?
14. Is there something wrong with reality, as Turkle suggests, given that so many prefer to escape from it in order to be happy? Is happiness best achieved by escape or by engagement? Consider this question in relation to particular clients.
15. Do your clients know how to find happiness as autonomous consumers? Do you try to improve their skills? Consider this question in relation to particular clients.
16. What are the 'aspirational ages' of *your* clients? Are they as low as Klein suggests? Consider this question in relation to particular clients.
17. Do you agree with Feltham that we seem to live in an impatient and unthinking age where either impulse or apathy often rules? If so, does this reduce the sum total of human happiness and what is the role of the counsellor in challenging such tendencies?
18. How far do you agree with Aristotle that truly human happiness comes via 'ataraxia' – an actively lived integration of excellence and virtue? Should counsellors put this agenda at the centre of their work?
19. How far do you agree that there is a loss of public space, and that this loss is actually encroaching on personal happiness and identity?
20. Are you, on balance, an optimist or a pessimist concerning the prospects of individual happiness in a changing social and political world? Summarise the arguments and evidence of optimists and pessimists. Do counsellors have any role in relation to these larger changes?
21. Do you think that efforts should be made to actually measure gross domestic happiness and net (genuine) wealth? Are economists correct in seeking to improve on purely monetary measurements?
22. Are rising levels of recorded distress a sign of progress, professional appetite for new markets, fragmentation, or merely a change in methods of measurement? Or all of the above?
23. Do you see the growing focus on self as a sign of cultural progress or social and political decay? Or both? What evidence and argument seems most significant?
24. How far does personal development and happiness require democratic values and critical intelligence? What is the counsellor's role in developing these?

CHAPTER 6

Feeling Good and Being Good: Identity and Ethics

> unlike religion, the therapeutic ethos posits no values higher than the self. Nor does it offer a world view through which people can collectively share meaning. (Furedi 2004:91)

In previous chapters we have examined conceptions of identity, narratives of health, notions of reality and ideas of happiness as these relate to our efforts to identify and express ourselves. We have asked, in other words:

Who am I?
Who am I when I am *well*?
Who am I when I am *real*?
Who am I when I *feel good*?

I now want to move to the related question:

Who am I when I am *being good*?

The aim, throughout, will be to show how all these questions and agendas are intimately interrelated and that Aristotle's welding together of excellence and virtue, in the Greek concept of 'ataraxia', was essentially correct. We certainly hear a great deal about the need for 'excellence', in work contexts at least. Less is heard about the importance of virtue. But recent scandals within large corporations suggest that virtue may indeed need to be rehabilitated if there is to be any real kind of excellence.

'In both Britain and the United States, the funding of studies of corporate crime has all but disappeared' (Monbiot 2001:300). It does appear that much of the 'boom' of the late 1990s was more to do with dishonest accounting and greedy expectations, than honest work. Economies, and, more important, *people*, may be damaged at least as much by such ethical failings as they are by any failure to achieve other forms of excellence.

There is, as we shall see, a moral dimension to everything. We can always be asked 'is what you do morally trivial?' Perhaps the entire culture is drenched in moral triviality? 'charity itself has been reduced to a postmodern gesture of having fun on behalf of the world's immiseration' (O'Neil 1995:20). The alternative, though, does not have to consist in humourless, stuffy, starchiness or holier-than-thou snobbery.

Who is an authority concerning ethics?

Generally, when counsellors consider ethical questions, they do so in the context of professional codes of practice. In this respect, their concern about ethics is no different from the interest that any other category of professionals shows, and ought to show, when seeking to maintain professional standards. Codes of practice, generally, are set out in some detail. These codes may include long lists of 'dos' and 'don'ts', or, when these become unwieldy, underlying principles, values, and even personal moral qualities that are considered to be desirable or essential in good professional practice.

There will be a complaints procedure, something about training, continuing professional development, supervision, monitoring and so on. The codes will be revised from time to time. There will be recurrent concerns about implementation and management. To repeat, this process of quality control is a feature of *any* kind of professional activity and, for that matter, of any kind of staff management. It is important, but it does not get to the real heart of ethical matters, as they ought to preoccupy counsellors and therapists. At its worst, quality control has more to do with protection of the status of the profession than it relates to genuine protection of the client. But within the best codes of practice, people take the practice at least as seriously as the code, and make genuine efforts to implement, monitor, manage and ensure that the profession is genuinely accountable.

So much for codification. However, within counselling I wish to argue that ethics is not just a matter of professional codes of practice. It is far more central than this. There are also the questions of client ethics, client values and their relation to client wellbeing, the wider social responsibilities and social roles of the counsellor, and the negotiation of ethical issues between counsellor and client. The ethical or unethical values and behaviour *of the client* may be central to their personal development, but sadly, this is almost never recognised within the contemporary practice of counselling. The counselling, to put it crudely, is amoral. The reason is that so often the social context within which it operates has become essentially amoral.

Ethics, and the serious business of addressing people to the importance of ethical issues, has become 'nobody's job' – except for that of a few priests. This is serious for that majority of non-believers, in Europe at least, who do not attend church, and who no longer believe that the church is an essential source of moral authority or an important arena within which ethical issues should be discussed.

For some believers, of course, there can be no ethics without God, and therefore, to their mind, a society is bound to become amoral when it loses its faith in God. But for secular humanists, who seriously want to construct a good society through essentially cooperative human efforts and without divine assistance, the current focus on 'excellence' without much corresponding attention to 'virtue' is a grave problem.

Within so much current secular humanist philosophy, ethics is separated from, and never emerges within, discussions about personal progress and development. We buy goods, establish skills-portfolios, change attitudes, purchase services, develop new habits, and build networks of contacts and activities. If all goes well and we are satisfied with the result, we 'develop' as persons. We become more of a 'someone', and we 'make something of ourselves'. It seems that we are all trying to make it in some way or another. We are all on the make. The trouble is that we are on the make, and making something – *for ourselves.* First, middle, last and foremost. The question is not so often seriously asked 'what are you going to make *for others*?' What we may do for ourselves may 'reflect on' and benefit others. And we may do for others, if this reflects well on and benefits ourselves.

And so the god within this essentially amoral universe becomes 'me'. I cooperate in society if this is really in my best long-term interests. I help others since this will help me and since I may need their help. I am altruistic because I hope for altruism from others were I to need it. The entire contractual culture is based on the notion that we are all looking after ourselves first and foremost. The contract is designed to ensure that what we do will assist other parties to the contract and, possibly, the wider society. But we are expected to sign up to it because it will do *us* some good. Its benefits – to us – will exceed our costs. And if they don't? Then we are thought to be poor market operators.

The marketplace, so classical economists argued, is full of selfish individuals. They are all trying to buy at the lowest price and sell at the highest price that they can possibly get away with. Fortunately, we are to believe, the market itself is a cleansing process on all this individual selfishness. It makes people work hard, and although it is based on greed, people are not exploited because the greedy seller will be undercut by someone else who will see the chance to sell for less. Our intentions may not be honourable, we may be self-seeking, and the market requires that we be self-centred. But the outcome will be the best of all possible worlds for society as a whole. The market will ensure innovation, efficiency, cost reduction, technological development, and a continued search for new marketing opportunities.

All we have to do is make sure that the codes of practice, the rules of the marketplace, the monitoring are all in place. We ensure that there is fair competition, freedom of information; and this community of self-centred and self-interested producers will deliver precisely what the community of self-centred and self-interested consumers wants to buy. Everyone will be happy. *The market system, we are to believe, is so good that no one actually has to* be *good.* People will nonetheless *do* good because the market will ensure that it is in their interests to do so.

A similar argument applies to the activities of individual *institutions*. These, too, are players in the market place and they too must seek to minimise their costs and maximise their gains when selling their goods and services. For example, consider the sale of counselling courses by universities and colleges in the counselling marketplace. From an ethical, and academic, perspective, counselling courses would be sold if the form of counselling on sale was considered to be of good quality and a social good in society. We would seek to educate students and clients concerning the desirability of these programmes. Ethical and academic considerations would predominate.

But, from a purely marketing perspective, the only thing that matters is that there is, for whatever reason, sufficient 'demand' for the courses. Perhaps people are, more than sensibly, hopeful that they will find employment after qualifying? Perhaps they ought to be advised of the virtues of rival courses? Perhaps they will be prepared to pay a substantial premium, compared with other courses, to attend as counselling students? In these circumstances it becomes 'rational' for university managers to increase the number, and price, of counselling courses. It is not rational, even if it would be ethical, to advise students that their employment expectations may be too high and that counselling was becoming, yet another, economic bubble. Hence, I believe, the explosion of counselling courses in the UK. Hence I fear their current decline as demand levels off and employment expectations are seen to be unrealisable. This is not to suggest that academic and ethical considerations have been entirely eroded within academe. But it seems beyond dispute that commercial considerations have become more important, that these often do conflict with academic and ethical criteria, and that the latter have suffered substantially as a result of the growth of the commercial ethic.

We have had around two centuries wherein this market 'ethic' has grown ever more central and powerful in its hold on our imagination (or the lack thereof). Its earliest protagonists were more aware of the dangers and limitations than its contemporary disciples: '"The government of an exclusive company of merchants," Adam Smith observed, "is, perhaps, the worst of all governments for any country whatever"' (Monbiot 2001:14). The 'free enterprise ethic' has certainly delivered technological innovation and no command economy alternative has proved itself to be superior. But for how much longer can we go on believing that, in order to *feel* good and *be* good, we don't need to think about actively *doing* good – for others as well as for ourselves?

> Eudaimonia is often rendered as 'happiness': but this is misleading, since it misses the emphasis on activity, and on completeness of life. (Nussbaum 1994:15)

> The very nature of the good is such that no one can seek his liberation without seeking the liberation of others. (de Silva 2000:117)

Aristotle took the view that virtue was absolutely essential for well-being. Counsellors certainly focus on the client's agenda for well-being. But *very little attention is paid to whether clients are interested in being virtuous and what the counsellor's role might be in addressing this question.* This reluctance is quite understandable given the extent to which we have become an amoral society. By amoral, I do not mean that nobody behaves ethically. On the contrary. What I am saying is that it is now very difficult to get any serious recognition of, discussion about, responsibility for, or leadership concerning the matter and manner of ethical behaviour. Instead of attention to individual or collective *conscience* we instead restrict ourselves to *codes of practice* to control people who, it is assumed, need their essentially amoral behaviour to be institutionally directed towards 'wealth creation'.

Counsellors are often, understandably, reluctant to be seen as ethical authorities: 'Training as a psychologist, so far as I can tell, does not provide any special understanding of the relative rights and obligations of persons towards each other' (Fancher 1995:170). Yet, as Dawes shows, psychologists are becoming increasingly overconfident in their presumption that they are capable of being 'expert' witnesses in court. They have no special capacity to determine the degree of responsibility and culpability of accused persons: 'There is no knowledge in psychiatry or psychology that would allow *anyone* to determine whether impulses are "irresistible".' (Dawes 1996:230).

Counsellors, on the other hand, tend to wish to avoid being seen as preachers or ethical judges. They do not wish to claim to be ethically superior individuals and they may certainly have no reason to make such a claim. They do not wish to force their own particular values onto clients who may not share these values. All this is well and good. I do not think that society would be making ethical progress if we were to create a new army of frowning, disapproving, finger wagging supposed 'authorities' who chose to pontificate about the sin and damnation of their morally inferior flock of disciples. We do not need someone to come down from a mountainside with another set of ten 'commandments', demanding that we all obey. *Ethical responsibility does not consist in obeying the commandments, injunctions or scolding of presumed ethical authorities.* And responsibility, of every kind, consists not just in choosing between options, but in construing the range of options from which to choose.

Ethical authorities and ethical authoritarianism

> We view ourselves as integrated mental entities with an agenda of intentions and actions, authors of our own destiny. In a moral universe, perhaps that is the only conceivable way to view other people too. (Broks 2003:61)

We need, essentially, to distinguish between an *authority* about ethics and an *authoritarian* concerning ethics. *Counsellors should not be ethical authoritarians; they should be ethical authorities.* This is an absolutely crucial point, and the distinction needs to be appreciated comprehensively and intimately. An ethical authority is not someone who preaches ethics, or who pretends to be ethically superior to others. An ethical authority, within counselling for example, is someone who has made a study of the role of ethics within the development of individuals and societies. An ethical authority can help a client examine the ethical dimensions of their problems and dilemmas. An ethical authority knows that there will not be much in the way of personal or social development without a full engagement with the ethical dimensions of this development.

Let us look at what happens to counselling when it fails in its grasp of the importance of ethics within personal development and fails, thereby, to provide a suitable ethical authority. For example, there is the agenda of personal development as 'growth'. Everyone wants more growth and so counselling, in many of its forms, offers you the prospect of more. Come to the counsellor, or the encounter group, and you will *grow*. You will become *more* of yourself. The therapist Rollo May (1976:255) spotted the problem years ago: 'Growth cannot be a basis for ethics, for growth is evil as well as good. Each day we grow towards infirmity and death.' Within person-centred therapy, growth is good. But the question, surely, is growth of *what*? There may be growth but *is the growth itself good? The only way we can answer the question is to see, first, that it is an ethical question.* With the 'growth centres' of the encounter group movement, the image of an oak tree was popular. We like oak trees. Great oaks from little acorns grow. The growth of oaks is good. You, too, could grow in this good way. But you are not an oak tree. Will any kind of personal growth be good? Rats can grow in numbers. Cancer is an unbridled growth where there is no harmony between the growth of the cancerous cells and the growth and well-being of other cells. Eventually, as a result of all this unbridled, unprincipled, uncontrolled, and uncoordinated growth, the host organism dies. 'Cancer is a growth. It is a disproportionate growth where some cells run wild growing' (May 1976:256). The question is not so much, shall we grow, but shall we *grow up*? Shall we grow to be wise and good? We do not grow in a social vacuum. Like cells we grow in a context of cells in harmony. Shall we add to this harmony? Shall we contribute to it? Shall we therefore ourselves be nurtured within it? Or shall we grow like a cancer and thereby threaten the overall wellbeing of the social context within which we exist? This question of appropriate personal growth in harmony with the social context of which we are a part is an intrinsically ethical question. *Personal development, therefore, is absolutely inseparable from ethical development*, and an ethical authority is someone who knows this, in detail, and who can assist others to explore the ethical issues.

'Being a self is inseparable from existing in a space of moral issues, to do with identity and how one ought to be. It is being able to find one's standpoint in this space, being able to occupy, to be a perspective in it' (Taylor 1996:112). Here is a crucial metaphor. We exist in a moral space. This is a fundamental contribution that sociologists, philosophers, anthropologists, ethicists and cultural theorists can make to counselling. We do not need priests to provide this ethical authority. There is no evidence that the behaviour of priests or believers is ethically superior to that of secular humanists.

> A funny thing is happening within the Anglican Communion. It is threatening to tear itself apart over a handful of people who live in monogamous, stable, long-term, loving relationships and are sufficiently religiously observant to want the church to bless them.
>
> While the rest of the world considers weightier matters of life and death, the church has converted an issue most of the western world now regards as a private and personal matter into an obsession. (*Guardian*, 'Gay Communion' 17 June 2003, p 17)

We do not need God to provide ethical foundations since *societies do not exist at all except within a moral space.* Indeed, the priestly view that there is no ethics without God is itself a sign of a *lack* of knowledge and faith concerning the centrality of ethics within human secular life.

The Christian ethic itself remains deficient in many ways:

- The teaching that there is justice on Earth flies in the face of obvious realities. It may falsely lead us to believe that, if we are good, then good things will necessarily happen to us. We may then imagine that, if bad things happen, it must be our fault. This is a recipe for self-flagellation that only adds to our woes.
- The teaching that the world already is a just world takes away our responsibility to work for justice.
- The teaching that some are 'saved' encourages us to project our own fantasies of superiority onto the 'bad' other.

Real faith requires accepting that, as adults, we are not protected by a cosmic father figure who will rectify all wrongs either here on in the after life. Real faith requires coming to terms with the fact that much occurs by chance and that nature is neither supportive nor hostile but more nearly 'indifferent' to our fortunes, were it capable of expressing any feelings about the matter.

> All religions teach that we live in a Just World where goodness is rewarded and badness punished. Since the evidence that rewards and punishments are handed out fairly in this life is rather slim religions require an after life to save this hypothesis
>
> *The Skeptical Intelligencer* vol 3, no 1, July 1998; on line at www.dorothyrowe.com.au

Without ethics, though, there is no society at all. *Codes of practice alone will be no defence against self-centred individuals devoid of conscience.* It is just too easy to evade, avoid and entirely ignore such codes – and get away with it. Without a basic *trust* that people will generally stick to their word, even when they are not forced into it, then we have no basis for cooperating at all. *Without such trust, there can be no market, no contract, no economy, no well-being, whether individual or social.*

The myth of ethical neutrality

> In *The Battle for Human Nature*, Barry Schwartz describes how modernists' conceptions of social science are obliterating the traditional language of morality.[1] (Gergen 1991:246)

> Psychotherapy involves applying the value system of the therapist to the dilemmas of the clients . . . his or her value system is more important to you than training, credentials, or even professional degrees.'[2] (Dineen 1999:147)

Because we have become, understandably, tired of the Victorian legacy of moralising, preaching, commandments and ethical authoritarianism we have sought to purge ethical discourse from professional discourse – except within professional codes of practice. The ethical wellbeing of individuals is not considered to be the job of care professionals. Instead we have engaged in the fiction that we can, and should, be 'ethically neutral'. We leave it to clients to get on with their own ethical agendas. Who are we to judge? As consumers they must seek their own salvation in their own lights. We will restrict ourselves to factual matters.

But this is absurd. To repeat, it is impossible to talk about personal development, individual dilemmas, options and frustrations, without engaging with, and taking a view about, ethical questions. *We cannot take a neutral view because there is no neutral view to take.* You cannot be neutral about exploitation, for example, because if a person is being exploited, to their detriment, then your 'neutrality' is itself an (ethically unacceptable) standpoint which is therefore far from neutral. This is obvious in relation to extreme examples of unethical behaviour. For example, it would be absurd to claim that 'I am ethically neutral and value free as regards the Holocaust. I just look at the facts and the points of view of all concerned.' The pretence of ethical neutrality is simply an unethical way of describing and relating to amorality.

> All forms of discourse or rhetoric which purport to be 'value-free' and yet which attempt to give direction to our lives are riddled with moralistic maxims disguised as matters of fact. (Smail 1987:17)

> Technicism seems to be value-free but is shot through with values. (Barnett 1994:170)

> Often the refrain of 'effectiveness' and 'efficiency' operates as a good way of concealing that no real thought has been given to the question of ends . . . (Blake et al. 1998:55)

I don't think that Blake is right here. More often, when managers talk about effectiveness and efficiency, they *do* have clear views about ends; it is just that they don't want you to talk about them, question them, challenge them or modify them in any way.

The cognitive therapist operates with all kinds of implicit value judgements about what is self-defeating, unrealistic, acceptable and unacceptable. The person-centred therapist works from a coherent ethic concerning what the good life ought to consist of. This ethic needs to be made clear and needs to be challenged since it is overly individualistic, selfish and hedonistic. Likewise, psychodynamic therapists adopt an implicit, powerful and highly influential ethical position concerning what are 'realistic' compromises between the demands of the id, the world and the conscience of the superego.

As Sardar (2002:115) observes, one of the troubles with amoral secularism is that: 'People are free floating individuals, children and adults, over-endowed with rights and with no accepted language in which to discuss their responsibilities to anyone or anything beyond themselves.' *If we do not get serious about the need for ethical authorities we will end up once again with ethical authoritarians.* The backlash against amoral individualism and consumerism is growing both within Christian and Islamic communities. *Their recognition of amorality is significant, serious and deserves respect.* Their remedies, involving a return to simplistic medieval fantasies, and finger wagging authoritarians, are to be deplored. But if they triumph, as they might, then 'we' secular amoralists will only have ourselves to blame.

The problem is that this amorality has been around for quite a few decades. It is now so ubiquitous that it has become invisible. Here is Rollo May (1973:56) again, describing the growth of the problem as far back as the 1920s:

> Those of us who lived in the 1920s can recall the evidences of the growing tendency to think of the self in superficial and oversimplified terms. In those days 'self-expression' was supposed to be doing whatever popped into one's head, as though the self were synonymous with any random impulse. To 'be yourself' was then an excuse for relaxing into the lowest common denominator of inclination.

The 1920s were a hedonistic period. Critics felt that traditional ethical authorities had failed. They looked at World War I. They were critical of what had happened as a result of all this talk about character building, duty and dignity. People had become mere fodder for the machine guns. They had deprived themselves of the chance of joy and happiness. They were so buttoned up and repressed that they did not express their emotions, they did not show to themselves, or to others, what they really thought, felt and wanted. They were dead masks hiding the real human being inside. Away with all this ethical authoritarianism. It was time for a return to Dionysus.

Sure enough, the self-help books of the time changed their ethical agendas. Victorian and Edwardian texts had focused on character building, forbearance, deferred gratification (sometimes deferred to a life after death), duty and all the rest. They distinguished between present distraction and future distinction. They argued that a dissolute self would become a disintegrated self. They considered that there could be no real human freedom without responsibility, courage, maturity, self-discipline and insight. They saw a role for refinement, understatement, cultivation and a 'sensible temper' as a means of dealing with the great pleasures and the (much more frequent) great pains of life.

From the 1920s on, though, we start to see the agenda move away from 'character' towards 'personality'. This is developed by the Dale Carnegie programme advising on how to make friends and influence people, how to make something of oneself. We start to talk of *carving* a place in society rather than *finding* and *accepting* one's social position. This was proclaimed as an end to ethics, towards a more 'value-free' stance. But it was more a change of ethical perspective towards a more individualist, introspective and self-centred agenda.

> R. Susman (1979) 'Personality and the Making of Twentieth Century Culture', in J. Higham and P. K. Conkins (eds) *New Directions in American Cultural History.* Baltimore, Johns Hopkins University Press p 220 has suggested that one of the key changes in identity formation . . . occurred with the shift from the proclamation of virtues of character to those of personality. (Featherstone 1991:115)

This change, as Susman observes, can even be documented within the work of individual self-help writers. In 1899, O. S. Marsden wrote *Character; The Greatest Thing in the World.* This, you may predict, explored and recommended traditional Victorian values. In 1921, he published *Masterful Personality.* This is much more familiar to modern readers. Its themes are the same as contemporary 'how to' books. How to attract friends, and be charming, influential and fascinating.

As we came through to the 1960s this revolt against traditional values and praise of hedonism and individual atomism grew mightily. Somehow or another, it was imagined, we could develop ourselves without worrying ourselves with ethical matters. The ethical route was to reject the Victorian ethic, which had proved itself to be ethically deficient. Fritz Perls, a guru of 1960s gestalt, encounter and personal development, was fierce in his criticism of the old order. Our grandparents, in their efforts to build character, were simply smothering themselves – and others. What they presented to the world was not a really valuable human being. It was pretence. It was hypocritical. It was domination and oppression. It was life killing. It was everything that the human potential movement sought to escape from:

> Self-conquest is socially esteemed as 'character'. And certain aspects of our civilisation are probably due to character: namely the vast empty facade, the mere quantity, the imposing front; for these constitute the ever-needed proofs of dominating men and nature, they are proofs of potency. But grace, warmth, strength, good sense, gaiety, tragedy: these are impossible to persons of character. (Perls et al. 1979:419)

If this was character building then who wanted to be imprisoned within the straightjacket of 'character'? So the message was 'let go', 'let it out', 'let it all hang loose', relax, just be, just go with the flow, wake up to the world around you, live in the now. And so on.

Of course, insofar as we become overly obsessed with the future and imprisoned by the past, an attention to the here and now can be ethically and humanly desirable. But past and future have their place. It is precisely our ability to make *positive* use of imagination and memory that distinguishes us from the bovine existence of a cow chewing the cud in a field. And, in any case, as physiologists and neurologists have shown convincingly, even our perception of the present 'moment' is itself constructed by future intentions and past memories and experiences.

Ram Dass wrote 'Be Here Now' as a celebration of present moment living (Dass 1971). But what, actually, do we mean by here and now? Its language usage varies enormously, and rightly so. 'Now' might mean today, this minute, this week, this epoch in history, this century. 'Now' is longer if you are a cultural theorist, longer still if you are a historian, longest of all if you are a geologist or above all a cosmologist. Likewise with 'here'. So how here and now do we want to be? How now can we be? The now of electrons as they sequentially light up the TV screen/cathode ray tube? The now of a single frame on a film? Of course not. These moments are beyond our range of here and now apprehension. Moments are only moments at all within a wider context of meaning and intention.

Abraham Maslow (1908–70) was an important therapist authority, who himself had explored and proposed the stages of 'self-actualisation'. But he was of an earlier generation, and was less than impressed with the 'be here now' agenda of the 1960s. He thoroughly disapproved of this hedonistic carnival which sought to throw off the ethical constraints and 'hypocrisies' of earlier generations: 'Maslow called his activist students and colleagues members of the "Spit on Daddy Club". As far as he was concerned, they were overindulged, underdisciplined, ungrateful and impolite' (Herman 1995:273).

If we assume that results, outcomes and consequences matter, some attention needs to be paid to the ethics and character of those who propose a new kind of ethic and character. We cannot expect counsellors to be morally superior beings. They may help if they can merely assist us to explore moral issues. But it does rather matter if they prove to be morally dissolute, inferior even? So many of the personal growth gurus of the 1960s fell to drink or other forms of dissipation. Of Perls for example: 'Referring again to Perls Shepard (1975:96) claims that he had a "justly deserved reputation for being indifferent, at best, to children and was a failure as a father"' (Dryden & Feltham 1992:260).

Ethics within schools of counselling

There is an ethic underlying every school of counselling, regardless of how far its practitioners are aware of it. Each has its strengths and limitations. Each has a crucial influence on practice. Each requires careful examination and assessment. It, surely, is a moral failure to elicit, pander to and manipulate cheap responses from people, whatever the context, but particularly so in relation to therapy. We have seen, in a previous chapter, Rogers' description of personal development as involving tears and the release of 'pent-up' emotion. But are emotions like water against a dam? Is this an appropriate metaphor? And is it the case that the *control* of emotion indicates that the feelings of the person concerned are less powerful and less authentic? On the contrary, many novelists have shown that the greatest power, pathos (as opposed to bathos) of emotion involves the control of emotion. 'Self-restraint is healthful and beneficial; it is even a virtue. This is why we find self-discipline to have been one of man's earliest moral attainments' (Jung 1995:38).

We are human, and we find and express ourselves when we exercise suitable self-control, not when we behave like animals. This does not require that we become in any way false, frustrated, artificial or hypocritical. Passion does not require that we behave like infants. Mature adult choice may only be possible and meaningful for those who wish to, and learn to, exert some degree of control over their passions. Mature adults exist within, and are created from, mature communities. Civilisation does not 'block' mature identity and expression, it creates it. The compromises that living in communities requires do not prevent authentic self-expression since there is no authentic individual self prior to, or outside of, history, culture, society and community. 'The fact that a feeling is uncontrolled is no indication whatsoever that it is any deeper than a feeling that is disciplined. We must not assume that someone whose feelings are modulated and controlled is not a passionate person' (Peck 1983a:156).

At every stage we need to examine and assess the adequacy of the ethics underlying different schools of counselling. Here for example, is an illustration from Roberto Assagioli (1980:112), doyen of psychosynthesis: 'Many women find their self-identification in wifehood, and even more so in motherhood – they consider themselves, function and live only as the mother. This kind of self-identification does not give the experience of the pure self.' Here, says Assagioli, a woman can over-identify in the role of wife and mother. The underlying ethic is that women can, and should, be more than just a wife and a mother. Fair enough. The general consensus has now become that people deserve more than just two roles, although the value and importance of the roles of wife and mother are perhaps *under*estimated these days. But what is this 'pure self'? Is there a 'pure' self free of all roles? If, as this book seeks to argue, there is no such final pure entity then people may damage themselves, and behave unethically, in chasing after an almost saintly, yet illusory, status of 'pure' identity somehow distinct from their actual roles.

Here is Martin Heidegger (1995:312), referring, from an existentialist perspective, to the problem of inauthenticity: 'Dasein[3] makes no choices, gets carried along by the nobody, and thus ensnares itself in inauthenticity.' Certainly we consider it unethical to avoid taking responsibility when the responsibility is indeed, our own. Self-discipline involves recognising that 'easy' choices (where there is just one overwhelmingly preferred option) are nonetheless choices. It is an instance of 'bad faith' to believe that there is no choice just because the choice is clear, or painful, or limited. Decisions made without conscious deliberation may nonetheless be decisions for which we should take responsibility.

We have seen Passons' efforts to show how clients can become more responsible by using language where personal responsibility is suitably honoured. Many person-centred counsellors have gone down this route which, as I say, takes a strong, albeit implicit, ethical stance. But what if counsellors ask clients to 'own' problems that they ought not to own because they are mainly beyond their powers to control or influence? Surely to do so is not just an *incorrect* understanding of the client's predicament. It is also an *unethical* pressure on the client, to carry a burden that is beyond their *capacity* to carry.

A counsellor may seek to defend themselves by saying that they did not realise this, that they had meant well, but had merely misunderstood the client's predicament. But then it can be charged that the counsellor *ought* to have known better, that counsellor training *ought* to explore both the limits to, as well as the opportunities for, personal responsibility.

Existentialists often refer to the 'angst' that arises when we confront the extent to which we are responsible for our lives. To some degree this may be misplaced in that we may be *over*estimating the degree to which we actually are responsible. Also we may in any case by making too much fuss about this responsibility. Nietzsche, as we have seen, was rather scornful about the supposedly terrible problems faced by contemporary humanity. More recently, Maslow expressed similar criticism: 'Existentialism in its European version: Maslow called it "high IQ whimpering on a cosmic scale"' (Herman 1995:265).

It may be immoral and cowardly to be overly negative and miserable about our circumstances. It may, likewise, be ethically unacceptable to take an overly positive view of society when this involves failing to engage with real and pressing problems. We have a duty to face up to such problems and, if we don't, then we may be morally culpable. A child can be innocent without moral reproach. But an adult who remains innocent may be *guilty* of innocence and should therefore be prepared to take responsibility for some of the consequences.

Rollo May, for example, was rightly concerned that Carl Rogers' ethical philosophy, which so much structured his counselling, was naïve, false, and therefore positively dangerous. Far from helping adults find their inner child, it infantilised adults at precisely the time when they needed adult maturity, courage and wisdom to deal with their problems.

Rogers took a highly positive view about the goodness of people and the opportunities within society. May asked: 'I wonder how you square your statements with the famous Milgram experiments at Yale? How also do you deal with Philip Zimbardo's 1971 'prison' experiments at Stamford?' (Greening 1984:16). The Milgram experiment showed the extent to which people would blindly follow authorities even when their own conscience, and the evidence before them, indicated that they were doing great damage. The Zimbardo experiment showed how easily people settled into destructive group norms and polarised in confrontation with others. Neither piece of research gives us any cause to be sanguine about the prospects of human progress and personal development. For that matter, neither does our history. To repeat, it is only since the Enlightenment that humanity has got at all serious in its belief about the likelihood, never mind the inevitability, of progress. 'A colleague tells me that when you had a discussion with Martin Buber in Michigan you said, "Man is basically good", and Buber answered, "Man is basically good – and evil"' (Ibid.:21).

Ethics and beliefs in progress

> Our ethics and systems of justice, our entire moral order, are founded on the notion of society as a collective of individual selves – autonomous, introspective, accountable agents. If this self-reflective, moral agent is revealed to be illusory, what then? (Broks 2003:49)

Evolution is about adaptation, not progress. In future, the best way to adapt may be to be lichen or an ant. Both have survived and prospered for far longer that human beings and may yet outlive us, even though they have not 'progressed' very much. Throughout most of our history human beings have generally seen history as an essentially cyclical process, like the weather and the seasons. There are good times. There are bad times. Mainly the agenda has been about survival more than celebration. Our ancestors generally assumed that in the long run there was no reason to think that the good times would increase or that the bad would decline. In the long run, in any case, we are all dead.

Hence, in earlier times, much of the hope we managed to assemble concerned itself with the good and just life we would, hopefully, live after we had died. For the past few hundred years, though, we have been more confident about the likelihood of progress arising from technological advance. This confidence has, of course, been shaken from time to time; particularly during the disasters of two world wars and the threat of nuclear annihilation. If humankind does in fact fail to 'advance' it looks as though it will be because of ethical rather than technological deficiencies. Because of our moral inadequacies, (traditional vices like greed, selfishness, laziness, impatience) we may yet misuse technology in such a way that it does more harm than good.

> We [The USA] have 50% of the world's wealth but only 6.3 per cent of its population. In this situation, our real job in the coming period . . . is to maintain this position of disparity. To do so, we have to dispense with all sentimentality . . . we should cease thinking about human rights, the raising of living standards and democratisation. (George Kennan, US strategic planner, 1948, in Pilger 2003:101)

At the turn of the millennium one country, beyond all others, has the power to shape, or shatter, prospects of global progress. The above observation by

George Kennan, made half a century ago, is chilling. We want, of course, to believe that those with power and influence will use it to good effect. Abraham Lincoln spoke of democracy as government *of* the people, *by* the people, *for* the people. The USA speaks of the need to spread democracy throughout the world. Perhaps it should begin in its own backyard? 'So far, America has not done very well in producing the sort of citizen who can interact well with distance cultures. In consequence, Americans are insular and ignorant to a degree unparalleled in Europe, where a plurality of Western cultures, at least, is a fact of everyday life' (Nussbaum 1997:116).

Gerrymandering is not new, or marginal, in the USA, it is a part of the system. Constituencies are adjusted into tortuous shapes in order to ensure that the incumbent stays in power. Money produces more response from government than a vote at the ballot box. Neither are the European democracies a shining example of ethical integrity. And then, of course, there is the rest of the world!

> While they appear to be able to exempt themselves from national law, multinational companies also remain immune from international human rights law, which applies only to states. They may use the law as if they were human beings, in other words, but in key respects they are no longer subject to it. (Monbiot 2001:12)

We talk about the problem of crime and how to deal with it. It is very hard to accept that many of the most powerful crooks do not break the law at all. Instead many make the law, use and abuse the law, evade the law. They do not rob the bank, they own the bank and collude with companies to tell lies to shareholders about the reality of these companies. They pay themselves ever more, regardless of whether or not their company turns a profit. This problem is not at the margin of society; it is endemic. This is what some of our leaders are doing to us and for themselves. A common fantasy, as provided in school history courses, is that once upon a time there was injustice but, after political agitation and political reform, western nations become democratic. So now we have justice and fairness?

> Researchers[4] have shown that belief in a just world is so widespread that people blame victims of misfortune even when their fate is clearly beyond their control. (Swann 1996:144)

> That ideal of self-realisation, gloriously expressed over a century ago in John Stuart Mill's *On Liberty*, still carries a powerful appeal, and it squares with other values – democracy, freedom of speech, equal opportunities – which we all hold dear and to which all Western regimes at least pay lip-service. (Porter 1997:1)

In fact we are still at the very earliest *beginnings* of the process of establishing democracy as envisaged by Lincoln. It is not all clear that any real progress is currently being made in providing much in the way of justice, opportunity and political representation in any Western nation. Nor will we make much progress unless and until we recognise the extent of the problem. In fact, though, people are, arguably, more apathetic about politics than they have ever been. Turnouts at elections, and membership of political parties, continue to decline.

'The standard reading of the last two decades chronicles a move from radical politics to a preoccupation with self' (Cohen & Taylor 1992:17). Social progress, or the lack of it, is of fundamental relevance to ethics and its relation to identity. We find ourselves and feel good about ourselves to the extent that we live in communities that we believe in, that we are committed to, that we think will support us and which deserve our support. We feel undermined, insecure, destabilised, decentred and depressed if we discover that our leaders are liars and crooks who are more concerned about appearances than realities and who are not actually democrats at all. Moreover, it is so much more difficult to be good when one fears that others will merely take advantage of you if you try to be virtuous. Leaders are enormously important in the example they set. A great leader, of nations, institutions, or companies, inspires, uplifts, provides hope, engenders loyalty, reassures, supports, and encourages others to behave well and be the best they can be. A corrupt leader spreads corruption in a society and the corruption feeds off itself bringing more and more individuals into its web.

Ethics and corruption

> The fact that a corrupt and corrupting society may well have formed the patient's beliefs about the good life, and even about herself, makes it necessary for the philosopher to be not too quickly trusting. (Nussbaum 1994:27)

The more corrupt a society becomes, the more it disintegrates. And the more the society disintegrates, the more the integrity of individual identities disintegrates. Crime becomes the only way of survival and of establishing one's identity and status. Commerce itself becomes impossible without a degree of trust, since protocols, ethical codes of practice and laws are not sufficient in themselves to engender cooperation:

> Trust is one of the most powerful factors affecting a country's economic health. Where trust is low individuals and organisations are more wary about engaging in financial transactions . . . but there is a negative correlation between trust and religious belief . . . If you can't rely on others, you have to rely on a higher power. (*New Scientist* 10 May 2003:36,37)

The evidence is strong that people feel good about themselves and develop a strong sense of identity when they feel good about, and identify with, an organisation, a nation, a principle, a cause, a project – something that is larger than themselves but which becomes a part of themselves. *We like to work on something that is being done well, is worth doing and which will be recognised and appreciated as good. We are damaged, and may suffer a crisis of identity, when the work is badly done and is not really worth doing in any case.* Many suffer because, at root, this is their view of their predicament.

'We accept our destiny to work, to fight, to die for ideal aims. At the grave of a hero who has done these things, we end, not with sorrow at the inevitable loss, but with the contagion of his courage; and with a kind of desperate joy we go back to the fight' (Oliver Wendell Holmes, in Reinfeld 1964:140). Here are fine words. Even the words on their own can inspire, except when the reader has been too hollowed out by cynicism. But few us feel wealthy enough in spirit to aspire to the role of 'hero', even in the most limited of ways. It is hard to see how one can exercise courage in response to absurd, and/or morally trivial tasks. Courage may, though, be needed to cope at all. Cynicism is an obvious option, and follows on all too easily from unrealistic and utopian ideals: 'Escape through irony and critical self-awareness is in any case itself an illusion; at best it provides only momentary relief' (Lasch 1980:174). We saw that Klein made the ironic proposal that, in the fact of injustice, all that is left is a vaguely sarcastic way to eat pizza pops. It is not a solution. It hollows us out all the more.

Tom Morris provides ethical consultancy to senior executives from the Fortune 500 group of companies. Rather than offering a new acronym, or this year's 'five step' remedy for all ills, he seeks to reinstate traditional virtues in boardroom agendas. He compares (1997:207) ancient forms of wealth with modern tinsel equivalents:

Ancient Good	Modern counterfeit
Wisdom	Cleverness
Dignity	Glamour
Truth	Expediency
Beauty	Titillation
Goodness	Pleasantness
Character	Personality
Reputation	Fame
Respect	Fear

Instead of trying ever more sophisticated ways to manipulate appearances, he recommends Socrates' injunction: 'The way to gain a good reputation is to endeavour to be what you desire to appear' (Morris 1994:241). He suggests that treating people as human beings, subjects of their own affairs who deserve respect and attention, would be in everyone's long-term interests and that we cannot go on treating people as objects of manipulation: 'Neglect of what is genuinely human is the major reason why so many people in American business right now feel more victimised than helped by the latest management techniques and company-wide processes for improvement' (Morris 1997:109). He deplores (Ibid.:156) the subversion of democracy by corporate lobby interest groups: 'much of modern corporate political involvement has not been entirely salutary, to put it extremely mildly. So much recent lobbying activity has been driven by exclusively short-term, bottom-line, narrowly self-interested mentality that the results for the nation as a whole have often been destructive.'

Despair, though always tempting, ought not to be allowed to engulf us. *We have no cause to complain more than any of our ancestors, who lived through the same tangles of vice and virtue.* If we are more encumbered it may be that our main problem is our ever rising expectation that things can, and will, only get better.

> Our very sense of disillusionment arises from the fact that we expect more of ourselves than our forbears did of themselves. Human behaviour that we find repugnant and outrageous today was accepted as a matter of course yesteryear. (Peck 1983a:267)

> We cannot live our dreams. We are lucky enough if we can give a sample of our best, and if in our hearts we can feel that it has been nobly done. (Oliver Wendell Holmes in Reinfeld 1964:138)

Adversity can prevent us from bringing out our best. But it can also, in itself, provide us with an opportunity to show ourselves, and to the world, what we are really made of: 'Of the civil war: It left us feeling through life that pleasures do not make happiness and that the root of joy as of duty is to put out all one's powers towards some great end' (Ibid.:120).

There are so many hard truths that have to be accepted, when searching for moral courage. Our individual powers are far less than we would wish, though possibly far more than, at our most despairing, we may imagine. We are forced to live with ambiguity and uncertainty about the nature of the 'great end' towards which we hope to be working. The whole point about courage is that the success of one's endeavours is far from guaranteed and that it is impossible to predict with any confidence what the outcome will be, even with the best-laid plans. There are too many unforeseen, unforeseeable and unintended consequences; the interconnected efforts of many actors combine in such a way that the net result is not securely in anyone's hands.

The sociologist Norbert Elias (1897–1990) described this process which he called 'figuration'. In every society and community of individuals working, cooperating and competing together each has their own version of events, their own plans, hopes, values, priorities and intentions. All these individual actions and negotiations come together to produce – who knows what? Perhaps all we can say for sure is that the end result will not conform to anyone's plan or creation. The net result will follow a somewhat blind course, though it will not be random, chaotic or independent of all these efforts either. Hence the experience of those with far more power than the rest of us. Even these find that, as they pull on the levers of power, the response of the institution they control is forever surprising them. Everyone is in control. No one is in control. Some, certainly, are far more equal than others.

Morris (1997:140) suggests that: 'The greatest challenge we face nowadays in our intricately interconnected world society is to be truly universal in our ethical concerns.' Likewise Nussbaum (1997:52) proposes that: 'We must educate people who can operate as world citizens with sensitivity and understanding.' But the prospect overwhelms us. We cannot even figure out the figuration process of unanticipated consequences within small communities of action and interaction. How, then, do we figure out what to do within a global community? And how do we 'cooperate with', or challenge, the power of global corporations who are now larger and more powerful than some entire nation states? There are reasons for hope: 'There has been a massive growth in the number of co-operative organisations working at a global level'. (Giddens 1998:140).

de Silva suggests an even more fundamental way forward. We should forget our self-preoccupation, live by our ideals, tolerate uncertainty, and get on with committed action. So, of course the outcome is uncertain. What else do you expect? 'Self-conceit according to the Buddha can take three forms: "I am superior to others", "I am equal to others", "I am inferior to others"' (de Silva 2000:65). Find yourself by losing yourself. Live by your values and test them in action. Be prepared to be flexible but don't confuse flexibility with withdrawal!

'In ancient Latin, virtu meant "strength". In even more ancient Greek, there was a word, *arete*, that meant both "ethics" and "excellence"' (Morris 1997:151). It is so often useful to look at the roots of keywords. They often provide us with a clue to some of their essential qualities. Virtue is associated with strength. Strength relates to courage, commitment and action. We cannot be virtuous therefore by hiding in a corner, counting our moral assets and principles, rehearsing our values but doing nothing.

'The study of drives and emotions cannot be separated from the "social values" in terms of which they are satisfied and restrained' (de Silva 2000:97). We discover, and test, our values, our motives and our feelings through action, through active commitment, in a social context, and not merely in our heads. Emotion divorced from action is an indulgence. The word emotion is rooted in 'moving *out*'. It is not about endlessly contemplating one's navel and nursing one's feelings in an introspective reverie. Emotions are welded together with thoughts, with actions, with values. All these ingredients must stay cemented together or else each lacks integrity and loses its meaning and purpose. Without emotion though, without feeling, the life can drain from our lives. Our very sense of identity is threatened: 'In Cotard's syndrome, however, the core has dissolved. Cognition is decoupled from feeling and, consequently, thoughts and actions have no fixed moorings. There is no "I" left to claim ownership. It disintegrates; the fragments drift apart' (Broks 2003:100).

Existentialists have had a great deal to say about despair. We may despair because we never make any commitment. We may despair because we are no longer committed to the commitments we thought we had made. We may despair because we nonetheless hide ourselves within the daily habits that we no longer believe in:

> Camus' character (in *L'Etranger*) fights off the necessity to make decisions by detachment. He imagines himself to be free by not choosing and assumes that that is what he wants to do. Conversely, it is possible that what one does as a matter of routine is hardly what one wants to do, but is instead a shield against productive changes in one's life. (Sloan 1987:89)

We may despair because we forget what it was that brought excitement and commitment to our lives: 'Married people don't usually feel lucky, the way they did when they first met' (Bandler 1985:63). We may despair because we take others who are close to us far too much for granted: 'One thing that has always amazed me is that people are seldom nasty to strangers. You really have to know and love someone before you can treat her like dirt and really make her feel bad about small things' (Ibid.:64). We may not despair at all, yet still remain stuck and lacking in any real humanity or vitality: 'For most people "getting stuck" is wanting something and not getting it. However, there is another kind of of being stuck that no one notices: Not wanting something and not having it' (Ibid.:98).

Ethics and language

Rosen (1977:225) argued that counsellors and therapists, far from facilitating and enabling people to explore problems in their own language, were substituting 'psychobabble' in place of ordinary language and were thereby impoverishing clients. 'What appears to be occurring in the therapeutic culture of the seventies is the suppression of natural narrative speech itself, the suppression of language in its richest, most associative, most unpredictable, revealing and hence therapeutic form.' But perhaps it is unfair to single out counsellors and therapists as being linguistic imperialists? Perhaps this kind of power projection is something we are all guilty of? We all tend to prefer those around us to interpret and understand events and people as we do. At the very least, we want others to understand our own understandings. If they are to see things as we do, an excellent beginning is to get others to talk about these events with our vocabulary, our metaphors, our narrative, our descriptions of cause and effect, and our connotations.

It is a sure sign that we are not interested in understanding other points of view when we abolish the use of the word 'understanding' altogether. Education[5] is about sharing, and thereby developing, everyone's (differing) understandings. Training is about ensuring that trainees understand the task in the same way as the trainer understands it. *Since, in training, there is only one kind of understanding, we don't have to talk about understanding at all.* Indeed, we don't wish to, since trainees may then introduce extraneous agendas, priorities, interpretations and understandings that distract us from the task in hand and the priorities and programmes as previously prepared and accredited.

Barnett (1994) argued that people's autonomy is seriously under threat since they are so much treated as objects of manipulation rather than as autonomous adults. *The language of technology is replacing the language of humanity. In so doing, it is also destroying our ability to think about ethical questions.* If people cannot find the language that would assist them to *talk* about themselves as human beings, then they will be undermined in their ability to *think* of themselves as human beings. Clearly an important way of removing autonomy is to replace people's own means of talking about and making sense of their lives with one's own language. 'To learn to communicate as a matter of practising skills or techniques, by contrast, is to learn to play on people's susceptibilities, to manipulate them and achieve certain effects (in this sense the skilled communicator is indeed effective)' (Blake et al 1998:57).

In this triumphant technological age, it is tempting to imagine that everything can be 'solved' and dealt with by dealing with it as though it was a technological problem. We ask, what are the costs? What are the benefits? What are the resources? Obstacles? Alternatives? Facts? We key in the assumptions, add a few probability estimates, and generate the best, or least-worst, option.

We are so familiar with the notion that all 'real' and foundational explanation concerns matter in motion that we can hardly imagine that ethical considerations were once seen to be a central component in any important explanation. Here, for example, is Sidgwick in a letter to Darwin on receiving and reading his *Origin of Species*:

> 'Tis the crown and glory of organic science that it *does*, through *final causes* link material to moral. You have ignored this link and, if I do not mistake your meaning, you have done your best in one or two pregnant cases to break it. Were it possible (which thank God it is not) to break it, humanity, in my mind, would suffer a damage that might brutalise it, and sink the human race into a lower grade of degradation than any into which it has fallen since its written records tell of its history.

A technological approach has now embraced not just the marketplace, but governments, public services, organisations and institutions of all kinds, including health care. Generate your quality adjusted life years and you will be able to calculate life or death matters just as you can calculate recipes for biscuits. Quality control is exercised over biscuits, so why not extend these principles to human beings, to their lives and to the technological, professional, detached, and specialist assessment of its quality?

Technological language has grown so much in the last century that it has begun to displace other ways of talking and thinking about ourselves and our lives. We all 'retroflect' (as Perls described it); we see ourselves as subjects acting on ourselves as objects of manipulation. And the manipulation is described in purely instrumental terms. As a result *the language that we could use to describe ethical and spiritual matters has atrophied.* We hardly know how to speak about ethics. Instead, *our ethical assumptions are buried in our language so that it is difficult even to locate them, never mind assess them.*

> For Aristotle, praxis, or enlightened and moral social activity, was not to be confused with *techne*, or technological activity . . . as Habermas has said, the catastrophe of modern times (and of modern sociological and psychological theory) is that praxis has been reduced to techne. (Wilbur 1981:162)

We use the *language of technique*, and *this language routinely hides the ethical assumptions that we have implicitly made in order to justify what we do.* Because the assumptions are hidden they are difficult to assess. We are not invaders; we are liberators. We are not terrorists; we are freedom fighters. I am firm; thou art stubborn; she is pig headed. We are principled; they are bloody-minded. We are taking a firm stand; they are troublemakers. We are persistent; they are obsessed. We are brave; they are foolish. We are determined; they are fanatical. We are neutral and detached; they are negative and biased. We, in short, are right; and they are wrong. God, if we have one, is, of course, on our side.

Much of our language is designed to persuade at least as much as to inform. And the best way of persuading is to persuade others and ourselves that there are no serious alternatives to the line we are taking. If we send soldiers to another country the question is obvious, *should* we be doing this? If we *invade* another country, the answer is obvious, we should *not* be doing this. The answer is so obvious because it is implicit in the negative connotations associated with the language. Conversely, if we *liberate* a country, it is clear that this is an ethically desirable action. The ethical desirability is wrapped up in the language. *If you accept the language, or fail to notice that it is so ethically loaded, then you will accept the ethical position taken.* You may not even notice that there is an ethical issue at all. By buying into the language you will have bought in to the ethics, without even realising it. A great deal of seemingly 'neutral' technical language is in fact intensely full of ethical assumptions and connotations. For example, 'quality adjusted life years' become a technocratic, and seemingly neutral means of settling fundamental ethical issues about health care priorities.

Modern warfare is full of pseudo-neutral descriptions of the gory business that it truly is. We have 'collateral damage' rather than dead civilians. We have only ministries of *defence*. There are no ministries of *attack*. There used to be ministries of *war* and, although this is an honest enough description, the bloody connotations became too uncomfortable and so a more anodyne alternative was found, designed to dissociate us from uncomfortable truth. Killing is a systematic managerial process and the managerial/technocratic language used to describe it is the same as that used to account for any other production process of input/output optimisation.

The language we use reveals the position we are taking; our perspectives; our priorities and our values. As embodied human beings, who must always be occupying some position or another in the world, we can never adopt an independent, 'neutral', detached or dispassionate view, because no such view exists, even in principle. We can only *pretend* to such a view by using pseudo-neutral language. This will bury the ethical assumptions and priorities implicit in the perspective taken.

Even the most seemingly 'detached' scientist studies one topic rather than another and has made this a priority over all the other possibilities. He is interested in the topic, presumably because he finds it intrinsically interesting and also because it becomes in his interest, as a professional, to pursue it successfully. He has decided, with more or with less conscious deliberation, that this vocation is a worthwhile way of using his or her time and energy.

Technology may be used for good or ill. But most training and discussion concerns the technology rather the ethical aspects of the activity. The ethical implications tend to be either ignored by technologists or prejudiced within the pseudo-neutral language used. A chicken is given added bulk by injecting it with water. We might say that this reduces the price of the chicken. This is a neutral, factual account? Or is it? What if, instead, we say that it substantially adds to the price of the water? We may say that the process 'adds value' to the production process. Is this a neutral account? Or is it more accurate to say that the process reduces the real value of the chicken, and of the researcher who *inflicted* this process on the world? Perhaps it is honest to say that the process reduces the value for the customer who thought she was buying a chicken but was buying 40–50 per cent added water? Which accountant will be paid to provide a *true* and *fair* account of this (foul?) process?

This matter of the *burial of ethical assumptions within pseudo-neutral language* is crucially important to counsellors since clients are bringing them ethical issues to respond to all the time. However, the clients may well be unaware of the ethical assumptions they are making. They will probably want the counsellor to share their own ethical presuppositions without even clarifying what these are. They will want the counsellor to support their interests and accept their perspectives. They may well not say so, and they may not believe that this is their position. The counsellor, too, may wish to imagine that she is more independent of the client's values and interests than is really the case.

Language is continuously tilting, prejudicing and making invisible underlying ethical issues. *We may imagine that language is the neutral and transparent means of describing various human battlegrounds. But it is far more the actual battleground itself.* When people are in conflict, their language will be in conflict. There will be a battle of narratives. They will see matters differently and will want others to see, and speak, of the issue as they do. They will even want 'the other' to see themselves and each other differently. So often conflicts remain intractable because people cannot agree even how to talk about the issue, and so are a long way from agreeing on what to do about it.

Couple counselling, and much other counselling, concerns essentially ethical disputes; narrative battles about who should and should not have done, or did and did not do, what to whom. Counsellors cannot be 'value-free' or ethically neutral in relation to these ethical questions which are interwoven with other aspects of individual wellbeing and development. Counsellors can help by assisting clients in seeing the variety of ways in which they might talk about, and think about, their predicament. They can help by showing the client that all these narratives are saturated in value-laden assumptions. They can help in assisting clients with values-clarification. But *counsellors can only do this if they are themselves able to deconstruct the language used.* Moreover, counsellors can only act with ethical integrity if they recognise their wider ethical obligations and don't merely empathise with client perspectives.

Generally people think that God, or right, is on their side and they have an explanation and justification for their decisions. (Even if this has to be invented post hoc.) Everyone tends to think that they are ethically neutral and reasonable and that others are pig-headed. Self-esteem, perhaps, requires this, at least to some degree? We are inclined to think, obviously, that we are right. If I didn't think I was right about (whatever), then I would not think what I think. I would think and do something else.

When counsellors are faced with couples at war with each other, it is quickly obvious that there are two sides to the questions being discussed. The counsellor will be told that the other party has not merely been hurtful, they have also been morally reprehensible and wrong. But this lack of unanimity about perspectives and ethics will be equally true in issues brought to the counsellor by a single client. It can be assumed that people close to the client will *not* see contentious issues in the same way as the client. The client may well fail to know how others see them. The counsellor may have great difficulty finding out when they have no contact with other interested parties in the client's life.

What should be clear, though, is that 'neutrality' does not exist for the counsellor any more than it does for any other human being. Also, that it may not be in society's interest, and it may not be ethically right, to promote the interests and collude with the prejudices of the client. The ethical issues are fundamental to the agenda of counselling. They are part of the subject matter of counselling. They do not merely concern the manner in which the counselling is conducted. Ethics is (to use Aristotle's terminology), a *praxis.* It cannot, and should not, be reduced to the *techne* of codes of practice.

Ethical issues are generally made all too 'obvious' and/or invisible by the language we adopt to describe the problem. If we talk of a 'terrorist', our ethical perspective is clear – this is a 'bad' person. A terrorist is a person who attempts to settle a political dispute through killing people. However, the armed forces also comprise persons who attempt to settle a political dispute through killing people. The difference is that soldiers are better organised, obey orders rather than take responsibility, have more lethal weapons, and kill far more people.

It sometimes seems that we are more concerned about ethical rationalisation than ethical truth. We probably *need* to believe that what we are doing, whether alone or in organisations, is good and is well done. Rationalisation may well be more important to us than reason. We all seem to think that we are one of the good people, and perhaps this is necessary for our survival. No tribe, in history, has believed itself to be the bad, wrong and barbaric team. All have had a battery of reasons to explain and morally justify their actions. Even criminals tend to have good retionalisations to show that what they are doing, although it may seem bad, is not really so bad. Society is unjust. Society is amoral, it gives you a hard time. In all these circumstances, the only way to survive and show that you are a somebody is to commit crimes. It's a matter of respect, looking after your own, and maintaining self esteem. The Mafia chief says, 'I do not threaten, I merely make people offers they will not refuse'.

> If you can trick yourself into believing something that isn't true, you must be convincing, says Robert Trivers of Rutgers University in New Brunswick, New Jersey. He thinks that the same evolutionary forces that make straightforward deception a useful ability may also select for self-deception. Trivers even goes so far as to suggest that the conscious mind is largely just a 'social front, maintained to deceive others'. Truth, he argues, is stored in the unconscious, while the conscious is full of fabrication. That way, when you spin your yarn, all the telltale signs of deceit will be absent: no sweaty palms, no fidgeting, no shifty eyes. (*New Scientist*, (2001) vol 172 no 2322, 22 December:70)

This kind of rationalisation may assist us to justify 'bad' and competitive behaviour. It may also be useful in helping us to be 'good', to cooperate and stay loving and loyal: 'Not everybody lied to themselves about how wonderful their partner was, but those who did were much more likely to have an enduring relationship, the researchers found' (Ibid.).

We find ourselves in the first person and we assume that we, above all others, are persons. I am, first, a person myself and I am the only person I know in the first person. The persons who are closest to us are also persons. We treat them as persons, we empathise with their personal take on the world and we imagine what it is to be them, from their own first person perspective. Then there are those other persons who are less like us, who disagree with us and who, therefore, seem less like persons than we do.

The 'stubborn' ones we try to negotiate with, or better still, persuade. The pig-headed are more like pigs than persons. Perhaps they are more like rats? If so, shouldn't we exterminate them? Perhaps they are not really people at all; or not so much and so obviously persons, and personable, as we are. They are 'beyond the pale' and perhaps therefore they are beyond moral discourse, moral concern, human interest and any possibility of empathy.

Five hundred dead Chinese equals 50 dead French equals five dead in our town. That is the journalistic view. But why blame the journalists?[6] Presumably they are just responding to the perspective, and news priorities, of their readers? Everyone is human but some, we believe,[7] are more human than others. The less-than-fully-human need and deserve less concern, less respect, less empathy, less ethical treatment. They become faceless 'collateral damage'. They can be paid a dollar a day to make our shoes and we won't even think about it. Our grandchildren, let us hope, will be as horrified to read this in their history books as they will feel when reading about slaves and children climbing chimneys and working in coal mines.

Ethical imperatives are most intensive in relation to persons who are one of 'us'. Words that position people in relation to each other, like 'we', may seem innocuous, simple and neutral. But they are loaded with connotations, emotional meanings, expectations, obligations and entitlements, duties and rights. Identity likewise is strongly formed according to the words that position you in society. Who are you? Are you one of us? I am a brigadier in the British Army. I am a prefect at Eton College. I try to survive cleaning shoes on the street.

Ethics, identity, and language, then, are all inextricably linked. All require careful delineation if we are to act wisely and ethically. Ethics, moreover, is not an 'add-on' to our mental map of the world, but fundamentally shapes what we see and the way we see it.

Are we disinterested, dissociated or committed?

Social scientists have tended to retreat from the messy language of *praxis* and reduce their studies to *techne*. This withdrawal from human dialogue, and preference for managerial and professional diagnosis, diminishes humanity. It destroys any prospect of democracy and replaces it with the management and manipulation of public opinion. It thereby becomes exploitative, bureaucratic and unjust. Far from being detached, disinterested and ethically neutral, it is amoral and therefore *wrong*.

Individuals worn down by this alienating process may, of course, resort to counselling. But the underlying cause of the problem then remains unchallenged. In any case, counsellors may be increasingly forced into, or actively prefer, technocratic to humanist interventions. Technological language does not make scientific prejudice and power ploys disappear. All it does, as Foucault has shown, is make professional interest and prejudice *invisible*. The 'neutral', technological jargon merely hides the ethical stance and human interests at work. 'The confusion between the terms "subject" and "object" in quantitative psychology (in which we call people "subjects" but treat them as "objects", and we pretend to be objective but are still always deeply subjective) is a symptom of how deep a moral problem there is' (Banister et al. 1994:5). This (mis)use of language to turn people into objects is the first step towards exploiting them and treating them in an amoral fashion. Far from being ethically neutral, the pretence that the observer and her language is neutral and disembodied, is ethically wrong. It is this abuse that Habermas and other critical theorists of the Frankfurt school have so consistently challenged.

> To reduce human action to a constellation of terms such as 'performance', 'competence', 'doing' and 'skill' is not just to resort to a hopelessly crude language with which to describe serious human endeavours. In the end, it is to obliterate the humanness in human action. It is to deprive human being of *human* being. (Barnett 1994:178)

Jürgen Habermas has been recognised as a major critic of the modernist/technicist tendency to reduce human beings to objects of manipulation. He is also a defender of modernism against the drift of postmodernists towards nihilism and subjectivism. He acknowledges that naïve concepts of identity, rationality and objectivity cannot stand the sceptical onslaught from postmodern (and earlier) critics. But what of the prospect that there is no identity, only masks and presentations? Are we to believe that there is no rationality, only rationalisations? And that there are no objective facts, only subjective opinions? This prospect seems intolerable. Habermas seeks to argue that it is also untrue. He acknowledges, though, that we must sharpen up our understanding of truth, identity and rationality, if we are to preserve and renew our belief in our capacity to act responsibly, and to make sense both of our world and ourselves.

Habermas's solution emphatically does *not* follow the Cartesian route of going deeper into ourselves in isolation, and building up our view of the world from foundations of certain knowledge. We do not start from self, clarify our raw data and reasoning processes, and then build connections with our world. On the contrary, we need to understand that identity, reasoning and knowledge are all very substantially *social* processes. They can only be adequately understood from a social and sociological perspective. Habermas refers to 'communicative reason' and 'communicative action'. Reason and action are welded together; one is not conceptually coherent in the absence of the other. We are, after all, *embodied* creatures. Neither reason nor actions take place except as forms of *communication*, which is itself, of course, an inherently *social* process.

Habermas observes that we are social creatures, that we make sense of our selves, others and our world in a social context, via cooperation, via communication. This communication is not merely linguistic. It is often non-verbal arising from our cooperating with each other in joint ventures. It always takes place in a social *context* of one kind or another. I gesture to you to take a seat at the table, and contained within this gesture are many kinds of shared, tacit, knowledge and understanding about what is going to happen next and what this shared eating together signifies.[8] Certainly we disagree and conflict at times. But a great deal of our everyday survival depends on the fact that we *do* understand each other. We know what we are doing, what we are intending to do and what it all means within a larger social context whose meanings we also share and understand. In our focus on, and inevitable preoccupation with, areas of disagreement and misunderstanding, we lose sight of the larger context of consensus, cooperation, agreement and understanding.

Ethics, therefore, the questions about how we are to live with each other, how we are to treat each other, what we can expect to give to, and receive from, each other, is not just a matter of technical codes of practice. It lies at the heart of social formation which itself constructs identities, reasons and knowledge. Much of our identity emerges from our ethics.

> In communicative action, the very outcome of interaction is even made to depend on whether the participants can come to an agreement among themselves on an *intersubjectively valid* appraisal of their relations to the world. On this model of action, an interaction can succeed only if those involved arrive at a consensus among themselves, a consensus that depends on yes/no responses to claims potentially based on grounds. (Habermas 1997:106)

If we can't understand each other, we can't cooperate at all and therefore there is no society to belong to. All that we have is a bunch of individuals who can make no sense of each other. They cannot help each other because they cannot even make sense of what the other is doing, trying to do or wanting to do. Manifestly, though, we often do make sense of each other. *We merely need to look around at the complex interactions and interdependencies of our society and culture to know that the extreme nihilism and subjectivism of some postmodernists must be false.*

Our society may be far from perfect but if we have managed to achieve all this together we can't be quite as stupid, irrational or imaginary as some claim. *Habermas, then, in stark contrast to Descartes, builds identity, reason and knowledge not on the fact of private thought, but on fact of public action, interaction and cooperation.* 'Intersubjective understanding, because it is a communicative experience, cannot be carried out in a solipsistic manner. Understanding (*Verstehen*) a symbolic expression fundamentally requires participation in a process of reaching understanding. (*Verständigung*)' (Ibid.:112). *I* understand because *we* understand. Because we have been working together to try to understand. Even when, as now, I appear to be most cut off from society and privately ruminating in front of a word-processor, I am not sitting in Cartesian isolation. In fact I have had to steep myself in the communications from thinkers over many centuries, and respond both via speech and writing. I am not ploughing a lonely furrow. I am picking up where others left off; seeking to disseminate practical ideas more widely and passing on to others the opportunity to respond and develop further this discussion.

'Processes of reaching understanding are aimed at a consensus that depends on the intersubjective recognition of validity claims; and these claims can be reciprocally raised and fundamentally criticised by participants in communication' (Ibid.:136). We may disagree, but the very process of disagreement exists in the larger context of our trying to make sense of each other and learn from each other. Also, we can genuinely discuss our agreements and disagreements only insofar as we recognise the capacity of the other to have a genuine discussion with us, to have genuine, coherent views and experiences that are worth discussing. To make a serious case against the ideas of another is to complement, to some degree at least, their own formation of ideas. Clearly they are interesting enough to justify our efforts to challenge them.

Habermas reminds us (Ibid.:125) that every utterance always takes place within a social context and that we must understand the context if we are to make sense of what people say. 'In everyday communication an utterance never stands alone; a semantic content accrues to it from the context the speaker presupposes that the hearer understands. The interpreter too must penetrate that context of reference as a participating partner in interaction.' The meaning of words, sentences, actions, all depend to a great degree on context. They are all embedded in the social. The meanings of even the most fundamental and day to day words are heavily determined by context: 'The meaning of sentences in which terms such as 'I' and 'you', 'here' and 'now', 'this' and 'that' appear varies with the situation of speech' (Ibid.:124).

I have previously shown that 'here' and 'now' mean very different things to geologists, historians and journalists. Likewise, *the very meaning of the question 'who am I?' is hugely determined by the context.* 'I' exists in relation to 'you' and 'we', and so the nature of 'I' is greatly influenced by context. But that emphatically does *not* imply that 'I' can just mean anything at all. There are principles and patterns to the usage (and abuse) of 'I'.

> If we assume that the human species maintains itself through the socially co-ordinated activities of its members and that this co-ordination has to be established through communication – and in certain central spheres through communication aimed at reaching agreement – then the reproduction of the species *also* requires satisfying the conditions of a rationality that is inherent in communicative action. (Ibid.:397)

Our very survival depends on our ability to communicate, to cooperate, understand, to share a society, projects, and ethics. 'A process of self-preservation that has to satisfy the rationality conditions of communicative action becomes dependent on the integrative accomplishments of subjects who co-ordinate their actions via criticisable validity claims' (Ibid.:398). If I am to preserve myself I had better help to preserve society. If I am to understand *for myself*, I had better try to understand *with you*. If I am to understand myself I had better try to understand you, because all these processes are interconnected. I simply cannot achieve one without the other. *Societies, and the ethics that construct them, far from constraining the development of individuals, are essential if individuals are to develop at all.* 'Communicative reason does not simply encounter ready-made subjects and systems; rather, it takes part in structuring what is to be preserved' (Ibid.:398).

For Habermas, communication, cooperation and mutual efforts to understand do not merely take place *within* a society. They are, more profoundly, *the very means by which societies and individuals are constructed, and maintained.* Ethics, far from being an add-on, a subject for the occasional debate, lie at the very heart of the process of cooperation, mutual respect and identify formation.

Even my *autonomy* is not in fact autonomous from the society of which I am a part. An autonomous individual, acting with agency and responsibility, is not someone acting independently of, and outside of, or beyond, society. Responsible, autonomous individuals negotiate intelligently with the people and communities around them, of which they are a part. If others have any doubt about it, (and generally they do not), *I can show that I am responsible by the account of my actions and ideas that I am able to give, if asked.* I don't show that I am responsible by making some strange Cartesian claim that, half a second before doing something, I had a first person experience of a 'decision'.

We do not run our lives in our minds, a split second before running them in the material world. If we tried we would cripple ourselves and we would not make ourselves any more responsible. I do not become more responsible by having the thought of an action just prior to doing the action. As a tennis player, for example, I am fully responsible for returning your volley low across the net. I may or may not have had a mental image of some kind prior to the action. (In the case of tennis this is undesirable; it is much better to watch the ball than an image in your head.) Either way, I am responsible. I am an autonomous player though, as such, integrated within, and a part of, the social and cultural, rule-based, system that is tennis.

But ethics, identity, responsibility and autonomy can all be undermined when we give up trying to understand other people and instead decide to treat them as objects of manipulation. Then we see them as passive objects of *our* agendas. They must follow our programme. They must develop the skills that *we* consider important. They must see things as we see them. They must understand that we are the ones that understand, that we do the understanding around here, and that their understandings only matter when they are *our* understandings.

In such a situation human respect, cooperation, and genuine dialogue cease to exist. Instead we have specialist, expert, professional observers – us – and relatively naïve and unknowing objects of observation – them. We observe what others do and infer why. We are not much interested in the other's understanding of what they are doing and why since we assume that they are, to a substantial degree at least, and compared with ourselves, ignorant, lacking in awareness, self-awareness, knowledge and understanding. This process of *diagnosis and control*, rather than *dialogue and cooperation*, is manipulative, undemocratic, disrespectful – intrinsically unethical. 'According to the presuppositions of the communicative model of action, the agent possesses just as rich an interpretative competence as the observer himself' (Ibid.:118).

So what are the prospects for democracy and humanity? How much dialogue in fact exists? How many good[9] managers are there, who are genuinely interested in the suggestions, understandings, agendas and intentions of their staff? Do we listen and seek consensus? Or do we manage appearances, prey on weaknesses and blind spots, and colonise the language with our own concepts and metaphors? Many in the Frankfurt School were pessimists about the social prospects. Adorno and Horkheimer, for example, described the predicament of alienation, bureaucracy and dehumanisation but saw no real solution in sight. Earlier still, and prior to the Frankfurt programmes, Max Weber was less than optimistic about the possibilities of genuine human progress given the misuse of science and technology, against the interests and well being of the majority. 'Weber too shares in the pessimistic appraisal of scientific civilisation. He mistrusts the rationalisation processes set loose and detached from ethical value orientations, which he observes in modern societies – so much so that in his theory of rationalisation, science and technology forfeit their paradigmatic status' (Ibid.:155).

But Habermas himself is more of an optimist. Ironically, given his stress on the importance of dialogue, shared life-worlds, and respect for 'ordinary' understandings, Habermas' own language is not always terribly accessible. It may often be daunting and intimidating even to fellow academics. It would be preferable if communicative reason was more overtly linked to communicative action and if the language used succeeded more often in communicating to a wider audience. 'The term "life-world" is that of Jürgen Habermas and it captures the point that what is at issue is an education for the world of human life' (Barnett 1994:178).

Habermas seeks to protect the enlightenment agenda that progress is possible, that we can, and should, cooperate, that we can make sense of others and ourselves and make a world more fit for human beings. But, in so doing, we need to abandon naïvety about identity, reason and objectivity. 'Too much of the world still starves, dies young and is wasted by systematic greed and evil for anyone to write the obituaries of philosophy, ideology and humanism' (O'Neil 1995:196).

After all the postmodern scepticism, sophistication and cosmopolitanism, certain truths remain intact: 'The ideal cure for the effects of poverty is money, social justice, and a social order which minimises the distance between classes' (Sabo & Havens 2000:83).

Questions for Counsellors

1. When purchasing, or selling, a counselling course, what relative weight do you give to commercial, academic and ethical considerations?
2. What, if anything, do you think is missing from counsellor codes of practice as regards the counsellor's ethical responsibilities?

3. How far, if at all, do you agree with Aristotle that virtue is essential to human wellbeing?
4. Do you think it is useful to distinguish between ethical authoritarianism and ethical authorities? Are counsellors generally ethical authorities, authoritarians, or amoral?
5. Do you think counsellors should be ethical authorities? How far do they succeed within this role at present and what can, and should, be done to assist them? How do you introduce the discourse of 'ought' in your dialogue with clients?
6. How far do you agree that 'personal growth' needs to be in harmony with social context? What specific examples of this principle can you think of?
7. How far do you agree with Taylor that 'Being a self is inseparable from existing in a space of moral issues, to do with identity and how one ought to be.'?
8. How far do you agree with Barnett that 'Technicism seems to be value-free but is shot through with values.'?
9. How far do you think that society needs to return to 'traditional' values? Which values deserve rehabilitation? Which were always a false currency and need to be continually rejected?
10. Which of your clients do you consider were behaving unethically? Did they suffer as a result? What did you do about it? What, on reflection should you have done about it? What instances come to mind?
11. How far, in your view, do the underlying ethics of person-centred, cognitive-behavioural, and psycho-dynamic schools of counselling differ? What are the merits and demerits of each? What is missing from each and all of them?
12. Which of your clients could become more human, and more ethical, if they *expressed* their feelings more? Which of your clients could become more human, and more ethical, if they *controlled* and *inhibited* their feelings more? What examples come to mind?
13. How far do agree with Peck that 'We must not assume that someone whose feelings are modulated and controlled is not a passionate person.'?
14. Do you see existential 'angst' as a courageous confrontation with human responsibility? As 'high IQ whimpering on a cosmic scale'? Which is closest to your own ethical position on the matter?
15. How far do you think people can be guilty of innocence, naïvety and romanticism? Do any examples from your own experience come to mind?
16. How far do you agree that we find ourselves and feel good about ourselves to the extent that we live in communities that we believe in, that we are committed to, that we think will support us and which deserve our support?
17. How far do you think the personal problems presented by your clients are the result of ethical, social or political failings? What specific examples come to mind?
18. How far do you agree with Nussbaum that 'a corrupt and corrupting society may well have formed the patient's beliefs about the good life, and even about herself.' What instances of this problem come to mind from your own client experience?
19. How far do agree with Lasch that 'Escape through irony and critical self-awareness is in any case itself an illusion; at best it provides only momentary relief'?
20. Do we have more or less reason to despair than – which generation of ancestors? Are we primarily suffering, or progressing, via rising expectations? Are our expectations rising?
21. How far do you agree with Rosen that what has occurred as a result of the therapeutic culture is 'the suppression of natural narrative speech itself, the suppression of language in its richest, most associative, most unpredictable, revealing and hence therapeutic form.'?
22. What, in your own words, is your understanding of Aristotle's distinction between *praxis* and *techne*? How relevant and important, do you think, is this distinction in the twenty-first century?
23. What ethical assumptions are buried in the language used by your clients? What examples come to mind?
24. What ethical assumptions are buried in the language you use with your clients? What examples come to mind?
25. Do you think that your clients are bringing to you narrative battles to address – some, most or all of the time? What do you about it? What specific examples come to mind?
26. How often do you, should you, challenge the ethical perspective of clients? What specific examples come to mind?

27. What experience and training do you have, and do you need, to assist clients in values-clarification and language deconstruction? What specific examples come to mind?
28. Can you envisage instances where you should stand up for the interests of society against the interests as perceived by the client? What specific examples come to mind?
29. How far do you agree that ethical rationalisation appears to be more important than ethical reasoning?
30. How far do you consider you should challenge client concepts of 'the good' when, in your view, their beliefs are not good for anyone?
31. Who, in your view, carries any particular authority concerning ethics and what is good?
32. What is, and what is the importance of, *dialogue* in preserving humanity, identity and ethical values? What do you think are its prospects?
33. How far do counsellors have a role in assisting clients to become good citizens?

CHAPTER 7

What Was It Like For You? – Measuring and Assessing Change in Identity

I shall argue in this chapter that the identity of counselling needs to be fundamentally reconstructed. In developing this argument, I hope to clarify our understanding of the nature of *personal* identity; what it is to be a person and what is, and is not, involved in treating someone as a person. This change in the identity of counselling will be in the long-term interests both of counsellors and of clients. But it will not take place unless counsellors change the way they see themselves, their clients, their practice, and the nature of this practice.

> 'The pursuit of truth in some directions is even injurious to happiness, because it compels us to take leave of delusions which were pleasant while they lasted'. (A. E. Houseman, quoted in Dineen 1999:130)

> 'That scepsis, that passion not to be fooled and not to fool anyone else, does not seem to be as fundamental a part of all psychologists' mental equipment as it was half a century ago.'[1] (Paul Meehl, former President of American Psychological Association, quoted in Dineen 1999:115)

Persons and reasons versus treatments and results

How far can we know another person? How far do we need to know ourselves in order to know another person? Do counsellors have superior ways of knowing clients than the rest of us? How well do they need to know clients in order to assist them? What evidence is there that they have knowledge of clients and that they can assist them?

To begin with I want to summarise the current position as regards research into counselling, and then move on to ask:

1. Where do we go from here?
2. What has been missing within counselling and how can these gaps be filled?
3. How far could, and should, we tackle the problem of research by thinking differently about the very identity of counselling?

4. If counsellors saw themselves differently how would that affect the way they see clients?

I want to argue that *if counselling is to change it will need to embrace a sociological, cultural and philosophical imagination. It will need to see itself as a personal and cultural activity more than a psychological or quasi-medical treatment.* It will need to accentuate its concern for *dialogue* and *cooperation*, as opposed to *diagnosis* and *control.* In doing so, it would do well to draw on ideas about reason, identity and communication developed by Jürgen Habermas who seeks to relate democratic practice with personal development; social solidarity with individual self-esteem; intellectual understanding with cooperative inquiry.

As a diagnosis and treatment, evidence for the efficacy of counselling is very poor. But as a form of dialogue, a cultural product, counselling may have an honourable and secure future. To ask if counselling is effective may be a bit like asking if a novel by Dickens, or a Mills and Boon author, or a play by Shakespeare, is effective. *Questions concerning effectiveness may themselves prove to be ineffective questions,* at least in some circumstances. The line of questioning may be inappropriate to the reality of the product. People talk about what they got out of Shakespeare and what good they found in him. But does it make sense to ask if Shakespeare is *effective*?

Likewise, we might best ask what we got from a particular counsellor and what there was to be got from her, rather than ask whether she was effective. The management perspective consists in asking what is *effective* and wanting desired *outcomes.* The human perspective asks for, and engages in dialogue with, the *reasons* that people do what they do. *Managers look for results. People look for, and discuss, reasons,* (and the process of doing so is an intrinsic part of what it is to be human).

We may, in any case, be wiser to look for the reasons people seek counselling rather than boasting about the results since, as we shall see, the outcomes of talking programmes, from a managerial perspective, are generally disappointing. 'The bitter truth is that most experimental psychological knowledge is either trivial or contradictory or both' (Pilgrim & Treacher 1991:64).

I have written elsewhere (Howard 1996) about the difficulties experienced by psychologists in developing interesting insights about human beings. Efforts to research the effectiveness and insights of counselling have run into very substantial obstacles. It is not at all clear that counsellors pay much attention to the research studies into the efficacy of counselling. Perhaps that is just as well. They would find the subject extremely demoralising. 'An anti-intellectual emotional stance seems integral to therapeutic culture today. It is not therapeutics as such, but its peculiarly strident celebration of emotionalism that lends it a strikingly anti-intellectual character' (Furedi 2004:159).

The problem is not diminished when, as we shall see, counselling organisations, like the British Association for Counselling and Psychotherapy, seek to turn a sow's ear into a silk purse, by drawing unwarrantedly optimistic conclusions from a very disheartening set of data. 'As Frank Farley, a past president of the APA,[2] says, "the science side of psychology is in selling ourselves in the market"'[3] (Dineen 1999:131).

There seems to be both individual and collective denial concerning the essential failure to demonstrate efficacy in counselling. Counsellors are reluctant to address the problem and are certainly little inclined to inform clients who themselves, once committed to counselling, want to believe that something good will come out of the process. There is nothing new in this. Patients have always been predisposed to have faith in the powers of their chosen healer. How, otherwise, could they proceed? And, after a substantial commitment of time, money, physical pain and/or heartache, patients have always wanted to look for positive outcomes wherever these might be found. They can always console themselves by thinking that, without this treatment, they would have been even worse off. This might well be true, since the very existence of faith in a health programme can itself be healing and helpful, as every placebo study has shown. 'people enter therapy when they are extremely unhappy, they are less likely to be unhappy later, independent of the effects of the therapy itself. In fact, even if the therapy has been downright harmful, people are less likely to be as unhappy later as when they entered therapy.' (Ibid.:125).[4]

'Counselling' is very large umbrella term beneath which shelter many different and often profoundly opposed views about human beings and how to treat them. There are managerialists of one kind or another, who seek to diagnose, treat, train and control. There are humanists who wish to enable, negotiate, respect, and 'empower' – though this has now become a greatly abused and over-used word. I shall argue that those who offer counselling of a more humanist variety ought to be assessed in the same way that other *cultural* producers are assessed. In the process, as we shall see, many of the questions about efficacy will need to be recast. Instead of asking clients about the *effects* that counselling had on them, perhaps we would get more to the heart of the matter of counselling by asking clients for the *reasons* they chose counselling and the *reasons* they did, or did not, value the experience?

Critics use sophisticated forms of discourse to discuss the quality of cultural products. There is plenty of room for individual opinion, though criticism is not merely an expression of opinion. There are criteria, but they are cultural, aesthetic and ethical rather than psychological or medical.

Avant-garde critics may not agree with laypersons. Perhaps most of us prefer tepid middlebrow cultural products to more demanding works? So it is with art, literature and music; so it may also be with counselling. In counselling, as in art, there will no doubt be some who will want to have their prejudices protected rather than face anything that makes serious demands upon them.

The same dilemmas concerning the state funding of arts, of popular culture versus élite arts, may emerge concerning the state funding of counselling. When people talk about how to make meanings in their lives, some will seek much more sophisticated, subtle, cosmopolitan and demanding narratives than others. Some will settle for a few homilies, others may wish to wrestle with Nietzsche. In either case, talk of 'efficacy' and 'outcomes' tends rather to miss the heart of the matter. The true nature and quality of humanist counselling, literature, art, music as cultural products is not understood by discourse about outcomes and efficacy. Another kind of discourse is needed, and humanist counsellors might be wiser to look at how quality issues are dealt with in the arts and humanities rather than in the social and natural sciences or within technologies of management or healthcare.

Professionals versus amateurs

If there is one conclusion that researchers in any topic tend to agree on, it is that there needs to be more research! Given the number of different kinds of theory and practice within counselling it is true enough that the effectiveness of many has been little studied. On the other hand it is a mistake to conclude that no general observations can yet be made about efficacy in counselling. Time and time again different studies come out with essentially the same results. Essentially they show that there is no conclusive evidence that professional counselling 'works' better than other, less expensive professional *and non-professional* interventions. 'The belief that simply providing more services will lead to improved outcomes has been shown to be delusional'[5] (Kimberly Hoagwood from National Institute of Mental Health, quoted in Dineen 1999:130).

Research also shows that no particular school of counselling scores significantly better than any of its rivals. Of course, it must be asked, what are we saying when we say that counselling does, or does not, 'work'? What are the criteria for success? This is, of course, a huge question. Suffice it to say, at this stage, that *whatever* the defined outcome, non-professionals and other professionals tend to achieve it as well as counsellors. So, professional counselling does not work in that it does not appear to provide any ingredients that cannot be found, more readily and more cheaply, elsewhere. Hence Dawes' observation:

> We should not be pouring out resources and money to support high-priced people who do not help others better than those with far less training would, and whose judgements and predictions are actually worse than the simplest statistical conclusion based on 'obvious' variables. Instead, we should take seriously the findings that effectiveness of therapy is unrelated to the training or credentials of the therapist . . . Virtually all the research – and this book will reference more than three hundred empirical investigations and summaries of investigations – has found that these professionals' claims to superior intuitive insight, understanding, and skill as therapists are simply invalid. (Dawes 1996:5, 8)

Time and time again, though, researchers do show that clients are inclined to be happy with, and appreciative of, the efforts made by counsellors. This positive response may well itself have a positive influence on the well-being of clients.

There is, in other words, a strong placebo ingredient at work in counselling as in most other medical and personal care interventions. *Counselling is definitely likely to be better than nothing.* This should hardly come as a surprise or be a cause of any celebration. Nothing is not very much at all, and so when counselling is compared with nothing it often, but not always, does better. 'Studies consistently show that therapists tend to see more improvement than anyone else, followed closely by their clients. Friends, family and other observers come in a distant, and often unimpressed, third' (Dineen 1999:97).

It now seems certain that most medical interventions, throughout history, were based on ignorance rather than knowledge of the human body. They contained no active ingredients, did not help the patient, and may often have harmed them. It is equally certain that these interventions were often better than nothing, since nothing is an intolerable prospect when we are sick, diseased or ill at ease. We have to believe that something can be done; that somebody is doing something; that the somebody of choice knows what they are doing; and that the result will be better than nothing.[6] 'Prioleau et al. (1983) suggest that only placebo controls, in which clients genuinely believe they are receiving treatment that will help them and in which the treatment does not comprise any other "active ingredients" apart from this belief, can operate as true controls in testing the effectiveness of therapy' (McLeod 1994:133).

But when counselling is matched against, even just the superficial pretence of something comparable, its performance is disappointing: 'If anything, the history of psychotherapy research shows that when a psychotherapy finally confronts a credible placebo, it rarely wins' (Erwin 1997:154). To say that the research *results* concerning counselling are not conclusive is not the same as saying that the *research* itself is inconclusive. Counsellors make this error of logic over and over again. Researchers have not yet shown that counselling works. Counsellors obviously assume that counselling does work. And so counsellors conclude that researchers have not done any conclusive research, and that they will only have done so when they have shown conclusive evidence of the efficacy of counselling.

'The American Psychological Association has stated that it is "important, perhaps imperative, that psychology begin *to assemble a body of persuasive evidence* bearing on the value of specific educational and training experience"'[7] (Dineen 1999:103). Nobody wants to entertain the possibility, indeed the high likelihood, that researchers *have already shown conclusively* that counselling, in most of its current forms, is *a weak and inconclusive intervention.* In case you have any doubts about this, I now consider the position as summarised by a variety of commentators. This will be hard hitting information and acutely painful for those counsellors who still hope to be buttressed by research. *But be patient and you will see that I am not seeking to bury counselling, merely to (radically) reconstruct it.*

> Despite a volume of research which by now amounts to a total of several hundred published studies (Smith et al. 1980) there are a number of serious methodological

> problems associated with attempts to assess the effectiveness of counselling or therapy (Kazdin, 1994). As a result, it is often hard to interpret whether these studies as a whole do or do not given unequivocal support to the idea that counselling or therapy is generally helpful. (McLeod 1994:121)

McLeod concludes that more research is needed. He is, himself, a researcher and so has an interest in keeping the business in business. Researchers are not yet able to say that they have found any active ingredients, but urge that they should keep on looking. Yet for how long?

> Most of the studies reviewed by Hattie et al. (1984) were comparison group designs which showed that non-professionals were equally effective as highly trained professional counsellors . . . It would be only moderately interesting to discover that non-professional volunteers were more effective than no treatment. It is very interesting to discover that these volunteers produce outcomes that are the equal of those reported by the professionals. (Ibid.:134)

Notice this, non-professional volunteers do as well as trained counsellors. They are better than nothing, as you might expect, *and* they are as good as the professionals. As McLeod says, this is *very* interesting. It raises the profound question, do counsellors yet deserve to claim professional status at all if they cannot improve on the performance of amateurs? Do counsellors and counselling organisations take much interest in this research? Of course they don't. It is not in their professional interests to do so. Counselling, if it is claimed to be a form of treatment, is where medicine was in the Middle Ages. At that time a layperson could fiddle about in a plausible looking way with someone's brain and they would do no more harm or good than the 'professional' brain surgeon. Now, at last, medicine really is a profession, with a real knowledge base that is far in advance of a layperson's. Even the thought that an amateur brain surgeon could be as good as a professional is laughable. But research continues to show that amateur '*mind*scapers' are, regularly and repeatedly, just as good as accredited counsellors. 'Strupp and Hadley[8]: Professionals were no more effective than untrained professors' (Dineen 1999:103). Does that lead the British Association for Counselling and Psychotherapy, and other agencies, to withdraw their accreditation programmes? Of course not. But it *should* if the interests of clients, as opposed to accredited counsellors, were being protected.

> there are as many *certified* charlatans and exploiters of people as there are uncertified. (Rogers 1980:244)

> One hundred and fifty four comparisons from 39 studies indicated that clients who seek help from paraprofessionals are more likely to achieve resolution of their problems than those who consult professionals. [Hattie 1984] . . . In general, there was no difference between the outcome of patients treated by trained and untrained persons. [Berman & Norton 1985] (Bergin & Garfield 1994:171)

This is a lot of research work. Over and over again amateurs are doing as well as professionals. It ought to be leading would-be counselling professionals to ask absolutely fundamental questions about the nature of their practice. I see little evidence of this. On the contrary there appears to be a collective process of denial. Get the mechanisms into place, produce codes of practice, develop minimal hours of training and supervision, produce all the appearances of professional status and perhaps counselling can pass itself off as a profession?

The paraphernalia of professional status can easily be produced, but *this tells us nothing whatever about whether an activity really has a genuine knowledge and skill base and really is a profession.* 'Quality standards' can be, and are, produced for astrologers and could easily be applied to any medieval medical practice you care to think of. We could produce codes of practice, continuing professional development programmes, and all the rest, for phrenologists, sorcerers, witches, wailers and gnashers of teeth. You name it. All the accountrements, dressings, procedures, pomp and circumstance of professional status could be put in place. But the quality of the would-be 'profession' would not be improved one iota.

'It is also a proposition to be taken seriously that psychotherapy (at least in all its established professional pretentiousness) offers only polished illusions (see Szasz 1988; Smail 1984, 1987) (Dryden & Feltham 1992:257). These conclusions are repeated over and over again:

> Nonprofessional and inexperienced therapists appear to do quite well compared with trained and experienced individuals. (Roth and Fonagy 1996:287)
>
> There is only a modest relationship between training and outcome, or between experience and outcome, although the evidence for the latter is stronger than that for the former. (Ibid.:37)
>
> Therapist training, experience, technique and outcome: Orlinsky and Howard (1980): Professional qualification was not associated with outcome, but greater experience was. (Ibid.:346)

Compare this with the view taken by the British Association for Counselling and Psychotherapy media department press release: 'This most recent BACP membership survey shows that members themselves are increasingly seeking higher professional qualifications. This is good news for the public.'

Experience helps, as you might expect. Indeed it would be very surprising indeed if we learnt nothing from, and could show no benefit as a result of, long experience. But even the effects of experience are not very large: 'Overall, the meta-analytic reviews of psychotherapy that have proved correlational data have not suggested a substantial relationship between experience and outcome . . . it would seem that little empirically solid data has been added to the debate over whether experience and training make a difference in client outcome (Bergin & Garfield 1994:170–1).

Certainly it is the case that professional qualification is not associated with outcome but you can be sure that this will not affect the stampede towards professional qualification. *Think of all the time and money being spent on training that cannot demonstrate a better than amateur result.* Erwin (1997) acknowledges that clients might do just as well if they turned to amateur sources. But everyone is very busy. Maybe there is nowhere else they can go? In any case, 'counselling' – whatever it might mean in practice – is the flavour of our time and so perhaps is the major beneficiary of placebo effects: 'Most of the various forms of psychotherapy, *as far as anyone knows*, are not more effective than credible placebos' (Erwin 1997:145). 'Perhaps they could obtain such benefits from talking to spouses or friends, or to their clergy, or even to the "psychic counsellors" who advertise on American television, but many people do not want to do any of these things. For these people, professional psychological treatment, whatever its defects, is all that is left' (Ibid.:161).

As a result of this growth in the demand for counselling, the UK's National Health Service has been under increasing pressure to supply counsellors within primary health care as a part of the range of services offered in general practice. In a very short space of time, counsellors, of one kind or another, were to be found working alongside medical practitioners, practice nurses and other ancillary staff such that, at the time of writing,[9] 50 per cent of GP surgeries now employ counsellors. This is an enormous growth in resourcing. Is it worth all the expense? Does it 'work'? 'Very few investigations demonstrate any consistent benefit to patients from counselling, and no studies show generic counselling to add to standard general-practice care' (Roth & Fonagy 1996:261).

Is it scandalous to have introduced a new intervention, on such a scale and at such expense, with so little evidence of its efficacy? Roth and Fonagy (1996:262) think *not*:

> While there is little evidence for the value of generic counselling in contrast to treatment as usual, this does not imply that generic counselling is of little value within primary care settings. Rather it may suggest that general practitioners have considerable generic counselling skills, though clearly this may not be the most cost effective use of their time.

In other words, doctors, despite, until recently, having had little training in communication – never mind counselling – and despite their often somewhat technological focus, do as well as counsellors in counselling. They have 'generic counselling skills'. Roth and Fonagy offer no evidence for this, but it may well be, given the performance of amateur counsellors, that many or most of us have 'generic counselling skills'. We all, presumably, unless we are real hermits and introverts, learn something over the years about how to talk to people and even how to listen to, attend to, and cooperate with others.

Roth and Fonagy suggest that counselling by GPs, for all their 'generic skills' may not be cost effective. Rowland and Tolly (1995) examine this question in more detail. Their conclusions is that counsellors do *not* provide better value for money than GPs:

Case Study

	Counsellor option	GP option
Percentage feeling happier	80	45
Cost per 1 per cent feeling happier	£1.21	£0.11
Percentage coping better	77	40
Cost per 1 per cent coping better	£1.26	£0.17

(Tolley and Rowland 1995:182)

Counsellors get better results than GPs but look at the costs involved! More clients are happier with the counsellor, and more are 'coping better'. *Given that clients are getting far more time and attention from counsellors than doctors can provide, these results are not surprising.* The results are nearly twice as good but the cost per 1 per cent coping better is more than *700 per cent* greater with counsellors. It costs *1,100%* more for 1 per cent to feel happier with a counsellor than with a GP. *Counsellors bring an extra smile, but at a prohibitive price*!

The results are similarly disappointing in a more recent major study:

A statistical summary (or meta-analysis) of the results found that:

- Counselling reduced psychological distress more than usual GP care in the short-term (six weeks to 6 months).
- The overall benefits were modest in size.
- Counselling was no better than usual GP care in the long-term (over 8–12 months).

Although patients often report satisfaction with their treatment, such measures may not provide clinicians and service managers with the information they need: did the treatment significantly improve patients' well-being and functioning? (Bower et al. 2001)

The British Association for Counselling and Psychotherapy (BACP) spun this into a more positive summary: 'Professional counselling services can help take the pressure off GPs – this report shows professional counselling is not only efficacious, it is efficient . . .' (BACP Deputy Chief Executive Alan Jamieson). Likewise, BACP stated that: 'A new study to be summarised in the *BMJ* on 2nd December [2001] shows that the most effective help for the treatment of DEPRESSION lasting less than a year is COUNSELLING' (From Phillip Hodson Head of Media Relations). Compare this with the Bower et al.'s (2001) actual study of counselling in Primary Care:

One study compared counselling and usual GP care in the management of chronic depression (i.e. symptoms of six months duration or more). A mix of psychodynamic and cognitive-behavioural counselling was used. Results indicated NO BENEFITS ASSOCIATED WITH COUNSELLING at six or twelve month follow-up.

Table 7.1

BACP media relations department	Research evidence
Workplace counselling is effective in relieving the symptoms of both anxiety AND depression.	Anxiety (Post-Traumatic Stress Disorder): there is good evidence that generic counselling is not particularly effective in those who develop this condition. (Roth & Fonagy 1996:169) Depression: The superiority of psychotherapeutic treatment over medical treatment is small and unreliable across studies. (Roth & Fonagy 1996:101)
All styles of counselling turn out to be helpful.	Parloff, in reviewing nearly 500 rigorously controlled studies, concluded that 'the research evidence . . . has not met the needs of policy makers and does not greatly enhance the credibility of the field of psychotherapy.'[1] (Dineen 1999:235)
Successful results can be achieved after as little as 3–8 sessions of counselling	Depression: The efficacy of brief interventions is poor in the longer-term. (Roth & Fonagy 1996:100)

Note: [1] Parloff, M. B. (1982) 'Psychotherapy Research Evidence and Reimbursement Decisions: Bambi Meets Godzilla'. *American Journal of Psychiatry*, 139(6), June:721.

It is very interesting indeed to compare some of the press releases of the BACP with more sober descriptions of research evidence. For example compare the entries in Table 7.1.

Throw more time and attention at a patient and they benefit a little, as might be expected. But the benefit tends not to last. Given all the other demands for resources within the National Health Service, it is not obvious that this growth of resourcing of counselling is the best use of tax payers' money. Patients/clients obviously much prefer 6 × 50 minutes from a counsellor than 1 × 6 minutes from a GP. But: *Are the worried well from middle class backgrounds displacing health care attention away from the severely ill so that they themselves can receive more time and attention?* Mental health services, at the time of writing, are close to collapse in London. People suffering from chronic, severe, and deeply disabling mental illness receive remarkably little time and attention. The Royal College of Psychiatrists has repeatedly expressed concern about the lack of funding.

> There are worries that scarce resources have been appropriated for less disabling conditions (Patmore & Weaver, 1991) and that psychotherapy services are sometimes seen as providing expert help to those with mild difficulties while those with more severe and complex health needs are relatively neglected. (Roth & Fonagy 1996:39).

All must have prizes?

In defence of counselling, it is argued that this profession is in the early stages of its development. There are many fundamentally different forms; they cannot all be expected to work. Perhaps *one's own* preferred school of counselling is best? Perhaps evidence will soon be available to show how efficacious it really is? The evidence so far suggests otherwise:

> What has really challenged counsellors in relation to the theories they adhere to is the still widely accepted finding, from psychotherapy outcome research, that in terms of effectiveness there is little if any difference between the different models (Luborsky et al., 1975 *Archives of General psychiatry*, 32, 995–1008).
>
> in fact no evidence exists which demonstrates that some theoretical approaches to therapy are more effective than others (A. E. Kazdin, 'Comparative outcome studies of psychotherapy: methodological issues and strategies', *Journal of Consulting and Clinical Psychology*, 54:729–57, 1986). (Spinelli 1994:76)

This evidence repeats, over and over again. It is conclusive that no brand of therapy can be shown to be better than all the others.

> One of the most difficult findings to conceptualise theoretically or to use practically is the continuing and frequent lack of difference in the outcomes of various techniques. With some exceptions, which we will consider, there is massive evidence that psychotherapeutic techniques do not have specific effects; yet there is tremendous resistance to accepting this finding as a legitimate one. (Bergin & Garfield 1994:822)

Notice this, from the enormous meta-analysis of research over 30 years by Bergin and Garfield: There is a *continuing* and *frequent* failure to show difference in outcomes. There is *massive* evidence that there are no specific effects. There is *tremendous* resistance from counsellors. They do not wish to accept this finding. So how do they respond? By attacking Bergin and Garfield or others? Not at all. They have nothing to attack with. Were they to attack they would be crushed; their position would become all the more obviously unsustainable. So, instead, counsellors simply *ignore* all this research work and therefore *fail to draw the essential conclusions about the identity of counselling that I wish, later, to argue for.*

Meanwhile BACP's media relations department cherry picks results and spins its own conclusions.[10]

'Group and family treatment methods show few differences in results as compared with individual methods' (Bergin & Garfield 1994:822). 'There is no evidence that individual therapy has superior outcomes to group therapy' (Feltham 1995:90). Group and family treatments tend to be cheaper. But the message is ignored.

Psychodynamic and person-centred counsellors have felt particularly challenged by researchers since they have been less inclined to clarify outcomes in the way that cognitive behaviourists like to do.

> overall the trend has been away from the non-directive orientation. This has largely been due to evidence indicating that therapy oriented entirely by the traditional

client-centred, non-directive approach to treatment has not produced very large effect sizes . . . Research evidence has also significantly undermined the notion that interpretation in general, and transference interpretation in particular, is the key to efficacy in this approach. (Bergin & Garfield 1994:824)

As Bergin and Garfield observe, the concept of 'transference', so central within psychodynamic counselling, has been *significantly undermined* by research evidence. Given the substantial costs and training requirements of psychodynamic schools their future looks decidedly bleak. Psychodynamic approaches have peaked in numbers and status of practitioners. They are now in headlong decline and it is hard to see how this decline will be averted. Universities are even closing down whole departments of psychodynamically oriented training programmes.

So is the future to be found among cognitive-behavioural practitioners?

Cognitive-behavioural approaches show little advantage over others in many instances. (Bergin & Garfield 1994:822)

Common factors loom large as mediators of treatment outcomes. The research base for this conclusion is substantial and multidimensional, and we must attend to its import. While there is some resistance to acknowledging the importance that common factors have, possibly as Frank (1976) states because 'little glory derives from showing that the particular method one has mastered with so much effort may be indistinguishable from other methods in its effects'. (Ibid.:167)

Again, notice the emphatic nature of this conclusion. There is *substantial* and *multidimensional* evidence of the importance of common factors as opposed to specific schools of therapy. Counsellors do not wish to face up to this since, quite obviously, there is *little glory* in thinking that all the time and money one spent in one's very particular training may count for so little. 'Behaviour therapy and cognitive therapy – are both simply glorified common sense' (Stuart Sutherland). (Dryden & Feltham 1992:193).

Insofar as cognitive therapy works, is it because 'common sense' is pretty effective also? Is cognitive therapy, as Fancher argues, an essentially middlebrow intervention attractive to clients who are themselves middlebrow?

'This is not to say that techniques are irrelevant but that their power for change is limited when compared with personal influence' (Bergin & Garfield 1994:181). Clearly it is difficult to pin down which factors are having which effects in therapy. There is so much variation between theory, practice, therapists, clients, aims and outcomes. How, then, can we draw conclusions that apply in any general way? One option would be to carry out a *very large* study indeed such that one could at least see if there was positive net change of some sort, even if one could not pin down all the causes. Such research has, in fact, been conducted. The largest study that I am aware of is the Fort Bragg Demonstration Project[11] (Dineen 1999). Huge numbers were involved: $80 million was spent involving 42,000 clients over five years. Yet, as Dineen

(1999:128) observed: 'these results should raise serous doubts about some current clinical beliefs about the effectiveness of psychological services . . . there is scant evidence of its effectiveness in real-life community settings.' In case this was not enough, a replication study was carried out: 'Stark County replication study: children receiving no mental-health services improved at the same rate as the children who received many services' (Ibid.:129).

Somehow or another the American Psychological Association managed not to report the results of these studies in their 'public education' campaigns but instead focused on consumer surveys which, yet again, showed clients were generally 'satisfied' with their counselling experiences.

> Rather than being the best suited to evaluate therapy, psychologists and their clients are the least able to answer the questions:
>
> - Is therapy effective?
> - Is it any better than friendship?
> - Do high-paid professionals do a better job than minimally trained counsellors?
> - Does training and experience improve a therapist's skill?
> - Is therapy always safe?
> - Do professionals know more about human nature than the rest of us?
> - Would people naturally get worse without professional treatment?
>
> They say yes to all these questions while scientific studies that address them conclude with a resounding NO! (Dineen 1999:99)

Clients may be happy, but funding bodies, health managers, insurance companies and researchers, increasingly, are not. Clients may also be amazed at the 'memories' that therapists help them to 'recover' yet: 'there is no evidence that recovered memory techniques can reveal memory of real events or accurately elaborate factual information about past experiences' (Royal College of Psychiatrists)[12] in Dineen 1999:252)

> As we collect more and more data on the types of therapies involved in recovered-memory therapy, we cannot avoid the conclusion that this is bad therapy.[13] (Ibid.:108)
>
> In 1968, the psychiatrist Herbert Spiegel gave a live demonstration designed to show how easily such false memories can be implanted. (Ibid.:64)

Addicts may praise the 'helpful' influence of their therapist, yet: 'The American treatment of alcoholism follows a standard procedure that appears impervious to emerging research evidence (which shows no evidence of effectiveness), and has not changed significantly for at least two decades'[14] (Ibid.:210).

Clients and therapists may agree concerning some of the insights they have gained, but research is always restricted to the *present* lifetimes of clients rather than previous lifetimes!

'Many of my patients have discovered that the cause of their phobias, fears, and even aversions were rooted in some traumatic event of a previous lifetime.' (Psychologist Edith Fiore, in Dineen 1999:58)

'Ruth White is a Transpersonal Psychologist accredited by the UK Council for Psychotherapists. Ruth describes herself as a 'spiritual consultant'. For fortyfive years she has been the channel for her discarnate guide, Gildas, *in cooperation with whom she has developed workshops and written a number of books. *Gildas: A discarnate teaching guide, whose last incarnation was as a monk in 14th Century France. (Flyer for 'Soul Celebration'; workshop at Dartington Hall, Devon, 3–5 October 2003)

Resourcefulness versus resources

Personal influence matters more than 'techniques' but the personal influence of counsellors is not demonstrably more significant than the personal influence of anyone else. And, in any case, maybe personal influence is less important than the more general, tacit and continuous *social* influence of social context, social opportunity, social resources, or the *lack* thereof. 'Personal growth is reserved for the rich, and social control is reserved for the poor, in the 'land of the free' (David Pilgrim, in Dryden & Feltham 1992:233).

The highly resourceful, and highly resourced, tend to gain a disproportionate share of counselling resources. They understand the language, they want the time and attention, and they, perhaps, are best placed to make best use of the counsellor's message: 'Making the best of what you already have ('positively connoting the experience') can be helpful if you already have quite a lot. It can have a hollow ring if you are poor. (Ibid.)

It is useful to think about how to be more proactively resourceful when you already have a good deal of personal and material resources to be resourceful with. But when you are relatively destitute of resources, and overwhelmed by the social forces around you, perhaps the best thing is just to keep your head down, or hold on to anyone who is prepared just to hold your hand? 'Sometimes our choices are irrelevant – and the poorer and more powerless we are the more this claim becomes true' (Ibid.:234).

Counselling focuses on the task of mobilising the powers of the client so that they can better tackle their problems. That is fine when the client does have real power, and when this power is sufficient to overcome social constraints and the powers of others. 'The emphasis on *individual* responsibility, strengths or cognitive ingenuity becomes more and more relevant the richer and more powerful the client' (Ibid.). But what if the client does not have the power? What if, despite the power of the client, others have far more power and will use it against the client? What if the power and insight of the *counsellor* is not, in any case, all that great? What, after all, do counsellors know that is all that special, concerning the circumstances, opportunities, constraints, and tragic contexts within the life of their clients?

Does counselling provide new and useful languages for people to explore their problems, or does it disempower clients by taking away from them their own language? 'F. Newman (1991, *The Myth of Psychology*, Castillo) suggests that the received language of psychology is alien and unhelpful to oppressed people, who are better empowered by using language which is their own and methods which emanate from their own experience' (Feltham 1995:148).

Is counselling an essentially middle class activity? 'In Britain, for example, the majority of counsellors are middle-class women, and much counselling (certainly counselling skills training) resembles, perhaps is often barely distinguishable from, the social skills and social graces of the middle class' (Dryden & Feltham 1992:260).

Does counselling provide a critique of the inanities of contemporary secular life? Or is it just another feature of this inanity, banality and tepid mediocrity? 'as a whole the profession has failed to put across any credible, unified view of what it does' (Ibid.:262).

In search of 'objectivity'

It is not at all certain that there is a unified view to put across given the vast diversity in values, methods, concepts, narratives and vocabularies among different schools of counselling. Yet efforts to systematise and to provide training manuals continue. Here for example, is Dryden and Feltham in another publication, *Developing Counsellor Training* (1994). They propose a scoring system for trainers. For example: 'Score 6 Therapist seemed to understand the patient's "internal reality" thoroughly and was adept at communicating this understanding through appropriate verbal and non-verbal responses to the patient' (Dryden and Feltham 1994:140).

The key word here is 'seemed'. In the trainer's opinion the therapist 'seemed' to understand the patient's 'internal reality'. But is there *a* reality to understand and in what respects can it be said to be 'internal'? Given that, as we have seen, trained and experienced practitioners do not score better outcomes than amateurs, *on what basis do trainers presume to 'score' trainee performance at all?* If a mere opinion is being offered, or a dialogue is taking place, the discussion may be useful. But to give a 'score' is to presuppose a methodology and a degree of objectivity, accuracy and efficacy that is simply not supported by any research evidence. However, as Feltham (1995:13) acknowledges: 'philosophical texts taking questionable therapeutic constructs to task are still rare.' In any case, the evidence suggests that, even when there are therapy protocols, therapists do not themselves adhere very closely to the methods of any particular school, and tend to be somewhat eclectic: 'Studies suggest that therapists vary considerably in the degree to which they adhere to therapy protocols' (Roth & Fonagy 1996:347).

It has to be assumed that the trainer knows best if scoring is to be justified at all. But there simply is not research evidence to support this assumption.

The research itself, however, often gets tangled up in making the very same assumption: 'There is a problem with the assumption, an assumption that guides much positivist research, that the psychologist knows best' (Banister et al. 1994:104).

Researchers, we are to believe are neutral, dispassionate and effective even if therapists are not. But time and time again we find, if we look, that the researcher's own partialities and preferences structure the way in which research is conducted and interpreted. Dineen, for example, (1999:126) shows Seligman's chart of 'improvement' which grossly exaggerates the result by using the old device of truncating the axis on the chart. She, likewise, provides (1999:92) an instance of a researcher actually overriding the perspectives of clients when these clash with the researcher's own agenda: 'Of these women, who were categorised as rape victims, 73 per cent did not define their experience as "rape". Mary Kiss, the psychologist conducting the study, defined it as rape, stating that the women themselves didn't recognise what had really happened to them.'

It is high time that we faced up to this tendency of human beings to 'interact' with the data they collect/create. We need to accept that researchers, being human beings, cannot possibly avoid having interests, preferences, values and prejudices of their own. 'Research questions are structured by personal and political interests that need to be explored rather than hidden away, for it is when they are concealed that they do the most damage' (Banister et al. 1994:9).

Repeatedly I find that researchers draw relatively positive interpretations from data that, in my opinion, simply do not support the interpretation. For example, we have seen Roth and Fonagy concluding that counsellors perform no better than general practitioners but that this is because doctors themselves 'have considerable generic counselling skills'. Where is the evidence for this? And how do doctors manage to exercise these considerable skills in a six-minute interview that must focus, generally, on medical symptoms presented by the patient? Certainly there is now more training for doctors on 'people skills'. But many doctors, traditionally, have preferred to focus on the *science* of medicine rather than its art. They may learn their bedside manner over the years, but many other kinds of professionals and staff learn how to relate to people via their work. If doctors can claim 'considerable generic counselling skills' let's see the evidence.

'One of the features of measurement in quantitative methodologies is that it attempts to screen out interpretation, and to imagine that it is possible to produce a clear and unmediated representation of the object of study' (Banister et al. 1994:2). Dryden and Feltham's scoring system of counsellor performance is a case in point. The process is *entirely* a matter of personal interpretation. *No methodology is even proposed.* But, once the result is sedimented into a number, it takes on an aura of accuracy and objectivity that is simply not supportable by the evidence, by the (non-existent) methodology, or by any other careful examination of the process.

> Research is always carried out from a particular standpoint, and the pretence to neutrality in many quantitative studies in psychology is disingenuous. It is always worth considering, then, the 'position of the researcher', both with reference to the definition of the problem to be studied and with regard to the way in which the researcher interacts with the material to produce a particular kind of sense. (Banister et al. 1994:13)

The position of researchers into counselling is that they are generally counsellors themselves, or highly sympathetic to counselling. They are also highly sympathetic to the continuation and growth of research. So even though they rarely announce that counselling 'works' and even though they go on producing very strong evidence that counselling is a very weak intervention, they generally manage to find something to console both counsellors and funders of research.

This weak response to the strong evidence of the weakness of counselling does nothing at all to strengthen either counselling or research. The fear, I presume, is that if a stronger, more critical, voice was taken more seriously the entire enterprise of counselling could face collapse. Government, other funding bodies, counselling students, clients; all would turn away and find some other way of filling in their time.

In fact, this backlash is already well under way. Health maintenance organisations in the USA have begun to rebel against spiralling costs and now demand to see evidence of the efficacy of particular brands of counselling before agreeing to fund it via insurance schemes. Rosters of approved psychologists have been created and even then there are severe restrictions on the number of visits that can be funded and on the problems that will be considered suitable for treatment.

Lambert's (1986) study concluded that, even where there was a defined improvement, only 15 per cent could be ascribed to a specific treatment:

Factors for Change, per cent of improvement due to:	
Spontaneous improvement	40
Placebo effect	15
Common nonspecific factors	30
Specific treatment	15

(Lambert 1986)

It is no wonder, then, that insurance companies are becoming increasingly reluctant to fund such effete, yet expensive, treatment programmes.

Treatment *of* a client versus treatment *as* a person

In the short run, I am sure, many agencies and many counsellors would face a major crisis if they accepted how flimsy and illusory was the professional clothing they imagine they are wearing. But in the longer term, I am equally convinced, *this crisis has simply got to be faced* and gone through if counselling is to provide a coherent account of itself and draw in the kinds of insights it so desperately needs from, for example, cultural theorists, philosophers, sociologists and anthropologists. Banister is highly critical of much research and its false claims to objectivity, neutrality and validity. But he is not seeking to destroy the livelihoods of researchers. On the contrary, he seeks to get them to raise their game so that it relates to what we now know, from postmodern theorists, about the nature of objectivity, evidence, neutrality and the importance of identity. Researchers, if they are to produce more constructive and significant results, must deconstruct their own practice. They must acknowledge its limitations if they are to play to its strengths:

> Ethnographic researchers thus recognise that they are part of the social world they are studying, and that they cannot avoid having an effect on the social phenomena being studied. The issue is: '*rather than engaging in futile attempts to eliminate the effects of the researcher, we should set about understanding them*' (Hammersley and Atkinson 1983:17) (Banister et al. 1994:36)

> There is a strong argument that ethnographies should be very much like narrative writing, with an emphasis on theme and illustration: it is essential to make clear the pattern of events and the researcher's understanding. (Ibid.:45)

Like every *constructive* postmodernist,[15] Bannister is not seeking to pull us all down into relativism and nihilism. He is not saying that research conclusions are merely a matter of opinion. He is not suggesting that they carry no more authority than the opinions or anecdotes of laypersons, amateurs or anyone else: 'Acknowledging the multiplicity of readings (or accounts of the account) does not mean that all readings are equal. Otherwise we are stuck in the quagmire of relativistic nihilism which disempowers us from using the research to say anything' (Banister et al. 1994:65). But if we are to become more real, more authentic, more objective and more empathic, we need to develop a sophisticated and cosmopolitan understanding of what postmodern concepts mean, how they can, and cannot, be used, and what are their strengths and limitations. We need to clarify underlying philosophies, value systems, and rules of evidence. We need to deconstruct key concepts, not in order to destroy or discard them, but in order to toughen them up so that they are rugged enough to deal with contemporary, sceptical, critiques: 'The psychotherapist carries on his work with an almost wholly unexamined "philosophical unconscious" Alan Watts (1975 *Psychotherapy East and West*, Vintage)' (Feltham 1995:115).

I am sure that this is true, and it is high time that psychologists and counsellors on this insular and essentially anti-intellectual island brought their philosophical unconscious into consciousness. For example, social science, and especially psychology, is shot through with positivism and naïve empiricism, yet most psychologists demonstrate no knowledge of what positivism is, and do not explain how it is relevant to their own work. They imagine that they are anti-metaphysical, though they give no account of the nature of metaphysics. And so they appear entirely unaware of the underlying metaphysics of positivist empiricism, instrumentalism and mechanistic materialism.

This metaphysical weakness has enormous practical consequences. Positivist psychologists, as a result of their underlying philosophy, are able to say more and more about less and less. They provide numbers to 'prove' it, except that actually the numbers prove nothing. Yet positivists show no interest or competence in key concepts like meaning, narrative and personality. They rarely ask what it is that makes someone a *person* rather than a machine. They shy away from the question in case they get sucked into some kind of psychological dualism and are forced to talk of mental 'worlds' or some other kind of superannuated vitalism.

> The reason most orthodox Western psychology cannot tell you one interesting point about the meaning of your life is that it has proudly restricted itself to empiric-analytic enquiry, i.e. inquiry *based on* sensory, objectified, subhuman modes and processes. The liberating insight is that an individual's life as a mental being is a life of trans-empirical, hermeneutical exchange. (Wilbur 1981:277)

Positivists fail to notice the crucial problem involved in studying experience: 'Experience is a first-person business. Science operates in the third person' (Broks 2003:139). So they either ignore experience and study only behaviour (the choice of 'hard' behaviourists), or they imagine that experience can be inferred purely by observing behaviour ('soft' behaviourism). Alternatively positivist psychologists abandon psychology and seek to understand experience purely by focusing on brain states. Physiology is an important area of study, but we never observe, or understand, experience just by focusing on brain states.

I understand you in a social world of interaction, cooperation, institutions, dialogue and symbolic representations. I do not understand you by trying to map the physiology of 100 billion brain cells flashing 'on' and 'off'. Likewise, I understand how to use word processors and word processing software by learning about keyboarding skills and software rules. I do not learn word processing by learning about computer circuitry even though, obviously, there could be no software without the hardware. I do not learn about poetry by close study of patterns of ink stains on paper. 'Robert Frost said that "Poetry is what is lost in translation. It is also what is lost in interpretation." Likewise, consciousness is lost in translating from first-person experience to third-person description of brain states' (Broks 2003:141). We can, and should, do better than this and move on to: 'Ethnogenic method – the study of human sense making. New paradigm research. Research done *with* rather than *on* people' (Blackman & Walkerdine 2001:106).

If we want to get serious about the quality of our research, we have to get serious about *qualitative* research and its nature. There are no quick fixes or easy answers. But at least we could make a start if we began to ask the right questions. 'Harre equated the role of the social scientist to that of a grammarian, studying the rules of language that exist within the social world' (Ibid.). Banister acknowledges that: 'Research would be so much easier if researchers did not have to interact' (Banister et al. 1994:109).

But the fact is that researchers *do* interact. They are part of the social world they investigate. They influence what they observe. They cannot exist as 'flies on a wall'. They have their own agendas, prejudices and preferences. They can still, nonetheless, do a worthwhile job. But only if they abandon the pretence that they are gods and admit that they are human. All this should have been obvious for years, and would have been but for the blinkered perceptions of positivist researchers. For example the Hawthorne effect was documented years ago, way back in 1927. Researchers found that, whatever variables they tweaked when looking at work performance, the performance continued to improve. Eventually they realised that the most important influence on the women workers being studied, was the researchers themselves! The very fact that they kept on turning up to see how these women were getting on had a huge influence on morale and productivity.

Banister provides a long, and immensely practical, list of proposals concerning how qualitative research should be conducted, and it is, as I will try to show, of considerable relevance to the identity and practice of counselling, counsellors and their clients.

Impatience with mechanism, positivism and materialism in science has grown in recent years but it is by no means new. Weber spoke of the disenchanting understandings provided by mechanism. Romantics lamented Newtonianism from Blake right through to nineteenth-century romanticism. Wilhelm Dilthey (1833–1911) distinguished between natural science and 'Geisteswissenschaften', the sciences of the spirit, or human sciences.

Natural science, Dilthey argued, focused on explanation (Erklärung), in terms of causes and generalisations. But the human sciences should seek understanding (Verstehen). This required researchers to engage actively with the structures of a person's life that were given in their lived experience. For Dilthey, our lives were inherently meaningful and connected experiences. We could only understand another if we engaged in this meaning and interconnection. We could do not do so if we broke experience down into atomistic units linked by crude 'associations' of ideas, stimulus-response etc.

First person versus third person perspectives

> In teaching psychologically meaningfully, an essential goal must surely be to help students become present to themselves, so that they are able to engage with the material from their own personal standpoint. (Pilgrim 1983:92)

However, in seeking to be a science, psychology tries to adopt a 'third person' perspective. It positively discourages students from being 'present' in their studies. They should try to absent themselves as personable individuals with personal agendas. Students' own personal perspectives are not part of the curriculum of a degree in psychology. The discussion concerns 'it', 'he', 'she', 'they', 'the subject' rather than 'you' and 'I'.

Behaviourists, in particular, tried to ignore first person experience since it seemed unreachable by science. They did not want to say 'This is how *you* or *I* see it?'. Rather they wanted to demonstrate that 'this is how it *is*'. But in trying to achieve such objectivity they were in fact succumbing to naïvety about the nature of knowledge of other persons and how it can be achieved.

I try to see, as you see, by talking and listening to you. But we are all talkers and listeners. Psychologists could not claim particular authority as regards the art of conversation. Behavioural social scientists focused instead on observing what people *did*. They looked upon people as 'doers', portfolios of skills, dispositions to respond. That, after all, is what interests managers of human beings. Managers already know what their staff mean to them and how they mean to employ them. So psychology could, perhaps, help managers if it helped them work out how to manage people. It could also, in so doing, help itself to a lucrative status within academe, commerce and politics.

Managers already understand what they want from staff and they seek to instil this understanding on to others so that they will behave accordingly. *The manager provides the first person understanding and the staff respond with suitable third person behaviour.* The manager provides the meanings, understandings, the first person mission and vision. The manager is the first person; staff are employed to be third persons; their first person perspectives are not of interest – unless, of course, these perspectives themselves need to be 'managed'. Unscheduled personal staff perspectives on the company are liable to get in the way of the corporate mission. They are a distraction. *But, just sometimes, we seek to learn about other first person perspectives rather than merely impose our own first person perspective upon others.* Sometimes we want to learn from, rather than just control, the understandings of others.

Behaviourists tried to bracket off action from understanding but it cannot be done. Their fantasy of an 'impersonal' perspective was in fact a management perspective. There is no such thing as 'pure' behaviour. Speech and behaviour are just noise and movement until they are understood. Only meaningful sounds can be speech. Only meaningful actions can be behaviour. Speech and action differ from noise and movement only because they consist in the creation of, and response to, meaningfulness. But meaning is not something that sticks inherently to objects and actions; it is inherent only to persons who make or accept meanings. There are meanings only because there are persons who understand as they do and who construct a world of meaning within and around them.

Nothing means anything in the abstract. Things mean what they mean always to particular persons who understand as they do. Meaning making is an inherently first person activity which is not, at all, to say that you can sensibly make anything you like of anything whatever. The theory of relativity, for example, like everything else, has to be understood in the first person. But most people are incapable of understanding it very much at all.

We learn about people, theories and things in active first person participation and interaction rather than as disembodied third person aliens. We are persons, first and foremost. We live in the first person from first to last in our being in the world. We are, none of us, ever, neutral, disembodied, impersonal observers. We can never achieve 'impersonality' however much we may pretend otherwise.

Understanding is always a personal act, achieved by persons, from a personal perspective. How then, can counselling researchers and psychologists progress if they pretend to study persons in the third person as third persons themselves? *We ought not to be surprised if all this third person effort produces third rate results.*

Personal experience and understanding is more akin to the process of characterisation and story telling of a novelist than the sterile observation and presupposition of the behaviourist. The thin assumptions of behaviourists lead to a thin picture of subjects. Now, therefore, almost all behaviourists describe themselves as *cognitive* behaviourists, they attend both to behaviour and cognition – thoughts, feelings, intentions, all that difficult mental and first person material that behaviourists sought to avoid. 'Most of the people who used to consider themselves behavioural therapists now identify themselves as cognitive-behavioural' (Bergin & Garfield 1994:824). The question then arises, how is cognition to be studied, how impersonal can such a study be and who can claim to research into, and thereby understand, cognition with any particular authority?

As the Hawthorne experience, previously described, showed so conclusively, the very activity of trying to study people affects the results of the study. Researchers are not merely *observing*; they are *interacting*. The subjects of research themselves have understandings of the identity of the researchers and the agenda of the research. The *researchers themselves have to give an account of themselves to the people being studied*. This understanding itself affects behaviour in ways that may be hard to predict.

First persons as language users, not ghosts in a machine

In trying to make sense of intentions, feelings and thoughts, researchers rightly avoid getting enmeshed in Descartes' metaphysics. Few subscribe to a Cartesian mental 'world' of mental stuff existing parallel with the physical world. Dualism has expired as a useful way of construing selves, minds, persons and identities.

But to understand experience, identity, and first person existence, to 'get inside' the world as it is seen and understood by another, we cannot simply talk about the behaviours, habits and responses of passive objects of manipulation. Above all we have to have a sophisticated understanding of the way in which *language* is used, and we must ourselves learn to use it in a sophisticated way. The notion of first person experience is itself a linguistic concept. 'I', 'you', 'he', 'she', 'it', 'they' – all these are first and foremost constructed by, and embedded within, our language. If there is another 'world' as well as the physical, it is linguistic more than mental.[16]

Yet who are the most accomplished and proficient users of language? Who most pays attention to the subtleties of language, of its many denotations and connotations, cadences, allusions and metaphors? Certainly not scientists and social scientists. They seek to apply a kind of conceptual 'bleach' to their language; emptying it of all its implicit and tacit suggestions, implications and innuendoes. They try to keep it simple, direct and unambiguous.[17] They want to cleanse and purify it of the unpredictable, ambiguous, multifaceted and uncontrollable. They like to write in the third person about third persons. They like to keep themselves, as persons, out of the script. They try to keep the narrative out. The story of the research is not seen as a part of the story. The focus instead is on the methods and the results. There are no anecdotes, no asides, no agendas, assumptions, values, no sub-texts, no gaps, mysteries or guesses, no interactions, no multiple readings and interpretations by the multiplicity of characters, of persons, who were actually engaged in a personal and interpersonal interaction.

This impersonal treatment of persons, by those who foolishly seek to be non-persons, does not succeed in producing neutrality, objectivity, detachment or truth about other people. Instead it produces results that are every bit as impoverished, incorrect and irrelevant as the metaphysical and methodological assumptions themselves. This is not science; it is a false scientism. It is a methodology that works well enough for inanimate objects; our technological progress is recognition enough of that. But it does not work for subjects, for animate and animated individual persons, and for living, valued and evaluating social communities.

This mechanistic and materialistic impersonalism, devoid of concern for language, society, meaning and its negotiation, is not merely *inadequate* as a way of understanding people, it is also, and just as important, *immoral*. If, in day-to-day life, I treat you as a mere object, you are likely to take great personal offence. If I treat you in this way as your manager you may not appreciate it, though you may decide that there is nothing much you can do about it.

Yet not even psychologists engage very actively with the language using activities of their 'subjects', which ought to be surprising given that what particularly distinguishes human beings is their capacity to use language. But talking to people requires active *engagement*, whereas if we remain in a voyeuristic mode we can pretend to be dispassionate, 'passive' – and 'scientific' – *observers*. 'It is understandable, though not surprising, that language, the medium through which social life is maintained, is absent from most studies in psychology' (Banister et al. 1994:8).

We can study bodies as complex physical objects and produce worthwhile results. Medical progress is a testament to that. But we cannot study persons in this way since persons are not just physical bodies. We are embodied, of course we are. A body is a necessary condition of there being a person; we have never met a disembodied person. But the identity of persons is negotiated, is multifaceted; is social as well as personal; is linguistic as well as behavioural and physical; is intentional and meaningful as well as inert; and is plastic more than fixed or solid. *Persons are subjects, not just complicated objects.* 'People are not "social facts", inhabiting the place, institution etc, and just waiting to be studied and to reveal their all' (Ibid.:39).

So, if we are to get to know another person we cannot simply observe them, we have to encounter them. We have to engage in some kind of dialogue with them. I can observe a rock, manipulate it and increase my understanding. But I cannot just observe you because it is rude and wrong and I know that you are also observing me unless I hide myself behind a one way mirror. Our non-verbal interaction will affect what and how we observe. Also, I am extremely limited in what I can learn about you if I avoid the use of language and the consequent negotiation of meaning. So I get you to talk, and I have to talk myself, though I may try to restrict myself to questionnaires, and thereby limit the sophistication, flexibility and extent of our active interaction.

'The knower is part of the matrix of what is known' (Ibid.:84). *If I am really to get to know you I will have to introduce myself.* I will have to make myself present to you. I will have to get into conversation with you and I will therefore need to know the art of conversation, something that science knows little of and scientists tend to shy away from. I can, of course, know *of*, or *about*, you by reading or hearing descriptions of you provided by other people, and there is nothing intrinsically wrong with knowing *of* other people. My concern, though, is that this crucial distinction – between knowing a person and knowing *of* a person – is rarely made or recognised. 'All too often we analyse interviews as disembodied voices but interviews are interactions between embodied people' (Ibid.:68).

Even when introducing an anonymous questionnaire, a narrative account is generally given. This usually involves praising the 'power' of this research 'tool' way beyond anything suggested by the evidence. Subjects are invited to subject themselves to the authority of the questionnaire, of the form to be filled in, and to accept that *here is yet another part of their life where they are not allowed to engage in a human relationship.*

Human beings should not be seen merely as 'objects of study'. They have a right to speak for themselves and in their own language. Research protocols, questionnaires and other research 'instruments' tend to take away people's own language and own ways of accounting for themselves. Thus our own perspectives, experiences, concerns, priorities, preferences and needs tend to be lost.

The research agenda: are we asking the wrong questions?

As a result of this naïvety about people, and ignorance of the nature of the concept of a person, social scientists make elementary errors that remain invisible to them. They imagine that knowledge exists independently of power, action, interaction and intention. They fail to see how facts emerge from human agendas more than the other way round, and that what we 'find' may often be the result of the method we used to find it.

Banister and others argue that, because of these continued failings within social science research generally, and research into counselling in particular, we need to look again at the methods of research we use. If we are to improve the quality and significance of our research we ought to accept the need for *qualitative* research methods. But what does this actually mean in practice, other than the avoidance of numbers, quantities, when these throw no light on our understandings of other people? To begin with, Bannister argues, we need to stop pretending that we are third person impersonalities when we are first person individuals: 'It is generally desirable in writing up qualitative reports to use the first person (e.g. 'I'), rather than reporting the research in the more traditional stylised impersonal fashion' (Ibid.:161).

We must accept that we have a class background, a gender and an agenda. We do not look in on people and their communities from an objective and absolute 'outside' since we are not outsiders at all. We are all active citizens in a social and socially constructed world that we all share. We should not pretend to be impersonal and we should not describe a world devoid of persons since it is the fact that we *are* persons that makes us human and that comprises our social world. 'science conveys a picture of the world from which a real human psyche appears to be excluded – the very antithesis of "the humanities"' (Jung 1996:13).

Yet it is hard to believe that psychologists, as currently trained and constructed, are sufficiently well placed to engage in this kind of qualitative, participative and narrative engagement; this meeting of minds with other minds via a personal encounter with other persons. A novelist and poet would be better equipped to describe persons, experiences and events of personal significance. A conversationalist would be better able to talk with and about them. An activist of whatever kind, or anthropologist, or biographer could better account for experiences that they had actually experienced.

Researchers have not demonstrated that professional counsellors do better than amateurs or that counselling is a very strong intervention. To put it another way, they *have* shown that counselling is rather weak when construed as a form of treatment. But are the wrong questions being asked? Is the nature of counselling being misconstrued? *Is counselling a weak form of treatment because it should not be seen as a treatment at all?* Do we need to change our view of counselling, research and the clients/'subjects' of this research? Certainly the traditional research approach of trying placebo controls seems to have run into the sand: 'we have concluded that the typical placebo controls are so conceptually and procedurally flawed that they have essentially failed in their purpose of helping to isolate the active therapeutic ingredients. It is time to discontinue placebo controls and design studies with more meaningful comparison groups' (Bergin & Garfield 1994:152).

Placebo groups must not be identifiable. Subjects, obviously, are not supposed to know if they belong to a control or a real therapy group. So the pretend 'therapist' in a control group must convince clients that they are receiving the 'real thing'. Such deception raises ethical questions. It is in any case very difficult to achieve. People know the difference between receiving therapy and the non-specific chat offered in a control group.

If we were to relocate counselling into the arts and humanities, and take it out of '*social* science', what would be the consequences of research into its efficacy? People may claim to have been inspired and informed. Or they may consider that the work in question was shallow, superficial, false, indulgent, a light distraction, a confused muddle, or whatever. Others may agree or disagree with the assessment. We may, or may not, convince them with the force of our experience, ideas, and evidence. Debate may, or may not, be mature, sensitive, respectful and informed, or egocentric, introverted, ignorant and inattentive.

The humanities, at their best, can integrate self and society. They can inspire, change and enlarge us in some way, or remind us how small, anxious, divided and uncertain we are. Artistic creation can bring us more to life. *Arguably, the greatest humanists still have far more to say of significance about what it is to be a human being, in the personal, individual, first person sense, than any social scientist has yet managed in the third person.*

If counselling attached itself to the humanities project, how, then, could and should it be assessed? Psychologists, psychotherapists and counsellors would no longer see themselves like technicians, looking for and rectifying faults in a machine. Counsellors would not provide repairs, interventions and treatments. *Therapy would not be so much a treatment, rather a way of treating people.* Therapists would be assessed in the way that novelists, playwrights, painters, musicians and other professionals within the humanities are assessed.

They would all have been trained and educated, in a more or less relevant way, but the training would not in itself be a measure, or guarantee, of competence or success. Some would be trained and educated but would fail to produce work that interested or impressed either mass or sophisticated audiences or critics. Some would become marginally or hugely successful in a mass market and make lots of money. Of these, some would be praised by critics, others would derided or ignored. Some would succeed with more sophisticated audiences and critics, more often with limited financial success. Others, very occasionally, might offer something that everyone praised.

The critical response might be consensual or bitterly divided, but it would be more than a mere expression of opinion. Criteria would be debated, creativity would be applauded, and coherence of argument and expression would be expected. Some would work closely, and well or badly, within established conventions. Others would be highly creative and innovatory, with more or less success and acclaim. Each humanist artist, be they composer or counsellor, would, above all, succeed or fail as an *individual.* Their previous school of training would be less significant than their current practice. *Research has, in any case, shown that all this is already the case.*

A growing number of social science researchers have expressed frustration with the ideas, methods and rules of evidence that have been used within social science. Growing numbers, indeed, argue that it is a myth to go on believing that psychology is a science at all. For example, Gough and McFadden (2001) argue that critical research needs to change its agenda very fundamentally. According to Gough and McFadden (2001:47), researchers should move away from the old, and failed, methods and:

- emphasise the variation, complexity and often contradictory qualities in human experience;
- situate individuals/research participants within wider social contexts;
- offer knowledge which is partial, incomplete and critical;
- challenge aspects of existing inequalities in society;
- make visible pertinent personal and contextual elements within research; and
- deconstruct the myth of (social) psychology as science.

Instead of observing people as though they were merely inarticulate animals, we have to meet them personally as language-using persons. If we want to understand them with any sophistication, and with suitable respect, then *we cannot simply give them a questionnaire or form to fill in.* We have to be prepared to converse with them, so that they are free to introduce their own agendas, priorities and perspectives in their own words. If we are to meet others, understand them and learn from them, we have to accept that each of us brings with us our own tacit understandings and experiences with which we try to make sense of each other.

There will have to be some mutual acceptance and understanding of this tacit knowledge if we are to understand each other at all. We have to understand that the language we use is itself a form of performance and action and that in a genuine dialogue we continually modify our understanding and agenda in the light of what is said and understood by the person we are talking to. *If we are seriously trying to learn from each other then we do not merely try to manipulate the other person into filling in our form or questionnaire for us.*

We have to be prepared to examine the language people use, but we cannot, and we have no right, to determine entirely in advance the nature of this language. We have to understand that *human beings have been carrying out research on each other, developing their understanding of each other, since, and before, the time we evolved from apes.* We are fools if we believe that the research methods used by our ancestors are without validity and efficacy, and that we can supplant these methods 'as scientists' within a single generation. Human efforts to understand each other are highly problematic but they have worked sufficiently well for human beings to construct enormously complex structures and systems of cooperation and codependence. The language we use in daily life reflects this history and sophistication. The bleached language of scientific discourse has all the subtlety burned out of it. It works on rocks, but it cannot be expected to work when the subject of study is the human language user herself.

Hence we may make more progress in understanding others if we look at the language usages of the literary critic more than that of the social scientist. Mikhail Bakhtin (1895–1975) for example: 'For Bakhtin, the self–other relation was dialogic in that the self does not exist as a fixed, finished and finalised datum, but is in a state of constant activity' (Swingewood 1998:114). Bakhtin, like Habermas, stressed democratic dialogue as central to the formation and understanding of self, and as the only way of emancipating ourselves from managerial monologues, deformations and manipulations. Bakhtin, like the later Wittgenstein, saw meaning arising from interaction between speakers and listeners, not as welded permanently into words, or protocols or theories of would-be authorities. 'In this dialogue a person participates wholly and throughout his whole life: with his eyes, lips, hands, soul, spirit, with his whole body and deeds. He invests his entire self in discourse, and this discourse enters into the dialogic fabric of human life' (Bakhtin 1984 in Swingewood 1998:115).

We will have to accept that the language people use to account for themselves and their world is complex, subtle, multiple, contrary and often contradictory. It is full of allusions, connotations, tacit understandings, questions, and uncertainties. Questionnaires and form filling may seek to flatten out this complex reality. But, as a result they produce tidy, and dehumanising, social science *fictions*. Hence the paradox; *the fiction created by novelists, in its subtle sensitivity to the refinements and details of characterisation, may be closer to the facts about what it is to be a person than anything produced by social science.*

Modernism, instrumentalism, positivism and managerialism turned creative subjects into passive objects. In the process, identity, integrity, authenticity, humanity were lost. Social science was too often an ignorant servant of such tendencies and actively prevented, rather than actually promoted, human understanding. Thus argued philosophers and sociologists concerned to promote and explore hermeneutics, that is, meanings as collectively, culturally and historically negotiated. Hans-Georg Gadamer (1900–2002) was a major leader of this hermeneutic turn, along with Heidegger, Habermas, Ricoeur, Merleau-Ponty, Wittgenstein, and many others.

For Gadamer, we did not understand others as objects of clinical observation or research. We did not understand them by treating them as instrumental to our own purposes or as bodies to be manipulated. On the contrary we understood others by recognising that all of us were active participants, placed in, and prejudiced by, our history, culture, and shared concerns and intentions.

Genuine human understanding is more likely to be fluid, fragmented, and subject to continual change through negotiation. Language is emphatically not, however, an entirely personal, individual, private or mental phenomenon. On the contrary, it is a *social* activity, a *public* reality that emerged from the need for human beings, inherently social creatures, to communicate and cooperate with one another. In their efforts to respond to this reality, Gough and McFadden (2001:52) describe an approach to discourse analysis that:

> attends closely to the 'repertoires' deployed in everyday conversation. It is assumed and frequently illustrated that speakers will draw upon a wide range of (sometimes competing) metaphors, images, and idioms in different conversational contexts; indeed the same speaker may well use conflicting repertoires during one social encounter. Such analyses are often sophisticated expositions of the complex and contradictory workings of discourse/ideology as reproduced in everyday talk.

Qualitative research

Scientists work *on* human beings. But to work *on* someone has not unlocked, and is not going to unlock, their identity as persons since the very methodology consists in treating people as impersonal objects of observation, modification and manipulation. Humanists, on the other hand, work *with* human beings. Critical social science researchers are attempting to move closer to this paradigm of study by changing quite fundamentally their research methods. They refer to *action* research as a *partnership* between the researchers and laypersons. The latter are no longer seen as 'subjects', or objects, of study but are instead often considered to be 'co-researchers'.

The research is prefaced with the word *action* since it is assumed that words without action are of little value and that human beings are ethical beings committed to making changes in the world around them. The research is collaborative and the agenda is not therefore defined in advance by professionals, but negotiated in discussion with laypersons. Obviously the professionals have ideas and priorities of their own, but these are *discussed with*, rather than *imposed upon*, the laypersons invited to participate. This discussion includes agreeing to the agenda, to what kind of action and change participants believe to be important, and to what information is relevant to this change agenda. Gough and McFadden (2001:67) make practical observations concerning how this practical research agenda can be most intelligently and ethically conducted:

- *Personal reflexivity* requires that the researcher make visible their individuality and its effects on the research process . . .
- *Functional reflexivity* relates to one's role as a researcher and the effect this may have on the research process. It focuses attention on the different identities presented with the research and the interactions between researcher and participants.
- *Discipline reflexivity* involves a critical stance towards the place and function of the particular research project within broader debates about theory and method.

The question can, of course, be asked, *how* can anyone be so superhuman as to be self-aware of all the ways our identity structures what we do and how we do it? The answer is that there is no superhuman perspective to take. As humans we can try to be as self-aware as we can, but our identity is itself a moving process, shaped by, as well as shaping, our language, the place we are in, our place within it, the people with whom we interact. But *as humans we have to identify ourselves, with all the limitations and uncertainties of this identity, if we are to identify and meet with others.* There simply is no perspective of objective, neutral, Olympian detachment and certainty available to us when it comes to meeting with, and understanding, other people.

Qualitative, critical, action research has been the subject of increasing attention in the past ten years. It is easy to see it as a new phenomenon, a new methodology and ideology. From a professional perspective most familiar with positivist constructions of social science it is indeed new. But it is important to remember that *this qualitative methodology is precisely the way in which people have always sought knowledge of others in their everyday lives.* For example, and most relevant, consider research into counselling. How do clients and potential clients go about assessing whether counselling is for them and, if so, what form of counselling is best? What they do *not* do is read research journals. Indeed counsellors don't often read these either. Instead, and above all, they rely on personal recommendation, personal contact, and word-of-mouth accounts from people they know and trust. These will be trusted above all if they themselves have been the clients of a recommended counsellor.

Both in private life and in our commercial transactions *we mainly trust the judgements and recommendations of people we trust*, rather than relying on protocols, procedures and 'quality standards'. *Word of mouth carries most weight, whether in the board room, the living room, or on the street.*

We ask around, we ask open-ended questions, we rely on word of mouth, though we also make eye contact and watch body language. We have a conversation with people whose perceptions we trust. We ask 'what did you make of it?' and 'what did you get out of it?' and we listen and discuss attentively. We let others find their own words to describe what was good and useful and what was not. We judge for ourselves. We all, of course, vary in our capacity for judgement. So it is in counselling as it is in art and in daily life.

This is a rational strategy and were we to read the counselling research literature we would still return to the word of mouth approach. Why? Because research does not tell you whether *any particular* counsellor will be the right one *for you.* On the contrary, research confirms that personal qualities count for more than experience, that training does not correlate with results, that counsellors don't necessarily do what they say they do or have been trained to do. Research outcomes are described in such general terms that it is hard to relate them to any specific agenda a client may have.

None of this means that nothing of value can be obtained from counselling, but it does mean that we must very much rely on our own resources in seeking and assessing the value we get from counselling. Such self-reliance is far from being foolproof and, by definition, it cannot work if we are fools. But *most of the big decisions we make in our lives depend similarly on our own, ultimately personal, judgement.* We confide, we consult, we educate ourselves, we discuss, but then we have to decide. Shall I choose this counsellor? Shall I read this book? Shall I go and see this play? What do I want to get out of it? What is it all about? What could I make of it? What could it make of me? What could I learn from it? Would I enjoy, or value, it? What do I mean by enjoy, or value, in this instance?

There are no neat, easy or final answers to these questions, but we are perfectly capable of asking them in an intelligent and systematic way. We find our answers as best we can and we are perfectly capable of refining our understanding, consulting, reading, studying and researching more deeply and widely if we so choose. Our tastes and values may be naïve and simple, average or avant-garde. They may be indulgent and infantile, mature and honourable, informed or ignorant or, more often, a contrary and contradictory mixture of all these. Despite, and within, all the uncertainties and subjectivity, we get on with making such decisions as human beings have always done. We do not believe that everyone's opinion is as good as everyone else's. We generally, perhaps unavoidably, over-estimate the accuracy of our own judgement.

Consider how manifestly absurd it would be if we applied positivist social research methodology to those humanities with which we are familiar. The positivist, let us imagine, says 'I will not read this novel until you can demonstrate what are the outcomes, and I need to know whether the writer is trained, supervised and accredited. Is this a professional writer and can it be demonstrated that this professional writer achieves better outcomes than amateur writers?' We can see that these questions cannot produce meaningful, interesting or relevant answers. They reveal our ignorance of the nature of the humanities. No one can say for sure whether a particular book, symphony, work of art, or discussion will be right for you or will produce particular outcomes. No one can say for sure whether it will make you happier or healthier or whether you ought to be doing something else altogether.

But a great deal can be said about what a particular discussion, in particular circumstances, with a particular individual *might* be able to achieve and what you in particular might be able to give to and get from it. It cannot sensibly be said what counselling in general can do. At least, the general answers that can be given will not do much to influence your decision making any more than a general discussion about novels can help you.

Some general questions, which appear to be providing an objective overview, in fact take us right out of a sensible understanding of a debate altogether. It is just ignorant and absurd to say, 'Is this novelist properly trained and supervised?' Or 'Can this painter demonstrate positive therapeutic or learning outcomes?' Or 'Will this musician make me happier, more satisfied or more resourceful?' Or, 'Is this the most effective *school* of dance?'

Positivists may not appreciate or understand the point but, quite often, *one of the least effective questions is to ask whether something is effective.* It presupposes that we are passive objects of (effective or less effective) forces acting on us. It fails to understand that personal understanding, personal development, personal therapy and support, is a dialogue, is active, is open, is personal, is negotiable, is fluid. That is what makes it alive and that is why it cannot, and does not need to be, 'pinned down'. Pinning down is something that professional control-freaks, managers and bureaucrats like to do but it does not empower us, it is not therapeutic, it does not help us to understand each other or ourselves. It is dehumanising and therefore unethical.

In summary, I hope it is clear that:

1. Positivist research has shown that counselling is a very weak intervention.
2. Careful analysis of methodologies should convince us that counselling should not be seen as an 'intervention' at all.
3. Counselling belongs within the humanities and should be assessed, chosen or avoided accordingly.
4. The humanities are not understood if we measure them in terms of their 'effects'.
5. By changing our understanding of the identity of counselling, we also thereby sharpen our understanding of the nature of human identity.
6. We *understand* individual identity by seeing it as embedded in the social.
7. We *value and promote* individual identity by *participating with* individuals rather than *working on* them.
8. We *see* another when we *meet* them rather than merely by *observing* them. We need to stop working *on* people and start to work *with* them.
9. We meet another when we make ourselves visible to them and, in the process, when we are visible to ourselves.
10. We need to distinguish between knowing a person and knowing *of* a person.
11. We never 'finally' meet or pin down others or ourselves and that should be a cause for celebration rather than regret or frustration. It demonstrates that we are still alive!

Similar observations can be made about education, its nature and its values, as opposed to mere training. Indeed it could be said that counselling is itself a primarily educational and cultural activity rather than a technical training process. Perhaps I should say that counselling and education *ought* to be parts of the larger humanist project; they are often, currently, a process of technical and managerial training and behavioural modification. As such they become just another instance of the dehumanisation, unjust and undemocratic management and manipulation that has become so much more prevalent in the last century and which has been described throughout these pages.

Future prospects

In summary, then, there is good news and bad news for counsellors and would-be counsellors. The bad news it that research does not support their efforts to professionalise and accredit. Artists, humanists, cannot expect to make a living merely by declaring that they are trained and accredited. They will be judged by their work first and last.

The bad news is that counselling is a weak and ineffective intervention. But the good news is that counselling should not be seen as an 'intervention' at all. It is more a dialogue, an education, a serious meeting of human beings concerning fundamental goals, identities, meanings and values.

The bad news is that we have a great deal more to learn about how to operate as counsellors. This is also good news since it would be very dispiriting to think that people can really be squashed into the shallow constructs of humanity currently on offer within counselling schools.

The good news is that people already know a great deal about how to understand and cooperate with each other. Counsellors need to draw from a huge range of other disciplines and from the substantial understanding that 'ordinary' lay-people develop of each other in order to function as social beings.

People will decide for themselves who can help them in painting the story of their lives just as they will decide for themselves which paintings to put on their wall. There is no particular reason why governments should subsidise them in these activities and, if they do, the decision will be more to do with cultural than with medical criteria. *There is certainly no reason, or justification, for accrediting or licensing the painters of either physical or psychological spaces.*

Counselling has a great deal to do with trying to achieve a well-lived life. It, therefore, needs to look much more widely at the huge cultural legacy of those who have approached this question from so many different directions and with so many different methods, practices and vocabularies.

The assessment of counselling should not, therefore, be anchored in outcomes but should instead address intentions, priorities, meanings and human values. Counselling is *all* about values that contribute to a well-lived life – to genuine human wealth and well being. The good life is seen as such not because of its outcomes. The only long-term outcome is that we die. The good life, rather, is assessed according to the number, and nature, of 'goods' that are seen to be *intrinsically* good in their own right rather than because of any consequences they may have.

Counselling is attractive because dialogue is attractive. Dialogue is indeed a good in its own right. Socrates tried to establish who he was, where he was going, what was true, beautiful, important and right. Why bother? *His answer was that these activities were intrinsic to being human and were intrinsically good in their own right.* Within such dialogue he was not so much *seeking* the good life, he was, rather, *in the very process of seeking*, actually *living* the good life.

So people will choose counselling, if they do, because that is what they want to do. The discussion will be intrinsically worthwhile to them. It may increase their understanding, though it may not necessarily make them behave very differently. I go to a play and find it inspiring. Can I *demonstrate* that this play produced measurable and important outcomes? No, of course I can't. I can talk about why I think it was inspiring and why that is important. I can relate this to possible changes in behaviour, or to views about who ought to be role models. But there is nothing measurable that will be decisive or which will give any decisive understanding as to why I think this was a good play.

Counselling is, or can be, an arena where people treat each other as human beings and where we respect the humanity of others. Counselling is not, or need not be, yet another way of treating people as operatives, producers and consumers who deliver outcomes and who have benefits delivered to them. *The rampant instrumentalisation and bureaucratisation of society is such that we can hardly think straight about an activity being a good in its own right. Everything, we imagine is a means to some other end, some other outcome.* Everything is a preparation for the 'delivery' of something else. But, lest we forget, life is an end in itself. If our whole lives become a preparation for future delivery then when will we actually live? *Life is not a preparation; not even for death. But life becomes a deathly, deadly, business when we are all turned into proletarians, seeking nothing other than to increase productivity, deliveries, outcomes and evidence.*

In our endless wealth creation we have forgotten what wealth is, what is intrinsically worthwhile. We are greatly in need of more *activity that is not so much delivering an outcome but which is, in itself, a worthwhile outcome.* Counselling can be its own worthwhile outcome. But *what we need, above all, is not more counselling but more humanity, more dialogue, at home, at work and in communities.*

Quality standards in counselling should focus on the quality of the experience itself. Yet, as they stand, quality standards do not even say anything about the *truth* of counselling theories, never mind evidence or efficacy. Therefore counsellors can be accredited who focus on the alleged 'past lives' of clients as much as early childhood or present or future options.

Counselling, then, to repeat, ought to be about dialogue rather than treatment. Dialogue is about being treated *as* a person, rather than being treated *by* a professional. Such personal, human, and humane contact and treatment is, in our alienating society, a real treat. The questions that matter in such a human encounter concern what *you make of it* as a cultural product rather than what *it makes of you.* So perhaps we should not despair that therapy is an ineffective treatment, since perhaps it was always a mistake to see it as a treatment at all. *Shakespeare, arguably, is an equally ineffective treatment. But perhaps we should treat ourselves both to Shakespeare and to therapy from time to time?* Therapy, like literature, is full of the good the bad and the mediocre. Perhaps it is statistically unavoidable that most is mediocre (relative to the best)? Perhaps this fact, too, does not have to be a cause for despair?

Research, then, shows that therapy cannot promise to make people 'better'. But perhaps we have no right, or reason, or need, to feel better. *Perhaps we would not feel so bad if we stopped imagining that we have any need, or right, to feel better*! Perhaps introspection, stocktaking and reflection are just something that, as human beings, we find intrinsically worthwhile. Likewise, we find dance, music, theatre etc intrinsically interesting and worthwhile. We don't engage in them and enjoy them because of what they may lead on to or because they make us feel good. They don't lead on to anything. They don't necessarily make us feel happy.

Even the very idea of feeling better is itself banal. Why should we feel better? What does 'better' as a genetic concept, even mean? We may feel sadder after watching a tragedy. But our appreciation and evaluation is not determined by whether we feel one particular emotion or another. Likewise, to ask what is the *destination* of a dance is an absurd question. In dancing we are not trying to get to a particular place in a room; but the movement is worthwhile in itself. Likewise, therapy can be something we greatly value, for what others might think are good or bad reasons, even though it 'goes' nowhere and 'delivers' no particular 'outcomes'.

Life consists in more than solving problems and achieving outcomes. In some ways, perhaps, counselling is just one way in which we stay alive. What are the 'outcomes' of a dialogue, or a conversation? To ask the question merely reveals that you don't understand why human beings value, enjoy and seek out dialogue.

Questions for Counsellors

1. How much attention do you pay to research into counselling? Do the results disturb you? Or does this research seem mainly irrelevant to you?
2. Do you think that asking if counselling is 'effective' is itself an effective line of questioning? In what circumstances should/should not we ask such a question?
3. Do you think of a counsellor as more like an artist than a social scientist? Can the quality of artistic work be measured in 'outcomes' and, if not, what do you propose?
4. Do you believe that, despite the evidence, experienced and trained counsellors are better than amateurs? If so, what is the basis of this belief?
5. Do you think that, given the research evidence, there is a justification for continued state funding of counselling?
6. Given that clients appear to want counsellors, and that they are happy to have received counselling, do the benefits appear to justify the costs? How is such a decision to be taken? How should the NHS make such a cost–benefit calculation?
7. Given the 1100% extra cost in making clients 'happy', when comparing counsellors with general practitioners, are BACP correct to suggest that counselling 'is not only efficacious, it is efficient'?
8. Do you agree with Patmore and Weaver that there are worries that scarce resources have been appropriated for less disabling conditions?
9. If you are assessed as 'seeming to understand a patient's internal reality' on what basis do you accept, or challenge, this assessment?
10. What is your opinion of the efforts of health maintenance organisations to control the costs of counselling? Do you think that such developments are likely, and desirable, in the UK?
11. How far, if at all, do you agree that researchers have essentially been asking the wrong questions? If so, what questions ought they to be asking?
12. Do you think that control groups are possible and desirable when researching counselling? If so, what form should they take?
13. How far do you agree that scientists study in the third person but that persons must be understood on a first person basis?
14. What does Banister mean when he says that 'The knower is part of the matrix of what is known'? How far do you agree with this statement?

15. How far do you think people have a right to give an account of themselves in their own language? What instances come to mind?
16. What do you think novelists and poets can offer in our understanding of persons that counsellors and scientists cannot?
17. Should counsellors and/or psychologists see themselves as scientists or artists? Explain and justify your answer.
18. Compare and contrast 'qualitative' with 'quantitative' research methods.
19. How do you describe the potential benefits of counselling to particular clients? Be specific concerning the individuals that come to mind. What kind of evidence could you offer these individuals, or is 'evidence' irrelevant?
20. Do you agree that counselling is often more of a cultural product than a social or medical service? If so, explain the similarities.
21. How are, and how should, cultural products be assessed, by whom and with what criteria? What specific examples come to mind?
22. Should governments subsidise people in their efforts to paint the story of their lives? Or do you reject this metaphor and, if so, why?
23. In your own counsellor practice and training, where do you draw inspiration in the search for a well-lived life?
24. Do you agree that counselling is, at its best, an 'intrinsic good' and that we seek to make sense of our lives because we are human beings rather than because we search for a particular 'outcome'?

CHAPTER 8

Transcending Self: Identity, Society and the Transpersonal

> You and I are psychologically in bad shape because our physical world is bent out of shape. (Hillman & Ventura 1993:125)

> The 'West' (including Japan) increased income per head fourfold in 1950–2001. The gap between the West and the rest grew but the rest still experienced a threefold rise in income per head. West: 2.8% c.f. rest 2.2% average growth per year. Measured by the benchmark favoured by the World Bank of income of $2 a day or less, adjusted to cater for differences in purchasing power, the proportion of the world's population in poverty dropped from 56% in 1980 to 23% in 2000. (*Economist* (2003) 'Liberty's Great Advance', 28 June–4 July, from OECD report 2002)

Throughout this book I have sought to show that personal and social dimensions of identity and development are part of one whole story. This chapter will explore more carefully and directly the intimate way in which selves and societies are intertwined. In the process we will need to address some related questions. For example, what does it mean when people talk about 'transcending' their individual circumstances?

How far, in order to be persons, and become fully human beings, can we, should we, and *must* we, seek to be social beings, ethical individuals and political persons? How far can we, and should we, escape from the confines of a self-centred 'ego' and achieve some kind of 'transpersonal' experience and commitment? What is meant by 'spiritual' and 'transcendental', that is of value in understanding ourselves and in achieving a well-lived life?

It is beyond dispute that personal and social development interconnects. Yet counselling still tends to focus too much on individual dynamics and neglect the ways in which social contexts construct and constrain individuals. And so, in considering individual prospects, it is relevant to ponder the likely future of individual communities, institutions, nations and the planet as a whole. For example, is a particular depressed client suffering because of some personal 'deficiency'/'abnormality' or because they have a realistic view of the tough and damaging future that awaits them?

Personal prospects and social trends

> Psychotherapeutic culture tends to focus on the internal world of the psyche and its cognitive and emotional processes. Little attention is paid to the world in which the person lives, and so people's problems are generally interpreted as personal or, at most, as family problems. (van Deurzen 1997a:94)

Hillman and Ventura's (1993) book was entitled, provocatively, *We've had One Hundred Years of Psychotherapy, and the World's Getting Worse.* They argued that psychotherapy could not ultimately help individuals in a world that was actively damaging people faster than counsellors could possibly 'repair' them. Hillman and Ventura asserted that counsellors needed to be more politically aware and astute if they were to contribute to human wellbeing. Many others have argued along similar lines.[1]

Certainly if the world really is getting 'worse' then this will be greatly detrimental to individual development, wellbeing and integrity. At its worst, if the ship of state is sinking, then comfortable conversations in the first class lounge only delay, but cannot prevent, the inevitable. Counsellors dealing with stress at work, for example, might do best to focus on the institutional causes of stress rather than merely trying to mop up the individual effects. Otherwise they may actually be *colluding* with, rather than genuinely alleviating the effects of, unjust, inhumane and destructive workplace environments.

Certainly counselling is vulnerable to being co-opted as a form of social control. *Social oppression, moreover, becomes all the more insulting when it is dressed up in the language of liberation.* Employers increasingly adopt an informal style and talk of teamwork, cooperation, creativity and empowerment. But employees may discover that they have less support, autonomy and control than from overtly authoritarian employers, and must work for longer hours and be continuously available. And if they do not? Then it is they who are the mavericks, who are not good team players, who are not 'owning', 'sharing' and participating in the corporate mission. George Orwell would, I think, have relished writing a satire on the way in which the language of humanistic counselling has been co-opted by those who already have too much power and who are abusing the power they have.

The *Economist*, on the other hand, as quoted above, for example, takes a much more positive view of personal, social and global prospects. Clearly these are very large debates that are not going to be settled in one chapter of one book! But I do think that counsellors need to have at least a basic awareness of the shape of the main arguments concerning social trends, especially insofar as these have a most direct effect on the wellbeing of clients. My own view is that optimists and pessimists (some of each) have important points to make that impact very strongly on the possibility of individuals developing their humanity, maturity, integrity and wellbeing.

Rowe (1996:167) copies a *Punch* cartoon (23 May 1984) which illustrates the connection between the personal and the political. It depicts a corporate 'fat cat', behind a large desk, who explains that: 'I love the absolute power that goes with my job. It allows me to be myself.' The lowly member of staff who is being spoken to looks less than enthusiastic. Power can indeed be an aphrodisiac and altogether raises levels of testosterone, energy, enthusiasm, confidence and wellbeing. And power is relative as well as absolute. What really makes us resourceful is not just that we have resources but that we have *more* resources than our neighbours can command. Only then can we enjoy *exclusive* goods, services, holiday locations and all the rest. And the whole point about an exclusive kind of lifestyle is that most people, by definition, are excluded from it.

But social exclusion appears to be highly destructive of the wellbeing and development of excluded individuals. If we are excluded from most of life's opportunities how are we to 'make something of' ourselves? Is crime to be our only option? Should we just make the best of our lot? Can the poor man at the gate find his way to a kingdom of heaven as easily as the rich man in his castle? Or is the rich man in fact excluded from such a kingdom just as a camel can never pass through the eye of a needle? How much inequality will produce the optimal amount of wellbeing for rich and poor alike? How much inequality in fact exists?

Even the *Economist*, that beacon of capitalist free enterprise, expresses concern about some of the destructive effects of wealth creation as currently practised:

> The really damaging perception now is that many of these mega-incomes have been gained through the abuse of power – and that, in some cases, they are also being preserved by the use of that moneyed power in politics. Worse still, the perception is largely correct. (*Economist* (2003) 'Pigs, Pay and Power', 28 June–4 July)

> Corruption, by firms and individuals seeking to exploit governments' vast powers, is indeed a big problem for democracies all over the world. (*Economist* (2003) 'Pro-market, Not Pro-business', 28 June–4 July)

Even the *Economist* accepts that beyond a certain degree, inequality can become abusive, corrupting and damaging to all concerned. Even the rich, in the longer term, may not be safe if public spaces erode, crime increases, and there are ever fewer places that can be visited in safety.

'With the exceptions of Switzerland and Japan, throughout the developed world violence has increased at an astonishing rate since 1950'. (James 1998:26). James argues that many people are depressed because the world is becoming an increasingly depressing place to live in. If so, we will only feel better when we change our world sufficiently enough for us to have *good reason* to feel better. 'A lot of people are depressed because they have good reason to be. A lot of people have dull, meaningless lives, and they're unhappy. Talking to a therapist won't change that, unless it results in the person living differently' (Bandler 1985:29).

Sennett, likewise, poses some hard social questions that impact directly on individual wellbeing and development. To develop as persons we need a degree of security, we need to be able to make long-term plans and develop long-term commitments. But Sennett paints a social context that is preventing increasing numbers of us from achieving these basic goals and meeting these fundamental needs. He asks:

> How can long term goals be pursued in an economy devoted to the short term? How can mutual loyalties be sustained in institutions which are constantly breaking apart or continually being redesigned? (Sennett 1998:10)

> How can a human being develop a narrative of identity and life history in a society composed of episodes and fragments? (Ibid.: 26)

He provides a poignant account of one individual who is trying to teach his children the importance of commitment: 'Rico suddenly erupted on the plane, "You can't imagine how stupid I feel when I talk to my kids about commitment. It's an abstract virtue to them; they don't see it anywhere"' (Ibid.:25). Commitment, Sennett argues, is central to our identity formation, to our wellbeing, to common civility, civic pride and individual security. Yet how can we be committed, and how can others be committed to us, in an economy that does not value or reward commitment in any way? And what happens to our morale when, despite our best efforts to move 'forward', the economy appears to be propelling us backwards?

> The economist Simon Head has calculated that for the bottom 80 per cent of the American working population, average weekly wages (adjusted for inflation) fell by 18 per cent from 1973–1995, while the pay of the corporate elite rose 19 per cent before taxes, and 66 per cent after the tax accountants had worked their magic. (Ibid.:54)

> Today more people lose than gain through making company job changes; 34 per cent significantly lose, 28 per cent significantly gain. (Ibid.:86)

We like to think that there is justice and fairness in our world, and that we will be rewarded for our efforts. But instead it appears that corruption and greed continue to be rewarded the most, and that honesty and integrity are exploited more than respected. If true, this is hugely damaging to our feelings towards each other and to our view of ourselves. How can we trust and commit to each other when trust and commitment are merely abused and betrayed? But how can we function as individuals if we have no reason to trust? How can we function as individuals if we cannot find projects to which, and persons to whom, we are committed?

How can we succeed, together and separately, in the longer term, if success is measured by narrow, short-term, individual and selfish criteria? And if only a few are defined as 'successes', what becomes of that majority who, failing to achieve celebrity and exclusivity, are deemed to be failures? 'Failure is the great modern taboo. Popular literature is full of recipes for how to succeed, but largely silent about how to cope with failure' (Ibid.:118).

It is argued that we are only left behind by social change if we fail to keep up with the changes. The rate of change in the economy increases; we must continually retrain to keep abreast of such change. And then we will have our fair share?

> It is estimated that by 2010, of people aged twenty-five, 41 per cent of those in the United States will have a four-year college degree, 62 per cent at least a two year college degree; the rates for Britain and Western Europe are predicted to be about 10 per cent lower. Yet only a fifth of jobs in the American labour force require a college degree, and the percentage of these highly qualified jobs is only slowly rising. (Ibid.:89).

> The value of educational credentials begins to fall as a higher percentage of each generation achieves graduate status (up to 6% in the early 1960s to almost 30% in the early 1990s) when there is no corresponding expansion of elite jobs. (Coffield & Williamson 1997:13)

The 'good life' is there to be earned, we are told. Yet more and more educational qualifications produce fewer and fewer returns. What do you say to an arts graduate, the comedian asks. The answer? 'Burger and fries please'. We must become more competitive in an increasingly competitive world. Reorganisation, continuous change, quality assurance, management of change is essential. 'Deadwood' must be removed. But does it work?

> The AMA (American Management Association) found that repeated downsizings produce 'lower profits and declining worker productivity'; the Wyatt study found that 'less than half the companies achieved their expense reduction goals; fewer than one third increase profitability and less than one in four increased their productivity.' (Sennett 1998:50)

We will feel good about our world and ourselves, perhaps, if there is a good life to work towards. But otherwise? 'A middle-class standard of life generally now requires two adult wage-earners' (Ibid.:57). And what happens to our morale when cheats, cynics, criminals, tyrants and opportunists appear to prosper? 'The really successful ones seem the most adept at walking away from disaster, leaving others to hold the bag; success consists in avoiding the reckonings of the accountant's bottom line' (Ibid.:79).

The *Economist*, as quoted above, argues that there has been substantial economic progress since 1950. *But what has the position been since 1980, or 1970?*

> Briefer vacations and longer working hours combined to produce an increase of 30 working days per year from 1967 to 1987. (Swann 1996:132)

> Between 1960 and 1986, the time parents spent with their children dropped 10 hours per week for whites and 12 hours per week for African Americans. (Ibid.:133)
>
> Since, 1964, participation in parent-teacher associations has plummeted from 12 million to 7 million. Volunteering help for various community activities has become increasingly rare. (Ibid.:135)
>
> In a survey conducted during the 1980s, 70 percent of Americans reported feeling a void in their lives because they had many acquaintances but few close friends. In addition, 41 percent reported that they had fewer close friends than they did in the recent past. (Ibid.:136)

Are all these signs of a serious decline in 'real' wealth and wellbeing that may be occurring even as gross domestic product is increasing? If counsellors see more children should they attend to child dynamics or to absent working parents? If clients are chronically exhausted will words from a counsellor assist, or a longer holiday – free from faxes, emails and mobile phones? If clients seek to befriend their counsellor should the counsellor reciprocate or encourage the client to build a community of real friends? Or should the counsellor acknowledge that the problems are primarily social and that therefore the solutions, likewise, must be social rather than psychological? If a client is pessimistic should we encourage them to be more optimistic? Will we provide *reasons* for optimism?

> Such pessimism is well-founded – over the past few decades, the possibilities for escaping poverty have become increasingly remote. (Ibid.:141)
>
> The foreclosure of community, and the trivialisation of the self and family are the rubble upon which we construct our glass corporations. (O'Neil 1995:18)

There are many apocalyptic warnings of dehumanisation, exploitation of people and planet, and spiritual poverty in the midst of material abundance. Who is to be believed? Certainly the questions matter. O'Neil (1995) is particularly pessimistic concerning the influence of postmodern capitalism on the possibilities of achieving any kind of identity, decency and personal humanity:

> Style rewrites the mind, appropriates authority and narrativity in order to subject writing to writing – grammatology without end. (O'Neil 1995:15)
>
> Experience surrenders to the autonomy of the instant which in turn cracks all memory. (Ibid.:22)
>
> The suspension of a common sense and of public discourse fractions human speech into aggressive 'mini-logues' that, in my view, distract us from the corporate monologue which is, in fact, well served by the postmodern Babel of tongues. (Ibid.:194)

Designer spirituality

> The numerous efforts to persuade everybody to be the brother of everybody, indiscriminately, on a mass scale, have not met with much success. (Zeldin 1998:388)

Brooks (2000) seeks to argue, not quite seriously, that the new elite is more humane, sensitive and caring than its predecessors. But the 'care' that he describes is more of the 'designer' variety than the genuine article. The exploiter who pretends to be your friend and buddy is, if anything, even more obnoxious than one who does not bother to peddle such illusions. 'To calculate a person's status, you take his net worth and multiply it by his anti-materialist attitudes' (Brooks 2000:50). Re-enter the Marxist tycoon. Re-enter the materialist who claims not to be one. Re-enter the consumers who buy goods that make endless consumer 'statements' that their owners are not really consumers. 'A capacious kitchen with durable appliances is a sign that you do your own chores, sharing the gritty reality of everyday life, just as Gandhi and Karl Marx would have wanted you to' (Ibid.:89).

> Grocery stores provide brochures delineating the company's notions about community. Ice cream companies now possess their own foreign policy doctrines. These stores offend us if they dwell overmuch on utilitarian concerns – such as what a great bargain we are getting – but they win our loyalty if they appeal to our idealistic hopes. Volvo advertises a 'car that can not only save your life, but help save your soul as well.' Toyota counters with a slogan for its line of trucks that reads, 'Haul some concrete. Move some lumber. Save the world.' Johnnie Walker Scotch announces, 'In a crass and Insincere World, Something That Isn't.' (Ibid.:100)

> We educated elites surround ourselves with the motifs of lives we have chosen not to live. (Ibid.:96)

In a materialist world, élite consumers, some at least, have caught on to the idea that materialism is not the only kind of wealth. There are all kinds of books around claiming that we suffer from spiritual poverty, that we are alienated, and that we cannot find our true selves unless we mend our ways. So *designer spirituality has become a major growth area within the postmodern economy.*

> Everything the old gentry tried to make smooth, we in today's educated gentry try to make rough. They covered over ceiling beams. We expose them. They buried bulky stone chimneys in plaster and paint. We unearth stone chimneys and admire massive rocky hearths. (Ibid.:83)

> We will buy chicken legs, just like everyone else, but they'll be likely to be free-range chickens that in life were treated better than Elizabeth Taylor at a health spa. (Ibid.:97)

> The beauty of such a strategy is that it allows us to be egalitarian and pretentious at the same time. (Ibid.)

Trungpa (1973), among others, showed that this kind of 'spiritual materialism' is in no way new and carries a large romantic element. 'Spirituality', in any case, is an extremely problematic concept. It is hardly surprising that many shun it altogether for fear of being swallowed up by New Age mysticism or other kinds of dogmatism, irrationality or romantic reverie. But many, who do not wish to subscribe to ecclesiastical medievalism, or sign up to any particular theology, nonetheless seek spiritual forms of 'wealth' and identity, and are dissatisfied with material consumerism and retail therapy. Where are they to turn? So often spirituality is associated with pleasant experiences of peace, serenity, and oneness with the world.

> Spiritual needs. We all have a deep need for a sense of uniqueness, union, usefulness, understanding. (Morris 1999:108)

> Spirituality is fundamentally about two things: depth and connectedness. (Morris 1997:174)

Is that what spirituality is about? Yes, and no, perhaps. 'Meditation isn't to disappear into the light. Meditation is to see *all* of what we are. As long as there's any state of mind you prefer to any other state of mind, that's your hell. So, we sit and we say "There's my restlessness," and we see it as the old demon. Not something to be afraid of, just the demon' (Levine 1979:97). Is a holy person a wholly 'good' person or a person who sees themselves whole – warts and all? And what does spirituality have to do with our identity? Quite a lot, it seems: 'We keep thinking that we are the contents of our mind, but actually we are the space in which these contents are happening' (Levine 1984:120).

Here we are, trying to make ourselves more solid, more of a 'somebody'. And here are various transcendentalists telling us, yet again, that 'really' we are just a 'space'! Religions have often spoken of the need for us to recognise our essential 'nothingness'. This reminds me of the old Jewish joke: The rabbi praying, says, 'Lord, I am nothing'. The senior rabbi asserts, 'Lord, I am nothing, *nothing*'. The caretaker says 'Lord, I am nothing, *nothing*, NOTHING!'. The rabbis, angry, observe, 'Who does he think he is to think that he is more of a nothing than we are!' Spiritual competitiveness once again.

> Being at one with our surroundings is a unique experience and thus might merit the word 'spiritual', but when this word takes on the connotations of superior virtue and contact with mysterious powers the experience itself with all its wonderment is degraded. (Dorothy Rowe, online at: http://www.dorothyrowe.com.au/spirit_psych_what_spirit.htm)

We will compete about everything and perhaps competition is nowhere fiercer than among those who wish to become more spiritually 'advanced'. It is no wonder that many shrink back from this kind of fantasy and indulgence. But will our consideration of identity be adequate if we ignore constructs of spirituality?

> The doctrines of egolessness and of transience, along with that of suffering, form the central base of the philosophy of the human person in Buddhism. (de Silva 2000:83)
>
> But then what is the conventionally existent I that undergoes help and harm? Within the Buddhist schools there are many different assertions on what the person who undergoes help and harm is. (Gyatso (Fourteenth Dalai Lama) 1984:163)

Notice that the Dalai Lama refers to 'many different assertions' concerning the nature of the person. It appears that, as we have already seen, we can be identified in many ways, with many assertions, in many different contexts, and are not just 'nothing' or 'space', useful though these latter concepts may be in some circumstances. What we make of each other and ourselves varies and changes a great deal.

But for many who seek a spiritual dimension to their identity such complication is unwelcome. They seek to escape. They want magic powers and/or magical defences against uncertainty. They want something simple to hold on to. All the time, they simplify: 'what we identify as the Christian tradition actually represents only a small selection of specific sources chosen from among dozens of others' (Hardy 1987:126). Of course, a degree of simplification is inevitable and essential if we are to make sense of ourselves and our world. But, too often, our efforts to simplify become simplistic, and pathos descends into bathos.

In a disenchanting world there has long been a romantic urge for the heroic, adventurous, remote, mysterious, and idealised. We seek passion, mystery, enchantment and the miraculous, within ourselves and all around us. We seek to add chapters, metaphors, and adventures to the story of our lives.

This entire book, for example, can itself become a binge eating festival of consumption of the concepts of self that have been developed over many centuries. Ideas can be *collected*, and *assembled* like any other sets of goods, possessions or commodities. But this is to abuse the purpose of this book since, in my view, ideas are *tools* and, as such, they are of no use unless they are used, put to some good purpose. Like so much else, it is what *you*, very personally, *make* of all these self-constructs that really matters. And there is no reason why you should, or will, make the same of this text as other readers. If this account is coherent at all, though, there will, I hope, be some commonality and coherence of response.

The search for the miraculous is commonplace among spiritual seekers. But perhaps we above all need to see that the whole of life is something of a miracle, even at its most dejected and depressing. 'Everything is a miracle when you give it your full attention and yet everything is still quite ordinary' (Stevens 1977:255).

Transcending oneself

'Spirituality', variously defined and understood, has long been an important agenda within some schools of psychotherapy. Most notably, Roberto Assagioli (1888–1974) a contemporary of Freud, juxtaposed his psycho*synthesis* with Freudian psycho*analysis*. Freudian analysis consisted in examining the components of self and understanding individual dynamics. Assagioli's synthesis involved making connections between ourselves and the larger picture of which we were a part. For Assagioli, our central task was not to clarify what it was, people, places, principles, projects, with which we identified; rather we needed to learn to *dis*identify. 'We are dominated by everything with which our self is identified. We can dominate and control everything from which we dis-identify ourselves' (Assagioli 1980:111).

As Buddhists have long argued, much of our suffering arises from 'attachment'. We try to have and to hold that which we wish to permanent. But everything changes, nothing is permanent, and we suffer as we try to stop the rise and fall of this tide of change. So disidentification has its place. It allows us to take a larger perspective, to look *in* on our situation, our alliances and our accoutrements rather than always looking out *through* them. But if we are always trying to look down on our lives from Mount Olympus we may once again find that we are foolishly trying to play at being a God when we are a mere mortal human being. We *withdraw* from commitment, action and involvement and become mere *spectators* concerning the imagined story of our lives.

'What am I then? What remains after discarding from my self-identity the physical, emotional and mental contents of my personality, of my ego? It is the essence of myself – a centre of pure self-consciousness and self-realisation. I am a centre of awareness and power' (Ibid.:119). Yes and no. We are not simply awareness and power. Freedom involves choice and choice involves *limiting* ourselves and *excluding* all those options that we *might* have chosen. It involves standing by, for, and understanding, all the choices we have made with all their, often inevitably, limiting consequences. 'A basic tenet of Gestalt psychology is that a person is inseparable from his environment' (Passons 1975:49). If we are inseparable from our environment then there is a limit to which we can, and should, disidentify ourselves from all our accoutrements. If someone asks you who you are and you reply merely that you are a 'centre of awareness and power', then the questioner may see you as rather too airy and unreal for your own, or anyone else's, good.

'Human persons . . . exist only in a certain space of questions, through certain constitutive concerns' (Taylor 1996:50). Taylor speaks of space, but the space is less ethereal. There are questions and concerns. We identify with them. We stand by and for them. We might, *in extremis*, even be prepared to fight and die for them. This may sometimes be folly but sometimes it may be courageous and honourable. And not all romantics are of the airy, ethereal, withdrawing sort. Many saw that the most important means of self-expression was not via Cartesian 'mind-stuff', quietly pursued in aesthetic introspection, but in action, commitment, active involvement in the people and causes around us: 'Goethe, Schiller, Schelling, Hegel, Coleridge, and Emerson – common to all was a fundamental conviction that the relation of the human mind to the world was ultimately not dualistic but participatory' (Tarnas 1991:433).

More prosaically, symbolic interactionists within sociology, like John Dewey, George Mead and Charles Cooley, argued that the self was not fundamentally to be found in psychology but was a sociological phenomenon. Minds, selves were not found in the Cartesian fashion by looking 'inwards', neither were we even born with a mind. Rather we made up our mind by deciding what we were going to do, with whom, where and why.[2] Identity arose from experience and was constructed and reconstructed piece by piece in an essentially social process of engagement, commitment and interaction. So we certainly could not *dis* identify with all these social accoutrements, since we only identified ourselves by creating our various social identities. 'We can replace the Cartesian dictum *cogito ergo sum* with *communicamus ergo sum*, for without co-ordinated acts of communication, there is simply no "I" to be articulated' (Gergen 1991:242).

So perhaps it is worth rephrasing Hamlet's *to be*, or *not to be* by asking whether *to identify, or to disidentify*? Perhaps we need to do both? But which option do we choose, in what circumstances and for what reasons? Perhaps the answer can sometimes be found by asking what it is that we might be *running away from*? We may cultivate an 'inner' life, and disassociate from the world around us, because the social world frightens, appals or dismays us. On the other hand we may become social activists since we are terrified at the prospect of sitting alone with ourselves, even for a moment. Wherever the locus of our attention, the question can sometimes be asked, to good purpose, 'what am I *avoiding*?' 'The left has too often served as a refuge from the terrors of the inner life' (Lasch 1980:46).

Of course, we may just be exercising a positive preference, without necessarily feeling any fear of the alternatives. Introverts more easily feel reconnected with themselves, and at home, when alone; extraverts find themselves most comfortably when in contact with others. One identifies mostly with their 'inner life', the other with the external. Either way, though, we may resist *changes* to anything in our lives with which we have identified. Wilber et al. observe that: 'My experience teaching Buddhist psychology and *Vipassana* meditation has made it equally clear that clinging to a sense of personal continuity and self-identity results in chronic discontent and psychic conflict' (Wilbur et al. 1986:17).

Anchoring oneself

We seek continuity, in order to create some stability and predictability in our world, and so we suffer when that which seemed central to our identity changes or disintegrates. It is wise, then, to avoid *clinging* to personal continuity. But we surely need to seek and establish some integration, stability and continuity of self and world. Otherwise we risk dissolution into chaos. We can make too much of ourselves, but it is unwise to make nothing of ourselves. *Meditation, then, can be positively dangerous for some persons who, far from being weighed down by their own weight, are just too ethereal for their own, or anybody else's good.* We don't want to be bogged down on the ground we occupy, but it is important to ensure that our feet are actually attached to the ground – at least some of the time. 'In my experience, Buddhism can exert a special attraction for individuals with borderline organisation. In part the attraction seems to be precisely the *anatta* or no-self doctrine. It helps explain and rationalise, if not actually legitimate, their lack of self-integration, their feelings of inner emptiness, of not having a cohesive self' (Ibid.:31).

Viorst (1986:62) expresses similar concerns: 'As part of a magical, mystical whole with claims to perfect enlightenment, he tries to find augmentation of the self. As part of a joyful, blissed out whole which banishes "negative thoughts", he tries to retrieve the rapture of infantile narcissism.' A person who has made nothing of themselves and their lives may well be strongly attracted to a doctrine that states that we are just an airy space and that nothing lasts. *If nothing lasts, then perhaps it doesn't matter that we have done nothing, created nothing, achieved nothing*? Except that it *does* matter. It is an ultimate funk, an act of bad faith, to withdraw from commitment and involvement in the world merely because, in the long run, we are all dead.

The history of spiritual practice is full of such quietist avoidance, failure to make a mark, or lay down foundations or take a stand. The turf we stand on can only be of infinitesimal significance compared with the universe as a whole. But it's our turf. It's where we stand, like it or not. With a spiritual perspective we seek to take a broader view. But we look out on a vast vista using just one pair of eyes, placed within one head, on one body at one place at a time. With imagination we can try to extend the range of our understanding, but not by pretending that we can look out from everywhere at once or from nowhere at all.

The quietist might try to live in the whole cosmos at large, but individual human beings can only really have an impact within a small universe of concern, a limited universe of discourse. Spirituality might provide a worthwhile perspective on this small turf, and help us to place it in its appropriate larger context. But if we try, in creative imagination, to be everywhere, we end up being nowhere, doing nothing, and making nothing of ourselves. Thus, in our search for the miraculous infinite, we end up achieving infinitely less than those who just cultivated their own garden and protected their own household.

Freud, aware of such dangers, was highly dismissive of spirituality. He saw it as a regression, an attempt to return, in imagination to that kind of 'oceanic awareness', peace, and oneness that, Freud argued, we could only experience in the womb. This certainly does appear, sometimes, to be the reality of some people's spiritual yearning. They want security, peace, and *an escape from the pangs of person-hood with all its painful limitations*: 'Practitioners of meditation, often swimming in the rhetoric of transformation, may fail to recognise the regressive nature of much of their experiences' (Wilbur et al. 1986:56).

Jung, on the other hand, was highly critical of Freudian reductionism and emphatically did not believe that all spiritual yearnings could be reduced and trivialised in this way. Indeed, Jung even dared to use the 'G' word that, for many, is hopelessly encumbered with theological dogmas. 'The individual who is not anchored in God can offer no resistance on his own resources to the physical and moral blandishments of the world' (Jung 1996:360).

As the Dalai Lama observes, there is no unanimity concerning the nature of self among those with a concern for spirituality. Wilbur highlights the dangers of quietist withdrawal and avoidance, but sometimes (1981:279) appears to succumb himself: 'Hui-neng summarised the entire essence of Zen as "Inwardly, no identity; outwardly, no attachment" . . . *property* and *persons* are, beyond their temporary usefulness, ***nothing but*** "stick points" or "blockages" to higher consciousness. They are ways of defending and fortifying the separate self against transcendence.' I highlighted 'nothing but' because I think it is generally dangerous to say that something is nothing but something else. If that were so why would we use different words with different meanings? Property and persons can indeed be 'stick points'. We can be encumbered and entrapped by our constructed identity. We may sometimes need to move on. But cherished ideas about, and commitments to, projects, properties and persons have their place. We sometimes want, need, and *should* be a 'somebody', and not just a more-of-a-nothing-than-thou. Holiness is one thing. Holier than thou is another. A disciple was asked 'Who are you?' and responded 'I have no idea'. The Zen teacher observed, 'you are, of course, free to cling to that idea of no idea'. And people often do.

Identity concerns boundaries. We can create a great deal of pain for ourselves when we cling overmuch to lines drawn between 'us and them', 'me and you', 'his and hers', self and other. As Robert Frost observed in his poem 'Mending Wall':

> Something there is that doesn't love a wall,
> That sends the frozen-ground-swell under it,
> And spills the upper boulders in the sun;
> (Frost 1968:33)

But boundaries also have a place and we need to know when it is time to draw a line and when it is better to rub it out, or see it for what it was, a partial construction, and sub-division, of underlying unity. 'The boundary between self and other causes fear, the boundary between past and future causes anxiety, the boundary between subject and object causes desire . . . the aim of mystics is to deliver men and women from their battles by delivering them from their boundaries' (Wilbur 1981:334). Boundaries do indeed cause fear and anxiety because boundaries, if they are worth establishing, are worth defending. Life depends utterly on the boundary-making of the cell walls that facilitate and block the movement of chemical messengers. The mystic may pay more attention to the whole, and see it as greater than the sum of its parts. But 'selves' are no more illusory than cells. One comprises the building blocks of an organism, the other of a society. Both have their place. From the householder's, ruler's, merchant's and warrior's perspective, self is of major concern, though we can all benefit from the mystic's injunction to sit loose to the self we think we are. Home, nation, company, comrades are being quite falsely and wrongly disparaged, abused and insulted if they are dismissed as merely illusions. And what would the mystic do, where would they find alms, how would they live, but for the worldly work of non-mystics?

'When the self sense dies, all that dissolves is not a real entity but a simple boundary, a boundary that was never real, a boundary that was only imaginary' (Ibid.:337). This is unacceptable. And it is false. The boundary between self and other is no more imaginary than the boundaries between cells. When people we care about, and have spent our lives with, die it is an abuse of language, and of humanity, to say that there was no real entity there in the first place. The real entity was real enough. It (he or she) was a real person, embodied, and with a mind to say, and to do, this or that, in response to who or whatever. True, a certain softening of (our understanding of and attachment to) these boundaries, is appropriate and useful. Parfit (1984:282) makes one such attempt: 'Thinking hard about these arguments removes the glass wall between me and others. And, as I have said, I care less about my death. This is merely the fact that, after a certain time, none of the experiences that will occur will be related, in certain ways, to my present experiences. Can this matter all that much?' Obviously it *does* matter to some, not inconsiderable, degree. We would, rightly, be seen as callous, unfeeling or, more likely, dishonest, if on losing our mother or spouse, we claimed to have lost only an illusion and made light of it. Such loss is real and grief is the only respectful and healing response.

'So long as we are preoccupied with our wants and fears, our identities, we are confined within the narrow prison of the self, cut off from the world, from life . . . And the way to release is by realising that what we call self is in fact ephemeral, a phenomenon in constant change' (Hart 1982:133). Yes and no. Self-hood, our own personal perspective, can be something of a prison. But it *is* our perspective, if we don't take it, who will? If we won't be ourselves, who will? And do we really want to avoid suffering by hiding as space, in space, as a form of non-being? Moreover, whether we want to or not, do we have any right to 'space ourselves out' in this way? We have duties, obligations, a world to live, a place and more to occupy; and a project and more, to choose, commit to, and complete. Spirituality, then, is a trap, a dead-end, a form of avoidance *and* a means of emancipation. 'A. Ellis[3] has been one of the main critics of psychologically dysfunctional religiosity' (Feltham 1995:106). Over and over again, those who would identify themselves cross swords with those who seek to *dis*-identify. Here is Fromm: 'Still another form of trying to heal the suffering of separateness lies in building up one's own Ego, as a separate, fortified, indestructible "thing". One then experiences oneself as one's own property, one's power, one's prestige, one's intellect' (Fromm et al. 1977:89). Making something of oneself can indeed become something of a trap, and Fromm explores the extent to which we define ourselves in terms of what we have accumulated and made into 'us-and-ours'.[4] But it can also be a trap to make nothing of oneself and try to be more of a nothing than other 'not-selves'. Here, in contrast, is Elliott (2003:27) describing G. H. Mead's various forms of *identified* selves: 'The "me" is the socialised self, made up of the internalised attitudes of others as experienced in the early years of life. The "I", as Mead uses the term, is the unsocialised self, an assortment of personal desires, needs and dispositions.' Mystics would say that we need to float free of both 'me' and 'I'. But that seems unwise, though Mead's boundary between the socialised and unsocialised self is, in any case, far less hard and fast than it appears. After all, the self emerges from a social context; there never is a self prior to, or outside of, the social world of which it is a part. 'At the moment of enlightenment the cognitive structures that maintain our individual egos collapse. The mind is no longer dominated by an abstract sense of "I" or by goal seeking or time dependent constructs of self' (Hey 1988 in Mace 1999:198).

Neurologists are now beginning to discover the physiological concomitants of meditation and 'transcendental' experience. Spiritual practitioners who claim to have lost a sense of self, space and time, as ordinarily understood, do indeed register reductions in the blood supply to the parietal lobes of the brain, that are concerned with orientation, sense of self, and space–time location.[5] 'Neuro-theologists' seek to relate the claims of mystics to the concomitant changes in the brain and are confident that their understanding both of the brain and of mystical experiences will be increased as a result.

But the question remains, however possible it undoubtedly is to transcend ordinary boundaries of self, space and time, in what circumstances, and for what reasons, is such transcendence actually *desirable*?

'The ego covers over the fragmentation of the psyche through narcissistic illusions of perfection and completeness' (Elliott 2003:137). Neurologists may indeed confirm that the changes in experience induced by meditation were 'real' in that they correlated to relevant physiological change. It would be far more surprising if such correlation was *not* found. But the 'mind bending' might still, on occasions, in some circumstances, be avoidance, an indulgence, and a somewhat juvenile party trick. 'Minds emerge from process and interaction, not substance. In a sense we inhabit the spaces between things. We subsist in emptiness. A Beautiful, liberating thought and nothing to be afraid of. The notion of a tethered soul is crude by comparison' (Broks 2003:56).

Broks is a neurologist, willing to break free of mechanistic and materialistic language. I think he is right in that persons are not just physical and not just mental, and not just individual and not just social. When making up our minds we make up our minds *about* something or someone. In so doing, we forge links of interconnection, patterns of understanding that are indeed about relation, perspective, process and interaction. Meditation may help us achieve such insights, but it may also leave us more spaced out than is good for us:

> Meditation, in other words, tends to undo those intermediate level self-structures that the borderline or psychotic is in need of creating and strengthening in the first place. (Wilbur et al. 1986:154)

> Someone caught in role confusion or role conformist pathology, or who is having a difficult time establishing formal self identity, is particularly vulnerable to using meditation, and various meditation groups, in a cultic fashion, pledging allegiance to the particular meditative 'in-group' as an acting out of unresolved identity neuroses.
>
> In sum: meditation is not a structure-building technique, nor a script analysis-technique, nor a Socratic-dialoguing technique. It cannot substitute for these techniques, nor should it be used as a way to spiritually bypass (Welwood, 1984) any major work needed on those levels. (Ibid.:156)

The role of 'peak experiences'

Vulnerable individuals, seeking to 'transcend' themselves, can easily succumb to the authority of cult leaders. They may blindly identify themselves with their new-found community; collapse subtle realities into simplistic homilies, and inflict their own claims to 'salvation' on others. They will, of course, busily form schisms with those who, though similar in their perspective, do not quite know 'The Truth' as known by the truly enlightened.

Such bickering has been observable throughout the history of Christianity ever since the Roman Emperor Constantine (280–337) became a convert, thereby giving Christians real power. As Nietzsche observed, one would be more inclined to believe that Christ was a redeemer if Christians looked rather more redeemed, and redeemable. As it is, they tend to lag behind, and actively oppose social change, and identify with conservative, authoritarian, dogmatic and intolerant principles and practices.

Quite apart from the implausible theological ideas, Christian ethics have often been equally objectionable. Christian perspectives have, too often, constituted an escape from the subtleties, mysteries and complexities of an ever-changing, endlessly perplexing and often rather frightening world. It is true that more liberal thinkers within Christianity share a willingness to 'not know' and to embrace a suitable humility about dogma. In this respect they are much closer to non-theistic secular transcendentalists than they are to Christians of a more 'fundamentalist' bent.

Hence I do not think it is at all certain that, on balance, Christianity has been a force for good within humanity and for the formation of all our identities. It is interesting to speculate about what would have become of Christianity if Constantine had not become a convert. What if he had remained in the view that Christianity offered just one 'take' on reality, among many others in the Roman Empire, rather than the One and Final Truth? Perhaps our subsequent history would have been more benign and enlightened? There is no way of knowing. But Hellenism, that body of humanist and classical ideas associated with ancient Greece, does appear, in many respects, more attractive, cosmopolitan, coherent and tolerant than Hebraism, to use the binary explored by Matthew Arnold.

A respect for a spiritual[6] apprehension of life can and should be differentiated from interest in theology, belief in supernatural deities, or any kind of wish to join a Church. In a postmodern era many people take a 'pick and mix' approach to spiritual matters. At its worst this can be superficial, arbitrary, ignorant and chaotic. At its best it can be ecumenical in the positive sense of seeking what is of abiding significance beneath all the details of history. As the dictionary shows, 'spirituality' denotes and connotes in a variety of ways. I do not think we need the supernatural, the ghostly, or the dogmatic connotations.

What is there within spiritual experience that may be of biological value? Charlton (2000:197), for example, refers to the role of 'peak experiences': 'The peak experience seems to function as a means of focusing attention. The characteristic emotion asserts that the marked insight is something we should dwell upon, puzzle over, sort out – *do* something about. It is not – or should not be – simply a passive feeling of happiness and insight.'

'Peak experiences are the result of a "significant alarm" going off in the brain. When things are working properly, this alarm will only be triggered when something "important" has happened that is worthy of sustained attention' (Ibid.:205). With a peak experience, we feel that something is 'coming together' in some way. We may feel we have had some kind of breakthrough, there may be elation, or peace, or acceptance. The details and variations lie way beyond the capacity of neurologists to map them. But Charlton is surely right to warn that peak experiences are not an infallible guide to 'truth': 'Peak experience insights have the potential to mislead as well as to enlighten. The easy induction of pseudo-profound insights by intoxicants serves as a warning of the potential pitfalls' (Ibid.:204).

Charlton describes one of his own 'peak experiences'. He dreamt that he had discovered the secret to his own wealth and success. It was buried in the words *Oh Colonel Flastratus*! and the precise manner in which these words were stated. As he observes: 'The only "funny" thing about *Oh Colonel Flastratus*! was the surrealist absurdity of my having attached significance to it' (Ibid.:190). Likewise I can think of many occasions when something has 'come together' for me. A bulb lights up in my brain as it were. I think, 'yes, that's it!' I feel that I have made a breakthrough about something I was unsure about. But then the cold light of day requires that this bright idea be subjected to test. My own scrutiny involves rejecting most candidate ideas. They were not so brilliant as they seemed when I was half-asleep or half-awake. Then there is the test that comes when others scrutinise the results. More candidates fall by the wayside. 'Aha, that's it!' signifies the birth of another 'cod roe' of an idea. Only a small minority ever develops into fully-grown cod! The elation of a breakthrough is rare.

> The first tendency of an individual is to be connected, involved, outgoing, and engaged with the world, but punishment, the loss of approval, and physical harm soon batter these life tendencies and create a foundation for ambivalence. (Sloan 1987:128)

Equally rare is the sense of peace and 'at-oneness'. More often, the world can seem to be a threat, and the body is then placed into 'alarm' mode, ready to fight or flee. In such circumstances we may feel separate from, at odds with, and threatened by the world. Or, if we are stronger and more confident, there may be an opportunity to successfully hunt down something (or someone) that we would wish to make a part of us and ours. Or we may successfully fight back and feel triumphant, elated. Or we may be defeated and lapse into depression and despair.

In a more spiritual mode of being-in-the-world the boundaries between self and world may feel much more loose and arbitrary. We feel at one with everything and everyone around us. At its most profound, an experience like this can lead me to feel that everything and everyone around me is my brother and sister. So what is the truth? The postmodern view is that there is not just a single truth at all. *A fight–flight approach to the world is appropriate when there is fighting or fleeing to be done. A sense of deep trust, union, and peace and at oneness with everyone and everything around me is suitable when I am safe and secure enough to trust my environment to this degree.*

But the idea that we can *always* feel at one and at peace, and *always* feel our identities merged into a warm bath of worldly love and care, seems more like a divine than a human agenda! Spiritual seekers talk about the wish to become 'enlightened'. The secular perspective of self as separate from, and permanently at odds with, its environment, is seen as a cage, a trap, an illusion. It leads to chronic suffering and insecurity. If only, the seeker imagines, we could find a place where we always felt at peace, at one, at home.

If only. But people often feel threatened because they *are* threatened. They may feel insecure because they *are* insecure. They may feel angry because they need to mobilise themselves against injustices that they may well be right to challenge. Life is not always like a still millpond into which we can stare, meditate and merge. It is often a violent, raging storm, or a restless chopping, heaving uncertainty.

'No one who wants to be enlightened will ever be enlightened because what we are enlightened *from* is that someone wishing to be enlightened' (Levine 1979:78). We cannot be at peace if we think we always can, and should, feel at peace. We cannot lose ourselves if we think we always should feel an oceanic integration of self and world. In any event, why all this obsession with feeling good, at one and at peace all the time? Why on earth should we feel at one with the universe all the time? 'The British psychologist Michael Billig and his colleagues have studied the values, goals, and ideals to which people are committed in their everyday lives.[7] They found the typical condition of the individual to be internal conflict: for each belief there exists a strong countertendency' (Gergen 1991:72).

In this respect at least, Freud's picture of self as being more or less regularly at war with itself, seems more or less correct. The most peace we can find will be when we are at peace with not always feeling at peace. The fight–flight response has its place and so there is absolutely no point in developing a meta-level, second-order fight–flight reaction in response to our fight–flight response. There is no point in getting tense about being tense. There is no wisdom in running away from the need to run away, or fighting against the need to fight!

This capacity for second order, reflexive responses, where we turn back and look in on ourselves, is both the blessing and the curse of being a human being. We can have thoughts and feelings about our thoughts and feelings. We can feel pain in response to our pain; we can get tense because we are tense. We can thus greatly complicate our experience. Thoughts about thoughts, feelings about feelings, can add greatly to our difficulties; or they can provide us with perspectives, insights and solutions way beyond the capacity of other animals. The results are positive or negative depending on our intelligence, character, and maturity and, above all, our wisdom. It is as easy for us to think about a thought as it is to think about anything else. We can, as it were, hold up mirrors to our activities and, in so doing, create any number of reflections. These will provide extra dimensions or distractions, or both.

And so, for example, many people place themselves under permanent stress because they do not just see 'themselves' walking down the street for example. They also see a kind of blueprint of 'themselves' and they are perpetually comparing themselves-as-they-see-themselves with themselves-as-they-think-they-should-be. The results of such comparison are generally unfavourable and I put myself into alarm mode as a result. I don't look as I should look. I do not act as I should act. I am two hundred metres behind where I 'should' be. '*Ideal-me' is always ahead of, and greatly outperforming, 'actual-me-that-I-can-see'*. For some, the tension, misery and self-punishment that results is unending. Such is the power of imagination.

The pains of life can be reduced, bur certainly not removed, when we are reconciled with the reality of pain and disappointment. This does not require us to approve of it! But we certainly add to pain by resisting it when it cannot be resisted.

> We almost never directly experience what pain is because our reaction to it is so immediate that most of what we call pain is actually our experience of resistance to that phenomenon. And the resistance is usually a good deal more painful than the original sensation. (Levine 1979:100)

> Tensing holds onto pain, which increases the pain while increasing the resistance to pain. There is pain and pain surrounding the pain. (Ibid.:101)

This is no mere word play. With our big brains we can put ourselves into a permanent state of fight–flight alarm with thoughts of tomorrow's uncertainties and yesterday's disappointments. Or we can place our problems into perspective, and be creative and intelligent concerning our options.

Transcending time

Bodies die and rot away. But the fact of death is difficult to grasp for minds and brains evolved to focus on our lives and loves. Death always exists beyond our event horizon. We are programmed to keep ourselves alive, to grow, gain and prosper; and we seem more than a little reluctant to come to terms with the fact of age, decay and death. No wonder, then, that so many philosophies and theologies have proposed that we don't really die at all but that some kind of essential self, some sort of non-physical homunculus, breaks free of the dying body, and floats away – non-physically – into some kind of heavenly eternity, or is re-incarnated into some other body.

Life after death is something that has seemed possible in that we can certainly imagine life going on after we have died, and we are confident that it will. We can imagine watching people as they attend our funeral, but we cannot at all imagine 'nothing at all', our non-being and non-existence. We may attempt to do so by thinking of, say, darkness, silence, loneliness; but all this is still very much a (frightening) something rather than nothing. We cannot imagine being dead since, to imagine at all, we must still be very much alive.

We can imagine watching and listening to others as they attend our funeral. We can imagine looking down from above the coffin, or by the door, etc. But evidence, and coherent thought about the matter, suggests that we will, in fact, attend our funeral only with our new found status as an inanimate, non-sentient, and decomposing, material object. We will be no more aware of our own funeral than the coffin that contains us.

Yet when people die who are close to us, and who are now physically existent only as a corpse or as ashes, it is very difficult to accept that they are really gone. Loved ones are remarkably willing to believe that the dead person is still communicating with them 'from the other side', in one form or another. For example, 'ouija' boards and other magical paraphernalia may be used as communication devices. People may watch a glass moving, 'by itself', around a table, from letter to letter placed in a circle. As it spells out a message, they will be convinced that here, indeed, is Uncle Jack, giving his customary advice.

Or Auntie Jill's views, about this and that, will be expressed through the voice of a 'medium' during a seance. Seekers will confabulate a coherent message from piles of gibberish.

It is extraordinary (or is it?) how very easily, when the bereaved have a mind to, they will believe in the lived 'presence' of an absent other, with remarkably few cues. *To a degree this is not merely understandable, but sensible, and it requires no supernatural explanation.* We build up a relationship with, and an understanding of, others who have been important to us over many years. This knowledge, and its importance, does not disappear when they are absent for a day, week, month or year. It is the same with death. The person is absent, and we slowly come to understand that their absence, this time, is different in that they can no longer be physically present.

But our understanding, and grasp of who they are for us, and what they mean to us, remains. Likewise, their place and significance in our lives does not disappear, and probably never will. Our *memory and imagination* concerning important people in our lives may dim a little, but remains long after they have died. Even when others are alive, their influence comes through memory and imagination, *at least as much as from direct communication.* Hence, when they have died, their significance to us remains very substantial. No wonder, then, that they may still seem to be 'present' for us. *Mere physical absence, whether temporary or permanent, does not remove the role and presence of significant others in our construction of our world and ourselves.*

People can influence us when they are absent at least as much as when they are present because we can remain actively, or tacitly, aware of how they would respond to our current joys, woes, opportunities and constraints. Like everyone else, the way I understand events around me is to a substantial degree informed by what I think important others would think. In writing this book, concerning the nature of 'self', I am constantly bearing in mind the various constructions of self that other people have offered. I have quoted their words extensively and those writers who are most significant to me do indeed have a kind of 'presence' for me.

There are key dead voices which are in fact more alive, and carry more weight, for me than most of the voices of the living. Many important thinkers thereby maintain a very significant presence in my life, even though I have never met them, and some have been dead for centuries. For me, for example, Socrates, hits the spot. For others it may be Elvis. *For some, Elvis is indeed alive!* Not, as they may think, as a body, nor as a ghost, but as a living icon, message, memory, movement, character, principle, story, inspiration.

Identity formation is strongly influenced by these role models and (imagined) confidentes. For each of us, there are key persons, alive or dead, who become mentors, counsellors, 'Gods' even. We seek to become whoever we model ourselves upon, be they celebrity, philosopher, real or imagined.

To repeat, I am not suggesting that there is anything remotely 'occult' or supernatural about this. It is just that persons are formed and described via their stories and their understandings. *Persons do not, like bodies, travel on a time line*. Books, like bodies, are material. But the story told, or the account provided, in the book, like the person expressed through the body, is not a material object. It is not a 'ghostly' or supernatural object either – it is not an 'object' at all. Persons are subjects, more than they are objects, and books, also, are stored under subject headings and not as different categories of objects – blue, red etc!

'Human beings can thus be seen not so much to live *in* time as to be living it' (Cohn 2002:67). Time, for a person, is a dimension of their identity. It is not a line upon which they travel. Over time, the nature of a person unfolds. A body is shaped within three dimensions. A person is shaped within four. Hence it is possible to describe a body within three spatial dimensions. But it is impossible to describe a person without substantial use of the time dimension, just as it is impossible to describe an understanding or a narrative that is not dimensioned by time. Bodies may be around six-foot long, two-foot wide and a foot and a half deep. Persons, their understandings and their story, are all this plus, say, 80 years long. And 80 years, moreover, within a particular place and time in history. All these comprise the very dimensions of our identity. The influence of a person may be far more than 80 years long since it may continue in the minds, perceptions and actions of others long after they have died and long after their names have been forgotten.

Hence, for example, I find the physical presence of burial mounds all over the Orkney Islands to be deeply moving. This is not because I share the theology and philosophy of people living 5,000 years ago. It is because I recognise that here is a human expression of people showing that other people mattered to them. My reaction is much the same in any burial area. I sense that I am in a 'sacred' space, not because I believe the theology, but because I recognise that these are spaces where people express, however 'imperfectly', that they matter to each other. *The 'spirit' (principle) of love, communion and concern is real enough, and does not require us to postulate a dualist view of non-physical phantoms.* And it really does matter, I think, to see that persons are eternal, as in, *formed* by time rather than *travelling* in time. Eternity is most sensibly construed as meaning not travelling along the time continuum, rather than 'an infinitely long time'.

When we recognise the eternal quality of person-hood we bring back some of the enchantment and magic that lies in the mystery of encountering each other and ourselves. This magic is does not consist in supernatural, and juvenile, fantasies that we can walk on water, make our dreams come true, defy nature, or survive as conscious entities beyond our own physical demise. But it does overthrow the kind of disenchantment that comes from believing, falsely, that we are just input-output machines, or merely consumers or producers. It allows us to *reinstate a sense of awe and reverence that is perfectly consistent with a 'scientific' view of the world. Science does not have to be equated with mechanism and materialism, and physics moved on from this grey, robotic, paradigm more than a century ago.* Unfortunately so much of twentieth-century social science modelled itself on nineteenth-century physics, without appreciating that physicists were conjuring with worlds more fantastic and awesome than could be imagined in the wildest of fairy tales.

Secular and transcendental identity

> Certainly, it must be conceded that we have not the least conception of the 'I', or of anything whatever, not even of the Notion itself, so long as we do not really think, but stop short at the simple, fixed general idea and the name. (Hegel, *Science of Logic*, Book III (The Notion), Section Three: The Idea)

Hegel argued that the 'I' needed a context of soul within which to attain coherence and direction, just as the eye needs a physical body within which to be embedded, to function and to be placed within context. 'The secret of what anything means to us depends on how we've connected it to all the other things we know. That's why it's almost always wrong to seek the "real meaning" of anything. A thing with just one meaning has scarcely any meaning at all' (Minsky 1987:64). A secular apprehension of self sees us as separate from and (often) at odds with the world and others. A spiritual apprehension stresses a sense of 'at oneness' with a larger context. Within a spiritual account, our own story is seen to be just one tiny part of an immensely larger narrative. We feel healed, whole, hale, healthy, holy (even) insofar as we sense our connection[8] to that larger context of which we are a part. We thereby feel more at home with our world and ourselves, less separate from and at odds with others. We might, though, be unwise to expect that everything will, as a result, consist in peace, love, harps and happiness without end! 'The only way in which the world can be grasped ultimately lies, not in thought, but in the act, in the experience of oneness.' (Fromm 1979b:67).

Which of these narratives – the secular or the spiritual – are 'true'? Which is most 'real'? Are we 'really' separate from and at odds with the world, or are we really 'at one' with one and all, beneath all our illusions of separation and struggle? How far do we see the universe in fragments merely because our minds are too small to grasp it as a single unity? Was Parmenides (c.515 BC) correct, and all those many others who have subsequently claimed that 'all is one'? Do we fragment experience into past, present and future because our minds cannot grasp its timeless singularity? Or was Democritus (c.460–c.370 BC) and subsequent atomists correct in asserting that 'in reality' there is just matter in motion?

Or is it not, rather, that spiritual and secular, identified and disidentified, associated and dissociated ways of being in the world, all have their place? Why don't we accept that there are many meanings, many ways of apprehending, and that many narrative meanings, *but by no means all*, have substantial validity, 'truth' and value? So, perhaps there is value in seeing ourselves *both* as separate from, *and*, at one with, our surroundings? For that matter, we might also see ourselves as *both* 'at one' with ourselves, *and* divided within ourselves. Adrenaline calls forth a narrative of separation, endorphins and oxcytocin herald a sense of oneness. Presumably we evolved with both kinds of response for very good reason?

We not only see *ourselves* in these very different ways. We also project similarly contrasting narratives onto inanimate *objects.* For example, to take a secular view: A ship in a storm *ploughs* through the ocean, is *lashed* by the wind and waves, but rises *triumphant, battered* but *unbowed,* to sail away on another day. Or, to put it in a more transcendental way, a ship *cooperates* with the movement of wind and waves, expresses its own nature *effortlessly* and *in harmony* with the nature *effortlessly* expressed by wind and waves. The waves *carry* the ship and all of nature *dances as one.*

Both the warlike and the cooperative accounts involve projecting the kinds of emotions that a human being might feel if, as warrior or monk, they were transformed into, or identified with, a ship. We know, of course, that ships feel neither anxious nor calm about rough sees. The ship's plates may make clanging or groaning sounds in severe weather but they are neither *complaining* nor *complacent.* Yet much of our interaction with inanimate objects and events consists in our 'animating' them in one way or another. Likewise with plants and animals we tend to be anthropomorphic; we project specifically human attributes upon non-human beings. Even a blob on a screen moving around inside a square on the screen can easily be seen as 'trying to get out of the box'. *It is remarkable how few cues we need to ascribe intentions and sentient reactions to objects that clearly are not sentient beings.*

We both project sentience upon, and identify ourselves with, important objects around us. We (men more than women perhaps) may wince when, for example, our car is dented – as though we ourselves had been scratched on the arm. We slip into thinking that the wind is being harsh, the sun is kind, our misfortunes were 'cruel', and so on. This is relevant to our construction of identity because our sense of who *we* are is in part determined by the kind of relationship we imagine that we have with people, with objects, events and the world around us.

At a more general level consider the following two statements:

1. 'Science helps us to *triumph* over nature.'
2. 'Science teaches us to *cooperate* ever more intimately with the workings of nature.'

Science can be compared with, and seen as, a 'weapon', a 'tool', or as a way of being 'receptive' to nature. Rather than choosing which of these 'contestant' theories is 'the winner' perhaps we would be wiser to consider what insights and blind-spots each may offer us? Perhaps we would be wiser to run with as many different kinds of meanings and explanations and 'truths' as provide value and insight for us? But this emphatically does *not* mean that we take on board just *any* and *every* explanation on offer to us.

In my view, advances in science are showing that the grey, robotic, disenchanting mechanism and materialism that is projected onto science does not have to accord with the 'reality'. Science does not require us to subscribe to old polarities of thinking that blind us to the subtleties and enchantment of existence. We do not, for example, have to think in terms of binaries like 'reason' versus 'emotion', or 'logic' versus 'intuition', or 'creativity' versus 'methodology'. And in changing our relationships in this way we change our view of ourselves, and fundamentally so. A scientist who stops being merely a 'warrior', or 'detached', or 'impartial', or 'logical' becomes a larger, more complex, more interesting and interested human being. An artist who starts to take a real interest in the workings of science can deepen her own artistry.

Science does not have to limit our self-concept into robotic, conditioned, and machine-like stimulus–response processes. It can, on the contrary, open up more mysteries than we ever thought existed. A writer might think, for example, that our 'stream of consciousness' provides a subtle and direct route into self-awareness, and may write accordingly. But a mystic will be far more sceptical and 'unknowing' concerning who they are. They question how far they 'choose', how far they have agency and autonomy, and whether human rationalisation explains very much about human action. They are at peace in a cloud of unknowing. Science is beginning to come down in support of the mystic. For example: 'Why do our mental processes so often seem to us to flow in "streams of consciousness"? Perhaps because, in order to keep control, we have to simplify how we represent what's happening' (Minsky 1987:51).

Our 'stream of consciousness', in other words, is a highly edited, simplified, partial and incomplete account of who we are and what we are about. Mostly, as the mystics observe, we have no idea of who we are and what we are doing. Our 'consciousness' is in many ways a mere epiphenomenon in relation to our lives, loves, actions and choices. We could not function at all as human beings if we were consciously 'aware' of all that we were doing and why. *Mostly we get on with our lives without knowing why or even who.*

Mechanical versus organic identities

Science can help us to understand aspects of the human spirit.[9] But many scientists are still bogged down with the idea that science presupposes mechanism and materialism. It leads them to make some extraordinary observations at times. For example: '*When we are asking someone to take responsibility, we are appealing to that part of the brain, the pre-frontal cortex*' (Steve Pinker, lecturing in Newcastle, 25 September 2002). This is an extraordinary statement. It is manifestly obvious that, when ordinary people ask each other to take responsibility, the very last thing they are doing is appealing to a bit of brain, or any other bit of body. *We appeal to persons, as persons. We do not appeal to bodies, bits of bodies, or to ghosts hiding inside bodies.* Only persons can make appeals and only persons can receive them. The fact that bits of brain will certainly be involved when we take responsibility is irrelevant as far as the appellant is concerned. The appeal process would not be changed one iota if it transpired that one person, by some miracle, had only sawdust in their head.

The appeal process was exactly the same when, for example, Aristotle convinced people that the site of the soul was in the heart.[10] People may imagine, falsely, that they appeal to bits of brain, bits of heart, or ghosts, but actually they appeal to persons. The concept of a 'person' is neither a material concept, nor a 'non-material' one. *A person is not, merely, a body and not, at all, a ghost.*

The concept of a 'person' is not understood by construing it as being a merely physical entity. There are all kinds of other concepts that are neither material nor non-material. The concept of 'material' is itself *immaterial* (irrelevant) to many concepts. Persons are, to put it crudely and within common parlance, neither animal nor vegetable nor mineral but abstract. *A 'person' is an abstract concept with animal, vegetable and mineral connections, requiring sociological, psychological, cultural, ethical, spiritual and anthropological forms of discourse.*

Likewise, a university is not merely bricks and mortar. This does not, of course, mean, that persons and universities operate in some ghostly non-physical way. They operate within societies, within ethical and spiritual discourse, and their operation is simply not understood without the use of such discourse. Above all persons and universities express themselves via *language. Persons are not just pieces of matter, yet they matter most crucially to each and all of us.*

Spirituality, then, by which I mean the recognition of the importance of transpersonal[11] perspectives on self, is not just an optional 'add-on' to the story of self. It is, in my view, an essential 'tool' (to take just one metaphor) for understanding the nature of self. The word 'spirituality', of course, is full of all kinds of unfortunate connotations, fantasies and superstitions. We have to pick our way with care in the spiritual firmament. But there is more chance of finding our humanity within such discourse than from a conceptual misuse of mechanistic and materialistic metaphors. Take this one, as another example: 'We are survival machines – robot vehicles blindly programmed to preserve the selfish molecules known as genes. This is a truth which still fills me with astonishment' (Dawkins 1989).

This is, in itself, an astonishing statement. It combines inappropriate metaphors with the implication that it is a straightforwardly 'factual' account, free of any figure of speech. '*We are survival machines*?' This is not so. We like to thrive as well as 'survive'. Mere survival, once achieved, soon leaves us bored and restless. We do not treat each other as machines or, if we do, we create great resentment. We wish to be treated in an ethical, respectful way, and we approach persons in ways that are fundamentally different from the way we approach machines.

It would not be acceptable if I were to seriously accuse anyone of being a 'robot' in daily life. I do not see it as any more acceptable, or any truer, to make a similar assertion within the pages of a book. The word 'machine' is juxtaposed and contrasted with persons. Words have to be understood within the binaries from which they gain meaning. The word 'machine' gains its meaning from the differences between organic individuals and mechanical objects. If we are all considered to be machines, then we are going to have to invent new words to distinguish real persons from robotic vehicles.

Likewise molecules cannot be 'selfish' (or unselfish) in that they cannot form intentions and are not sentient. Dawkins claims that this is not relevant because biologists use the word 'selfish' in a 'technical' way. But this won't do when he addresses himself to non-biologists who emphatically do *not* use 'selfish' in a 'technical' way and who will inevitably and unavoidably understand 'selfish' in the way laypersons use and understand 'selfish'. Only a certifiable sociopath will think that someone is 'really' a robot, in the sense that we understand this word in everyday life. These are dangerous thoughts that might lead, and I fear have led on occasions, to scientists treating human 'subjects' with disrespect.

These important linguistic distinctions cannot be simply short-circuited by the bald and emphatically non-technical assertion that we are 'really' machines. If we are really machines then Dawkins should really treat his family and others like any other metal object designated as a machine. Why does he not do so? If, as is no doubt the case, it is because he thinks that they are (fundamentally) different kinds of machine, then he has so much changed the meaning of the word 'machine' as to make it meaningless. Individuals have no right, or licence, to change the usage of such key words, like 'machine', 'selfish' and 'responsibility' and thereby make them mean something fundamentally different from their everyday meanings. If a new 'technical' meaning is wanted, then coin your own new technical word. Of course, if you do, you will not sell so many books. But you will not, therefore, in the process mislead so many readers.

It matters a great deal if we talk, think of, and see human beings as selfish robots. When we fail to see human beings as different from robots then we will have great difficulty in understanding why we should treat them any differently from robots. Moreover, *if we treat human beings in a dehumanising fashion we may indeed succeed eventually in dehumanising them.* Our victims will need to possess exceptional powers of endurance, courage and integrity if they are to successfully resist our inhuman and inhumane treatment.

On every occasion in history, when one tribe has treated another in an inhumane way, the process has begun as a result of the victims being seen as less than human. They become 'rats', 'vermin', 'monstrous appropriators', 'terrorist maniacs', 'barbarians' or whatever. A crucial part of what it is to be human is that we treat other people as human beings and are ourselves treated as human beings. Our identity, responsibility, dignity, our ability to see the world and others from our perspective, all these are to be recognised and honoured if we are to succeed in expressing our humanity. Human beings are created by civil contexts wherein human rights are taken seriously. Human beings can no doubt be destroyed, dehumanised, degraded when they are seen, and treated as, rats or robots. Inhumane individuals do indeed fail to see the humanity in others and are thereby able to treat them as objects, manipulate them, abuse them, torture them or kill them.

Therefore, a sense of reverence and awe for human beings and the world in which we live is not some kind of aesthetic or transcendental 'accessory' to a well lived human life. It is absolutely crucial if we are to establish and maintain our humanity and live an ethical life of dignity and wellbeing.

Taking a larger perspective

Within a transpersonal perspective, we can see problems as part of the flow of life, an expression of our humanity, rather than as obstacles to the living of our lives. We acknowledge that we are, as it were, 'probleming' rather than being *hit*, *blocked*, or *weighed down* by problems. Seeing the world in this way does not make us any less limited or vulnerable, but it does certainly change our attitude.

Within a transpersonal perspective, we see that our ideas about our identity can never provide a 'final' account of who we are. This becomes a source of celebration more than of concern. We see that there is more to identity, to choice, to autonomy, to cooperation, to dialogue, to the mystery of another, than can be contained within any of our philosophies. We thereby feel awe and wonder about ourselves, our lives and each other, without descending into irrationality. We see ourselves as part of a larger story the nature of which is essentially beyond us. We learn to stand by a particular perspective or move beyond it as necessary:

> Teaching someone how, and when, to associate or dissociate is one of the most profound and pervasive ways to change the quality of a person's experience, and the behaviour that results from it. Dissociation is particularly useful for intensely unpleasant memories. (Bandler 1985:43)

Within a transpersonal perspective, we can face up to, and learn from our contrary and contradictory perceptions, thoughts and feelings, without feeling despair or thinking that we must forever choose just one meaning or understanding. We can learn to enlarge our understanding by extending the variety, depth and range of our understandings:

> When a human being is incongruent in his behaviour, he is signalling that he has more than one model in his world. The overall task of the therapist is to assist the client in creating a new model of the world in which the two formerly conflicting models will operate in a co-ordinated, smooth way, allowing the client all the choices available in both of the previous models. The process of achieving meta-position is, then, the overall strategy for working with clients' incongruities, thereby transforming the source of their pain and paralysis into a resource for growth, energy and vitality. (Bandler & Grinder 1976:89)

Within a transpersonal perspective we may even find something coherent in the concept of 'prayer'. It ceases to be a banal, absurd and irreverent petition to some supernatural being, requesting special favours. Instead it becomes meditative in the sense that one becomes more calm, more reflective, more sensitive to a larger surrounding mystery to one's existence, more willing to wait to see what 'comes next' as a means of relating to one's opportunities and difficulties. We stop being endless 'doers' unto the world and open up to something of the mystery that is our own mind, never mind that larger mystery beyond us.

Cohn (2002) argues that many of our questions simply dissolve when we move from the mode of seeing ourselves as separate from the world. For example, why do we go on asking how far we can 'penetrate' what is 'real'? Cohn's suggestion (2002:77) is that: 'The question can only be asked when we see ourselves as separate from the world.' Cohn draws from Heidegger in this account[12] and quotes, not just from the classic *Being and Time* but from the less well-known Zollikoner Seminars:

> Thus I am, first of all, not related to your presence as an individual but dwell with you in the same Being-here. Being-with-each-other is not the relation of one subject with another. (Heidegger, M. (1987) *Zollikoner Seminare* Protokolle-Gespräche-Briefe. Ed. M. Boss. Frankfurt-am-Main: Klostermann) p 145 (Cohn 2002:36)

Heidegger argued that many of our questions about the relation between self and world arise from the Cartesian (and mistaken) assumption that we start with 'self' and then go out to find evidence of a 'world'. In fact we emerge from a world of which we are a part and from that build up a conception of self. 'World' is the more primordial concept.

> Another way of expressing the 'with'-character of human existence is by saying that the individual is a priori the member of a group. (Cohn 2002:40).

> The question of whether there is a world at all and whether its Being can be proved, makes no sense if it is raised by Dasein as Being-in-the-world; and who else would raise it? (Heidegger 1995:247)

But Heidegger does not equate a transpersonal awareness with floating above the surface of the planet in a perpetual state of infinite possibility. To be a person with agency, choice, freedom and responsibility is to have the courage to choose, knowing that, as soon as one does so, one rapidly *reduces* one's options, and *grounds* oneself down into a particular place and time. 'Heidegger reminds us that "freedom, however, *is* only the choice of *one* possibility – that is, in tolerating one's not having chosen the others and one's not being able to choose them"' (Cohn 2002:97). Kierkegaard (1989:66) was similarly aware of the deceptive dangers of equating spirituality with failure to commit to a finite and limited world:[13] 'Possibility seems greater and greater to the self; more and more becomes possible because nothing becomes actual. In the end it seems as though everything were possible, but that is the very moment that the self is swallowed up in the abyss.'

Our commitment has to be primarily here and now, because here and now is the place and time we occupy. Our understanding and imagination, though, will work best in the here and now when it is emphatically *not* confined to here-now limitations. As Cohn argues, to understand is to move out from our own narrow perception. To understand, also, is to *share* an understanding beyond our own private experience. 'Understanding and attunement cannot be separated, and in a "with-world" it cannot be individualised – which inevitably strains our Western imagination' (Cohn 2002:46).

Likewise, Minsky argues that meaning and understanding involves apprehending and linking multiple meanings, multiple understandings, and multiple perspectives. For only in this way is our understanding made more broad and deep. Habermas, too, stresses the social nature of understanding, via dialogue, community, empathy and mutual respect. Such understanding is most likely within an interdisciplinary liberal humanist perspective that has become ever more difficult to achieve in an academic world increasingly fragmented, instrumental and proletarian.

Smail is another who stresses, in all his writing, that 'making' something of oneself and expressing oneself is a socially embedded process: 'For most "ordinary" people, what power they have usually stems from their association with others – being part, that is, of a relatively powerful organisation or group' (Smail 1996:128). Smail, too, suggests (1996:184) that we be cautious in our assertions concerning the nature of our agency, insight and autonomy: 'The point is precisely that I am *not* in control of my actions in the way my running commentary assumes.'

Rowan Williams, the current Archbishop of Canterbury, will, of course, express this sentiment within a more overtly theological discourse. For example: 'As I said earlier, we need now to give ourselves the proper opportunities honestly to think through what has happened and to find what God has been teaching us in these difficult days' (Guardian (2003) 'The Statement From the Archbishop of Canterbury', 7 July).

We may claim insight from *within* ourselves when in fact we borrowed an idea from someone else – and forgot that we had done so. I have no doubt that we make this kind of mistake *very* often. Much less often these days, do we hear people claiming that something was *not* their idea but that it came from God. Theological discourse, of this kind ('it's not my idea but God's) poses great problems in a secular society. Rowan Williams suggests that we find out what God has been teaching us, in order to settle disputes about the appointment of homosexual bishops. Who is to judge, though, what 'God' is teaching? Fundamentalists are convinced that they can 'hear' him saying that homosexuality is a mortal sin. Liberals are sure that God is a liberal who is presumably most sympathetic to *Guardian* readers. The Bible makes all kinds of contradictory assertions.

In other words, *when believers claim that an idea was 'not mine but thine Oh Lord' they appear to express humility but they are in fact travelling on a very dangerous road.* First, because it is much harder to reconcile people, when all sides are convinced that God is on their side. Second, because there is, in any case, no logical basis to discuss or question such 'divine' authority. *We are all, thereby, paralysed and infantilised. 'Spiritual', as a discourse, therefore is highly problematic, especially when institutionalised and turned into a theology. It seems to combine highly significant insights concerning our relatedness to our world with medieval superstition and dogma.* I do not envy the role of the archbishop in seeking to reconcile what, I am sure, is often utterly irreconcilable.

Questions for Counsellors

1. Which of the following best describes what your clients are trying to achieve? To *find, improve, transform, transcend* themselves? Be specific with examples.
2. What role, if any, does 'God' have in the lives of clients and how do you include this within therapy? Be specific with examples.
3. Do you see some clients suffering primarily from a spiritual crisis? What do you understand by this expression and how do you respond? Be specific with examples.
4. Which of your clients might benefit from a philosophy that helps them to see themselves as *of* the world rather than in triumphant control *over*, or oppressed *beneath*, their circumstances? Be specific with examples.
5. How far do you agree with Gergen that: 'With the conversion of cultures to hierarchies in which upward scrambling becomes the meaning of life, the planet is being laid waste.'?
6. What do you see as the main positive and negative connotations around the concept of 'spirituality'?
7. What do you see as the main reasons for optimism and pessimism concerning the benevolent and destructive effects of social trends on personal development? Are you therefore, on balance, an optimist or a pessimist about personal and social futures?
8. How far do you agree with, and how do you assess Brooks' observation that 'To calculate a person's status, you take his net worth and multiply it by his anti-materialist attitudes'?
9. What, for you, does it mean to talk about taking a 'spiritual' perspective on self and world?
10. How far do you agree with Morris that spirituality concerns 'uniqueness, union, usefulness, understanding, depth and connectedness'?
11. Do you think that 'spiritual' perspectives are necessarily 'pleasant' perspectives?
12. How far do you agree with Levine that 'As long as there's any state of mind you prefer to any other state of mind, that's your hell' And that: 'We keep thinking that we are the contents of our mind, but actually we are the space in which these contents are happening.'
13. Is a holy person a wholly 'good' person or a person who sees themself whole – warts and all? Or does the concept of 'holiness' have no place in a postmodern secular world?
14. What do you see as the major strengths and weaknesses of Buddhist conceptions of identity?
15. To what extent do you think spiritual seekers after truth are in danger of becoming romantic refugees from reality?
16. What do you understand by sociologist observations that the secular materialist world is 'dis-enchanting' and alienating to the human part of human beings?
17. How far do you agree with Stevens (1977) that: 'Everything is a miracle when you give it your full attention and yet everything is still quite ordinary'?
18. For what reasons do you agree or disagree with Assagioli that 'We are dominated by everything with which our self is identified. We can dominate and control everything from which we dis-identify ourselves.'
19. 'I am . . .' How many different ways do contributors quoted in this chapter complete this sentence?
20. Which of your clients need to let go of and transcend their existing boundaries? Which need to clarify and strengthen them? Be specific with examples.
21. Which of your clients make too much/too little of themselves? Be specific with examples.
22. What do you understand by a 'peak experience' and how important are these for you and in the lives of your clients? Be specific with examples.

23. What do you understand by the concept of 'enlightenment'? How far do you agree with Levine that 'No one who wants to be enlightened will ever be enlightened because what we are enlightened *from* is that someone wishing to be enlightened'?
24. How far, and in what way, do you think it is useful to see time as a dimension of a person rather than a line upon which a person travels?
25. How far do you agree with Minsky that 'A thing with just one meaning has scarcely any meaning at all'? How many meanings concerning 'self' will you take away from this book?
26. Can science help us to become 're-enchanted' with the world or is it inherently 'dis-enchanting'? Discuss.

CHAPTER 9

Conclusion – Identities, Past, Present and Future

> mankind, instead of entering into a truly human condition, is sinking into a new kind of barbarism. (Adorno & Horkheimer 1999:back cover)

> Earlier this year, just before he was fired as environment minister, Michael Meacher gave a speech in Newcastle, saying: 'There is a lot wrong with our world. But it is not as bad as people think. It is actually worse.' (Engel 2003)

At the very beginning of this book I began with the questions – *Who do you think you are? What are you to make of yourself? What do others make of you? Do you make too much of yourself? How can you avoid self-obsession?* I also promised that I would seek to provide a larger canvas, and a wider range of colours, with which people can paint for themselves the story of their lives.

Obviously, therefore, I am not going to conclude with a 'blue-print' or try to provide final answers and foundational meanings to our questions about identity. In the previous chapter I quoted Minsky (1987:64): 'A thing with just one meaning has scarcely any meaning at all.' In this spirit I hope it is clear that there is not a single foundational meaning to our concepts of self, but many meanings and interconnections, many circumstances, many agendas and intentions. The picture that you can thereby paint concerning identity will, I hope, be cosmopolitan, sophisticated, subtle, flexible, context bound, integrated but far from chaotic or arbitrary. It will always be a work in progress rather than a final account since we cannot give final accounts of ourselves.

For as long as we are alive our story of self will move, change, develop, even when our circumstances are constrained. Any final account of ourselves has to be made by others after we have died, but there will be no more consensus about the accuracy of our obituaries than there is in our daily interactions with others. This, I think, is to be welcomed as adding to the mystery, subtlety, variety and endless fascination of being alive.

Aspects of the story of self, and the nature of our identities, is told by many professional specialists, artists and, not least, by all of us in our everyday lives. Psychologists do not have privileged knowledge of identities and the nature of humanity. Indeed sociologists, anthropologists, cultural theorists, philosophers and others appear to have offered a much wider, and more fertile, range of perspectives on identity than psychologists. Sarason (1981:37) looks at the overall record of psychology in understanding and humanising humanity and sees it as gravely inadequate: 'We [psychologists] have worshipped false Gods! Far from creating a just society, we had contributed to the levels of injustice! Far from loving our fellow man we, as individuals and collectivities, had unwittingly reinforced man's inhumanity to man (which includes men's inhumanity to women)!'

We have seen many concerns expressed about the threats to identity arising from an unjust, inhumane and rapidly changing world. Can parents help their children find themselves? 'Today, however, it is no longer the authority of parents that is the menace, but their aimlessness; it is not the struggle for power that matters most, but the search for a purpose in life' (Zeldin 1998:381). Can we find an underlying integrity within all the conflict, change, and diversity in postmodern life? 'Fragmentation, compartmentalisation, and a false sense of autonomy are modern diseases of thought and feeling' (Morris 1997:180). Can we integrate a wide range of narratives of self, or will we be pulled to pieces by the diversity and the accelerating rate of change? 'With social saturation, the coherent circles of accord are demolished, and all beliefs thrown into question by one's exposure to multiple points of view. This is no less true in academic matters of truth and objectivity than in our daily experiences of self' (Gergen 1991:xi).

Yet without some degree of integration in our understanding of ourselves and others how can we operate at all as individuals or as a society? 'Without certain shared definitions of human selves, the institutions of justice, education, and democracy could scarcely be maintained' (Ibid.:6). We have to have faith in the reality of free choice, intention, intelligence, reason and judgement if we are to identify ourselves and others and find ways of cooperating with each other. Yet Gergen is only one of many others quoted who have grave concerns about the possibilities of postmodern existence providing us with a humane and coherent future:

> Social saturation furnishes us with a multiplicity of incoherent and unrelated languages of the self. For everything we 'know to be true' about ourselves, other voices within respond with doubt and even derision. This fragmentation of self-concepts corresponds to a multiplicity of incoherent and disconnected relationships. These relationships pull us in myriad directions, inviting us to play such a variety of roles that the very concept of an 'authentic self' with knowable characteristics recedes from view. The fully saturated self becomes no self at all. (Ibid.:7)

It is all too easy to sink into despair as one confronts the details and processes of disintegration:

> What can prevent the proliferation of postmodern consciousness – a time when family members begin to feel that prayers are 'merely ritual,' lovers wonder whether words of profound devotion aren't a bit recherché, college students trade 'finding oneself'

> for 'networking', business executives wonder whether personal decisions are ever rational, scientists doubt the concept of 'objective truth', and politicians recognise 'realistic' to be a rhetorical device? (Ibid.:201)

Elliot (2003:131), likewise, is pessimistic about our chances of establishing a (sufficiently) stable identity given the pressures and options around us: 'In contemporary social conditions durable selfhood is replaced by a kind of supermarket identity.' What are we to do if we see ourselves as no more than consumers and producers? How do we establish an identity if there is so little that we are required to do and so much that we can merely watch? 'the self becomes a mere spectator, watching the endless images of mass culture' (Ibid.:141).

But other commentators observe that there is much that can be done to humanise human beings and assist them in achieving a well-lived life. Moreover, regardless of postmodern assertions about diversity and change, there is much that remains unchanging. Above all, and despite all the talk of diversity, power becomes ever more centralised, the global economy becomes ever more integrated and interdependent, and the consequences, for all us, become ever more important:

> Psychological programmes are, by and large, an extravagant distraction from the real problems that affect people's wellbeing. The more significant issues of poverty, nutrition, employment, medical care, education and even law enforcement are negatively affected as society's attention and resources get diverted to trivialised versions of violence and the self-indulgent whining of those already better off. (Dineen 1999:261)

Psychologists seek to play a central role in enlarging our understanding of ourselves and our world. But their extravagant claims about their own powers and insights may have already created a backlash. 'In a 1996 mail survey of nearly 1,000 mental-health care providers, 62 per cent of the responding psychologists reported earning less from their full-time practice than they did two years earlier. "Practitioners report decrease in earnings". *APA Monitor*, March, 1997:6' (Dineen 1999:301).

The postmodern self, we are told, is anxious, confused, undisciplined, lifeless, bored, drained and atomised. The postmodern self has sought psychology to help. But the achievements of psychologists and counsellors have been modest, and the cries for help have, on occasions, been misplaced: 'Society has accepted the bizarre idea that there must be some psychological solution to all of life's pain and that for a price one can buy it for oneself or even purchase it as a gift' (Ibid.:14). Theorising about self began centuries ago, and our language, inevitably, contain the remnants of all this theorising, both good and bad: 'Well into the eighteenth century, even into the nineteenth, ordinary people understood their emotional life in part in terms of humours. Even today, we speak of people as "phlegmatic" or "sanguine"' (Taylor 1996:191).

We seek to find ways of knowing who we are, we seek forms of language to describe who we are, and, all the time, perhaps, we are trying to find what seems missing within ourselves. Our making something of ourselves never seems to be final; but then perhaps that is just as well if we are to remain alive to ourselves and others? 'In Dasein there is undeniably a constant "lack of totality" which finds an end with death' (Heidegger 1962:286). Perhaps on our death bed we will, at last, have got ourselves 'sorted'? Except that, when we reflect on it, what could such final completeness and reconciliation possibly mean? 'For the most part, Dasein ends in unfulfilment, or else by having disintegrated and been used up' (Ibid.:288).

'Perfect peace' can only come when, as our life blood slips away, we no longer seek to get anywhere, defend anything, promote anything or preserve any boundary between a skin encapsulated body and the world around us. We will be as peaceful as an inanimate object when our body itself becomes an inanimate, albeit decomposing, object.

Until then, our peace will always be partial and temporary and our identities will always feel, to some degree, 'incomplete'. But this does not have to be a cause of modish postmodern despair. We can, and should, keep the faith with our legacy of Englightenment humanism. This should not look back to an imagined and idealised past, but should engage with, and defeat, the pessimism and latent despair or cynicism of postmodern nihilism. Habermas is one of the champions worthy of attention. Nussbaum is another: 'John Dewey insisted that a liberal education ought to produce "hospitality of mind, generous imagination, trained capacity of discrimination, freedom from class, sectarian or partisan prejudice and passion, faith without fanaticism"' (Nussbaum 1997:180). Of course the details of what constitute hospitality, generosity, discrimination etc are the subject of endless debate and final conclusions are not achievable, or appropriate or desirable. But we plunge ourselves into chaos, losing our culture and ourselves if we abandon all belief in the possibility of such virtues and insights.

The search for, promotion and protection of, humanity and individual identity, is one that is assisted by specialists from many disciplines. If there is one that, above all others, draws all these specialisms together, it is, or ought to be, philosophy; that meta-discipline that seeks to connect together the insights of, and relations between, all the others. This may seem a novel role for philosophy but it is far from being so:

> For just as there is no use in a medical art that does not cast out the sickness of bodies, so too there is no use in philosophy, unless it casts out the suffering of the soul. (Epicurus) (Nussbaum 1994:13)

> According to the Hellenistic philosophers . . . The upbringing of young people is held to be deformed in various ways by false views about what matters: by excessive emphasis, for example, on money, competition and status. (Ibid.:26)

> Philosophy in the hands of the Hellenistic thinkers no longer calmly contemplates the world: it plunges into the world, and becomes a part of it. And this changes philosophy. (Ibid.:36)

Philosophy is now seen as overly abstract and cerebral; a 'head-trip' with little connection with the lived struggle for identity, meaning and purpose that we all experience. But this is more to do with the current fragmentation of academe than with the reality of the subject. If we are to integrate, then thoughts, feelings and actions must all be pulled together. We must recognise ourselves as embodied and embedded within the world of which we are a part. We will have to recognise that our search for wealth, added value and a well-lived life is inseparable from our notions of goodness and what constitutes a 'good' life. Hellenistic philosophers were well aware of these basic interconnections:

> In every case the cognitive dimension of the emotions is stressed, and, in particular, their close connection with a certain sort of ethical belief, concerning what is important and what not. What I fear, for example, is connected with what I think worth caring about, with the degree of importance I ascribe to unstable things that can be damaged by the accidents of life. (Ibid.:38)

But philosophy, (from 'philo sophia', a 'love of wisdom') cannot provide any kind of blue-print or formula for finding our humanity. On the contrary, philosophy seeks to free us from a robotic existence of applying only formulae and procedures. That is what machines do, and to be human is, precisely, to be something more than a machine implementing formulae:

> If the act of tenderness can be resolved into its mechanical parts, then it should be possible to reassemble these parts into an act of tenderness. Yet, could this tenderness have developed fully without a naïve belief – at least a suspicion or hope – that the act of tenderness was a total, indivisible, and personal act? (Halmos 1981:203)

Tenderness, compassion, love, empathy, understanding, all that makes us human is likewise, I think, a total, indivisible and personal act. Humanity cannot be broken down into components and reassembled as, for example, 'communication skills'. For what we are then left with is a hollow shell of the real thing. People become play actors and manipulators, they treat each other as objects and, in so doing they betray their own humanity and ours.

This possible betrayal of humanity, I presume, has always been a feature of the human condition. But the forces of mechanisation and bureaucratisation that are at work today are, I suspect, more intense than they have ever been: 'Western man is in danger of losing his shadow altogether, of identifying himself with his fictive personality and of identifying the world with the abstract picture painted by scientific rationalism' (Jung 1996:82).

Far from finding integrity and authenticity, we can more easily find ourselves ground down into a soulless existence from which we attempt to escape via endless novelty and distraction. Cohen and Taylor (1992:153) provide an amusing and poignant account of the consequences in their own personal lives:

> A visit to either one of our respective homes at the moment would reveal a museum of half-abandoned relics from those escape routes and free areas. Here there is a health-food diet book and a half-empty muesli packet left over from the days when rejuvenation through food was eagerly tried. In the desk drawer are fragments of the unfinished novel which meant emancipation from the drudgery of academic life. The bookshelves are full of long-forgotten novels and psychological tracts which at the time of reading seemed to offer the key to personal happiness, being nice to our family and able to cope with life's burdens. Alongside the packets of Rizlas and torn cardboard on the living-room shelf are old boxes of incense sticks to remind us that tonight's taken-for-granted joint was only a few years ago seen as the doorway to new perception. Lying in an old shoe box are photos of the country cottage which was going to be the place to get away from it all. Hanging on the walls are Klee and Picasso reproductions bought in the days when it was important to have our aesthetic sensitivities fully catered for. Stuffed in the sock drawer are a few Indian beads we used to wear at pop festivals. Our annual bank-balance statements reveal payments or stop orders for causes we no longer even remember supporting. And in the cupboard under the stairs lie discarded travel brochures, half constructed model airplanes, wrinkled dahlia tubers, unfinished water colours, vegetarian recipe books, the remains of three hand-made candles, a smelly beer-stained polythene bucket, and a nasty pile of fetid mushroom culture. There are even deserted rooms in the house to remind us of the days when the fantasy of providing a communal haven for itinerant hippie student friends was still going strong.
>
> Gloomily surveying the debris of failed escapes, we must wonder if there is some route which is too pure or natural to be spoilt or – failing that – some hope of putting together some of the elements which by themselves have proved so susceptible to subversion, so incapable of furthering our quest for identity. Can there be one composite free area, which will be less precarious, and from which escapes will be unnecessary?

What are we to make of this account? Is it a chronicle of failure to free, or find, oneself? Or is it a sign of a well-lived life that moves on leaving still loved, albeit dog-eared, remains and reminders? Is it a sign of a scattered and 'scatty' individualism; or of a cosmopolitan life and energy? To me it is clear that Cohen's and Taylor's identities come through in all of this account. Both, I suspect, are more content as cosmopolitans than they pretend. This is not to say, though, that the problems they describe are not real and important:

> No sooner has a new road to the true self been encountered than it is boxed and packaged for sale in the escape-attempts supermarket, no sooner has a new vocabulary of meaning been articulated, than it is raided for concepts and slogans

> by calendar makers and record producers, no sooner have we begun acting in an entirely novel way than we see coming over the horizon a mass of others mimicking our every action. (Ibid.:225)

Anything that seems authentic, creative and personal is soon seized by someone, copied, mechanised and sold back to us. The traditional, too, in all its many forms, is repackaged and reproduced, but can never be seen in its original innocence and can never exert the authority it held when it faced no competitors:

> It was religion that gave overall meaning and enabled us to feel at home in society. But now religion itself has become one more life-world, a segmented aspect of existence. It occurs at certain times, on certain days and in certain places. Religious programmes line up alongside programmes on hobbies, holidays, sport and politics. (Ibid.:220)

Minsky argues, as we saw, that multiple meanings positively enrich our understanding, and that single meanings are thin, naïve and unrewarding. But Gergen sees us as being torn into fragments by all this multiplicity, since he believes that it is beyond our powers to pull multiple understandings and identities together into one interconnected and integrated picture. Cohen and Taylor (1992:221) share Gergen's concern:

> Instead of transforming our world, the new symbol system is dragged into it mutilated. Phrases from the vocabulary of dialectical materialism decorate the posters in our bedroom, sentences from the vocabulary of mysticism are woven into the rock songs on the juke box, concepts from the vocabulary of pantheism are held up for our titillation in cigarette advertisements. Instead of integrating all worlds, the new vocabularies find themselves sucked down into the grammars of everyday life. Meaning proves as illusory as true self.

We have never had so many ways of expressing our 'individuality'. Never have so many cultures, narratives, metaphors, practices and ideas been available to us at the press of a button. But do all these meanings and understandings enrich and enlarge our understanding, or leave us with a sense of meaninglessness? Sociologists argue the point. I place myself in the optimists' camp – believing that a coherent integration is possible. But I do not believe that it is at all easy. 'Only the immensely powerful, gifted or resourceful can keep going; the less lose out in the Darwinian struggle for identity and in a real sense their needs are frustrated' (Ibid.:225).

I do not believe that we have to be immensely powerful, gifted or resourceful if we are to keep going, though power, gifts and resources always help! Neither do I accept that 'escape' via celebrity-watching, fundamentalism, drugs, alcohol, cyber circuses or any other introverted hobby are the only solution. I do, though, agree with Sennett (1998:147) that societal threats to the integrity of identity are very real and that: 'a regime which provides human beings no deep reasons to care about one another cannot long preserve its legitimacy.' Also that there are grave threats to identity from those who would see us essentially as pieces of machinery: 'A person who speaks of human beings as objects of a certain kind of respect is, it might be said, separated by an enormous gulf from one who speaks of us as, for example, "complex stimulus-response systems"' (Cockburn 2001:24). There is indeed an enormous gulf between those who seek to *utilise* (use) human beings and those who like to *meet* them. The problem can be solved but the worst thing about it is that there is so little recognition of the extent to which we have dehumanised ourselves and each other with the way we think about, see and treat each other. *We have lost sight of the way in which we should approach others as persons and see them, at once, as persons.* We need not infer ghostly spirits; we should not observe pieces of machinery: 'I *see* the joy in another's face, I *see* the anger in another's eyes, I *see* people laughing at jokes and writhing in agony, and so on. I do not see flesh – "a body" – moving in certain ways, and on the basis of this "infer" that there is here a joyful person, or "interpret" this as a person in pain' (Ibid.:102).

We should see ourselves and each other whole, and generally it ought to be very difficult to do anything else. We should not see bits or components of another person, indeed we only separate these out as ideas when asked to analyse and reflect. 'it is the *human being herself* – not some part of her, or something that inhabits, and animates, her body – that thinks, gets angry, feels pain, and so on; and, closely linked with that, it is the *human being* that we pity, love or fear' (Ibid.:104).

In this sense, then, we should see the 'spirit', that is the underlying principle of the person, when we remember or recognise someone we know. We should avoid soul-destroying relationships with other people. We should be concerned about the spirit, the essential character of a person, though not in some medieval or metaphysical way: 'I suspect that many others in our society today think roughly as I do here. They have no great use for the word "soul", and do not think of human beings as having just the kind of value that is traditionally associated with that term' (Ibid.:106). Of course, we can treat people as machines and as objects. We can ignore them as persons and see them purely as producers or consumers. 'Science is showing us ways of controlling human behaviour that bypass the *person* – the *human being* – altogether: it does this, for example, in its discovery of mood-controlling drugs' (Ibid.:135).

The question is, when is it *wrong* to avoid making personal contact with a person, in all the many ways that we do avoid making personal contract? I can fix your leg and change the way your brain works without addressing you as a person at all. I can change your consciousness even more easily by simply hitting you over the head. Sometimes, such physical, or other impersonal, intervention is appropriate. On many occasions, though, our failure to respect the humanity and individuality of another is morally wrong. However we treat them, a person remains to be treated as a person if we choose to treat them as such. And this person is never found merely by looking into their brain, just as a university is never found merely by looking at architecture. 'The person is not to be found at the level of internal causes' (Ibid.:139).

Persons may take responsibility for their actions but they are never immune from the pressure all around them. 'The self is never secure, requires unremitting protection and nurture, is always in danger of being undermined, of withering away or exploding into nothingness' (Frosh 1991:187).

Even when it is relatively secure, our identity may change very considerably as a result of wider social change. Within one generation there have been enormous changes in what it means to be a woman and a man. For example:

> It appears to be the case that masculinity is now more than ever pluralistic in expression, including within its boundaries a wide range of contrasting identities and meanings: from the ever-suited politician, to the androgynous David Bowie or Boy George; from the leathered biker, to the company man in the company car; from the gay athleticism of 'gym queens', to the raunchy heterosexuality of the Chippendales; from the domestically traditional to the househusband. (Roseneil & Seymour 1991:112)

But there is no reason to despair about these changes, and many reasons to believe that they are assisting in the further humanisation both of men and women. We can enlarge our understanding within a postmodern global culture, we can benefit from the range and variety of understandings and interpretations available. We can accept Chaney's (2002:7) observation that: 'Familiarity with cultural variety has become standard rather than exceptional.' And we can see this as a cause for celebration rather than fear and despair. And counsellors, providing they keep up with their clients in their postmodern sophistication, can, as Cohn (2002:118) observes, find themselves a future within this more complex and kaleidoscopic world: 'We have seen how the understanding of a situation grows, not by narrowing down the target to a "cause" or a cluster of causes, but by extending the range of questioning and broadening the area of discovery. Only the client can do this, assisted by the therapist.'

Such multiplicity does not have to unhinge our thinking; it can enhance it. Such sophistication is, surely, evidence that we are improving our capacity to think, and moving on from dogmatic simplicities, intolerance and rigidity: 'Well-connected meaning-structures let you turn ideas around in your mind, to consider alternatives and envision things from many perspectives until you find one that works. And that's what we mean by thinking!' (Minsky 1987:64). Indeed, far from lamenting the loss of our naïvety, we could celebrate it. Much of what we thought was an explanation explained nothing. Much of what we previously found to be a satisfying account now fails to survive our sceptical enquiry. We should have no more reason to fear psychic disintegration than David Hume, that arch sceptic, did so many centuries ago. 'The idea of a single, central Self doesn't explain anything. This is because a thing with no parts provides nothing that we can use as pieces of explanation!' (Minsky 1987:50). So like Hume, we may fail to find 'myself' when we look 'inside'. But, further, we may conclude that such a simplistic conception of self explains nothing.

Simple answers concerning who I am may reassure the insecure while leaving the more confident feeling bored, dissatisfied, even depressed. Sophistication concerning our identity will attract the cosmopolitan and those who enjoy multiplicity, rapid change and experimentation. But the danger is that such experimentation and exploration can degenerate into irresponsible play-acting and deliberate dissembling concerning who we are. The postmodern opportunity to actively and endlessly play with one's identity can leave us slowly but steadily disconnected from any kind of reality, any sense of responsibility and any real connection with others.

Youngsters routinely present invented stories about themselves when they go to online chat-rooms. These can encourage creativity, but they can also lead to a loss of reality contact. Of course, children have always played with their identity when playing games and this is an important part of child development. But life is not just a game and it is useful, and important, as an adult, to distinguish between play and genuine personal contact.

The trouble is that, in a postmodern environment, adults play around with the illusion that they are making genuine personal contact all the time. Authenticity, for example, is under continuous threat from the media generally. News, documentaries, plays, films, dramas can put us in touch with what is going on in the world around us. They can also create fictions and illusions that leave us ever less in contact with anything real.

For example, the informality of media presentations has become a norm. Long gone are the days when radio newsreaders dressed in a dinner jacket. Now everyone who looks into an auto-cue, or who reads the news on the radio, is making 'personal' contact with you. Even the BBC Radio 4 news announcer ends by saying '*I hope you enjoy the rest of the evening.*' So that is reassuring isn't it? Someone is hoping that we are going to enjoy our evening. Except, of course, that they are hoping no such thing. Media performers are employed because they have presence, personality, character, and, above all, the capacity to create the illusion that they are addressing each viewer or listener personally. If we think about it for the briefest moment we realise, of course, that the person on television is not making eye contact with us, but with a lens. We also know that no one can, in any significant sense, hope that millions of listeners will enjoy the rest of their evening.

The language of personal informality has been appropriated, by both the media and by managers, so that it is now more often the language of impersonal management. 'Have a nice day' just lubricates daily interactions. It is not a genuine or personal blessing. But how much of a price do we pay when the reality is that so many, who appear to be establishing a personal relationship, are doing no such thing?

This problem of alienation from others and ourselves is manageable if there are times in our day when others really treat us as persons, presenting themselves as persons, and not just as robots delivering outcomes in prescribed roles. The problem is manageable if we are at least sometimes encouraged to present ourselves as ourselves and not merely as ciphers wearing the off-the-shelf identities on offer in the media or from our managers. *Above all, the problem of alienation, of loss of self, can be borne, and even overcome, if we can love and be loved.* Notice the first person usage 'love'; third person observers and dispassionate professionals prefer to talk about 'bonding'. *For if love means anything,*[1] *it above all involves seeing another as an individual person and being seen oneself as a person, in all one's mystery and multiplicity.* That requires a degree of attachment, respect and empathy such that one does not need to pretend to be someone else.

We can avoid alienation, being cut off from ourselves, if at least sometimes we are not just manipulating and being manipulated. We can cope with a certain amount of diagnosis and management, both from others and of others ourselves. But just sometimes, if we are to reclaim the human part of our own and other people's identity, a *genuine dialogue, a relaxed open ended conversation, or a wordless cooperation or sharing of the passing of the day, are really essential, even if we cannot find much real love.* Perhaps counsellors, if no one else, can provide genuine dialogue for those who are unable to find it anywhere else in their lives?

But *if we are to preserve ourselves* – (remembering y Gasset's observation quoted in my Introduction) – *we have to preserve our environment.* How well are we doing? Leaving aside the views of 'tree huggers' and the environmentalist lobby, I will end on what the Pentagon has to say about it, and on the nature of the threats we face:

> A secret [Pentagon] report, suppressed by US defence chiefs and obtained by *The Observer*, warns that major European cities will be sunk beneath rising seas as Britain is plunged into a 'Siberian' climate by 2020. Nuclear conflict, mega-droughts, famine and widespread rioting will erupt across the world.
>
> 'Disruption and conflict will be endemic features of life,' concludes the Pentagon analysis. 'Once again, warfare would define human life.'
>
> Climate change 'should be elevated beyond a scientific debate to a US national security concern', say the authors, Peter Schwartz, CIA consultant and former head of planning at Royal Dutch/Shell Group, and Doug Randall of the California-based Global Business Network.
>
> Already, according to Randall and Schwartz, the planet is carrying a higher population than it can sustain. By 2020 'catastrophic' shortages of water and energy supply will become increasingly harder to overcome, plunging the planet into war. (Mark Townsend and Paul Harris 22 February 2004, *The Observer*)

Here is a truly frightening prospect, but despair about it is not the remedy, is not an excuse, and ought not to be tolerated. This Pentagon account, and so much else in these pages, ought to show, finally and conclusively, that *if coun-*

sellors really are concerned about human wellbeing and personal development, they will need to look beyond the confines of one room and the individual stories told within four walls. We must all take on the larger vision of y Gasset and so many others mentioned in these pages. They have, I believe, so much of importance to offer us all.

So, here is your canvas and a large palette of colours. I hope that with them you are enabled to paint larger pictures of identity, of value to yourself and, (to those readers who are also counsellors), your clients. But beware of mixing too many colours too rapidly. Beware, to mix metaphors, of the danger of indigestion. Take your time with all this material, and focus on that which seems of most relevance and value to you and your circumstances.

Remember the story of the Western academic visiting a Buddhist monk. He was highly informed about spiritual practices world-wide but wanted to update his knowledge of this particular school of Buddhism. The monk began by offering him tea. Without words he kept on pouring tea until it overflowed. The Westerner asked what the monk thought he was doing trying to pour in more tea into a cup that was already full. The monk replied that he feared that this Western mind was itself already overflowing and that he could not see how he could pour in any more ideas.

So, as I reach my word count, I also think that I should not pour out any more. All that remains are the words and ideas so far. And now this book is in your hands, whoever you are, or think you are, to make of me, and of it, as you will.

Questions for Counsellors

1. Minsky argues that multiple meanings positively enrich our understanding, and that single meanings are thin, naïve and unrewarding. Gergen sees us as being torn into fragments by all this multiplicity. Where do you stand? Has your identity been enriched or shredded by this journey into self?
2. Cohen and Taylor argue that only the immensely powerful, gifted or resourceful can keep going and that the less lose out in the Darwinian struggle for identity. What do you think?
3. Sennett argues that a regime which provides human beings no deep reasons to care about one another cannot long preserve its legitimacy. Does contemporary society do enough to provide us with deep reasons to care for each other? Should it?
4. Cockburn argues for the need to speak of human beings as objects of a certain kind of respect. What kinds of respect are uppermost in your mind – and 'heart'? How well are we doing in prizing the intrinsic wealth of humanity in general and unique individuality in particular?
5. I suggest that we have lost sight of the way in which we should approach others as persons and see them, at once, as persons. How far, if at all, is this true and in what ways?
6. I argue that we should be concerned about the spirit, the essential character of a person, though not in some medieval or metaphysical way. Do you agree and, if so, how is this concern to be expressed?
7. What kind of soul-destroying forces do you observe operating on, and stunting the personal development of, individuals?
8. Frosh argues that the self is never secure, requires unremitting protection and nurture, is always in danger of being undermined, of withering away or exploding into nothingness. Do you agree and, if so, what ought we to do to protect identities from exploding into nothingness?

9. I argue that the postmodern opportunity to play actively and endlessly with one's identity can leave one slowly but steadily disconnected from any kind of reality, any sense of responsibility and any real connection with others. What do you think?
10. How much of a price do we pay when so many, who appear to be establishing a personal relationship, are doing no such thing?
11. Major themes in this book can be summarised thus: *Praxis cannot be reduced to techne* (Aristotle). *Verstehen cannot be reduced to erklaren.* (Weber) *Verstehen* requires *Verständigung* (Habermas). Can you explain each in accessible English?

Notes

Chapter 1 Introduction: Identity and Why It Matters

1. Salman Rushdie, *Imaginary Homelands* (London, Granta Books, 1991:12).
2. Clare & Thompson, *Let's Talk about ME* (London, BBC, 1981).
3. For convenience I shall refer to 'the counsellor' as 'she'. It is less cumbersome than 'he/she' or 'they'; most counsellors are female and this usage compensates for the years wherein 'he' has routinely been applied to 'he and she'.
4. Note that the word 'education' is rooted in the Latin 'e ducere' – 'to bring out'. Compare this with 'schooling', getting people into the proper formation, and 'training', putting material into them.
5. For example Derren Brown who, at the time of writing, is impressing T.V. audiences in the U.K.
6. i.e. Humans with 'taste', wisdom, discernment, sagacity!
7. Lyotard has described Kant as an early postmodern thinker, still of relevance today.

Chapter 2 In Search of Self – Counselling and Identity

1. Socrates philosophised in latter half of fifth century BC.
2. Arnold as a school inspector, also argued convincingly about the corrupting effects of paying teachers by results. He demonstrated that serious grade inflation occurred when funding was linked to student attendance and achievement. We have entirely forgotten this salutary message.
3. And included within the spam of virtually everyone's email inbox.
4. 'Public' schools in England are, of course, *private* schools.
5. Though perception itself is not at all simple and is itself a creative process, driven by previous experience and current intentions.
6. Howard (1996 and 2000).
7. A recent University of Oslo study found that university students awarded criminals sentences that were 20% lighter if they were told that the villains were 'handsome' or 'pretty'. *Economist* 24–30 May 2003.
8. Brazil has more 'Avon ladies' (900,000) than it has men and women in its army and navy (Ibid.).
9. More than 70% of those who come under the knife (for cosmetic surgery) now earn less than $50,000 a year (Ibid.).
10. Though always within a social and moral context of duties and obligations!

Chapter 3 Telling What's Wrong – Narratives and Metaphors of Sickness and Health

1. 'QALYs' – 'quality adjusted life years'.
2. E.g. 'Kaplan's quality of well-being scale'.

3. Who, though, could determine what is valuable if we decide that price alone is an inadequate measure of wealth and value?
4. However, we all tend to think that we are more 'balanced' than 'the others'. Whoever admits to taking an 'unbalanced' view?
5. Abraham Lincoln (1809–65).
6. Or, in 'sociologese', this 'mediation of virtually all human experience'.
7. The best selling computer games, selling by the millions, larger in volume than the film industry, allow players to rampage on the streets or in the air; hunting, killing and maiming. Such is our social progress, or need for relief from social stultification.
8. 'Us' being the consumer segment to which we belong and which is considered to comprise our identity.
9. Here 'we' go again.
10. The relation between individuality, identity, liberty and democracy was classically portrayed in Mill, *On Liberty* ([1859] 1989).
11. See, for example, quotations from Sands within these pages.
12. Likewise: 'sanity, sanctity, saintly'.
13. An agenda which, throughout this book, I am seeking to promote.
14. I, and I hope you too.
15. Followers of Rene Descartes and his dualist view of body and mind.
16. Aphorism attributed to Reinhold Niebuhr (1892–1971), American theologian.

Chapter 4 Truth Telling – Identity and Reality

1. The English linguistic philosopher, J. L. Austin, though far removed from French poststructuralism and deconstruction, made a similar point in relation to the concept of 'reality'.
2. Just sometimes, though, the psychologist will produce evidence that, rightly, challenges tacit, 'common-sense' understandings. Our 'folk wisdom' and socially agreed understanding may be commonly shared and may be seen as common-sense. But it may still prove to be a (possibly serious) *mis*understanding.
3. And even (relatively) 'simple' perceptions, of colourful coats for example, are not at all simple.

Chapter 5 Honoured and Esteemed? Identity and Happiness

1. 1991 'Diagnoses are not diseases', *Lancet*, 338, 1574–6.
2. See page 75.
3. *New Scientist*, vol 171, no 2304, 18/08/2001, p 42.
4. Low serotonin, James and others argue, is associated with high stress, anxiety and depression.
5. 'Square', or, for the benefit of younger readers, 'not cool'.

Chapter 6 Feeling Good and Being Good: Identity and Ethics

1. Barry Schwartz, *The Battle for Human Nature* (New York: Norton, 1986).
2. Pittman, F. (1994) 'A Buyer's Guide to Psychotherapy,' *Psychology Today*, Jan/Feb 52–3.

3. Dasein: [being-in-the-world, or, literally, 'being there'].
4. M. Lerner (1980) 'The Belief in a Just World: A Fundamental Delusion', *Psychological Bulletin*, 85:1030–51.
5. 'Education' – from 'e ducere' – to 'draw out' (as opposed to putting in).
6. Indeed, why blame anyone necessarily? My own headache does preoccupy me more than the suffering of millions of strangers. This is not something that I believe I should automatically apologise about.
7. We would not admit to any such belief, but belief is best measured in our actions more than in our rationalisations. We simply do not treat all human beings as human beings. The evidence is overwhelming. We do not treat friends and neighbours in the way we treat 'aliens'. If we did so we would be accused of inhuman and inhumane behaviour.
8. Compare this with Heidegger's account as described, for counsellors, in Howard (2000).
9. 'Good' as in 'virtuous' rather than merely 'skilled'.

Chapter 7 What Was It Like For You? Measuring and Assessing Change in Identity

1. Meehl, P. E. (1986) 'Psychology: Does Our Heterogenous Subject Matter Have Any Unity?', *Minnesota Psychologist*, Summer 4.
2. APA – American Psychological Association.
3. Farley, F. (1996) 'From the Heart'. *American Psychologist*, 51(8):774.
4. Dawes, R. M. (1994) *House of Cards: Psychology and Psychotherapy Built on Myth.* (New York: Simon and Schuster, p 44).
5. Hoagwood 'Interpreting Nullity' p 548.
6. In response to this yearning for knowledgeable professionals, the professionals themselves, and their researchers, tend to exaggerate the powers of new techniques. For example a leading British psychiatrist, William Sargant, claimed in 1967 that psychotropic drugs would eliminate mental illness by the year 2000.
7. *Report of the Task Force on the Evaluation of Education, Training and Service in Psychology.* Washington, DC: American Psychological Association, 1982) (Italics added).
8. Strupp, H. & Hadley, S. (1979) 'Specific Versus Nonspecific Factors in Psychotherapy'. *Archives of General Psychiatry*, 36:1125–36.
9. 2003.
10. Research into counselling is not, of course, the only activity subject to 'spin'. Research into drugs is another arena of Machiavellian manoeuvring. See, for example *New Statesman*, 11 March 2002.
11. Bickman, L. et al. (1995) *Evaluating Managed Mental Health Services: The Fort Bragg Experiment* (New York: Plenum).
12. Brandon, S. (1968) 'Reported Recovered Memories of Child Sexual Abuse', *British Journal of Psychiatry*, April.
13. Lief, H. I. & Fetkewicz, J. (1995) 'Retractors of False Memories: The Evolution of Pseudo-memories', *Journal of Psychiatry and Law*, 23: 411–36, p 432.
14. Peele, S. (1989) *Diseasing of America: Addiction Treatment out of Control* (Lexington, MA: Lexington Books).
15. I do not pretend to know what proportion of postmodern thinking is essentially nihilist.
16. I prefer to conceptualise a single world of single, individual, selves, rather than a 'multiverse' of parallel universes and endless sub-personalities. We do, though, indeed experience ourselves as fragmented and occupying different worlds, as well as unified and within just one space.

17. Yet, in cleaning language of its connotations, social scientists still manage, too often, to write very obscurely.

Chapter 8 Transcending Self: Identity, Society and the Transpersonal

1. For example: Fancher 1995, James 1998, Pilgrim & Treacher 1991, Sabo & Havens 2000, Smail 1987.
2. Notice this: '*Make up your mind*' in common, and correct, parlance does not mean '*spin yourself a web of non-physical Cartesian "mind-stuff"/consciousness*' etc. It means, '*make a decision, don't hang back, get out and* do *something*.'
3. Ellis, A. (1986) 'Do Some Religious Beliefs Help Create Emotional Disturbance?' *Psychotherapy in Private Practice*. 4(4):101–6.
4. Our acquisitiveness includes collecting status *experiences* as much as status *objects*.
5. See BBC Reith lecture 2, 2003.
6. **spir.i.tu.al** *adj* [ME, fr. MF & LL; MF *spirituel*, fr. LL *spiritualis*, fr. L, of breathing, of wind, fr. *spiritus*] (14c) **1:** of, relating to, consisting of, or affecting the spirit: incorporeal **2a:** of or relating to sacred matters **b:** ecclesiastical rather than lay or temporal **3:** concerned with religious values **4:** related or joined in spirit **5a:** of or relating to supernatural beings or phenomena **b:** of, relating to, or involving spiritualism: spiritualistic (1994 Merriam-Webster, Inc).
7. Billig, M. et al., *Ideological Dilemmas* (London: Sage, 1988).
8. See French and Latin roots of 'religion' in 're ligare' to reconnect, tie back.
9. By which I mean 'spirit' as in 'the principles concerning what is meant by being human and showing humanity'. I am not interested in 'freeing' some ghostly Cartesian homunculus. This really is an illusion well past its 'sell-by' date.
10. We still, of course, talk about getting to 'the heart', rather than 'the brain', of the matter, and that a person has 'no heart'. The language of 'soul' still relates to heart more than brains.
11. **trans.per.son.al** *adj* (ca. 1906) **1:** extending or going beyond the personal or individual **2:** of, relating to, or being psychology concerned esp. with esoteric mental experience (as mysticism and altered states of consciousness) beyond the usual limits of ego and personality (1994 Merriam-Webster, Inc).
12. See also Howard (2000).
13. For more detail see Howard (2000).

Chapter 9 Conclusion – Identities, Past, Present, and Future

1. The vast variety of connotations, perspectives, interests and agendas around love can be deconstructed almost without end.

Bibliography

Adorno, T. (1973) *The Jargon of Authenticity* (London: Routledge).
Adorno, T. W. & Horkheimer, M. (1944, 1999) *Dialectic of Enlightenment* (London: Verso).
Allport, G. W. (1961) *Pattern and Growth in Personality* (London: Holt, Rinehart and Winston).
Althusser, L. (1999) *Writings on Psychoanalysis* (Columbia University Press).
Anderson, M. & Savary, L. (1972) *Passages* (London: Harper & Row).
Appignanesi, R. & Garratt, C. (1995) *Postmodernism for Beginners* (Cambridge: Icon).
Argyle, M. (1987) *The Psychology of Happiness* (London: Methuen).
Argyle, M. & Henderson, M. (1985) *The Anatomy of Relationships* (Harmondsworth: Penguin).
Arnold, M. (1993) *Culture and Anarchy* (Cambridge: Cambridge University Press).
Assagioli, R. (1980) *Psychosynthesis* (London: Turnstone).
Assagioli, R. (1985) *The Act of Will* (Wellingborough: Turnstone Press).
St. Augustine (1998) *Confessions* (Oxford: Oxford University Press).
Bakhin, M. (1984) *Problems of Dostoevsky's Poetics* (Manchester: Manchester University Press).
Bandler, R. (1985) *Using Your Brain for a Change* (Utah: Real People's Press).
Bandler, R. & Grinder, J. (1975) *The Structure of Magic* (Palo Alto: Science and Behavior Books).
Bandler, R. & Grinder, J. (1976) *The Structure of Magic 2* (Palo Alto: Science and Behavior Books).
Bandler, R. & Grinder, J. (1979) *Frogs into Princes* (Utah: Real People's Press).
Bandler, R. & Grinder, J. (1981) *Trance Formations* (Utah: Real People's Press).
Bandler, R. & Grinder, J. (1982) *Reframing* (Utah: Real People's Press).
Banister, P., Burman, E., Parker, I., Taylor, M. & Tindall, C. (1994) *Qualitative Methods in Psychology* (Buckingham: Open University Press).
Barnett, R. (1994) *The Limits of Competence* (Buckingham: Open University Press).
Barthes, R. (1957) *Mythologies* (London: Uintage).
Baruch, G. & Treacher, A. (1978) *Psychiatry Observed* (London: Routledge).
Baudrillard, J. (1983) *Simulacca and Simulations* (Michigan: University of Michigan Press).
Baudrillard, J. (1994) *The Illusions of the End* (Cambridge: Polity).
Baudrillard, J. (1998) 'The Ecstasy of Communication', in W. McNeill and K. S. Feldman (eds), *Continental Philosophy* (Oxford: Blackwell).
Beck, A. T. (1976) *Cognitive Therapy* (New York: New American Library).
Becker, E. (1980) *The Birth and Death of Meaning* (Harmondsworth: Pelican).
Bentham, J. (1996) *Introduction to the Principles of Morals and Legislation* (Oxford: Oxford University Press).
Benton, T. & Craib, I. (2001) *Philosophy of Social Science* (Basingstoke: Palgrave Macmillan).
Berger, J. (1972) *Ways of Seeing* (Harmondsworth: Pelican).
Bergin, A. E. & Garfield, S. L. (1994) *Handbook of Psychotherapy and Behaviour Change* (New York: Wiley).
Berne, E. (1967) *Games People Play* (New York: Grove).
Berrios, G. E. & Freeman, H. (eds) (1991) *150 Years of British Psychiatry, 1941–1991* (London: Royal College of Psychiatrists).

Blackman, L. & Walkerdine, V. (2001) *Mass Hysteria: Critical Psychology and Media Studies* (Basingstoke: Palgrave Macmillan).
Blake, N., Smith, R. & Standish, P. (1998) *The Universities We Need* (London: Kogan Page).
Blumer, H. (1986) *Symbolic Interactionism* (Berkeley: University of California Press).
Blumer, H. (2000) *Selected Works* (Illinois: University of Illinois Press).
Blyth, R. H. (1976) *Games Zen Masters Play* (New York: New American Library).
Boethius, A. (c.520 AD, 1962) *The Consolations of Philosophy* (New York: Bobbs-Merrill).
Bohm, D. (1985) *Unfolding Meaning* (Gloucester: Foundation House).
Bond, T. (1995) *Standards and Ethics for Counselling in Action* (London: Sage).
Bourdieu, P. (1987) *Distinction: A Social Critique of the Judgement of Taste* (Cambridge, MA: Harvard University Press).
Bower, P., Foster, J. & Mellor-Clark, J (2001) *Quality: A Guide for Effective Commissioning and Clinical Governance in Counselling in Primary Care* (Manchester: University of Manchester).
Bowlby, J. (1988) *A Secure Base* (London: Routledge).
Boyle, N. (2000) *Who Are We Now?* (Edinburgh: T & T Clark).
Brandon, D. (1976) *Zen in the Art of Helping* (London: Routledge).
Brinich, P. & Shelley, C. (2002) *The Self and Personality Structure* (Buckingham: Open University Press).
Broks, P. (2003) *Into the Silent Land* (London: Atlantic).
Brooks, D. (2000) *Bobos in Paradise* (New York: Simon & Schuster).
Cahoone, L. (1996) *From Modernism to Postmodernism* (Oxford: Blackwell).
Callinicos, A. (1989) *Against Postmodernism* (Cambridge: Polity Press).
Cameron, D. (2000) *Good to Talk?* (London: Sage).
Carrithers, M. (1992) *Why Humans have Cultures* (Oxford: Oxford University Press).
Carrithers, M., Collins, S. & Lukes, S. (eds) (1985) *The Category of the Person* (Cambridge: Cambridge University Press).
Chaney, D. (1996) *Lifestyles* (London: Routledge).
Chaney, D. (2002) *Cultural Change in Everyday Life* (Basingstoke/New York: Palgrave Macmillan).
Charlton, B. (2000) *Psychiatry and the Human Condition* (Oxford: Radcliffe Medical Press).
Clare, A. W. & Thompson, S. (1981) *Let's Talk about Me: Critical Examination of the New Psychotherapies* (London: BBC).
Clare, A. W. (1980) *Psychiatry in Dissent* (Cambridge: Cambridge University Press).
Clark, E. (1988) *The Want Makers* (Falmouth: Hodder & Stoughton).
Cockburn, D. (2001) *An Introduction to the Philosophy of Mind* (Basingstoke: Palgrave, now Palgrave Macmillan).
Coffield, F. & Williamson, W. (eds) (1997) *Repositioning Higher Education* (Buckingham: Open University Press).
Cohen, D. (1977) *Psychologists on Psychology* (London: Routledge).
Cohen, D. (ed.) (1990) *Challenging the Therapeutic State* (New York: *Journal of Mind and Behavior*).
Cohen, S. & Taylor, L. (1976, 1992) *Escape Attempts* (London: Routledge).
Cohn, H. W. (2002) *Heidegger and the Roots of Existential Therapy* (London: Continuum).
Cooley, C. H. (1902) *Human Nature and the Social Order* (New York: Scribner's).
Copleston, F. (1991) *Aquinas* (Harmondsworth: Penguin).
Craib, I. (1994) *The Importance of Disappointment* (London: Routledge).
Csikzentmihalyi, M. (1992) *Flow: The Psychology of Happiness* (London: Harper & Row).

Cushman, P. (1997) *Constructing the Self, Constructing America* (Cambridge, MA: Perseus Press).
Dass, R. (1971) *Be Here Now* (New York: Crown Publications).
Davis, H. & Fallowfield, L. (eds) (1991) *Counselling and Communication in Health Care* (Chichester: Wiley).
Dawes, R. M. (1996) *House of Cards* (New York: Simon & Schuster).
Dawkins, R. (1989) *The Selfish Gene* (Oxford: Oxford University Press).
Deleuze, G. (1989) *Cinema 2: The Time-Image* (London: Continuum).
Deleuze, G. & Guattari, F. (2002) *A Thousand Plateaus* (London: Continuum).
Derrida, J. (1998) *Of Grammatology* (Baltimore: Johns Hopkins University Press).
Derrida, J. (2001) *Writing and Difference* (London: Routledge).
de Silva, P. (1979, 2000) *An Introduction to Buddhist Psychology* (London: Macmillan, now Palgrave Macmillan).
Descartes, R. (1637, 1965) *Discourse on Method* (London: Everyman).
de Tocqueville, A. (1830) *Democracy in America*, Chapter XIII 'Why the Americans Are So Restless in the Midst of Their Prosperity'.
Dhiravamsa, V. (1975) *The Way of Non-attachment* (London: Turnstone).
Dineen, T. (1999) *Manufacturing Victims* (London: Constable).
Doerner, K. (1981) *Madmen and the Bourgeoisie: A Social History of Insanity and Psychiatry* (Oxford: Basil Blackwell).
Dryden, W. & Feltham, C. (eds) (1992) *Psychotherapy and its Discontents* (Buckingham: Open University Press).
Dryden, W. & Feltham, C. (1994) *Developing Counsellor Training* (London: Sage).
du Gay, P., Evans, J. & Redman, P. (eds) (2000) *Identity: A Reader* (London: Sage).
Eagleton, T. (1996) *The Illusions of Postmodernism* (Oxford: Blackwell).
Edgar, A. & Sedgwick, P. (eds) (1999) *Key Concepts in Cultural Theory* (London: Routledge).
Egan, G. (1986) *The Skilled Helper* (California: Brooks/Cole).
Elias, N. (2000) *The Civilising Process* (Oxford: Blackwell).
Eliot (1994) 'Burnt Norton' in Eliot, T. S. (1944) *Four Quartets* (London: Faber & Faber).
Elliott, A. (2003) *Concepts of the Self* (Cambridge: Polity Press).
Engel, M. (2003) 'Road to Ruin', *Guardian*, 24 October.
Erikson, E. (1968, 1994) *Identity, Youth and Crisis* (New York: Norton).
Erikson, E. (1977) *Childhood and Society* (St Albans: Paladin).
Erwin, E. (1997) *Philosophy and Psychotherapy* (London: Sage).
Eysenck, H. (1953) *Uses and Abuses of Psychology* (Harmondsworth: Penguin).
Eysenck, H. (1986) *The Decline and Fall of the Freudian Empire* (Harmondsworth: Pelican).
Fancher, R. T. (1995) *Cultures of Healing* (New York: Freeman).
Farrell, B. A. (1981) *The Standing of Psychoanalysis* (Oxford: Oxford University Press).
Featherstone, M. (1991) *Consumer Culture and Postmodernism* (London: Sage).
Feldenkrais, M. (1977) *Awareness through Movement* (Harmondsworth: Penguin).
Feltham, C. (1995) *What is Counselling?* (London: Sage).
Feltham, C. (1999) *Controversies in Psychotherapy and Counselling* (London: Sage).
Feng, G. & English, J. (1982) *Tao te Ching* (London: Wildwood House).
Ferguson, M. (1983) *The Aquarian Conspiracy* (London: Granada).
Ferrucci, P. (1982) *What We May Be* (London: Turnstone).
Ferrucci, P. (1990) *Inevitable Grace* (Wellingborough: Thorsens).
Foucault, M. (1980) *Power/Knowledge* (Brighton: Harvester).
Foucault, M. (1990) *The History of Sexuality Vol 1* (Harmondsworth: Penguin).
Foucault, M. (1991) *Discipline and Punish* (Harmondsworth: Penguin).
Franck, F. (1979) *Everyone* (London: Wildwood House).

Frankl, V. (1987) *Man's Search for Meaning* (London: Hodder & Stoughton).
Freire, P. (1975) *Pedagogy of the Oppressed* (Harmondsworth: Penguin).
Freud, A. (ed.) (1991) *The Essentials of Psychoanalysis* (Harmondsworth: Penguin).
Freud, S. (1962) *Two Short Accounts of Psychoanalysis* (Harmondsworth: Penguin).
Freud, S. (1985) *Civilisation and Its Discontents* (Freud: Vol. 12) (Harmondsworth: Penguin).
Fromm, E. (1956, 1979a) *The Sane Society* (London: Routledge).
Fromm, E. (1977) *Psychoanalysis and Religion* (London: Yale University Press).
Fromm, E. (1979b) *The Art of Loving* (London: Unwin).
Fromm, E. (1979c) *To Have or To Be* (London: Abacus).
Fromm, E. (1979d) *Th Art of Loving* (London: Unwin).
Fromm, E., Suzuki, D. T. & De Martino, R. (1977) *Zen Buddhism and Psychoanalysis* (London: Condor).
Frosh, S. (1991) *Identity Crisis: Modernity, Psychoanalysis and the Self* (Basingstoke: Macmillan, now Palgrave Macmillan).
Frost, R. (1968) *Robert Frost Selected Poems* (Harmondsworth: Penguin).
Furedi, F. (2004) *Therapy Culture* (London: Routledge).
Gadamer, H.-G. (1989) *Truth and Method* (London: Sheed & Ward).
Gallway, W. T. (1986) *The Inner Game of Tennis* (London: Pan).
Garfinkel, H. (1967) *Studies in Ethnomethodology* (London: Longmans).
Gendlin, E. T. (1978, 1982) *Focusing* (New York: Bantam).
Genosko, G. (1996) *Guattari Reader* (Oxford: Blackwell).
Gergen, K. J. (1991) *The Saturated Self: Dilemmas of Identity in Contemporary Life* (New York: Basic Books).
Giddens, A. (1991) *Modernity and Self-Identity* (Cambridge: Polity Press).
Giddens, A. (1992) *The Transformation of Intimacy* (Cambridge: Polity Press).
Giddens, A. (1998) *The Third Way: The Renewal of Social Democracy* (Cambridge: Polity Press).
Goffman (1969) *The Presentation of Self in Everyday Life* (Harmondsworth: Penguin).
Gough, B. & McFadden, M. (2001) *Critical Social Psychology* (Basingstoke/New York: Palgrave, now Palgrave Macmillan).
Gray, J. (2002) *Straw Dogs* (London: Granta).
Greening, T. (ed.) (1984) *American Politics and Humanistic Psychology* (San Francisco: Saybrook).
Gyatso, T. (1984) *Kindness, Clarity and Insight* (New York: Snow Lion Publications).
Habermas, J. (1989) *The Theory of Communicative Action: The Critique of Functionalist Reason* (Cambridge: Polity Press).
Habermas, J. (1990) *The Philosophical Discourse of Modernity* (Cambridge: Polity Press).
Habermas, J. (1995) *Postmetaphysical Thinking* (Cambridge: Polity Press).
Habermas, J. (1997) *The Theory of Communicative Action Vol 1* (Cambridge: Polity Press).
Hadfield, J. (1964) *Psychology and Morals* (London: Methuen).
Hall, S. (ed.) (1997) *Representation: Cultural Representations and Signifying Practices* (London: Sage).
Halmos, P. (1981) *The Faith of the Counsellors* (London: Constable).
Harding, D. (1972) *On Having No Head* (New York: Harper & Row).
Hardy, J. (1987) *Psychology with a Soul* (London: Routledge).
Harré, R. (1998) *The Singular Self* (London: Sage).
Hart, W. (1982) *Vipassana Meditation* (London: Harper & Row).
Hay, D. (1982) *Exploring Inner Space* (Harmondsworth: Pelican).
Hebdige, D. (1979a) *Subculture: The Meaning of Style* (London: Routledge).
Hebdige, D. (1979b) *Hiding in the Light: On Images and Things* (London: Routledge).
Hegel, G. W. (1971) *Philosophy of Mind* (Oxford: Oxford University Press).

Hegel, G. W. (1994) *Phenomenology of Spirit* (Pennsylvania: Penn. State University Press).
Heidegger, M. (1995) *Being and Time* (Oxford: Blackwell).
Herman, E. (1995) *The Romance of American Psychology* (Berkeley: University of California Press).
Hillman, J. & Ventura, M. (1993) *We've had One Hundred Years of Psychotherapy, and the World's Getting Worse* (San Francisco: Harper).
Hoagwood, K. (1997) 'Interpreting nullity. The Fort Bragg experiment – a comparative success or failure?' *American Psychologist*, 52, 546–50.
Hofstadter, D. (ed.) (1986) *The Mind's I* (Harmondsworth: Penguin).
Hopson, B. & Scally, M. (1981) *Lifeskills Teaching* (London: McGraw-Hill).
Hopson, B. & Scally, M. (1984) *Build Your Own Rainbow* (Leeds: Lifeskills Associates).
Horney, K. (1978) *Self-Analysis* (London: Rontledge).
Horwitz, A. V. (2002) *Greating Mental Illness* (Chicago: University of Chicago Press).
House, R, & Totton, N. (eds) (1997) *Implausible Professions* (Ross on Wye: PCCS Books).
Howard, A. (1991) *Getting Through to You* (Bath: Gateway).
Howard, A. (1996) *Challenges to Couselling and Psychotherapy* (Basingstoke: Macmillan now Palgrave Macmillan).
Howard, A. (2000) *Philosophy for counselling and Psychotherapy* (Basingstoke: Macmillan, now Palgrave Macmillan).
Hudson, L. (1978) *Human Beings* (St Albans: Paladin).
Hume, D. (1985) *Essays Moral, Political and Literary* (Indianapolis: Liberty Fund).
Hume, D. (2003) *An Enquiry Concerning the Principles of Morals* (Oxford: Oxford University Press).
Hume, D. (2004) *Treatise of Human Nature, An Enquiry Concerning the Principles of Morals, Essays Moral and Political* (New York: Dover Publications).
Illich, I. (1994) *Limits to Medicine* (New York: Marion Boyars Publishers).
Ingleby, D. (ed.) (1981) *Critical Psychiatry* (Harmondsworth: Penguin).
Irigaray, L. (1985) *This Sex Which is One* (Ithaca, NY: Cornell University Press).
Ives, C. & Gishin, T. (2002) *Critical Sermons of the Zen Tradition* (Basingstoke: Palgrave, now Palgrave Macmillan).
James, O. (1998) *Britain on the Couch: Treating a Low Serotonin Society* (London: Arrow).
James, W. (1909) *The Varieties of Religious Experience* (London: Longmans).
Jenkins, J., Oatley, K. & Stein, N. (1998) *Human Emotions* (Oxford: Blackwell).
Jordon, N. (1968) *Themes in Speculative Psychology* (London: Tavistock).
Jung, C. G. (1958, 1996) *The Undiscovered Self* (London: Routledge).
Jung, C. G. (1979) *Man and His Symbols* (London: Aldus).
Jung, C. G. (1995) *Modern Man in Search of a Soul* (London: Ark).
Kant, I. (1991) *Critique of Pure Reason* (Amerst, NY: Prometheus).
Kellner, D. & Antonio, R. J. (1999) *Crisis of Modernity* (London: Sage).
Kennedy, I. (1983) *The Unmasking of Medicine* (St Albans: Paladin).
Kenneth, R. & Jones, P. (1975) *Sociology in Medicine* (London: English Universities Press).
Kidd, W. (2002) *Culture and Identity* (Basingstoke: Palgrave, now Palgrave Macmillan).
Kierkegaard, S. (1989) *The Sickness unto Death* (Harmondsworth: Penguin).
Kierkegaard, S. (1992) *Either/Or* (Harmondsworth: Penguin).
Kiev, A. (1972) *Transcultural Psychiatry* (Harmondsworth: Penguin).
Klein, N. (2001) *No Logo* (London: Flamingo).
Kopp, S. (1981) *The Hanged Man* (London: Sheldon Press).
Kornfield, J. (2000) *After the Ecstasy, The Laundry* (New York: Random House).

Kosko, B. (1993) *Fuzzy Thinking* (London: Flamingo).
Krishnamurti, J. (1979) *The Penguin Krishnamurti Reader* (Harmondsworth: Penguin).
Krishnamurti, J. (1986) *Last Talks at Saanen* (London: Gollancz).
Lacan, J. (1994) *The Four Fundamental Concepts of Psychoanalysis* (New York: State University of New York Press).
Laing, R. D. (1969a) *Self and Others* (Harmondsworth: Penguin).
Laing, R. D. (1969b) *Knots* (Harmondsworth: Penguin).
Laing, R. D. (1973) *The Divided Self* (Harmondsworth: Penguin).
Lambert, M. J. (1986) 'Some Implications of Psychotherapy Outcome Research for Eclectic Psychotherapy, International Journal of Eclectic Psychotherapy, 5(1), 16–44.
Lasch, C. (1977) *Haven in a Heartless World: The Family Besieged* (New York: Norton).
Lasch, C. (1980) *The Culture of Narcissism* (London: Abacus).
Lasch, C. (1985) *The Minimal Self* (London: Picador).
Law, S. (2000) *The Philosophy Files* (London: Orion).
Layard, L. (2003) London School of Economics Lectures, 3–5 March.
Leavis, F. (1993) *The Great Tradition* (Harmondsworth: Penguin).
Levine, S. (1979) *A Gradual Awakening* (London: Rider).
Levine, S. (1984) *Meetings at the Edge* (New York: Anchor).
Levine, S. (1986) *Who Dies?* (Bath: Gateway).
Lewis, J. (2002) *Cultural Studies: The Basics* (London: Sage).
Locke, J. (1690, 1998) *An Essay Concerning Human Understanding* (Harmondsworth: Penguin).
Lyotard, J. F. (1984) *The Postmodern Condition* (Manchester: Manchester University Press).
Mace, C. (1999) (ed.) *Heart and Soul: The Therapeutic Face of Philosophy* (London: Routledge).
Mack, J. (2003) *The Museum of the Mind* (London: British Museum Press).
McGee, B. (1997) *Confessions of a Philosopher* (London: Weidenfeld & Nicolson).
McGuire, W. (ed.) (1979) *The Freud/Jung Letters* (London: Picador).
McLeod, J. (1994) *Doing Counselling Research* (London: Sage).
McNeill, W. & Feldman, K. S. (1998) *Continental Philosophy* (Oxford: Blackwell).
Maharshi, R. (1972) *Spiritual Teaching* (London: Shambhala).
Mann, T. (1924, 1999) *The Magic Mountain* (London: Vintage).
Marcuse, H. (2002) *One Dimensional Man* (London: Routledge).
Marinoff, L. (1999) *Plato not Prozac* (New York: HarperCollins).
Marinoff, L. (2002) *Philosophical Practice* (San Diego: Academic Press).
Marx, K. & Engels, F. (1998) *Communist Manifesto* (Oxford: Oxford University Press).
Maslow, A. (1976) *The Farthest Reaches of Human Nature* (Harmondsworth: Penguin).
Maslow, A. (1998) *Towards a Psychology of Being* (New York: Wiley).
May, R. (1953, 1973) *Man's Search for Himself* (London: Souvenir).
May, R. (1976) *Power and Innocence* (London: Fontana).
Mead, G. H. (1972) *Movements of Thought in the Nineteenth Century* (Chicago: University of Chicago Press).
Melman, S. (2001) *After Capitalism: From Managerialism to Workplace Democracy* (New York: Knopf).
Mill, J. S. (1989) *On Liberty:* with *Subjection of Women* and chapters *On Socialism* (Cambridge: Cambridge University Press).
Mill, J. S. (1998) *Utilitarianism* (Oxford: Oxford University Press).
Minsky, M. (1987) *The Society of Mind* (London: Heinemann).
Monbiot, G. (2001) *Captive State* (London: Pan).
Monbiot, G. (2004) 'The Corporate Stooges Who Nobble Serious Science', *Guardian*, 24 February.

Moore, M. (2001) *Stupid White Men* (London: Penguin).
Morris, T. (1994) *True Success* (New York: Putnam).
Morris, T. (1997) *If Aristotle ran General Motors* (New York: Henry Holt).
Morris, T. (1999) *Philosophy for Dummies* (New York: Wiley).
Mowbray, R. (1995) *The Case Against Psychotherapy Registration* (London: Trans Marginal Press).
Murray Parkes, C. (1987) *Bereavement* (Harmondsworth: Penguin).
New Scientist (2003) 1 March: 92.
Nussbaum, M. (1986) *The Fragility of Goodness* (Cambridge: Cambridge University Press).
Nussbaum, M. (1994) *The Therapy of Desire* (Princeton: University Press).
Nussbaum, M. C. (1997) *Cultivating Humanity* (Cambridge, MA Harvard University Press).
O'Hear, A. (2001) *Philosophy in the New Century* (London: Continuum).
O'Neil, J. (1995) *The Poverty of Postmodernism* (London: Routledge).
Ortegay Gasset, J. (2000) *Meditations on Quixote* (Illinois: University of Illinois Press).
Pagels, E. (1982) *The Gnostic Gospels* (Harmondsworth: Penguin).
Palmer, S. (1997) *The Future of Counselling and Psychotherapy* (London: Sage).
Parfit, D. (1984) *Reasons and Persons* (Oxford: Clarendon Press).
Parker, I. (1989) *The Crisis in Modern Social Psychology* (London: Routledge).
Passons, W. R. (1975) *Gestalt Approaches in Counselling* (New York: Holt, Rinehart and Winston).
Peck, M. S. (1983a) *The Road Less Travelled* (London: Hutchinson).
Peck, M. S. (1983b, 1988) *People of the Lie* (London: Rider).
Perls, F. (1978) *The Gestalt Approach* (Palo Alto: Bantam).
Perls, F., Hefferline, R. F. & Goodman, P. (1979) *Gestalt Therapy* (Harmondsworth: Pelican).
Pilger, J. (2003) *The New Rulers of the World* (London: Verso).
Pilgrim, D. (ed.) (1983) *Psychology and Psychotherapy* (London: Routledge).
Pilgrim, D. & Treacher, A. (1991) *Clinical Psychology Observed* (London: Routledge).
Polanyi, M. (1958) *Personal Knowledge* (London: Routledge).
Porter, R. (1997) *Rewriting the Self* (London: Routledge).
Porter, R. (2002) *Madness A Brief History* (Oxford: Oxford University Press).
Power, M. (1997) *The Audit Society* (Oxford: Oxford University Press).
Raabe, P. (2001) *Philosophical Counselling* (Westport: Praeger).
Rabinow, P. (1991) *The Foucault Reader* (Harmondsworth: Penguin).
Radford, J. & Kirby, R. (1975) *The Person in Psychology* (Bungay: Methuen).
Rainwater, J. (1981) *You're in Charge* (Wellingborough: Turnstone).
Ram Dass & Gorman, P. (1985) *How Can I Help?* (London: Rider).
Ramachandran, V. S. (2003) 'Neuroscience – The New Philosophy', Reith Lecture no. 5, London: BBC.
Reinfeld, F. (1964) *The Great Dissenters* (New York: Bantam).
Ricoeur, P. (1974) '*Political and Social Essays*', (Ohio: Ohio University Press).
Ricoeur, P. (1992) *Oneself as Another* (Chicago: University of Chicago Press).
Rogers, C. (1961, 1979) *On Becoming a Person* (London: Constable).
Rogers, C. (1970) *Encounter Groups* (Harmondsworth: Penguin).
Rogers, C. (1980) *A Way of Being* (Boston: Houghton Mifflin).
Rorty, R. (1990) *Philosophy and the Mirror of Nature* (Oxford: Blackwell).
Rosen, R. D. (1977) *Psychobabble* (New York: Avon).
Roseneil, S. & Seymour, J. (eds) (1999) *Practising Identities: Power and Resistance* (Basingstoke: Macmillan, now Palgrave Macmillan).
Roth, A. & Fonagy, P. (1996) *What works for Whom? A Critical Review of Psychotherapy Research* (New York: Guilford).
Rousseau, J. J. (1993) *Emile* (London: Dent).

Rowan, J. (1990) *Subpersonalities* (London: Routledge).
Rowan, J. (1993) *The Transpersonal* (London: Routledge).
Rowe, D. (1992) *Wanting Everything* (London: Harper Collins).
Rowe, D. (1994) *Time on Our Side* (London: Harper Collins).
Rowe, D. (1996) *Guide to Life* (London: Harper Collins).
Rowe, D. (1997) 'Love in the Line of Fire', *Guardian*, 24 October, online at: www.dorothyrowe.com.au
Ryle, G. (2000) *The Concept of Mind* (Harmondsworth: Penguin).
Sabo, A. & Havens, L. (eds) (2000) *The Real World Guide to Psychotherapy Practice* (Cambridge, MA: Harvard University Press).
Sacks, O. (1985) *The Man Who Mistook His Wife for a Hat* (London: Duckworth).
Salmon, P. (1985) *Living in Time* (London: Dent).
Sands, A. (2000) *Falling for Therapy* (Basingstoke: Macmillan now Palgrave Macmillan).
Sarason, S. (1981) *Psychology Misdirected* (New York: Macmillan, now Palgrave-Macmillan).
Sardar, Z. (2002) *The A–Z of Postmodern Life: Essays on Global Culture in the Noughties* (London: Vision).
Sartre, J. P. (1965) *Nausea* (Harmondsworth: Penguin).
Sartre, J. P. (1996) *Being and Nothingness* (London: Routledge).
Satir, V. (1983) *Peoplemaking* (London: Souvenir).
Scambler, G. (ed.) (1991) *Sociology as Applied to Medicine* (London: Baillière Tindall).
Schopenhauer, A. (1995) *The World as Will and Idea* (London: Everyman).
Seneca, L. (1997) *Dialogues and Letters* (Harmondsworth: Penguin).
Sennett, R. (1986, 2003) *The Fall of Public Man* (Harmondsworth: Penguin).
Sennett, R. (1998) *The Corrosion of Character* (New York: Norton).
Sheridan, A. (1980) *Foucault* (London: Tavistock).
Shotter, J. (1975) *Images of Man in Psychological Research* (London: Methuen).
Silverman, H. J. (ed.) (1990) *Postmodernism – Philosophy and the Arts* (London: Routledge).
Skinner, B. F. (1971, 1979) *Beyond Freedom and Dignity* (Harmondsworth: Penguin).
Sloan, T. S. (1987) *Deciding: Self-Deception in Life Choices* (London: Methuen).
Smail, D. (1984) *Illusion and Reality* (London: Dent).
Smail, D. (1987) *Taking Care: An Alternative to Therapy* (London: Dent).
Smail, D. (1993) *The Origins of Unhappiness* (London: HarperCollins).
Smail, D. (1996) *How to Survive without Psychotherapy* (London: Constable).
Spinelli, E. (1994) *Demystifying Therapy* (London: Constable).
Stevens, J. O. (1977) (ed.) *Gestalt Is* (Palo Alto: Bantam).
Stiglitz, J. (2002) *Globalization and Its Discontents* (Harmondsworth: Penguin).
Stones, R. (ed.) (1998) *Key Sociological Thinkers* (Basingstoke: Palgrave, now Palgrave Macmillan).
Storr, A. (ed.) (1986) *Jung, Selected Writings* (London: Fontana).
Storr, A. (1988) *Solitude* (London: Flamingo).
Storr, A. (1992) *Music and the Mind* (London: Collins).
Storr, A. (1998) *Selected Jung* (London: Fontana).
Sutherland, P. (ed.) (1997) *Adult Learning: A Reader* (London: Kogan Page).
Swann, W. B. (1996) *Self Traps* (New York: W. H. Freeman).
Swingewood, A. (1998) *Cultural Theory and the Problem of Modernity* (Basingstoke: Palgrave, now Palgrave Macmillan).
Swinton, J. (2001) *Spirituality and Mental Health Care* (London: Jessica Kingsley).
Szasz, T. (1973) *Ideology and Insanity* (Harmondsworth: Penguin).
Tarnas, R. (1991) *The Passion of the Western Mind* (London: Pimlico).
Taylor, C. (1996) *Sources of The Self* (Cambridge: Cambridge University Press).
Thoreau, H. (1992) Walden (London: Dent).

Thorne, B. (1991) *Person Centred Counselling* (London: Whurr).
Tillich, P. (1977) *The Courage to Be* (London: Collins).
Tolley, K. & Rowland, N. (1995) *Evaluating the Cost-Effectiveness of Counselling in Health Care* (London: Routledge).
Tonnies, F. (1975) *On Social Ideas and Ideologies* (London: Harper & Row).
Tonnies, F. (2001) *Community and Civil Society* (Cambridge: Cambridge University Press).
Trungpa, C. (1973) *Cutting Through Spiritual Materialism* (London: Shambhala).
Trungpa, C. (1976) *The Myth of Freedom* (London: Shambhala).
Turkle, S. (1997) *Life on the Screen: Identity in the Age of the Internet* (New York: Simon & Schuster).
van Deurzen, E. (1991) *Existential Counselling in Practice* (London: Sage).
van Deurzen, E. (1994) 'Monologue, Duologue, Dialogue', Paper presented at the Counselling and Intimacy Conference, School of Education, University of Durham.
van Deurzen, E. (1997a) *Everyday Mysteries* (London: Routledge).
van Deurzen, E. (1997b) *Paradox and Passion in Psychotherapy* (Chichester: Wiley).
Viorst, J. (1986) *Necessary Losses* (London: Simon & Schuster).
Walsh, S. (1990) 'Personal and Professional Threat: A Model of Self-Care for Clinical Psychologists', MSc Dissertation (Exeter: University of Exeter).
Walsh, P. (1993) *Education and Meaning* (London: Cassell).
Watts, A. (1975a) *Death* (Milbrae: Celestial Arts).
Watts, A. (1975b) *Psychotherapy East and West* (London: Vintage).
Whitaker, R. (2002) *Mad in America: Bad Science, Bad Medicine, and the Enduring Mistreatment of the Mentally Ill* (Cambridge, MA: Perseus Press).
WHO 1948 Preamble to the Constitution of the World Health Organization as adopted by the International Health Conference, New York, 19–22 June, 1946; signed on 22 July 1946 by the representatives of 61 States (Official Records of the World Health Organization, no. 2, p. 100) and entered into force on 7 April 1948.
Wilbur, K. (1981) *Up from Eden* (Boulder: Shambhala).
Wilber, K., Engler, J. & Brown, D. (1986) *Transformation of Consciousness* (London: Shambhala).
Wittgenstein, L. (1922, 1995) *Tractatus Logico-Philosophicus* (London: Routledge).
Wittgenstein, L. (1953, 1963, 2002) *Philosophical Investigations* (Oxford: Blackwell).
Wittgenstein, L. (1994) *Last Writings on the Philosophy of Psychology* (Oxford: Blackwell).
Wittgenstein, L. (1998) *Culture and Value* (Oxford: Blackwell).
Wolters, C. (1978) *The Cloud of Unknowing* (Harmondsworth: Penguin).
Wood, G. (1983) *The Myth of Neurosis* (London: Macmillan, now Palgrave Macmillan).
Zeldin, T. (1998) *An Intimate History of Humanity* (London: Vintage).
Zweig (2000) http://www.conniezweig.com/excerpt2.html at 2nd October 2002.

Index

www.ingramcontent.com/pod-product-compliance
Ingram Content Group UK Ltd.
Pitfield, Milton Keynes, MK11 3LW, UK
UKHW020202290926
15471UKWH00005B/1025

9 781403 933096